The

Daily Light

was presented to

....

....

....

by

....

....

....

date

....

Daily Light

Daily Light was first published
in Great Britian in 1794 by Samuel Bagster.
This edition published in 2007 by the

Trinitarian Bible Society

ISBN 978 1 86228 184 4   Black leather
ISBN 978 1 86228 185 1   Red leather
ISBN 978 1 86228 289 6   Paperback
ISBN 978 1 86228 290 2   Brown vinyl boards

All Scriptures herein taken from the Authorised Version. Rights in
the Authorised (King James) Version are vested in the Crown and
held by Royal Letters Patent, Cambridge University Press.

This edition of Daily Light
© 2007 Trinitarian Bible Society
Tyndale House, Dorset Road,
London SW19 3NN, UK

10M/01/07

Contents

Contents

Foreword

THIS REVISED EDITION of *Daily Light* is issued by the Trinitarian Bible Society using the Authorised Version, the faithful translation of the Holy Scriptures the original compilers of this book had employed.

Most of the words of Scripture in *Daily Light* are incomplete clauses and extracts removed and isolated from their contexts. Consequently, in this edition special care has been taken to ensure that the quotations are correctly stated and not misleading.

In modern literature italics are used for emphasis. However, in the Authorised Version, a translation of the Holy Scriptures noted for its accuracy, they are used to inform us that words have been added to the sacred text for the purpose of making the English clear and the original languages more explicit. For example 2 Peter 3.1 reads, 'This second epistle, beloved, I now write unto you; in *both* which I stir up your pure minds by way of remembrance'. If this is read without the italicised word, it makes good sense but it does not convey completely the full meaning of the verse, as in the original Greek the word 'which' is plural, something English is unable to express. The translators have therefore inserted the word '*both*' in italics to complete in English the meaning explicit in the original language.

In the *Translators to the Reader,* the translators of the Authorised Version wrote:

The Scriptures we are commanded to search (John 5.39, Isa. 8.20). They are commended that searched and studied them (Acts 17.11 and 8.28, 29). They are reproved that were unskilful in them, or slow to believe them (Matt. 22.29, Luk. 24.25). They can make us wise unto salvation (2 Tim. 3.15). If we be ignorant, they will instruct us; if out of the way, they will bring us home; if out of order, they will reform us; if in heaviness, comfort us; if dull, quicken us; if cold, inflame us.… Take up and read, take up and read the Scriptures.

For this purpose a Bible Reading Scheme is printed in this edition to encourage readers to read systematically through the Holy Scriptures and note the passages from which the extracts in *Daily Light* have been taken.

Preface

THE ORIGIN OF DAILY LIGHT is so closely bound up with the family of Bagster and the publishing firm of that name, that the proper background of the compilation of this most popular of all daily devotional books must necessarily include some account of Samuel Bagster, his antecedents and life.

Samuel Bagster was born on December 26, 1772, the second son of George and Mary Bagster of a Lyme Regis, Dorset-shire, family. Samuel Bagster's father, George Bagster, was a member of the congregation which assembled for worship under the pastorship of Dr. Andrew Gifford, a Baptist minister, notable antiquarian and assistant librarian at the British Museum. It was at these prayer meetings that George Bagster met his friend Mr. John Birch, whose daughter, Eunice Birch, became Samuel Bagster's wife.

When Samuel Bagster was seven years of age, his father sent him to school with the Rev. John Ryland, a Baptist minister who was the father of the well known Dr. Ryland, of Bristol. From his parents and from Rev. John Ryland, Samuel Bagster learned the precepts and practice of a devout Christian which sustained him throughout his life and which in turn he passed on to his children.

Samuel Bagster was indentured to a bookseller in the Strand and on completion of his apprenticeship he opened his own bookshop at No.81 Strand, London, on April 19, 1794, when twenty-one years of age. As one might expect from a high-principled and religious-minded man, he made it a rule that he would never sell any book which might be considered questionable in taste or subject: an attitude of mind by no means common in those days.

Samuel Bagster and Eunice Birch were married at the Parish Church of St. Giles in the Field on December 19, 1797. She was a brave woman of high principles and steadfast faith, a real helpmeet to her husband throughout their long married life. She died the day before her hundredth birthday on August 22, 1877, a few months after she had been honoured by a personal visit from Queen Victoria, who, it is said, knelt at Mrs. Bagster's bedside to receive the blessing of this, her revered and venerable subject.

Samuel and Eunice Bagster were blessed with twelve children, and it was Jonathan, their tenth child, who was mainly responsible for the idea and for the method by which DAILY LIGHT was compiled. He was the Editor-in-Chief, and his daughter Ann was his chief assistant. The practice of corporate daily worship had always been followed in the family, and it was the daily text that Jonathan Bagster selected that the family, joined together in prayer, were asked to illustrate by further applicable texts. The resultant Scripture quotations were then carefully considered, discussed and arranged by common consent of all those present, after which the manuscript would be laid aside for prayer and meditation to see if there would be any guidance for its further improvement. Sometimes it was weeks before it was felt that the reading for a particular day could not be improved and then that page would be sent to the printer to be set in type. Later it would be read and corrected and all the references would be verified. Each day for over two years the readings were compiled, corrected and improved in this way until the whole book was ready for publication in two volumes, one of the Morning readings and the other of the Evening readings.

Robert Bagster, one of Jonathan's sons, who as a lad was present with the family at these daily prayers, wrote these words many years after, 'Few are able to appreciate the heart-searching care with which every text was selected, the days, nay the weeks, of changes, alterations and improvements, until at last each page was passed to the printer. It has been said that each page was prayed over. This is true enough, but far less than the fact that portions were left over for weeks to see if any further guidance came. So this book stands to-day quite unrivalled, with not one word altered since those devoted people put it forth to the world. It has struck me as a wonderful thought that hundreds of thousands of Christians throughout the world, to its remotest corners, are each day reading the same page with its message of comfort and help.'

The truth of this last statement is amply borne out by the many letters that are still received which tell of the help that DAILY LIGHT has been, and still is, to the Missionaries from the frozen wastes of Canada and Alaska to the steaming heat of the jungles of Assam, Burma and tropical Africa and every climate between these extremes.

Thus the spirit of God-fearing devotion, passed down through successive generations, bears fruit which increases year by year and spreads to the very ends of the earth. The parable of the grain of mustard seed was never so aptly illustrated as by the story of DAILY LIGHT.

Abbreviations of the Books of the Bible

1 Chr.	1 Chronicles	**Ezek.**	Ezekiel	**Ne.**	Nehemiah
2 Chr.	2 Chronicles	**Ezr.**	Ezra	**Nu.**	Numbers
1 Co.	1 Corinthians	**Ga.**	Galatians	**Ob.**	Obadiah
2 Co.	2 Corinthians	**Ge.**	Genesis	**Phil.**	Philippians
1 Jn.	1 John	**Hab.**	Habakkuk	**Phlm.**	Philemon
2 Jn.	2 John	**Hag.**	Haggai	**Rev.**	Revelation
3 Jn.	3 John	**He.**	Hebrews	**Ro.**	Romans
1 Ki.	1 Kings	**Hos.**	Hosea	**Ru.**	Ruth
2 Ki.	2 Kings	**Isa.**	Isaiah	**Pro.**	Proverbs
1 Pe.	1 Peter	**Jas.**	James	**Ps.**	Psalms
2 Pe.	2 Peter	**Jer.**	Jeremiah	**Song**	Song of Solomon
1 Sa.	1 Samuel	**Jn.**	John	**Titus**	Titus
2 Sa.	2 Samuel	**Job**	Job	**Zech.**	Zechariah
1 Th.	1 Thessalonians	**Joel**	Joel	**Zeph.**	Zephaniah
2 Th.	2 Thessalonians	**Jon.**	Jonah		
1 Tim.	1 Timothy	**Jos.**	Joshua		
2 Tim.	2 Timothy	**Jude**	Jude		
Ac.	Acts	**Judg.**	Judges		
Am.	Amos	**Lam.**	Lamentations		
Col.	Colossians	**Lev.**	Leviticus		
Dan.	Daniel	**Lu.**	Luke		
Deu.	Deuteronomy	**Mal.**	Malachi		
Ec.	Ecclesiastes	**Mi.**	Micah		
Eph.	Ephesians	**Mk.**	Mark		
Est.	Esther	**Mt.**	Matthew		
Ex.	Exodus	**Na.**	Nahum		

Bible Reading Scheme

A concise course whereby one can read through
the whole Bible once in two years—the Psalms and
the New Testament twice

January

1	Ge. 1	Mt. 1
2	Ge. 2	Mt. 2
3	Ge. 3	Mt. 3
4	Ge. 4	Mt. 4
5	Ge. 5	Mt. 5
6	Ge. 6	Mt. 6
7	Ge. 7	Mt. 7
8	Ge. 8	Mt. 8
9	Ge. 9–10	Mt. 9
10	Ge. 11	Mt. 10
11	Ge. 12	Mt. 11
12	Ge. 13	Mt. 12
13	Ge. 14	Mt. 13
14	Ge. 15	Mt. 14
15	Ge. 16	Mt. 15
16	Ge. 17	Mt. 16
17	Ge. 18	Mt. 17
18	Ge. 19	Mt. 18
19	Ge. 20	Mt. 19
20	Ge. 21	Mt. 20
21	Ge. 22	Mt. 21
22	Ge. 23	Mt. 22
23	Ge. 24	Mt. 23
24	Ge. 25	Mt. 24
25	Ge. 26	Mt. 25
26	Ge. 27	Mt. 26
27	Ge. 28	Mt. 27
28	Ge. 29	Mt. 28
29	Ge. 30	Mk. 1
30	Ge. 31	Mk. 2
31	Ge. 32	Mk. 3

February

1	Ge. 33	Mk. 4
2	Ge. 34	Mk. 5
3	Ge. 35–36	Mk. 6
4	Ge. 37	Mk. 7
5	Ge. 38	Mk. 8
6	Ge. 39	Mk. 9
7	Ge. 40	Mk. 10
8	Ge. 41	Mk. 11
9	Ge. 42	Mk. 12
10	Ge. 43	Mk. 13
11	Ge. 44	Mk. 14
12	Ge. 45	Mk. 15
13	Ge. 46	Mk. 16
14	Ge. 47	Lu. 1.1–38
15	Ge. 48	Lu. 1.39–80
16	Ge. 49	Lu. 2
17	Ge. 50	Lu. 3
18	Ex. 1	Lu. 4
19	Ex. 2	Lu. 5
20	Ex. 3	Lu. 6
21	Ex. 4	Lu. 7
22	Ex. 5	Lu. 8
23	Ex. 6	Lu. 9
24	Ex. 7	Lu. 10
25	Ex. 8	Lu. 11
26	Ex. 9	Lu. 12
27	Ex. 10	Lu. 13
28	Ex. 11.1–12.21	Lu. 14

March

1	Ex. 12.22–51	Lu. 15
2	Ex. 13	Lu. 16
3	Ex. 14	Lu. 17
4	Ex. 15	Lu. 18
5	Ex. 16	Lu. 19
6	Ex. 17	Lu. 20
7	Ex. 18	Lu. 21
8	Ex. 19	Lu. 22
9	Ex. 20	Lu. 23
10	Ex. 21	Lu. 24
11	Ex. 22	Jn. 1
12	Ex. 23	Jn. 2
13	Ex. 24	Jn. 3
14	Ex. 25	Jn. 4
15	Ex. 26	Jn. 5
16	Ex. 27	Jn. 6
17	Ex. 28	Jn. 7
18	Ex. 29	Jn. 8
19	Ex. 30	Jn. 9
20	Ex. 31	Jn. 10
21	Ex. 32	Jn. 11
22	Ex. 33	Jn. 12
23	Ex. 34	Jn. 13
24	Ex. 35	Jn. 14
25	Ex. 36	Jn. 15
26	Ex. 37	Jn. 16
27	Ex. 38	Jn. 17
28	Ex. 39	Jn. 18
29	Ex. 40	Jn. 19
30	Lev. 1	Jn. 20
31	Lev. 2–3	Jn. 21

April

1	Lev. 4	Ps. 1–2
2	Lev. 5	Ps. 3–4
3	Lev. 6	Ps. 5–6
4	Lev. 7	Ps. 7–8
5	Lev. 8	Ps. 9
6	Lev. 9	Ps. 10
7	Lev. 10	Ps. 11–12
8	Lev. 11–12	Ps. 13–14
9	Lev. 13	Ps. 15–16
10	Lev. 14	Ps. 17
11	Lev. 15	Ps. 18
12	Lev. 16	Ps. 19
13	Lev. 17	Ps. 20–21
14	Lev. 18	Ps. 22
15	Lev. 19	Ps. 23–24
16	Lev. 20	Ps. 25
17	Lev. 21	Ps. 26–27
18	Lev. 22	Ps. 28–29
19	Lev. 23	Ps. 30
20	Lev. 24	Ps. 31
21	Lev. 25	Ps. 32
22	Lev. 26	Ps. 33
23	Lev. 27	Ps. 34
24	Nu. 1	Ps. 35
25	Nu. 2	Ps. 36
26	Nu. 3	Ps. 37
27	Nu. 4	Ps. 38
28	Nu. 5	Ps. 39
29	Nu. 6	Ps. 40–41
30	Nu. 7	Ps. 42–43

May		
1	Nu. 8	Ps. 44
2	Nu. 9	Ps. 45
3	Nu. 10	Ps. 46–47
4	Nu. 11	Ps. 48
5	Nu. 12–13	Ps. 49
6	Nu. 14	Ps. 50
7	Nu. 15	Ps. 51
8	Nu. 16	Ps. 52–54
9	Nu. 17–18	Ps. 55
10	Nu. 19	Ps. 56–57
11	Nu. 20	Ps. 58–59
12	Nu. 21	Ps. 60–61
13	Nu. 22	Ps. 62–63
14	Nu. 23	Ps. 64–65
15	Nu. 24	Ps. 66–67
16	Nu. 25	Ps. 68
17	Nu. 26	Ps. 69
18	Nu. 27	Ps. 70–71
19	Nu. 28	Ps. 72
20	Nu. 29	Ps. 73
21	Nu. 30	Ps. 74
22	Nu. 31	Ps. 75–76
23	Nu. 32	Ps. 77
24	Nu. 33	Ps. 78.1–37
25	Nu. 34	Ps. 78.38–72
26	Nu. 35	Ps. 79
27	Nu. 36	Ps. 80
28	Deu. 1	Ps. 81–82
29	Deu. 2	Ps. 83–84
30	Deu. 3	Ps. 85
31	Deu. 4	Ps. 86–87

June		
1	Deu. 5	Ps. 88
2	Deu. 6	Ps. 89
3	Deu. 7	Ps. 90
4	Deu. 8	Ps. 91
5	Deu. 9	Ps. 92–93
6	Deu. 10	Ps. 94
7	Deu. 11	Ps. 95–96
8	Deu. 12	Ps. 97–98
9	Deu. 13–14	Ps. 99–101
10	Deu. 15	Ps. 102
11	Deu. 16	Ps. 103
12	Deu. 17	Ps. 104
13	Deu. 18	Ps. 105
14	Deu. 19	Ps. 106
15	Deu. 20	Ps. 107
16	Deu. 21	Ps. 108–109
17	Deu. 22	Ps. 110–111
18	Deu. 23	Ps. 112–113
19	Deu. 24	Ps. 114–115
20	Deu. 25	Ps. 116
21	Deu. 26	Ps. 117–118
22	Deu. 27.1–28.19	Ps. 119.1–24
23	Deu. 28.20–68	Ps. 119.25–48
24	Deu. 29	Ps. 119.49–72
25	Deu. 30	Ps. 119.73–96
26	Deu. 31	Ps. 119.97–120
27	Deu. 32	Ps. 119.121–144
28	Deu. 33–34	Ps. 119.145–176
29	Jos. 1	Ps. 120–122
30	Jos. 2	Ps. 123–125

July

1	Jos. 3	Ps. 126–128
2	Jos. 4	Ps. 129–131
3	Jos. 5.1–6.5	Ps. 132–134
4	Jos. 6.6–27	Ps. 135–136
5	Jos. 7	Ps. 137–138
6	Jos. 8	Ps. 139
7	Jos. 9	Ps. 140–141
8	Jos. 10	Ps. 142–143
9	Jos. 11	Ps. 144
10	Jos. 12–13	Ps. 145
11	Jos. 14–15	Ps. 146–147
12	Jos. 16–17	Ps. 148
13	Jos. 18–19	Ps. 149–150
14	Jos. 20–21	Ac. 1
15	Jos. 22	Ac. 2
16	Jos. 23	Ac. 3
17	Jos. 24	Ac. 4
18	Judg. 1	Ac. 5
19	Judg. 2	Ac. 6
20	Judg. 3	Ac. 7
21	Judg. 4	Ac. 8
22	Judg. 5	Ac. 9
23	Judg. 6	Ac. 10
24	Judg. 7	Ac. 11
25	Judg. 8	Ac. 12
26	Judg. 9	Ac. 13
27	Judg. 10.1–11.11	Ac. 14
28	Judg. 11.12–40	Ac. 15
29	Judg. 12	Ac. 16
30	Judg. 13	Ac. 17
31	Judg. 14	Ac. 18

August

1	Judg. 15	Ac. 19
2	Judg. 16	Ac. 20
3	Judg. 17	Ac. 21
4	Judg. 18	Ac. 22
5	Judg. 19	Ac. 23
6	Judg. 20	Ac. 24
7	Judg. 21	Ac. 25
8	Ru. 1	Ac. 26
9	Ru. 2	Ac. 27
10	Ru. 3–4	Ac. 28
11	1 Sa. 1	Ro. 1
12	1 Sa. 2	Ro. 2
13	1 Sa. 3	Ro. 3
14	1 Sa. 4	Ro. 4
15	1 Sa. 5–6	Ro. 5
16	1 Sa. 7–8	Ro. 6
17	1 Sa. 9	Ro. 7
18	1 Sa. 10	Ro. 8
19	1 Sa. 11	Ro. 9
20	1 Sa. 12	Ro. 10
21	1 Sa. 13	Ro. 11
22	1 Sa. 14	Ro. 12
23	1 Sa. 15	Ro. 13
24	1 Sa. 16	Ro. 14
25	1 Sa. 17	Ro. 15
26	1 Sa. 18	Ro. 16
27	1 Sa. 19	1 Co. 1
28	1 Sa. 20	1 Co. 2
29	1 Sa. 21–22	1 Co. 3
30	1 Sa. 23	1 Co. 4
31	1 Sa. 24	1 Co. 5

September

1	1 Sa. 25	1 Co. 6
2	1 Sa. 26	1 Co. 7
3	1 Sa. 27	1 Co. 8
4	1 Sa. 28	1 Co. 9
5	1 Sa. 29–30	1 Co. 10
6	1 Sa. 31	1 Co. 11
7	2 Sa. 1	1 Co. 12
8	2 Sa. 2	1 Co. 13
9	2 Sa. 3	1 Co. 14
10	2 Sa. 4–5	1 Co. 15
11	2 Sa. 6	1 Co. 16
12	2 Sa. 7	2 Co. 1
13	2 Sa. 8–9	2 Co. 2
14	2 Sa. 10	2 Co. 3
15	2 Sa. 11	2 Co. 4
16	2 Sa. 12	2 Co. 5
17	2 Sa. 13	2 Co. 6
18	2 Sa. 14	2 Co. 7
19	2 Sa. 15	2 Co. 8
20	2 Sa. 16	2 Co. 9
21	2 Sa. 17	2 Co. 10
22	2 Sa. 18	2 Co. 11
23	2 Sa. 19	2 Co. 12
24	2 Sa. 20	2 Co. 13
25	2 Sa. 21	Ga. 1
26	2 Sa. 22	Ga. 2
27	2 Sa. 23	Ga. 3
28	2 Sa. 24	Ga. 4
29	1 Ki. 1	Ga. 5
30	1 Ki. 2	Ga. 6

October

1	1 Ki. 3	Eph. 1
2	1 Ki. 4–5	Eph. 2
3	1 Ki. 6	Eph. 3
4	1 Ki. 7	Eph. 4
5	1 Ki. 8	Eph. 5
6	1 Ki. 9	Eph. 6
7	1 Ki. 10	Phil. 1
8	1 Ki. 11	Phil. 2
9	1 Ki. 12	Phil. 3
10	1 Ki. 13	Phil. 4
11	1 Ki. 14	Col. 1
12	1 Ki. 15	Col. 2
13	1 Ki. 16	Col. 3
14	1 Ki. 17	Col. 4
15	1 Ki. 18	1 Th. 1
16	1 Ki. 19	1 Th. 2
17	1 Ki. 20	1 Th. 3
18	1 Ki. 21	1 Th. 4
19	1 Ki. 22	1 Th. 5
20	2 Ki. 1	2 Th. 1
21	2 Ki. 2	2 Th. 2
22	2 Ki. 3	2 Th. 3
23	2 Ki. 4	1 Tim. 1
24	2 Ki. 5	1 Tim. 2
25	2 Ki. 6	1 Tim. 3
26	2 Ki. 7	1 Tim. 4
27	2 Ki. 8	1 Tim. 5
28	2 Ki. 9	1 Tim. 6
29	2 Ki. 10	2 Tim. 1
30	2 Ki. 11–12	2 Tim. 2
31	2 Ki. 13	2 Tim. 3

November

1	2 Ki. 14	2 Tim. 4
2	2 Ki. 15	Titus 1
3	2 Ki. 16	Titus 2
4	2 Ki. 17	Titus 3
5	2 Ki. 18	Phlm.
6	2 Ki. 19	He. 1
7	2 Ki. 20	He. 2
8	2 Ki. 21	He. 3
9	2 Ki. 22	He. 4
10	2 Ki. 23	He. 5
11	2 Ki. 24	He. 6
12	2 Ki. 25	He. 7
13	1 Chr. 1–2	He. 8
14	1 Chr. 3–4	He. 9
15	1 Chr. 5–6	He. 10
16	1 Chr. 7–8	He. 11
17	1 Chr. 9–10	He. 12
18	1 Chr. 11–12	He. 13
19	1 Chr. 13–14	Jas. 1
20	1 Chr. 15	Jas. 2
21	1 Chr. 16	Jas. 3
22	1 Chr. 17	Jas. 4
23	1 Chr. 18	Jas. 5
24	1 Chr. 19–20	1 Pe. 1
25	1 Chr. 21	1 Pe. 2
26	1 Chr. 22	1 Pe. 3
27	1 Chr. 23	1 Pe. 4
28	1 Chr. 24–25	1 Pe. 5
29	1 Chr. 26–27	2 Pe. 1
30	1 Chr. 28	2 Pe. 2

December

1	1 Chr. 29	2 Pe. 3
2	2 Chr. 1	1 Jn. 1
3	2 Chr. 2	1 Jn. 2
4	2 Chr. 3–4	1 Jn. 3
5	2 Chr. 5.1–6.11	1 Jn. 4
6	2 Chr. 6.12–42	1 Jn. 5
7	2 Chr. 7	2 Jn.
8	2 Chr. 8	3 Jn.
9	2 Chr. 9	Jude
10	2 Chr. 10	Rev. 1
11	2 Chr. 11–12	Rev. 2
12	2 Chr. 13	Rev. 3
13	2 Chr. 14–15	Rev. 4
14	2 Chr. 16	Rev. 5
15	2 Chr. 17	Rev. 6
16	2 Chr. 18	Rev. 7
17	2 Chr. 19–20	Rev. 8
18	2 Chr. 21	Rev. 9
19	2 Chr. 22–23	Rev. 10
20	2 Chr. 24	Rev. 11
21	2 Chr. 25	Rev. 12
22	2 Chr. 26	Rev. 13
23	2 Chr. 27–28	Rev. 14
24	2 Chr. 29	Rev. 15
25	2 Chr. 30	Rev. 16
26	2 Chr. 31	Rev. 17
27	2 Chr. 32	Rev. 18
28	2 Chr. 33	Rev. 19
29	2 Chr. 34	Rev. 20
30	2 Chr. 35	Rev. 21
31	2 Chr. 36	Rev. 22

January

1	Ezr. 1	Ac. 1
2	Ezr. 2	Ac. 2
3	Ezr. 3	Ac. 3
4	Ezr. 4	Ac. 4
5	Ezr. 5	Ac. 5
6	Ezr. 6	Ac. 6
7	Ezr. 7	Ac. 7
8	Ezr. 8	Ac. 8
9	Ezr. 9	Ac. 9
10	Ezr. 10	Ac. 10
11	Ne. 1	Ac. 11
12	Ne. 2	Ac. 12
13	Ne. 3	Ac. 13
14	Ne. 4	Ac. 14
15	Ne. 5	Ac. 15
16	Ne. 6	Ac. 16
17	Ne. 7	Ac. 17
18	Ne. 8	Ac. 18
19	Ne. 9	Ac. 19
20	Ne. 10	Ac. 20
21	Ne. 11	Ac. 21
22	Ne. 12	Ac. 22
23	Ne. 13	Ac. 23
24	Est. 1	Ac. 24
25	Est. 2	Ac. 25
26	Est. 3	Ac. 26
27	Est. 4	Ac. 27
28	Est. 5	Ac. 28
29	Est. 6	Ro. 1
30	Est. 7	Ro. 2
31	Est. 8	Ro. 3

February

1	Est. 9–10	Ro. 4
2	Job 1	Ro. 5
3	Job 2	Ro. 6
4	Job 3	Ro. 7
5	Job 4	Ro. 8
6	Job 5	Ro. 9
7	Job 6	Ro. 10
8	Job 7	Ro. 11
9	Job 8	Ro. 12
10	Job 9	Ro. 13
11	Job 10	Ro. 14
12	Job 11	Ro. 15
13	Job 12	Ro. 16
14	Job 13	1 Co. 1
15	Job 14	1 Co. 2
16	Job 15	1 Co. 3
17	Job 16–17	1 Co. 4
18	Job 18	1 Co. 5
19	Job 19	1 Co. 6
20	Job 20	1 Co. 7
21	Job 21	1 Co. 8
22	Job 22	1 Co. 9
23	Job 23	1 Co. 10
24	Job 24	1 Co. 11
25	Job 25–26	1 Co. 12
26	Job 27	1 Co. 13
27	Job 28	1 Co. 14
28	Job 29	1 Co. 15

March

1	Job 30	1 Co. 16
2	Job 31	2 Co. 1
3	Job 32	2 Co. 2
4	Job 33	2 Co. 3
5	Job 34	2 Co. 4
6	Job 35	2 Co. 5
7	Job 36	2 Co. 6
8	Job 37	2 Co. 7
9	Job 38	2 Co. 8
10	Job 39	2 Co. 9
11	Job 40	2 Co. 10
12	Job 41	2 Co. 11
13	Job 42	2 Co. 12
14	Pro. 1	2 Co. 13
15	Pro. 2	Ga. 1
16	Pro. 3	Ga. 2
17	Pro. 4	Ga. 3
18	Pro. 5	Ga. 4
19	Pro. 6	Ga. 5
20	Pro. 7	Ga. 6
21	Pro. 8	Eph. 1
22	Pro. 9	Eph. 2
23	Pro. 10	Eph. 3
24	Pro. 11	Eph. 4
25	Pro. 12	Eph. 5
26	Pro. 13	Eph. 6
27	Pro. 14	Phil. 1
28	Pro. 15	Phil. 2
29	Pro. 16	Phil. 3
30	Pro. 17	Phil. 4
31	Pro. 18	Col. 1

April

1	Pro. 19	Col. 2
2	Pro. 20	Col. 3
3	Pro. 21	Col. 4
4	Pro. 22	1 Th. 1
5	Pro. 23	1 Th. 2
6	Pro. 24	1 Th. 3
7	Pro. 25	1 Th. 4
8	Pro. 26	1 Th. 5
9	Pro. 27	2 Th. 1
10	Pro. 28	2 Th. 2
11	Pro. 29	2 Th. 3
12	Pro. 30	1 Tim. 1
13	Pro. 31	1 Tim. 2
14	Ec. 1	1 Tim. 3
15	Ec. 2	1 Tim. 4
16	Ec. 3	1 Tim. 5
17	Ec. 4	1 Tim. 6
18	Ec. 5	2 Tim. 1
19	Ec. 6	2 Tim. 2
20	Ec. 7	2 Tim. 3
21	Ec. 8	2 Tim. 4
22	Ec. 9	Titus 1
23	Ec. 10	Titus 2
24	Ec. 11	Titus 3
25	Ec. 12	Phlm.
26	Song 1	He. 1
27	Song 2	He. 2
28	Song 3	He. 3
29	Song 4	He. 4
30	Song 5	He. 5

May			June		
1	Song 6	He. 6	1	Isa. 33	Rev. 3
2	Song 7	He. 7	2	Isa. 34	Rev. 4
3	Song 8	He. 8	3	Isa. 35	Rev. 5
4	Isa. 1	He. 9	4	Isa. 36	Rev. 6
5	Isa. 2	He. 10	5	Isa. 37	Rev. 7
6	Isa. 3–4	He. 11	6	Isa. 38	Rev. 8
7	Isa. 5	He. 12	7	Isa. 39	Rev. 9
8	Isa. 6	He. 13	8	Isa. 40	Rev. 10
9	Isa. 7	Jas. 1	9	Isa. 41	Rev. 11
10	Isa. 8.1–9.7	Jas. 2	10	Isa. 42	Rev. 12
11	Isa. 9.8–10.4	Jas. 3	11	Isa. 43	Rev. 13
12	Isa. 10.5–34	Jas. 4	12	Isa. 44	Rev. 14
13	Isa. 11–12	Jas. 5	13	Isa. 45	Rev. 15
14	Isa. 13	1 Pe. 1	14	Isa. 46	Rev. 16
15	Isa. 14	1 Pe. 2	15	Isa. 47	Rev. 17
16	Isa. 15	1 Pe. 3	16	Isa. 48	Rev. 18
17	Isa. 16	1 Pe. 4	17	Isa. 49	Rev. 19
18	Isa. 17–18	1 Pe. 5	18	Isa. 50	Rev. 20
19	Isa. 19–20	2 Pe. 1	19	Isa. 51	Rev. 21
20	Isa. 21	2 Pe. 2	20	Isa. 52	Rev. 22
21	Isa. 22	2 Pe. 3	21	Isa. 53	Mt. 1
22	Isa. 23	1 Jn. 1	22	Isa. 54	Mt. 2
23	Isa. 24	1 Jn. 2	23	Isa. 55	Mt. 3
24	Isa. 25	1 Jn. 3	24	Isa. 56	Mt. 4
25	Isa. 26	1 Jn. 4	25	Isa. 57	Mt. 5
26	Isa. 27	1 Jn. 5	26	Isa. 58	Mt. 6
27	Isa. 28	2 Jn.	27	Isa. 59	Mt. 7
28	Isa. 29	3 Jn.	28	Isa. 60	Mt. 8
29	Isa. 30	Jude	29	Isa. 61	Mt. 9
30	Isa. 31	Rev. 1	30	Isa. 62	Mt. 10
31	Isa. 32	Rev. 2			

July

1	Isa. 63	Mt. 11
2	Isa. 64	Mt. 12
3	Isa. 65	Mt. 13
4	Isa. 66	Mt. 14
5	Jer. 1	Mt. 15
6	Jer. 2	Mt. 16
7	Jer. 3	Mt. 17
8	Jer. 4	Mt. 18
9	Jer. 5	Mt. 19
10	Jer. 6	Mt. 20
11	Jer. 7	Mt. 21
12	Jer. 8	Mt. 22
13	Jer. 9	Mt. 23
14	Jer. 10	Mt. 24
15	Jer. 11	Mt. 25
16	Jer. 12	Mt. 26
17	Jer. 13	Mt. 27
18	Jer. 14	Mt. 28
19	Jer. 15	Mk. 1
20	Jer. 16	Mk. 2
21	Jer. 17	Mk. 3
22	Jer. 18	Mk. 4
23	Jer. 19	Mk. 5
24	Jer. 20	Mk. 6
25	Jer. 21	Mk. 7
26	Jer. 22	Mk. 8
27	Jer. 23	Mk. 9
28	Jer. 24	Mk. 10
29	Jer. 25	Mk. 11
30	Jer. 26	Mk. 12
31	Jer. 27	Mk. 13

August

1	Jer. 28	Mk. 14
2	Jer. 29	Mk. 15
3	Jer. 30–31	Mk. 16
4	Jer. 32	Ps. 1–2
5	Jer. 33	Ps. 3–4
6	Jer. 34	Ps. 5–6
7	Jer. 35	Ps. 7–8
8	Jer. 36, 45	Ps. 9
9	Jer. 37	Ps. 10
10	Jer. 38	Ps. 11–12
11	Jer. 39	Ps. 13–14
12	Jer. 40	Ps. 15–16
13	Jer. 41	Ps. 17
14	Jer. 42	Ps. 18
15	Jer. 43	Ps. 19
16	Jer. 44	Ps. 20–21
17	Jer. 46	Ps. 22
18	Jer. 47	Ps. 23–24
19	Jer. 48	Ps. 25
20	Jer. 49	Ps. 26–27
21	Jer. 50	Ps. 28–29
22	Jer. 51	Ps. 30
23	Jer. 52	Ps. 31
24	Lam. 1	Ps. 32
25	Lam. 2	Ps. 33
26	Lam. 3	Ps. 34
27	Lam. 4	Ps. 35
28	Lam. 5	Ps. 36
29	Ezek. 1	Ps. 37
30	Ezek. 2	Ps. 38
31	Ezek. 3	Ps. 39

September

1	Ezek. 4	Ps. 40–41
2	Ezek. 5	Ps. 42–43
3	Ezek. 6	Ps. 44
4	Ezek. 7	Ps. 45
5	Ezek. 8	Ps. 46–47
6	Ezek. 9	Ps. 48
7	Ezek. 10	Ps. 49
8	Ezek. 11	Ps. 50
9	Ezek. 12	Ps. 51
10	Ezek. 13	Ps. 52–54
11	Ezek. 14	Ps. 55
12	Ezek. 15	Ps. 56–57
13	Ezek. 16	Ps. 58–59
14	Ezek. 17	Ps. 60–61
15	Ezek. 18	Ps. 62–63
16	Ezek. 19	Ps. 64–65
17	Ezek. 20	Ps. 66–67
18	Ezek. 21	Ps. 68
19	Ezek. 22	Ps. 69
20	Ezek. 23	Ps. 70–71
21	Ezek. 24	Ps. 72
22	Ezek. 25	Ps. 73
23	Ezek. 26	Ps. 74
24	Ezek. 27	Ps. 75–76
25	Ezek. 28	Ps. 77
26	Ezek. 29	Ps. 78.1–37
27	Ezek. 30	Ps. 78.38–72
28	Ezek. 31	Ps. 79
29	Ezek. 32	Ps. 80
30	Ezek. 33	Ps. 81–82

October

1	Ezek. 34	Ps. 83–84
2	Ezek. 35	Ps. 85
3	Ezek. 36	Ps. 86
4	Ezek. 37	Ps. 87–88
5	Ezek. 38	Ps. 89
6	Ezek. 39	Ps. 90
7	Ezek. 40	Ps. 91
8	Ezek. 41	Ps. 92–93
9	Ezek. 42	Ps. 94
10	Ezek. 43	Ps. 95–96
11	Ezek. 44	Ps. 97–98
12	Ezek. 45	Ps. 99–101
13	Ezek. 46	Ps. 102
14	Ezek. 47	Ps. 103
15	Ezek. 48	Ps. 104
16	Dan. 1	Ps. 105
17	Dan. 2	Ps. 106
18	Dan. 3	Ps. 107
19	Dan. 4	Ps. 108–109
20	Dan. 5	Ps. 110–111
21	Dan. 6	Ps. 112–113
22	Dan. 7	Ps. 114–115
23	Dan. 8	Ps. 116
24	Dan. 9	Ps. 117–118
25	Dan. 10	Ps. 119.1–24
26	Dan. 11	Ps. 119.25–48
27	Dan. 12	Ps. 119.49–72
28	Hos. 1	Ps. 119.73–96
29	Hos. 2	Ps. 119.97–120
30	Hos. 3–4	Ps. 119.121–144
31	Hos. 5–6	Ps. 119.145–176

November

1	Hos. 7	Ps. 120–122
2	Hos. 8	Ps. 123–125
3	Hos. 9	Ps. 126–128
4	Hos. 10	Ps. 129–131
5	Hos. 11	Ps. 132–134
6	Hos. 12	Ps. 135–136
7	Hos. 13	Ps. 137–138
8	Hos. 14	Ps. 139
9	Joel 1	Ps. 140–141
10	Joel 2	Ps. 142
11	Joel 3	Ps. 143
12	Am. 1	Ps. 144
13	Am. 2	Ps. 145
14	Am. 3	Ps. 146–147
15	Am. 4	Ps. 148–150
16	Am. 5	Lu. 1.1–38
17	Am. 6	Lu. 1.39–80
18	Am. 7	Lu. 2
19	Am. 8	Lu. 3
20	Am. 9	Lu. 4
21	Ob.	Lu. 5
22	Jon. 1	Lu. 6
23	Jon. 2	Lu. 7
24	Jon. 3	Lu. 8
25	Jon. 4	Lu. 9
26	Mi. 1	Lu. 10
27	Mi. 2	Lu. 11
28	Mi. 3	Lu. 12
29	Mi. 4	Lu. 13
30	Mi. 5	Lu. 14

December

1	Mi. 6	Lu. 15
2	Mi. 7	Lu. 16
3	Na. 1	Lu. 17
4	Na. 2	Lu. 18
5	Na. 3	Lu. 19
6	Hab. 1	Lu. 20
7	Hab. 2	Lu. 21
8	Hab. 3	Lu. 22
9	Zeph. 1	Lu. 23
10	Zeph. 2	Lu. 24
11	Zeph. 3	Jn. 1
12	Hag. 1	Jn. 2
13	Hag. 2	Jn. 3
14	Zech. 1	Jn. 4
15	Zech. 2	Jn. 5
16	Zech. 3	Jn. 6
17	Zech. 4	Jn. 7
18	Zech. 5	Jn. 8
19	Zech. 6	Jn. 9
20	Zech. 7	Jn. 10
21	Zech. 8	Jn. 11
22	Zech. 9	Jn. 12
23	Zech. 10	Jn. 13
24	Zech. 11	Jn. 14
25	Zech. 12.1–13.1	Jn. 15
26	Zech. 13.2–9	Jn. 16
27	Zech. 14	Jn. 17
28	Mal. 1	Jn. 18
29	Mal. 2	Jn. 19
30	Mal. 3	Jn. 20
31	Mal. 4	Jn. 21

Daily Light

Morning and evening readings
from the Bible with additional readings
for special occasions

This one thing *I do*, forgetting those things
which are behind…I press toward the mark for the
prize of the high calling of God in Christ Jesus.

Father, I will that they…whom thou hast given me, be
with me where I am; that they may behold my glory,
which thou hast given me.—I know whom I have
believed, and am persuaded that he is able to keep that
which I have committed unto him against that day.—He
which hath begun a good work in you will perform *it*
until the day of Jesus Christ.

Know ye not that they which run in a race run all,
but one receiveth the prize? So run, that ye may obtain.
And every man that striveth for the mastery is temperate in all things. Now they *do it* to obtain a corruptible
crown; but we an incorruptible.—Let us lay aside every
weight, and the sin which doth so easily beset *us*, and let
us run with patience the race that is set before us, looking unto Jesus.

Phil. 3.13,14; Jn. 17.24; 2 Tim. 1.12; Phil. 1.6
§ 1 Co. 9.24–25; He. 12.1–2

The LORD, he *it is* that doth go before thee; he will be with thee, he will not fail thee.

If thy presence go not *with me*, carry us not up hence.—O LORD, I know that the way of man *is* not in himself: *it is* not in man that walketh to direct his steps.

The steps of a *good* man are ordered by the LORD: and he delighteth in his way. Though he fall, he shall not be utterly cast down: for the LORD upholdeth *him with* his hand.

I *am* continually with thee: thou hast holden *me* by my right hand. Thou shalt guide me with thy counsel, and afterward receive me *to* glory.—I am persuaded, that neither death, nor life, nor angels, nor principalities, nor powers, nor things present, nor things to come, nor height, nor depth, nor any other creature, shall be able to separate us from the love of God, which is in Christ Jesus our Lord.

Deu. 31.8; Ex. 33.15; Jer. 10.23 § Ps. 37.23–24
§ Ps. 73.23–24; Ro. 8.38–39

Sing unto the LORD a new song.

Sing aloud unto God our strength: make a joyful noise unto the God of Jacob. Take a psalm, and bring hither the timbrel, the pleasant harp with the psaltery.—He hath put a new song in my mouth, *even* praise unto our God: many shall see *it*, and fear, and shall trust in the LORD.

Be strong and of a good courage; be not afraid, neither be thou dismayed: for the LORD thy God *is* with thee whithersoever thou goest.—The joy of the LORD is your strength.—Paul…thanked God, and took courage.

Knowing the time, that now *it is* high time to awake out of sleep: for now *is* our salvation nearer than when we believed. The night is far spent, the day is at hand: let us therefore cast off the works of darkness, and let us put on the armour of light. Let us walk honestly, as in the day; not in rioting and drunkenness, not in chambering and wantonness, not in strife and envying. But put ye on the Lord Jesus Christ, and make not provision for the flesh, to *fulfil* the lusts *thereof*.

Isa. 42.10; Ps. 81.1–2; Ps. 40.3 § Jos. 1.9; Ne. 8.10; Ac. 28.15 § Ro. 13.11–14

Let my prayer be set forth before thee *as incense*; *and* the lifting up of my hands *as* the evening sacrifice.

Thou shalt make an altar to burn incense upon… And thou shalt put it before the vail that *is* by the ark of the testimony, before the mercy seat that is over the testimony, where I will meet with thee. And Aaron shall burn thereon sweet incense every morning… And when Aaron lighteth the lamps at even, he shall burn incense upon it, a perpetual incense before the LORD throughout your generations.

[Jesus] is able also to save them to the uttermost that come unto God by him, seeing he ever liveth to make intercession for them.—The smoke of the incense, *which came* with the prayers of the saints, ascended up before God out of the angel's hand.

Ye also, as lively stones, are built up a spiritual house, an holy priesthood, to offer up spiritual sacrifices, acceptable to God by Jesus Christ.

Pray without ceasing.

Ps. 141.2; Ex. 30.1,6–7,8 § He. 7.25; Rev. 8.4 § 1 Pe. 2.5 § 1 Th. 5.17

He led them forth by the right way.

He found [Jacob] in a desert land, and in the waste howling wilderness; he led him about, he instructed him, he kept him as the apple of his eye. As an eagle stirreth up her nest, fluttereth over her young, spreadeth abroad her wings, taketh them, beareth them on her wings: *so* the LORD alone did lead him.—*Even* to *your* old age I *am* he; and *even* to hoar hairs will I carry *you*: I have made, and I will bear; even I will carry, and will deliver *you*.

He restoreth my soul: he leadeth me in the paths of righteousness for his name's sake. Yea, though I walk through the valley of the shadow of death, I will fear no evil: for thou *art* with me; thy rod and thy staff they comfort me.

The Lord shall guide thee continually, and satisfy thy soul in drought, and make fat thy bones: and thou shalt be like a watered garden, and like a spring of water, whose waters fail not.—For this GOD *is* our GOD for ever and ever: he will be our guide *even* unto death.—Who teacheth like him?

Ps. 107.7; Deu. 32.10–12; Isa. 46.4 § Ps. 23.3–4 § Isa. 58.11; Ps. 48.14; Job 36.22

What wilt thou that I shall do unto thee?…
Lord, that I may receive my sight.

Open thou mine eyes, that I may behold wondrous things out of thy law.

Then opened he their understanding, that they might understand the scriptures.—The Comforter, *which is* the Holy Ghost, whom the Father will send in my name…shall teach you all things.—Every good gift and every perfect gift is from above, and cometh down from the Father of lights.

The God of our Lord Jesus Christ, the Father of glory…give unto you the spirit of wisdom and revelation in the knowledge of him: the eyes of your understanding being enlightened; that ye may know what is the hope of his calling, and what the riches of the glory of his inheritance in the saints, and what *is* the exceeding greatness of his power to us-ward who believe, according to the working of his mighty power.

Lu. 18.41; Ps. 119.18 § Lu. 24.45; Jn. 14.26; Jas. 1.17 § Eph. 1.17–19

Ye are not as yet come to the rest and to the inheritance, which the LORD your God giveth you.

This *is* not *your* rest.—There remaineth therefore a rest to the people of God.—Within the veil; whither the forerunner is for us entered, *even* Jesus.

In my Father's house are many mansions: if *it were* not *so*, I would have told you. I go to prepare a place for you. And if I go and prepare a place for you, I will come again, and receive you unto myself; that where I am, *there* ye may be also.—With Christ; which is far better.

God shall wipe away all tears from their eyes; and there shall be no more death, neither sorrow, nor crying, neither shall there be any more pain: for the former things are passed away.—There the wicked cease *from* troubling; and there the weary be at rest.

Lay up for yourselves treasures in heaven. For where your treasure is, there will your heart be also.—Set your affection on things above, not on things on the earth.

Deu. 12.9; Mi. 2.10; He. 4.9; He. 6.19–20
§ Jn. 14.2–3; Phil. 1.23 § Rev. 21.4; Job 3.17
§ Mt. 6.20–21; Col. 3.2

O death, where *is* thy sting?
O grave, where *is* thy victory?

The sting of death *is* sin.—But now once in the end of the world hath he appeared to put away sin by the sacrifice of himself. And as it is appointed unto men once to die, but after this the judgment: so Christ was once offered to bear the sins of many; and unto them that look for him shall he appear the second time without sin unto salvation.

As the children are partakers of flesh and blood, he also himself likewise took part of the same; that through death he might destroy him that had the power of death, that is, the devil; and deliver them who through fear of death were all their lifetime subject to bondage.

I am now ready to be offered, and the time of my departure is at hand. I have fought a good fight, I have finished *my* course, I have kept the faith: henceforth there is laid up for me a crown of righteousness.

1 Co. 15.55; 1 Co. 15.56; He. 9.26–28 § He. 2.14–15
§ 2 Tim. 4.6–8

We which have believed do enter into rest.

They...weary themselves to commit iniquity.—I see another law in my members, warring against the law of my mind, and bringing me into captivity to the law of sin which is in my members. O wretched man that I am! who shall deliver me from the body of this death?

Come unto me, all *ye* that labour and are heavy laden, and I will give you rest.—Being justified by faith, we have peace with God through our Lord Jesus Christ: by whom also we have access by faith into this grace wherein we stand, and rejoice in hope of the glory of God.

He that is entered into his rest, he also hath ceased from his own works.—Not having mine own righteousness, which is of the law, but that which is through the faith of Christ, the righteousness which is of God by faith.—This *is* the rest *wherewith* ye may cause the weary to rest; and this *is* the refreshing.

He. 4.3; Jer. 9.5; Ro. 7.23–24 § Mt. 11.28; Ro. 5.1–2 § He. 4.10; Phil. 3.9; Isa. 28.12

**Set a watch, O LORD, before my mouth;
keep the door of my lips.**

If thou, LORD, shouldest mark iniquities, O Lord, who shall stand?—They provoked his spirit, so that he spake unadvisedly with his lips.

Not that which goeth into the mouth defileth a man; but that which cometh out of the mouth, this defileth a man.

A whisperer separateth chief friends.—There is that speaketh like the piercings of a sword: but the tongue of the wise *is* health. The lip of truth shall be established for ever: but a lying tongue *is* but for a moment.—The tongue can no man tame; *it is* an unruly evil, full of deadly poison... Out of the same mouth proceedeth blessing and cursing. My brethren, these things ought not so to be.

Put off...anger, wrath, malice, blasphemy, filthy communication out of your mouth. Lie not one to another, seeing that ye have put off the old man with his deeds.—This is the will of God, *even* your sanctification.—In their mouth was found no guile.

Ps. 141.3; Ps. 130.3; Ps. 106.33 § Mt. 15.11
§ Pro. 16.28; Pro. 12.18–19; Jas. 3.8,10 § Col. 3.8–9;
1 Th. 4.3; Rev. 14.5

Let the beauty of the LORD our God be upon us: and establish thou the work of our hands.

Thy renown went forth among the heathen for thy beauty: for it *was* perfect through my comeliness, which I had put upon thee, saith the Lord GOD.—We all, with open face beholding as in a glass the glory of the Lord, are changed into the same image from glory to glory, *even* as by the Spirit of the Lord.—The spirit of glory and of God resteth upon you.

Blessed *is* every one that feareth the LORD; that walketh in his ways. For thou shalt eat the labour of thine hands: happy *shalt* thou *be*, and *it shall be* well with thee.—Commit thy works unto the LORD, and thy thoughts shall be established.

Work out your own salvation with fear and trembling. For it is God which worketh in you both to will and to do of *his* good pleasure.—Our Lord Jesus Christ himself, and God, even our Father, which hath loved us, and hath given *us* everlasting consolation and good hope through grace, comfort your hearts, and stablish you in every good word and work.

Ps. 90.17; Ezek. 16.14; 2 Co. 3.18; 1 Pe. 4.14
§ Ps. 128.1–2; Pro. 16.3 § Phil. 2.12–13; 2 Th. 2.16–17

The apostles gathered themselves together unto Jesus, and told him all things…they had done.

There is a friend *that* sticketh closer than a brother.— The LORD spake unto Moses face to face, as a man speaketh unto his friend.—Ye are my friends, if ye do whatsoever I command you. Henceforth I call you not servants; for the servant knoweth not what his lord doeth: but I have called you friends; for all things that I have heard of my Father I have made known unto you.

When ye shall have done all those things which are commanded you, say, We are unprofitable servants.

Ye have not received the spirit of bondage again to fear; but ye have received the Spirit of adoption, whereby we cry, Abba, Father.

In every thing by prayer and supplication with thanksgiving let your requests be made known unto God.—The prayer of the upright *is* his delight.

Mk. 6.30; Pro. 18.24; Ex. 33.11; Jn. 15.14–15
§ Lu. 17.10 § Ro. 8.15 § Phil. 4.6; Pro. 15.8

Think upon me, my God, for good.

Thus saith the LORD; I remember thee, the kindness of thy youth, the love of thine espousals, when thou wentest after me in the wilderness.—I will remember my covenant with thee in the days of thy youth, and I will establish unto thee an everlasting covenant.—I will visit you, and perform my good word toward you.—For I know the thoughts that I think toward you, saith the LORD, thoughts of peace, and not of evil, to give you an expected end.

As the heavens are higher than the earth, so are my ways higher than your ways, and my thoughts than your thoughts.—I would seek unto God, and unto God would I commit my cause: which doeth great things and unsearchable; marvellous things without number.—Many, O LORD my God, *are* thy wonderful works *which* thou hast done, and thy thoughts *which are* to us-ward: they cannot be reckoned up in order unto thee: *if* I would declare and speak *of them*, they are more than can be numbered.

Ne. 5.19; Jer. 2.2; Ezek. 16.60; Jer. 29.10; Jer. 29.11
§ Isa. 55.9; Job 5.8–9; Ps. 40.5

I will not fail thee, nor forsake thee.

There failed not ought of any good thing which the LORD had spoken unto the house of Israel; all came to pass.—God *is* not a man, that he should lie; neither the son of man, that he should repent: hath he said, and shall he not do *it*? or hath he spoken, and shall he not make it good?

The LORD thy God, he *is* God, the faithful God, which keepeth covenant and mercy with them that love him.—He will ever be mindful of his covenant.

Can a woman forget her sucking child, that she should not have compassion on the son of her womb? yea, they may forget, yet will I not forget thee. Behold, I have graven thee upon the palms of *my* hands.

The LORD thy God in the midst of thee *is* mighty; he will save, he will rejoice over thee with joy; he will rest in his love, he will joy over thee with singing.

Jos. 1.5; Jos. 21.45; Nu. 23.19 § Deu. 7.9; Ps. 111.5 § Isa. 49.15–16 § Zeph. 3.17

They that know thy name will put their trust in thee: for thou, LORD, hast not forsaken them that seek thee.

The name of the LORD *is* a strong tower: the righteous runneth into it, and is safe.—I will trust, and not be afraid: for the LORD JEHOVAH *is* my strength and *my* song; he also is become my salvation.

I have been young, and *now* am old; yet have I not seen the righteous forsaken, nor his seed begging bread.—For the LORD loveth judgment, and forsaketh not his saints; they are preserved for ever: but the seed of the wicked shall be cut off.—The LORD will not forsake his people for his great name's sake: because it hath pleased the LORD to make you his people.—Who delivered us from so great a death, and doth deliver: in whom we trust that he will yet deliver *us*.

Be content with such things as ye have: for he hath said, I will never leave thee, nor forsake thee. So that we may boldly say, The Lord *is* my helper, and I will not fear what man shall do unto me.

Ps. 9.10; Pro. 18.10; Isa. 12.2 § Ps. 37.25; Ps. 37.28; 1 Sa. 12.22; 2 Co. 1.10 § He. 13.5–6

They are without fault before the throne of God.

The iniquity of Israel shall be sought for, and *there shall be* none; and the sins of Judah, and they shall not be found: for I will pardon them whom I reserve.—Who *is* a God like unto thee, that pardoneth iniquity, and passeth by the transgression of the remnant of his heritage? he retaineth not his anger for ever, because he delighteth *in* mercy. He will turn again, he will have compassion upon us; he will subdue our iniquities; and thou wilt cast all their sins into the depths of the sea.

He hath made us accepted in the beloved.—To present you holy and unblameable and unreproveable in his sight.

Now unto him that is able to keep you from falling, and to present *you* faultless before the presence of his glory with exceeding joy, to the only wise God our Saviour, *be* glory and majesty, dominion and power, both now and ever. Amen.

Rev. 14.5; Jer. 50.20; Mi. 7.18–19 § Eph. 1.6; Col. 1.22 § Jude 24–25

**Thou hast given a banner to them that fear thee,
that it may be displayed because of the truth.**

Jehovah-nissi [*marg.* The LORD is my banner].—When
the enemy shall come in like a flood, the Spirit of the
LORD shall lift up a standard against him.

We will rejoice in thy salvation, and in the name of
our God we will set up *our* banners.—The LORD hath
brought forth our righteousness: come, and let us
declare in Zion the work of the LORD our God.—We are
more than conquerors through him that loved us.—
Thanks *be* to God, which giveth us the victory through
our Lord Jesus Christ.—The captain of their salvation.

My brethren, be strong in the Lord, and in the power
of his might.—Valiant for the truth.—Fight the LORD's
battles.—Be strong, all ye people of the land, saith the
LORD, and work…fear ye not.—Lift up your eyes, and
look on the fields; for they are white already to harvest.—Yet a little while, and he that shall come will
come, and will not tarry.

Ps. 60.4; Ex. 17.15; Isa. 59.19 § Ps. 20.5; Jer. 51.10;
Ro. 8.37; 1 Co. 15.57; He. 2.10 § Eph. 6.10; Jer. 9.3;
1 Sa. 18.17; Hag. 2.4,5; Jn. 4.35; He. 10.37

One thing is needful.

*T*here be many that say, Who will shew us *any* good? LORD, lift thou up the light of thy countenance upon us. Thou hast put gladness in my heart, more than in the time *that* their corn and their wine increased.

As the hart panteth after the water brooks, so panteth my soul after thee, O God. My soul thirsteth for God, for the living God.—O GOD, thou *art* my God; early will I seek thee: my soul thirsteth for thee, my flesh longeth for thee in a dry and thirsty land, where no water is.

I am the bread of life: he that cometh to me shall never hunger; and he that believeth on me shall never thirst.—Lord, evermore give us this bread.—Mary...sat at Jesus' feet, and heard his word.—One *thing* have I desired of the LORD, that will I seek after; that I may dwell in the house of the LORD all the days of my life, to behold the beauty of the LORD, and to enquire in his temple.

Lu. 10.42; Ps. 4.6–7 § Ps. 42.1–2; Ps. 63.1 § Jn. 6.35; Jn. 6.34; Lu. 10.39; Ps. 27.4

I pray God your whole spirit and soul and
body be preserved blameless unto the coming
of our Lord Jesus Christ.

Christ also loved the church, and gave himself for
it...that he might present it to himself a glorious
church, not having spot, or wrinkle, or any such thing;
but that it should be holy and without blemish.—
Whom we preach, warning every man, and teaching
every man in all wisdom; that we may present every
man perfect in Christ Jesus.

The peace of God which passeth all understanding.—Let the peace of God rule in your hearts, to the
which also ye are called in one body.

Our Lord Jesus Christ himself, and God, even our
Father, which hath loved us, and hath given *us* everlasting consolation and good hope through grace, comfort
your hearts, and stablish you in every good word and
work.—Who shall also confirm you unto the end, *that
ye may be* blameless in the day of our Lord Jesus Christ.

1 Th. 5.23; Eph. 5.25,27; Col. 1.28 § Phil. 4.7; Col. 3.15
§ 2 Th. 2.16–17; 1 Co. 1.8

Will God in very deed dwell with men on the earth?

Let them make me a sanctuary; that I may dwell among them.—I will meet with the children of Israel, and *the tabernacle* shall be sanctified by my glory. And I will dwell among the children of Israel, and will be their God.

Thou hast ascended on high, thou hast led captivity captive: thou hast received gifts for men; yea, *for* the rebellious also, that the LORD God might dwell *among them.*

Ye are the temple of the living God; as God hath said, I will dwell in them, and walk in *them*; and I will be their God, and they shall be my people.—Your body is the temple of the Holy Ghost *which is* in you.— Ye…are builded together for an habitation of God through the Spirit.

The heathen shall know that I the LORD do sanctify Israel, when my sanctuary shall be in the midst of them for evermore.

2 Chr. 6.18; Ex. 25.8; Ex. 29.43,45 § Ps. 68.18
§ 2 Co. 6.16; 1 Co. 6.19; Eph. 2.22 § Ezek. 37.28

Praise waiteth for thee, O God, in Sion.

To us *there is but* one God, the Father, of whom *are* all things, and we in him; and one Lord Jesus Christ, by whom *are* all things, and we by him.—All *men* should honour the Son, even as they honour the Father. He that honoureth not the Son honoureth not the Father which hath sent him.—By him therefore let us offer the sacrifice of praise to God continually, that is, the fruit of *our* lips giving thanks to his name.—Whoso offereth praise glorifieth me: and to him that ordereth *his* conversation *aright* will I shew the salvation of God.

I beheld, and, lo, a great multitude, which no man could number, of all nations, and kindreds, and people, and tongues, stood before the throne, and before the Lamb, clothed with white robes, and palms in their hands; and cried with a loud voice, saying, Salvation to our God which sitteth upon the throne, and unto the Lamb... Amen: Blessing, and glory, and wisdom, and thanksgiving, and honour, and power, and might, *be* unto our God for ever and ever. Amen.

Ps. 65.1;   1 Co. 8.6;   Jn. 5.23;   He. 13.15;   Ps. 50.23
§ Rev. 7.9–10,12

Who redeemeth thy life from destruction.

Their Redeemer *is* strong; the LORD of hosts *is* his name.—I will ransom them from the power of the grave; I will redeem them from death: O death, I will be thy plagues; O grave, I will be thy destruction.

As the children are partakers of flesh and blood, he also himself likewise took part of the same; that through death he might destroy him that had the power of death, that is, the devil; and deliver them who through fear of death were all their lifetime subject to bondage.

He that believeth on the Son hath everlasting life: and he that believeth not the Son shall not see life; but the wrath of God abideth on him.

Ye are dead, and your life is hid with Christ in God. When Christ, *who is* our life, shall appear, then shall ye also appear with him in glory.—When he shall come to be glorified in his saints, and to be admired in all them that believe.

Ps. 103.4; Jer. 50.34; Hos. 13.14 § He. 2.14–15 § Jn. 3.36 § Col. 3.3–4; 2 Th. 1.10

The only wise God our Saviour.

Christ Jesus, who of God is made unto us wisdom, and righteousness, and sanctification, and redemption.—Canst thou by searching find out God? canst thou find out the Almighty unto perfection? *It is* as high as heaven; what canst thou do? deeper than hell; what canst thou know?

We speak the wisdom of God in a mystery, *even* the hidden *wisdom*, which God ordained before the world unto our glory.—The mystery, which from the beginning of the world hath been hid in God, who created all things by Jesus Christ: to the intent that now unto the principalities and powers in heavenly *places* might be known by the church the manifold wisdom of God.

If any of you lack wisdom, let him ask of God, that giveth to all *men* liberally, and upbraideth not; and it shall be given him.—The wisdom that is from above is first pure, then peaceable, gentle, *and* easy to be intreated, full of mercy and good fruits, without partiality, and without hypocrisy.

Jude 25; 1 Co. 1.30; Job 11.7–8 § 1 Co. 2.7; Eph. 3.9–10 § Jas. 1.5; Jas. 3.17

When shall I arise, and the night be gone?

Watchman, what of the night? The watchman said, The morning cometh.

Yet a little while, and he that shall come will come, and will not tarry.—*He shall be* as the light of the morning, *when* the sun riseth, *even* a morning without clouds.

I go to prepare a place for you. And if I go and prepare a place for you, I will come again, and receive you unto myself; that where I am, *there* ye may be also... Let not your heart be troubled, neither let it be afraid. Ye have heard how I said unto you, I go away, and come *again* unto you.

Let all thine enemies perish, O LORD: but *let* them that love him *be* as the sun when he goeth forth in his might.—Ye are all the children of light, and the children of the day: we are not of the night, nor of darkness.

There shall be no night there.

Job 7.4; Isa. 21.11–12 § He. 10.37; 2 Sa. 23.4
§ Jn. 14.2–3,27–28 § Judg. 5.31; 1 Th. 5.5 § Rev. 21.25

**Thou wilt keep *him* in perfect peace,
whose mind is stayed *on thee*.**

Cast thy burden upon the LORD, and he shall sustain thee: he shall never suffer the righteous to be moved.— I will trust, and not be afraid: for the LORD JEHOVAH *is* my strength and my song; he also is become my salvation.

Why are ye fearful, O ye of little faith?—Be careful for nothing; but in every thing by prayer and supplication with thanksgiving let your requests be made known unto God. And the peace of God, which passeth all understanding, shall keep your hearts and minds through Christ Jesus.—In quietness and in confidence shall be your strength.

The work of righteousness shall be peace; and the effect or righteousness quietness and assurance for ever.—Peace I leave with you, my peace I give unto you: not as the world giveth, give I unto you. Let not your heart be troubled, neither let it be afraid.—Peace, from him which is, and which was, and which is to come.

Isa. 26.3; Ps. 55.22; Isa. 12.2 § Mt. 8.26; Phil. 4.6–7; Isa. 30.15 § Isa. 32.17; Jn. 14.27; Rev. 1.4

Let not the sun go down upon your wrath.

If thy brother shall trespass against thee, go and tell him his fault between thee and him alone: if he shall hear thee, thou hast gained thy brother... Lord, how oft shall my brother sin against me, and I forgive him? till seven times? Jesus saith unto him, I say not unto thee, Until seven times: but, Until seventy times seven.— When ye stand praying, forgive, if ye have ought against any: that your Father also which is in heaven may forgive you your trespasses.

Put on therefore, as the elect of God, holy and beloved, bowels of mercies, kindness, humbleness of mind, meekness, longsuffering; forbearing one another, and forgiving one another, if any man have a quarrel against any: even as Christ forgave you, so also *do* ye.— Be ye kind one to another, tenderhearted, forgiving one another, even as God for Christ's sake hath forgiven you.

The apostles said unto the Lord, Increase our faith.

Eph. 4.26; Mt. 18.15,21–22; Mk. 11.25 § Col. 3.12–13; Eph. 4.32 § Lu. 17.5

My Father is greater than I.

When ye pray, say, Our Father which art in heaven.—
I ascend unto my Father, and your Father; and *to* my
God, and your God.—As the Father gave me commandment, even so I do.—The words that I speak unto you I
speak not of myself: but the Father that dwelleth in me,
he doeth the works.

The Father loveth the Son, and hath given all things
into his hand.—Thou hast given him power over all
flesh, that he should give eternal life to as many as thou
hast given him.

Lord, shew us the Father, and it sufficeth us. Jesus
saith unto him, Have I been so long time with you, and
yet hast thou not known me, Philip? he that hath seen
me hath seen the Father; and how sayest thou *then*,
Shew us the Father? Believest thou not that I am in the
Father, and the Father in me?—I and *my* Father are
one.—As the Father hath loved me, so have I loved you:
continue ye in my love. If ye keep my commandments,
ye shall abide in my love; even as I have kept my Father's
commandments, and abide in his love.

Jn. 14.28; Lu. 11.2; Jn. 20.17; Jn. 14.31; Jn. 14.10
§ Jn. 3.35; Jn. 17.2 § Jn. 14.8–10; Jn. 10.30; Jn. 15.9–10

I will put enmity between thee and the woman, and between thy seed and her seed; it shall bruise thy head, and thou shalt bruise his heel.

His visage was so marred more than any man, and his form more than the sons of men.—He *was* wounded for our transgressions, *he was* bruised for our iniquities: the chastisement of our peace *was* upon him; and with his stripes we are healed.

This is your hour, and the power of darkness.— Thou couldest have no power *at all* against me, except it were given thee from above.

The Son of God was manifested, that he might destroy the works of the devil.—He…cast out many devils; and suffered not the devils to speak, because they knew him.

All power is given unto me in heaven and in earth.— In my name shall they cast out devils.

The God of peace shall bruise Satan under your feet shortly.

Ge. 3.15; Isa. 52.14; Isa. 53.5 § Lu. 22.53; Jn. 19.11 § 1 Jn. 3.8; Mk. 1.34 § Mt. 28.18; Mk. 16.17 § Ro. 16.20

**My soul cleaveth unto the dust:
quicken thou me according to thy word.**

If ye…be risen with Christ, seek those things which are above, where Christ sitteth on the right hand of God. Set your affection on things above, not on things on the earth. For…your life is hid with Christ in God.—Our conversation is in heaven; from whence also we look for the Saviour, the Lord Jesus Christ: who shall change our vile body, that it may be fashioned like unto his glorious body, according to the working whereby he is able even to subdue all things unto himself.

The flesh lusteth against the Spirit, and the Spirit against the flesh: and these are contrary the one to the other: so that ye cannot do the things that ye would.— Brethren, we are debtors, not to the flesh, to live after the flesh. For if ye live after the flesh, ye shall die: but if ye through the Spirit do mortify the deeds of the body, ye shall live.—Dearly beloved, I beseech *you* as strangers and pilgrims, abstain from fleshly lusts, which war against the soul.

**Ps. 119.25; Col. 3.13; Phil. 3.20–21 § Ga. 5.17;
Ro. 8.12–13; 1 Pe. 2.11**

The measure of faith.

Him that is weak in the faith.—Strong in faith, giving glory to God.

O thou of little faith, wherefore didst thou doubt?— Great *is* thy faith: be it unto thee even as thou wilt.

Believe ye that I am able to do this? They said unto him, Yea, Lord... According to your faith be it unto you.

Increase our faith.—Building up yourselves on your most holy faith.—Rooted and built up in him, and stablished in the faith.—He which stablisheth us with you in Christ...*is* God.—The God of all grace...after that ye have suffered a while, make you perfect, stablish, strengthen, settle *you*.

We...that are strong ought to bear the infirmities of the weak, and not to please ourselves.—Let us not...judge one another any more but judge this rather, that no man put a stumblingblock or an occasion to fall in *his* brother's way.

Ro. 12.3; Ro. 14.1; Ro. 4.20 § Mt. 14.31; Mt. 15.28 § Mt. 9.28,29 § Lu. 17.5; Jude 20; Col. 2.7; 2 Co. 1.21; 1 Pe. 5.10 § Ro. 15.1; Ro. 14.13

**It pleased *the Father* that in him
should all fulness dwell.**

The Father loveth the Son, and hath given all things into his hand.—God also hath highly exalted him, and given him a name which is above every name: that at the name of Jesus every knee should bow, of *things* in heaven, and *things* in earth, and *things* under the earth; and *that* every tongue should confess that Jesus Christ *is* Lord, to the glory of God the Father.—Far above all principality, and power, and might, and dominion, and every name that is named, not only in this world, but also in that which is to come.—By him were all things created, that are in heaven, and that are in earth, visible and invisible, whether *they be* thrones, or dominions, or principalities, or powers: all things were created by him, and for him.

Christ both died, and rose, and revived, that he might be Lord both of the dead and living.—And ye are complete in him, which is the head of all principality and power.—Of his fulness have all we received.

Col. 1.19; Jn. 3.35; Phil. 2.9–11; Eph. 1.21; Col. 1.16
§ Ro. 14.9; Col. 2.10; Jn. 1.16

Write the things which thou hast seen, and the things which are, and the things which shall be hereafter.

Holy men of God spake *as they were* moved by the Holy Ghost.—That which we have seen and heard declare we unto you, that ye also may have fellowship with us: and truly our fellowship *is* with the Father, and with his Son Jesus Christ.

Behold my hands and my feet, that it is I myself: handle me, and see; for a spirit hath not flesh and bones, as ye see me have. And when he had thus spoken, he shewed them *his* hands and *his* feet.—He that saw *it* bare record, and his record is true: and he knoweth that he saith true, that ye might believe.

We have not followed cunningly devised fables, when we made known unto you the power and coming of our Lord Jesus Christ, but were eyewitnesses of his majesty.—That your faith should not stand in the wisdom of men, but in the power of God.

Rev. 1.19; 2 Pe. 1.21; 1 Jn. 1.3 § Lu. 24.39–40; Jn. 19.35 § 2 Pe. 1.16; 1 Co. 2.5

Thou hast in love to my soul *delivered it* from the pit of corruption.

God sent his only begotten Son into the world, that we might live through him. Herein is love, not that we loved God, but that he loved us, and sent his Son *to be* the propitiation for our sins.

Who *is* a God like unto thee, that pardoneth iniquity, and passeth by the transgression of the remnant of his heritage? he retaineth not his anger for ever, because he delighteth *in* mercy. He will turn again, he will have compassion upon us; he will subdue our iniquities; and thou wilt cast all their sins into the depths of the sea.—O LORD my God, I cried unto thee, and thou hast healed me. O LORD, thou hast brought up my soul from the grave: thou hast kept me alive, that I should not go down to the pit.—When my soul fainted within me I remembered the LORD: and my prayer came in unto thee, into thine holy temple.—I waited patiently for the LORD…He brought me up…out of an horrible pit, out of the miry clay, and set my feet upon a rock.

Isa. 38.17; 1 Jn. 4.9–10 § Mi. 7.18–19; Ps. 30.2–3;
Jon. 2.7; Ps. 40.1,2

The things which are.

Now we see through a glass, darkly.—Now we see not yet all things put under him.

We have…a more sure word of prophecy; whereunto ye do well that ye take heed, as unto a light that shineth in a dark place, until the day dawn, and the day star arise in your hearts.—Thy word *is* a lamp unto my feet, and a light unto my path.

Beloved, remember ye the words which were spoken before of the apostles of our Lord Jesus Christ; how that they told you there should be mockers in the last time, who should walk after their own ungodly lusts.—The Spirit speaketh expressly, that in the latter times some shall depart from the faith, giving heed to seducing spirits, and doctrines of devils.

Little children, it is the last time.—The night is far spent, the day is at hand: let us therefore cast off the works of darkness, and let us put on the armour of light.

Rev. 1.19; 1 Co. 13.12; He. 2.8 § 2 Pe. 1.19; Ps. 119.105 § Jude 17–18; 1 Tim. 4.1 § 1 Jn. 2.18; Ro. 13.12

Him that was to come.

Jesus…made a little lower than the angels for the suffering of death…that he by the grace of God should taste death for every man.—One died for all.—As by one man's disobedience many were made sinners, so by the obedience of one shall many be made righteous.

The first man Adam was made a living soul; the last Adam *was made* a quickening spirit.—That *was* not first which is spiritual, but that which is natural; and afterward that which is spiritual.—God said, Let us make man in our image, after our likeness… So God created man in his *own* image, in the image of God created he him.—God…hath in these last days spoken unto us by *his* Son…the brightness of *his* glory, and the express image of his person.—Thou hast given him power over all flesh.

The first man *is* of the earth, earthy: the second man *is* the Lord from heaven. As *is* the earthy, such *are* they also that are earthy: and as *is* the heavenly, such *are* they also that are heavenly.

Ro. 5.14; He. 2.9; 2 Co. 5.14; Ro. 5.19
§ 1 Co. 15.45; 1 Co. 15.46; Ge. 1.26,27; He. 1.13;
Jn. 17.2 § 1 Co. 15.47–48

Things which shall be hereafter.

As it is written, Eye hath not seen, nor ear heard, neither have entered into the heart of man, the things which God hath prepared for them that love him. But God hath revealed *them* unto us by his Spirit.—The Spirit of truth…will shew you things to come.

Behold, he cometh with clouds; and every eye shall see him, and they *also* which pierced him: and all kindreds of the earth shall wail because of him. Even so, Amen.

I would not have you to be ignorant, brethren, concerning them which are asleep, that ye sorrow not, even as others which have no hope. For if we believe that Jesus died and rose again, even so them also which sleep in Jesus will God bring with him… For the Lord himself shall descend from heaven with a shout, with the voice of the archangel, and with the trump of God: and the dead in Christ shall rise first: then we which are alive *and* remain shall be caught up together with them in the clouds, to meet the Lord in the air: and so shall we ever be with the Lord.

Rev. 1.19; 1 Co. 2.9–10; Jn. 16.13 § Rev. 1.7 § 1 Th. 4.13–14,16–17

Serving the Lord with all humility of mind.

Whosoever will be great among you, let him be your minister; and whosoever will be chief among you, let him be your servant: even as the Son of man came not to be ministered unto, but to minister, and to give his life a ransom for many.

If a man think himself to be something, when he is nothing, he deceiveth himself.—I say, through the grace given unto me, to every man...not to think *of himself* more highly than he ought to think; but to think soberly, according as God hath dealt to every man the measure of faith.—When ye shall have done all those things which are commanded you, say, We are unprofitable servants: we have done that which was our duty to do.

Our rejoicing is this...that in simplicity and godly sincerity, not with fleshly wisdom, but by the grace of God, we have had our conversation in the world.—We have this treasure in earthen vessels, that the excellency of the power may be of God, and not of us.

Ac. 20.19;　Mt. 20.26–28　§ Ga. 6.3;　Ro. 12.3; Lu. 17.10　§ 2 Co. 1.12;　2 Co. 4.7

We have turned every one to his own way.

Noah...planted a vineyard: and he drank of the wine, and was drunken.—Abram...said unto Sarai his wife... Say, I pray thee, thou *art* my sister: that it may be well with me for thy sake.—Isaac said unto Jacob... *Art* thou my very son Esau? And he said, I *am*.—Moses...spake unadvisedly with his lips.—The men took of their victuals, and asked not *counsel* at the mouth of the LORD. And Joshua made peace with them.—David did *that which was* right in the eyes of the LORD, and turned not aside from any *thing* that he commanded him all the days of his life, save only in the matter of Uriah the Hittite.

Being justified freely by his grace through the redemption that is in Christ Jesus.—The LORD hath laid on him the iniquity of us all.

Not for your sakes do I *this*, saith the Lord GOD, be it known unto you: be ashamed and confounded for your own ways.

Isa. 53.6; Ge. 9.20–21; Ge. 12.11,13; Ge. 27.21,24;
Ps. 106.32–33; Jos. 9.14–15; 1 Ki. 15.5 § Ro. 3.24;
Isa. 53.6 § Ezek. 36.32

His name shall be called Wonderful.

The Word was made flesh, and dwelt among us, (and we beheld his glory, the glory as of the only begotten of the Father,) full of grace and truth.—Thou hast magnified thy word above all thy name.

They shall call his name Emmanuel, which being interpreted is, God with us.—JESUS: for he shall save his people from their sins.

All *men* should honour the Son, even as they honour the Father.—God...hath highly exalted him, and given him a name which is above every name.—Far above all principality, and power, and might, and dominion, and every name that is named, not only in this world, but also in that which is to come: and hath put all *things* under his feet.—He had a name written, that no man knew, but he himself...KING OF KINGS, AND LORD OF LORDS.

Touching the Almighty, we cannot find him out.— What *is* his name, and what *is* his son's name, if thou canst tell?

Isa. **9**.6; Jn. 1.14; Ps. 138.2 § Mt. 1.23; Mt. 1.21
§ Jn. 5.23; Phil. 2.9; Eph. 1.21–22; Rev. 19.12,16
§ Job 37.23; Pro. 30.4

The LORD's portion *is* his people.

Ye are Christ's; and Christ *is* God's.—I *am* my beloved's, and his desire *is* toward me.—I *am* his.—The Son of God…loved me, and gave himself for me.

Know ye not that…ye are not your own? For ye are bought with a price: therefore glorify God in your body, and in your spirit, which are God's.—The LORD hath taken you, and brought you forth out of the iron furnace, *even* out of Egypt, to be unto him a people of inheritance, as *ye are* this day.

Ye are God's husbandry, *ye are* God's building.—Christ as a son over his own house; whose house are we, if we hold fast the confidence and the rejoicing of the hope firm unto the end.—A spiritual house, an holy priesthood.

They shall be mine, saith the LORD of hosts, in that day when I make up my jewels.—All mine are thine, and thine are mine; and I am glorified in them.—The glory of his inheritance in the saints.

Deu. 32.9; 1 Co. 3.23; Song 7.10; Song 2.16;
Ga. 2.20 § 1 Co. 6.19–20; Deu. 4.20 § 1 Co. 3.9;
He. 3.6; 1 Pe. 2.5 § Mal. 3.17; Jn. 17.10; Eph. 1.18

Every *branch* that beareth fruit, he purgeth it.

He *is* like a refiner's fire, and like fullers' soap: and he shall sit *as* a refiner and purifier of silver: and he shall purify the sons of Levi, and purge them as gold and silver, that they may offer unto the LORD an offering in righteousness.

We glory in tribulations also: knowing that tribulation worketh patience; and patience, experience; and experience, hope: and hope maketh not ashamed; because the love of God is shed abroad in our hearts by the Holy Ghost which is given unto us.—If ye endure chastening, God dealeth with you as with sons; for what son is he whom the Father chasteneth not? But if ye be without chastisement, whereof all are partakers, then are ye bastards, and not sons... Now no chastening for the present seemeth to be joyous, but grievous: nevertheless afterward it yieldeth the peaceable fruit of righteousness unto them which are exercised thereby. Wherefore lift up the hands which hang down, and the feeble knees.

Jn. 15.2; Mal. 3.2–3 § Ro. 5.35; He. 12.7–8,11–12

Now we call the proud happy.

Thus saith the high and lofty One that inhabiteth eternity, whose name *is* Holy; I dwell in the high and holy *place*, with him also *that is* of a contrite and humble spirit, to revive the spirit of the humble, and to revive the heart of the contrite ones.

Better *it is to be* of an humble spirit with the lowly, than to divide the spoil with the proud.—Blessed *are* the poor in spirit: for theirs is the kingdom of heaven.

These six *things* doth the LORD hate: yea, seven *are* an abomination unto him: a proud look—Every one *that is* proud in heart *is* an abomination to the LORD.

Search me, O God, and know my heart: try me, and know my thoughts: and see if *there be any* wicked way in me, and lead me in the way everlasting.

Grace *be* unto you, and peace, from God our Father, and *from* the Lord Jesus Christ. I thank my God upon every remembrance of you.—Blessed *are* the meek: for they shall inherit the earth.

Mal. 3.15; Isa. 57.15 § Pro. 16.19; Mt. 5.3
§ Pro. 6.16,17; Pro. 16.5 § Ps. 139.23–24
§ Phil. 1.2–3; Mt. 5.5

> This God *is* our God for ever and ever:
> he will be our guide *even* unto death.

O LORD, thou *art* my God; I will exalt thee, I will praise thy name; for thou hast done wonderful *things*; *thy* counsels of old *are* faithfulness *and* truth.—The LORD *is* the portion of mine inheritance and of my cup.

He leadeth me in the paths of righteousness for his name's sake. Yea, though I walk through the valley of the shadow of death, I will fear no evil: for thou *art* with me; thy rod and thy staff they comfort me.—Thou hast holden *me* by my right hand. Thou shalt guide me with thy counsel, and afterward receive me *to* glory. Whom have I in heaven *but thee*? and *there is* none upon earth *that* I desire beside thee. My flesh and my heart faileth: *but* God *is* the strength of my heart, and my portion for ever.—Our heart shall rejoice in him, because we have trusted in his holy name.—The LORD will perfect *that which* concerneth me: thy mercy, O LORD, *endureth* for ever: forsake not the works of thine own hands.

Ps. 48.14; Isa. 25.1; Ps. 16.5 § Ps. 23.3–4;
Ps. 73.23–26; Ps. 33.21; Ps. 138.8

**In the multitude of my thoughts within me
thy comforts delight my soul.**

When my heart is overwhelmed: lead me to the rock *that* is higher than I.

O LORD, I am oppressed; undertake for me.—Cast thy burden upon the LORD, and he shall sustain thee.

I *am but* a little child: I know not *how* to go out or come in.—If any of you lack wisdom, let him ask of God…and it shall be given him.

Who *is* sufficient for these things?—I know that in me (that is, in my flesh,) dwelleth no good thing.—My grace is sufficient for thee: for my strength is made perfect in weakness.

Son, be of good cheer; thy sins be forgiven thee… Daughter, be of good comfort; thy faith hath made thee whole.

My soul shall be satisfied as *with* marrow and fatness…when I remember thee upon my bed, *and* meditate on thee in the *night* watches.

Ps. **94.19**; Ps. 61.2 § Isa. 38.14; Ps. 55.22 § 1 Ki. 3.7;
Jas. 1.5 § 2 Co. 2.16; Ro. 7.18; 2 Co. 12.9
§ Mt. 9.2,22 § Ps. 63.5,6

Hope maketh not ashamed.

I *am* the LORD…they shall not be ashamed that wait for me.—Blessed *is* the man that trusteth in the LORD, and whose hope the LORD is.—Thou wilt keep *him* in perfect peace, *whose* mind *is* stayed *on thee*: because he trusteth in thee. Trust ye in the LORD for ever: for in the LORD JEHOVAH *is* everlasting strength.—My soul, wait thou only upon God; for my expectation *is* from him. He only *is* my rock and my salvation: *he is* my defence; I shall not be moved.—I am not ashamed: for I know whom I have believed.

God, willing more abundantly to shew unto the heirs of promise the immutability of his counsel, confirmed *it* by an oath: that by two immutable things, in which *it was* impossible for God to lie, we might have a strong consolation, who have fled for refuge to lay hold upon the hope set before us: which *hope* we have as an anchor of the soul, both sure and stedfast, and which entereth into that within the veil; whither the forerunner is for us entered, *even* Jesus.

Ro. 5.5; Isa. 49.23; Jer. 17.7; Isa. 26.3–4; Ps. 62.5–6; 2 Tim. 1.12 § He. 6.17–20

The offence of the cross.

If any *man* will come after me, let him deny himself, and take up his cross, and follow me.

Know ye not that the friendship of the world is enmity with God? whosoever therefore will be a friend of the world is the enemy of God.—We must through much tribulation enter into the kingdom of God.—Whosoever believeth on him shall not be ashamed.—Unto you therefore which believe *he is* precious: but unto them which be disobedient, the stone which the builders disallowed, the same is made the head of the corner, and a stone of stumbling, and a rock of offence.

God forbid that I should glory, save in the cross of our Lord Jesus Christ, by whom the world is crucified unto me, and I unto the world.—I am crucified with Christ.—They that are Christ's have crucified the flesh with the affections and lusts.

If we suffer, we shall also reign with *him*: if we deny *him*, he also will deny us.

Ga. 5.11;   Mt. 16.24 § Jas. 4.4;   Ac. 14.22;   Ro. 9.33;
1 Pe. 2.7–8 § Ga. 6.14;   Ga. 2.20;   Ga. 5.24 § 2 Tim 2.12

The Lord *is* at hand.

The Lord himself shall descend from heaven with a shout, with the voice of the archangel, and with the trump of God: and the dead in Christ shall rise first: then we which are alive *and* remain, shall be caught up together with them in the clouds, to meet the Lord in the air: and so shall we ever be with the Lord. Wherefore comfort one another with these words.—He which testifieth these things saith, Surely I come quickly. Amen. Even so, come, Lord Jesus.

Wherefore, beloved, seeing that ye look for such things, be diligent that ye may be found of him in peace, without spot, and blameless.—Abstain from all appearance of evil. And the very God of peace sanctify you wholly; and *I pray God* your whole spirit and soul and body be preserved blameless unto the coming of our Lord Jesus Christ. Faithful *is* he that calleth you, who also will do *it*.

Be ye also patient; stablish your hearts: for the coming of the Lord draweth nigh.

Phil. 4.5; 1 Th. 4.16–18; Rev. 22.20 § 2 Pe. 3.14;
1 Th. 5.22–24 § Jas. 5.8

The choice vine.

My wellbeloved hath a vineyard in a very fruitful hill: and he fenced it, and gathered out the stones thereof, and planted it with the choicest vine...and he looked that it should bring forth grapes, and it brought forth wild grapes.—Yet I had planted thee a noble vine, wholly a right seed: how then art thou turned into the degenerate plant of a strange vine unto me?

The works of the flesh are manifest, which are *these*; Adultery, fornication, uncleanness, lasciviousness, idolatry, witchcraft, hatred, variance, emulations, wrath, strife, seditions, heresies, envyings, murders, drunkenness, revellings, and such like: of the which I tell you before, as I have also told *you* in time past, that they which do such things shall not inhereit the kingdom of God. But the fruit of the Spirit is love, joy, peace, longsuffering, gentleness, goodness, faith, meekness, temperance.

I am the true vine, and my Father is the husbandman. Every branch in me that beareth not fruit he taketh away: and every *branch* that beareth fruit, he purgeth it, that it may bring forth more fruit... Abide in me, and I in you... Herein is my Father glorified, that ye bear much fruit; so shall ye be my disciples.

Ge. 49.11; Isa. 5.1–2; Jer. 2.21 § Ga. 5.19–23 § Jn. 15.1–2,4,8

**The righteousness of God *which is* by faith of Jesus
Christ unto all and upon all them that believe.**

He hath made him *to be* sin for us, who knew no sin;
that we might be made the righteousness of God in
him.—Christ hath redeemed us from the curse of the
law, being made a curse for us.—Who of God is made
unto us wisdom, and righteousness, and sanctification,
and redemption.—Not by works of righteousness
which we have done, but according to his mercy he
saved us, by the washing of regeneration, and renewing
of the Holy Ghost; which he shed on us abundantly
through Jesus Christ our Saviour.

I count all things *but* loss for the excellency of the
knowledge of Christ Jesus my Lord: for whom I have
suffered the loss of all things, and do count them *but*
dung, that I may win Christ, and be found in him, not
having mine own righteousness, which is of the law, but
that which is through the faith of Christ, the righteousness which is of God by faith.

Ro. 3.22; 2 Co. 5.21; Ga. 3.13; 1 Co. 1.30; Titus 3.5–6
§ Phil. 3.8–9

The Spirit of adoption,
whereby we cry, Abba, Father.

Jesus...lifted up his eyes to heaven, and said, Father...Holy Father...O righteous Father.—He said, Abba, Father.—Because ye are sons, God hath sent forth the Spirit of his Son into your hearts, crying, Abba, Father.—For through him we both have access by one Spirit unto the Father. Now therefore ye are no more strangers and foreigners, but fellowcitizens with the saints, and of the household of God.

Doubtless thou *art* our father...thou, O LORD, *art* our father, our redeemer; thy name *is* from everlasting.

I will arise and go to my father, and will say unto him, Father, I have sinned against heaven, and before thee, and am no more worthy to be called thy son: make me as one of thy hired servants. And he arose, and came to his father.

Be ye therefore followers of God, as dear children.

Ro. 8.15; Jn. 17.1,11,25; Mk. 14.36; Ga. 4.6;
Eph. 2.18–19 § Isa. 63.16 § Lu. 15.18–20 § Eph. 5.1

Let us go forth therefore unto him without the camp, bearing his reproach. For here have we no continuing city, but we seek one to come.

Beloved, think it not strange concerning the fiery trial which is to try you, as though some strange thing happened unto you: but rejoice, inasmuch as ye are partakers of Christ's sufferings; that, when his glory shall be revealed, ye may be glad also with exceeding joy.—As ye are partakers of the sufferings, so *shall ye be* also of the consolation.

If ye be reproached for the name of Christ, happy *are ye;* for the spirit of glory and of God resteth upon you: on their part he is evil spoken of, but on your part he is glorified.

They departed from the presence of the council, rejoicing that they were counted worthy to suffer shame for his name.—Choosing rather to suffer affliction with the people of God, than to enjoy the pleasures of sin for a season; esteeming the reproach of Christ greater riches than the treasures in Egypt: for he had respect unto the recompence of the reward.

He. 13.13–14; 1 Pe. 4.12–13; 2 Co. 1.7 § 1 Pe. 4.14
§ Ac. 5.41; He. 11.25–26

The Lord Jesus Christ…shall change our vile body, that it may be fashioned like unto his glorious body.

Upon the likeness of the throne *was* the likeness as the appearance of a man above upon it. And I saw as the colour of amber, as the appearance of fire round about within it, from the appearance of his loins even upward, and from the appearance of his loins even downward, I saw as it were the appearance of fire, and it had brightness round about… This *was* the appearance of the likeness of the glory of the LORD.

We all, with open face beholding as in a glass the glory of the Lord, are changed into the same image from glory to glory, *even* as by the Spirit of the Lord.—It doth not yet appear what we shall be: but we know that, when he shall appear, we shall be like him; for we shall see him as he is.

They shall hunger no more, neither thirst any more.—They sing the song of Moses the servant of God, and the song of the Lamb.

Phil. 3.20,21; Ezek. 1.26–27,28 § 2 Co. 3.18; 1 Jn. 3.2 § Rev. 7.16; Rev. 15.3

Ye know that he was manifested to take away
our sins: and in him is no sin.

God...hath in these last days spoken unto us by *his*
Son...who being the brightness of *his* glory, and the
express image of his person, and upholding all things
by the word of his power, when he had by himself
purged our sins, sat down on the right hand of the
Majesty on high.—He hath made him *to be* sin for us,
who knew no sin; that we might be made the righteousness of God in him.

Pass the time of your sojourning *here* in fear: forasmuch as ye know that ye were not redeemed with
corruptible things, *as* silver and gold...but with the precious blood of Christ, as of a lamb without blemish and
without spot: who verily was foreordained before the
foundation of the world, but was manifest in these last
times for you.—The love of Christ constraineth us;
because we thus judge, that if one died for all, then were
all dead: and *that* he died for all, that they which live
should not henceforth live unto themselves, but unto
him which died for them, and rose again.

1 Jn. 3.5;　He. 1.1,2,3;　2 Co. 5.21　§ 1 Pe. 1.17–18,19–20;
2 Co. 5.14–15

**I have set before you life and death,
blessing and cursing: therefore choose life.**

For I have no pleasure in the death of him that dieth, saith the Lord GOD: wherefore turn *yourselves*, and live ye.

If I had not come and spoken unto them, they had not had sin: but now they have no cloke for their sin.

That servant, which knew his lord's will, and prepared not *himself*, neither did according to his will, shall be beaten with many *stripes*.

The wages of sin *is* death; but the gift of God *is* eternal life through Jesus Christ our Lord.—He that believeth on the Son hath everlasting life: and he that believeth not the Son shall not see life; but the wrath of God abideth on him.—Know ye not, that to whom ye yield yourselves servants to obey, his servants ye are to whom ye obey; whether of sin unto death, or of obedience unto righteousness?

If any man serve me, let him follow me; and where I am, there shall also my servant be: if any man serve me, him will *my* Father honour.

Deu. 30.19; Ezek. 18.32 § Jn. 15.22 § Lu. 12.47
§ Ro. 6.23; Jn. 3.36; Ro. 6.16 § Jn. 12.26

As thy days, *so shall* thy strength be.

When they shall lead *you*, and deliver you up, take no thought beforehand what ye shall speak, neither do ye premeditate: but whatsoever shall be given you in that hour, that speak ye: for it is not ye that speak, but the Holy Ghost.—Take therefore no thought for the morrow: for the morrow shall take thought for the things of itself. Sufficient unto the day *is* the evil thereof.

The God of Israel *is* he that giveth strength and power unto *his* people. Blessed *be* God.—He giveth power to the faint; and to *them that have* no might he increaseth strength.

My grace is sufficient for thee: for my strength is made perfect in weakness. Most gladly therefore will I rather glory in my infirmities, that the power of Christ may rest upon me. Therefore I take pleasure in infirmities, in reproaches, in necessities, in persecutions, in distresses for Christ's sake: for when I am weak, then am I strong.—I can do all things through Christ which strengtheneth me.—O my soul, thou hast trodden down strength.

Deu. 33.25; Mk. 13.11; Mt. 6.34 § Ps. 68.35;
Isa. 40.29 § 2 Co. 12.9–10; Phil. 4.13; Judg. 5.21

Awake, O north wind; and…blow upon my garden,
that **the spices thereof may flow out.**

No chastening for the present seemeth to be joyous, but grievous: nevertheless afterward it yieldeth the peaceable fruit of righteousness unto them which are exercised thereby.—The fruit of the Spirit.

He stayeth his rough wind in the day of the east wind.

Like as a father pitieth *his* children, *so* the LORD pitieth them that fear him.

Though our outward man perish, yet the inward *man* is renewed day by day. For our light affliction, which is but for a moment, worketh for us a far more exceeding *and* eternal weight of glory; while we look not at the things which are seen, but at the things which are not seen.

Though he were a Son, yet learned he obedience by the things which he suffered.—In all points tempted like as *we are*, *yet* without sin.

Song 4.16; He. 12.11; Ga. 5.22 § Isa. 27.8 § Ps. 103.13 § 2 Co. 4.16–18 § He. 5.8; He. 4.15

Thou God seest me.

O LORD, thou hast searched me, and known *me*. Thou knowest my downsitting and mine uprising, thou understandest my thought afar off. Thou compassest my path and my lying down, and art acquainted *with* all my ways. For *there is* not a word in my tongue, *but*, lo, O LORD, thou knowest it altogether… *Such* knowledge *is* too wonderful for me; it is high, I cannot *attain* unto it.

The eyes of the LORD *are* in every place, beholding the evil and the good.—The ways of man *are* before the eyes of the LORD, and he pondereth all his goings.—God knoweth your hearts: for that which is highly esteemed among men is abomination in the sight of God.—The eyes of the LORD run to and fro throughout the whole earth, to shew himself strong in the behalf of *them* whose heart is perfect toward him.

Jesus…knew all *men*, and needed not that any should testify of man: for he knew what was in man.— Lord, thou knowest all things; thou knowest that I love thee.

Ge. 16.13; Ps. 139.1–4,6 § Pro. 15.3; Pro. 5.21;
Lu. 16.15; 2 Chr. 16.9 § Jn. 2.24–25; Jn. 21.17

I will praise thee, O Lord my God, with all my heart: and I will glorify thy name for evermore.

Whoso offereth praise glorifieth me.—*It is a* good *thing* to give thanks unto the LORD, and to sing praises unto thy name, O most High: to shew forth thy lovingkindness in the morning, and thy faithfulness every night.

Let every thing that hath breath praise the LORD.

I beseech you...brethren, by the mercies of God, that ye present your bodies a living sacrifice, holy, acceptable unto God, *which is* your reasonable service.—Jesus...that he might sanctify the people with his own blood, suffered without the gate... By him therefore let us offer the sacrifice of praise to God continually, that is, the fruit of *our* lips giving thanks to his name.—Giving thanks always for all things unto God and the Father in the name of our Lord Jesus Christ.

Worthy is the Lamb that was slain to receive power, and riches, and wisdom, and strength, and honour, and glory, and blessing.

Ps. 86.12; Ps. 50.23; Ps. 92.1–2 § Ps. 150.6 § Ro. 12.1; He. 13.12,15; Eph. 5.20 § Rev. 5.12

Let us run with patience the race that is set before us, looking unto Jesus the author and finisher of *our* faith.

If any *man* will come after me, let him deny himself, and take up his cross daily, and follow me.—Whosoever he be of you that forsaketh not all that he hath, he cannot be my disciple.—Let us therefore cast off the works of darkness.

Every man that striveth for the mastery is temperate in all things. Now they *do it* to obtain a corruptible crown; but we an incorruptible. I therefore so run, not as uncertainly; so fight I, not as one that beateth the air: but I keep under my body, and bring *it* into subjection: lest that by any means, when I have preached to others, I myself should be a castaway.—Brethren, I count not myself to have apprehended: but *this* one thing I *do*, forgetting those things which are behind, and reaching forth unto those things which are before, I press toward the mark for the prize of the high calling of God in Christ Jesus.—Then shall we know, *if* we follow on to know the LORD.

He. 12.1–2; Lu. 9.23; Lu. 14.33; Ro. 13.12
§ 1 Co. 9.25–27; Phil. 3.13–14; Hos. 6.3

It is **good for a man that
he bear the yoke in his youth.**

Train up a child in the way he should go: and when he is old, he will not depart from it.

We have had fathers of our flesh which corrected *us,* and we gave *them* reverence: shall we not much rather be in subjection unto the Father of spirits, and live? For they verily for a few days chastened *us* after their own pleasure; but he for *our* profit, that *we* might be partakers of his holiness.

Before I was afflicted I went astray: but now have I kept thy word... *It is* good for me that I have been afflicted; that I might learn thy statutes.

I know the thoughts that I think toward you, saith the LORD, thoughts of peace, and not of evil, to give you an expected end.—Humble yourselves therefore under the mighty hand of God, that he may exalt you in due time.

Lam. 3.27; Pro. 22.6 § He. 12.9–10 § Ps. 119.67,71 § Jer. 29.11; 1 Pe. 5.6

If ye will not drive out the inhabitants of the land from before you…those which ye let remain of them *shall be* pricks in your eyes, and thorns in your sides, and shall vex you in the land wherein ye dwell.

Fight the good fight of faith.—For though we walk in the flesh, we do not war after the flesh: (for the weapons of our warfare *are* not carnal, but mighty through God to the pulling down of strongholds;) casting down imaginations…and bringing into captivity every thought to the obedience of Christ.

Brethren, we are debtors, not to the flesh, to live after the flesh. For if ye live after the flesh, ye shall die: but if ye through the Spirit do mortify the deeds of the body, ye shall live.

The flesh lusteth against the Spirit, and the Spirit against the flesh: and these are contrary the one to the other: so that ye cannot do the things that ye would.—I see another law in my members, warring against the law of my mind, and bringing me into captivity to the law of sin which is in my members.—We are more than conquerors through him that loved us.

Nu. 33.55;　1 Tim. 6.12;　2 Co. 10.3–5 § Ro. 8.12–13 § Ga. 5.17;　Ro. 7.23;　Ro. 8.37

If a man sin against the LORD, who shall intreat for him?

If any man sin, we have an advocate with the Father, Jesus Christ the righteous: and he is the propitiation for our sins: and not for ours only, but also for *the sins of* the whole world.—Whom God hath set forth *to be* a propitiation through faith in his blood, to declare his righteousness for the remission of sins that are past, through the forbearance of God; to declare, *I say*, at this time his righteousness: that he might be just, and the justifier of him which believeth in Jesus.

He is gracious unto him, and saith, Deliver him from going down to the pit: I have found a ransom.

What shall we then say to these things? If God *be* for us, who *can be* against us?... *It is* God that justifieth. Who *is he* that condemneth? *It is* Christ that died, yea, rather, that is risen again, who is even at the right hand of God, who also maketh intercession for us.

1 Sa. 2.25; 1 Jn. 2.1–2; Ro. 3.25–26 § Job 33.24 § Ro. 8.31,33–34

Whom having not seen, ye love.

We walk by faith, not by sight.—We love him, because he first loved us.—And we have known and believed the love that God hath to us. God is love; and he that dwelleth in love dwelleth in God, and God in him.—In whom ye also *trusted*, after that ye heard the word of truth, the gospel of your salvation: in whom also after that ye believed, ye were sealed with that holy Spirit of promise.—God would make known what *is* the riches of the glory of this mystery among the Gentiles; which is Christ in you, the hope of glory.

If a man say, I love God, and hateth his brother, he is a liar: for he that loveth not his brother whom he hath seen, how can he love God whom he hath not seen?

Jesus saith unto him, Thomas, because thou hast seen me, thou hast believed: blessed *are* they that have not seen, and *yet* have believed.—Blessed *are* all they that put their trust in him.

---

1 Pe. 1.8; 2 Co. 5.7; 1 Jn. 4.19; 1 Jn. 4.16; Eph. 1.13;
Col. 1.27 § 1 Jn. 4.20 § Jn. 20.29; Ps. 2.12

THE LORD OUR RIGHTEOUSNESS.

W e are all as an unclean *thing*, and all our righteousnesses *are* as filthy rags.

I will go in the strength of the Lord GOD: I will make
mention of thy righteousness, *even* of thine only.—I will
greatly rejoice in the LORD, my soul shall be joyful in my
God; for he hath clothed me with the garments of salvation, he hath covered me with the robe of righteousness,
as a bridegroom decketh *himself* with ornaments, and as
a bride adorneth *herself* with her jewels.

Bring forth the best robe, and put *it* on him.—To
her was granted that she should be arrayed in fine
linen, clean and white: for the fine linen is the righteousness of saints.

I count all things *but* loss for the excellency of the
knowledge of Christ Jesus my Lord...that I may win
Christ, and be found in him, not having mine own
righteousness, which is of the law, but that which is
through the faith of Christ, the righteousness which is
of God by faith.

Jer. 23.6; Isa. 64.6 § Ps. 71.16; Isa. 61.10 § Lu. 15.22;
Rev. 19.8 § Phil. 3.8–9

Oh…that thou wouldest keep *me* from evil.

Why sleep ye? rise and pray, lest ye enter into temptation.—The spirit indeed *is* willing, but the flesh *is* weak.

Two *things* have I required of thee; deny me *them* not before I die: remove far from me vanity and lies: give me neither poverty nor riches; feed me with food convenient for me: lest I be full and deny *thee*, and say, Who *is* the LORD? or lest I be poor, and steal, and take the name of my God *in vain.*

The LORD shall preserve thee from all evil: he shall preserve thy soul.—I will deliver thee out of the hand of the wicked, and I will redeem thee out of the hand of the terrible.—He that is begotten of God keepeth himself, and that wicked one toucheth him not.

Because thou hast kept the word of my patience, I also will keep thee from the hour of temptation, which shall come upon all the world, to try them that dwell upon the earth.—The Lord knoweth how to deliver the godly out of temptations.

---

1 Chr. 4.10; Lu. 22.46; Mt. 26.41 § Pro. 30.7–9
§ Ps. 121.7; Jer. 15.21; 1 Jn. 5.18 § Rev. 3.10; 2 Pe. 2.9

One star differeth from another star in glory.

By the way they had disputed among themselves, who *should be* the greatest. And he sat down, and called the twelve, and saith unto them, If any man desire to be first, *the same* shall be last of all.—Be clothed with humility: for God resisteth the proud, and giveth grace to the humble. Humble yourselves therefore under the mighty hand of God, that he may exalt you in due time.

Let this mind be in you, which was also in Christ Jesus: who…made himself of no reputation, and took upon him the form of a servant, and was made in the likeness of men… Wherefore God also hath highly exalted him, and given him a name which is above every name: that at the name of Jesus every knee should bow.

They that be wise shall shine as the brightness of the firmament; and they that turn many to righteousness as the stars for ever and ever.

1 Co. 15.41; Mk. 9.34–35; 1 Pe. 5.5–6
§ Phil. 2.5–6,7,9–10 § Dan. 12.3

**Be strong…and work:
for I am with you, saith the LORD of hosts.**

I am the vine, ye *are* the branches: he that abideth in me, and I in him, the same bringeth forth much fruit: for without me ye can do nothing.—I can do all things through Christ which strengtheneth me.—Strong in the Lord, and in the power of his might.—The joy of the LORD is your strength.

Thus saith the LORD of hosts; Let your hands be strong, ye that hear in these days these words by the mouth of the prophets.—Strengthen ye the weak hands, and confirm the feeble knees. Say to them *that are* of a fearful heart, Be strong, fear not.—The LORD looked upon him, and said, Go in this thy might.

If God *be* for us, who *can be* against us?—Therefore seeing we have this ministry, as we have received mercy, we faint not.

Let us not be weary in well doing: for in due season we shall reap, if we faint not.—Thanks *be* to God, which giveth us the victory through our Lord Jesus Christ.

Hag. 2.4; Jn. 15.5; Phil. 4.13; Eph. 6.10; Ne. 8.10
§ Zech. 8.9; Isa. 35.3–4; Judg. 6.14 § Ro. 8.31;
2 Co. 4.1 § Ga. 6.9; 1 Co. 15.57

The darkness hideth not from thee.

His eyes *are* upon the ways of man, and he seeth all his goings. *There is* no darkness, nor shadow of death, where the workers of iniquity may hide themselves.— Can any hide himself in secret places that I shall not see him?… Do not I fill heaven and earth? saith the LORD.

Thou shalt not be afraid for the terror by night…*nor* for the pestilence *that* walketh in darkness… Because thou hast made the LORD, *which is* my refuge, *even* the most High, thy habitation; there shall no evil befall thee, neither shall any plague come nigh thy dwelling.—He that keepeth thee will not slumber… The LORD *is* thy keeper: the Lord *is* thy shade upon thy right hand. The sun shall not smite thee by day, nor the moon by night. The LORD shall preserve thee from all evil.

Yea, though I walk through the valley of the shadow of death, I will fear no evil: for thou *art* with me.

Ps. **139.**12; Job 34.21–22; Jer. 23.24 § Ps. 91.5,6,9–10; Ps. 121.3,5–7 § Ps. 23.4

**The LORD hath said unto you,
Ye shall henceforth return no more that way.**

Truly, if they had been mindful of that *country* from whence they came out, they might have had opportunity to have returned. But now they desire a better *country*, that is, an heavenly.—Choosing rather to suffer affliction with the people of God, than to enjoy the pleasures of sin for a season; esteeming the reproach of Christ greater riches than the treasures in Egypt.—The just shall live by faith: but if *any man* draw back, my soul shall have no pleasure in him. But we are not of them who draw back unto perdition; but of them that believe to the saving of the soul.—No man, having put his hand to the plough, and looking back, is fit for the kingdom of God.

God forbid that I should glory, save in the cross of our Lord Jesus Christ, by whom the world is crucified unto me, and I unto the world.—Come out from among them, and be ye separate, saith the Lord, and touch not the unclean *thing*; and I will receive you.

He which hath begun a good work in you, will perform *it* until the day of Jesus Christ.

Deu. 17.16; He. 11.15–16; He. 11.25–26; He. 10.38–39; Lu. 9.62 § Ga. 6.14; 2 Co. 6.17 § Phil. 1.6

**They talk to the grief of
those whom thou hast wounded.**

I was but a little displeased, and they helped forward the affliction.

Brethren, if a man be overtaken in a fault, ye which are spiritual, restore such an one in the spirit of meekness; considering thyself, lest thou also be tempted.

He which converteth the sinner from the error of his way shall save a soul from death, and shall hide a multitude of sins.—Comfort the feebleminded, support the weak, be patient toward all *men*.

Let us not...judge one another any more: but judge this rather, that no man put a stumblingblock or an occasion to fall in *his* brother's way.—We...that are strong ought to bear the infirmities of the weak, and not to please ourselves.

Charity...rejoiceth not in iniquity.—Let him that thinketh he standeth take heed lest he fall.

Ps. 69.26; Zech. 1.15 § Ga. 6.1 § Jas. 5.20; 1 Th. 5.14
§ Ro. 14.13; Ro. 15.1 § 1 Co. 13.4,6; 1 Co. 10.12

**I am come that they might have life,
and that they might have *it* more abundantly.**

In the day that thou eatest thereof thou shalt surely die.—She took of the fruit thereof, and did eat, and gave also unto her husband with her; and he did eat.

The wages of sin *is* death; but the gift of God *is* eternal life through Jesus Christ our Lord.—If by one man's offence death reigned by one; much more they which receive abundance of grace and of the gift of righteousness shall reign in life by one, Jesus Christ.—Since by man *came* death, by man *came* also the resurrection of the dead. For as in Adam all die, even so in Christ shall all be made alive.—Our Saviour Jesus Christ, who hath abolished death, and hath brought life and immortality to light through the gospel.

God hath given to us eternal life, and this life is in his Son. He that hath the Son hath life; *and* he that hath not the Son of God hath not life.—For God sent not his Son into the world to condemn the world; but that the world through him might be saved.

Jn. 10.10; Ge. 2.17; Ge. 3.6 § Ro. 6.23; Ro. 5.17;
1 Co. 15.21–22; 2 Tim. 1.10 § 1 Jn. 5.11–12; Jn. 3.17

The judgment seat.

We are sure that the judgment of God is according to truth.—When the Son of man shall come in his glory, and all the holy angels with him, then shall he sit upon the throne of his glory: and before him shall be gathered all nations: and he shall separate them one from another, as a shepherd divideth *his* sheep from the goats.

Then shall the righteous shine forth as the sun in the kingdom of their Father.—Who shall lay any thing to the charge of God's elect? *It is* God that justifieth. Who *is* he that condemneth? *It is* Christ that died, yea rather, that is risen again, who is even at the right hand of God, who also maketh intercession for us.—*There is* therefore now no condemnation to them which are in Christ Jesus.

We are chastened of the Lord, that we should not be condemned with the world.

2 Co. 5.10; Ro. 2.2; Mt. 25.31–32 § Mt. 13.43; Ro. 8.33–34; Ro. 8.1 § 1 Co. 11.32

**The grace of our Lord was exceeding abundant
with faith and love which is in Christ Jesus.**

Ye know the grace of our Lord Jesus Christ, that, though he was rich, yet for your sakes he became poor, that ye through his poverty might be rich.—Where sin abounded, grace did much more abound.

That in the ages to come he might shew the exceeding riches of his grace in *his* kindness toward us through Christ Jesus. For by grace are ye saved through faith; and that not of yourselves: *it is* the gift of God: not of works, lest any man should boast.—Knowing that a man is not justified by the works of the law, but by the faith of Jesus Christ, even we have believed in Jesus Christ, that we might be justified by the faith of Christ, and not by the works of the law: for by the works of the law shall no flesh be justified.—According to his mercy he saved us, by the washing of regeneration, and renewing of the Holy Ghost; which he shed on us abundantly through Jesus Christ our Saviour.

1 Tim. 1.14; 2 Co. 8.9; Ro. 5.20 § Eph. 2.7–9;
Ga. 2.16; Titus 3.5–6

I am...the bright and morning star.

There shall come a Star out of Jacob.

The night is far spent, the day is at hand: let us therefore cast off the works of darkness, and let us put on the armour of light.—Until the day break, and the shadows flee away, turn, my beloved, and be thou like a roe or a young hart upon the mountains of Bether.

Watchman, what of the night? The watchman said, The morning cometh, and also the night: if ye will enquire, enquire ye: return, come.

I am the light of the world.—I will give him the morning star.

Take ye heed, watch and pray: for ye know not when the time is. *For the Son of man is* as a man taking a far journey, who left his house, and gave authority to his servants, and to every man his work, and commanded the porter to watch. Watch ye therefore...lest coming suddenly he find you sleeping. And what I say unto you I say unto all, Watch.

Rev. 22.16; Nu. 24.17 § Ro. 13.12; Song 2.17
§ Isa. 21.11–12 § Jn. 8.12; Rev. 2.28 § Mk. 13.33–37

**When thou has eaten and are full...
thou shalt bless the LORD thy God
for the good land which he hath given thee.**

Beware that thou forget not the LORD thy God.—One of them, when he saw that he was healed, turned back, and with a loud voice glorified God, and fell down on *his* face at his feet, giving him thanks: and he was a Samaritan. And Jesus answering said, Were there not ten cleansed? but where *are* the nine? There are not found that returned to give glory to God, save this stranger.

Every creature of God *is* good, and nothing to be refused, if it be received with thanksgiving: for it is sanctified by the word of God and prayer.—He that eateth, eateth to the Lord, for he giveth God thanks.—The blessing of the LORD, it maketh rich, and he addeth no sorrow with it.

Bless the LORD, O my soul: and all that is within me, *bless* his holy name. Bless the LORD, O my soul...who forgiveth all thine iniquities...who crowneth thee with lovingkindness and tender mercies.

Deu. 8.10; Deu. 8.11; Lu. 17.15–18 § 1 Tim. 4.4–5;
Ro. 14.6; Pro. 10.22 § Ps. 103.1–2,3,4

Jesus...was moved with compassion toward them.

Jesus Christ the same yesterday, and to day, and for ever.—We have not an high priest which cannot be touched with the feeling of our infirmities; but was in all points tempted like as *we are, yet* without sin.—Who can have compassion on the ignorant, and on them that are out of the way.—He cometh, and findeth them sleeping, and saith unto Peter, Simon, sleepest thou? couldest not thou watch one hour? Watch ye and pray, lest ye enter into temptation. The spirit truly *is* ready, but the flesh *is* weak.

Like as a father pitieth *his* children, *so* the LORD pitieth them that fear him. For he knoweth our frame; he remembereth that we *are* dust.

Thou, O Lord, *art* a God full of compassion, and gracious, longsuffering, and plenteous in mercy and truth. O turn unto me, and have mercy upon me; give thy strength unto thy servant, and save the son of thine handmaid.

Mt. 14.14;   He. 13.8;   He. 4.15;   He. 5.2;   Mk. 14.37–38
§ Ps. 103.13–14 § Ps. 86.15–16

**Henceforth I call you not servants;
for the servant knoweth not what his lord doeth:
but I have called you friends.**

The LORD said, Shall I hide from Abraham that thing which I do?—It is given unto you to know the mysteries of the kingdom of heaven.—God hath revealed *them* unto us by his Spirit: for the Spirit searcheth all things, yea, the deep things of God.—*Even* the hidden *wisdom*, which God ordained before the world unto our glory.

Blessed *is the man whom* thou choosest, and causest to approach *unto thee, that* he may dwell in thy courts: we shall be satisfied with the goodness of thy house, *even* of thy holy temple.—The secret of the LORD *is* with them that fear him; and he will shew them his covenant.—I have given unto them the words which thou gavest me; and they have received *them*, and have known surely that I came out from thee, and they have believed that thou didst send me.

Ye are my friends, if ye do whatsoever I command you.

Jn. **15**.15;   Ge. 18.17;   Mt. 13.11;   1 Co. 2.10;   1 Co. 2.7
§ Ps. 65.4;   Ps. 25.14;   Jn. 17.8 § Jn. 15.14

**Thou shalt call thy walls Salvation,
and thy gates Praise.**

The wall of the city had twelve foundations, and in them the names of the twelve apostles of the Lamb.

Ye are no more strangers and foreigners, but fellowcitizens with the saints, and of the household of God; and are built upon the foundation of the apostles and prophets, Jesus Christ himself being the chief corner *stone;* in whom all the building fitly framed together groweth unto an holy temple in the Lord: in whom ye also are builded together for an habitation of God through the Spirit.—If so be ye have tasted that the Lord *is* gracious. To whom coming, *as unto* a living stone, disallowed indeed of men, but chosen of God, *and* precious, ye also, as lively stones, are built up a spiritual house, an holy priesthood, to offer up spiritual sacrifices, acceptable to God by Jesus Christ.

Praise waiteth for thee, O God, in Sion.

Isa. **60.18**; Rev. 21.14 § Eph. 2.19–22; 1 Pe. 2.3–5
§ Ps. 65.1

Now he is comforted.

Thy sun shall no more go down; neither shall thy moon withdraw itself: for the Lord shall be thine everlasting light, and the days of thy mourning shall be ended.—He will swallow up death in victory; and the Lord GOD will wipe away tears from off all faces; and the rebuke of his people shall he take away from off all the earth.—These are they which came out of great tribulation, and have washed their robes, and made them white in the blood of the Lamb. Therefore are they before the throne of God, and serve him day and night in his temple: and he that sitteth on the throne shall dwell among them. They shall hunger no more, neither thirst any more; neither shall the sun light on them, nor any heat. For the Lamb which is in the midst of the throne shall feed them, and shall lead them unto living fountains of waters.—God shall wipe away all tears from their eyes; and there shall be no more death, neither sorrow, nor crying, neither shall there be any more pain: for the former things are passed away.

Lu. 16.25; Isa. 60.20; Isa. 25.8; Rev. 7.14–17; Rev. 21.4

The night cometh, when no man can work.

B lessed *are* the dead which die in the Lord...they...rest from their labours; and their works do follow them.—There the wicked cease *from* troubling; and there the weary be at rest.—Samuel said to Saul, Why hast thou disquieted me, to bring me up?

Whatsoever thy hand findeth to do, do *it* with thy might; for *there is* no work, nor device, nor knowledge, nor wisdom, in the grave, whither thou goest.—The dead praise not the LORD, neither any that go down into silence.

I am now ready to be offered, and the time of my departure is at hand. I have fought a good fight, I have finished *my* course, I have kept the faith: henceforth there is laid up for me a crown of righteousness, which the Lord, the righteous judge, shall give me at that day.

There remaineth therefore a rest to the people of God. For he that is entered into his rest, he also hath ceased from his own works, as God *did* from his.

Jn. 9.4; Rev. 14.13; Job 3.17; 1 Sa. 28.15 § Ec. 9.10; Ps. 115.17 § 2 Tim. 4.6–8 § He. 4.9–10

The light of the body is the eye: therefore when thine eye is single, thy whole body also is full of light.

The natural man receiveth not the things of the Spirit of God: for they are foolishness unto him: neither can he know *them*, because they are spiritually discerned.— Open thou mine eyes, that I may behold wondrous things out of thy law.

I am the light of the world: he that followeth me shall not walk in darkness, but shall have the light of life.—We all, with open face beholding as in a glass the glory of the Lord, are changed into the same image…*even* as by the Spirit of the Lord.—God, who commanded the light to shine out of darkness, hath shined in our hearts, to *give* the light of the knowledge of the glory of God in the face of Jesus Christ.

That the God of our Lord Jesus Christ, the Father of glory, may give unto you the spirit of wisdom and reve-lation in the knowledge of him…that ye may know what is the hope of his calling, and what the riches of the glory of his inheritance in the saints.

Lu. 11.34;   1 Co. 2.14;   Ps.119.18   § Jn. 8.12; 2 Co. 3.18;   2 Co. 4.6   § Eph. 1.17,18

He smote the rock, that the waters gushed out, and the streams overflowed.

All our fathers were under the cloud, and all passed through the sea; and were all baptized unto Moses in the cloud and in the sea; and did all eat the same spiritual meat; and did all drink the same spiritual drink: for they drank of that spiritual Rock that followed them: and that Rock was Christ.—One of the soldiers with a spear pierced his side, and forthwith came there out blood and water.—He *was* wounded for our transgressions, *he was* bruised for our iniquities: the chastisement of our peace *was* upon him; and with his stripes we are healed.

Ye will not come to me, that ye might have life.—My people have committed two evils; they have forsaken me the fountain of living waters, *and* hewed them out cisterns, broken cisterns, that can hold no water.

If any man thirst, let him come unto me, and drink.—Whosoever will, let him take the water of life freely.

Ps. **78**.20; 1 Co. **10**.1–4; Jn. **19**.34; Isa. **53**.5 § Jn. **5**.40; Jer. **2**.13 § Jn. **7**.37; Rev. **22**.17

They that feared the LORD spake often one to another:
and the LORD hearkened, and heard *it,* and a book of
remembrance was written before him for them that
feared the LORD, and that thought upon his name.

It came to pass, that, while they communed *together*
and reasoned, Jesus himself drew near, and went with
them.—Where two or three are gathered together in my
name, there am I in the midst of them.—My fel-
lowlabourers, whose names *are* in the book of life.

Let the word of Christ dwell in you richly in all wisdom; teaching and admonishing one another in psalms
and hymns and spiritual songs, singing with grace in
your hearts to the Lord.—Exhort one another daily,
while it is called To day; lest any of you be hardened
through the deceitfulness of sin.

Every idle word that men shall speak, they shall give
account thereof in the day of judgment. For by thy
words thou shalt be justified, and by thy words thou
shalt be condemned.—Behold, *it is* written before me.

Mal. 3.16; Lu. 24.15; Mt. 18.20; Phil. 4.3 § Col. 3.16;
He. 3.13 § Mt. 12.36–37; Isa. 65.6

The trees of the LORD are full *of sap*.

I will be as the dew unto Israel: he shall grow as the lily, and cast forth his roots as Lebanon. His branches shall spread, and his beauty shall be as the olive tree, and his smell as Lebanon.—Blessed *is* the man that trusteth in the LORD, and whose hope the LORD is. For he shall be as a tree planted by the waters, and *that* spreadeth out her roots by the river, and shall not see when heat cometh, but her leaf shall be green; and shall not be careful in the year of drought, neither shall cease from yielding fruit.

I the LORD have brought down the high tree, have exalted the low tree, have dried up the green tree, and have made the dry tree to flourish.

The righteous shall flourish like the palm tree: he shall grow like a cedar in Lebanon. Those that be planted in the house of the LORD shall flourish in the courts of our God. They shall still bring forth fruit in old age; they shall be fat and flourishing.

Ps. 104.16; Hos. 14.5–6; Jer. 17.7–8 § Ezek. 17.24 § Ps. 92.12–14

They shall be mine, saith the LORD of hosts, in that day when I make up my jewels.

I have manifested thy name unto the men which thou gavest me out of the world: thine they were, and thou gavest them me; and they have kept thy word... I pray for them: I pray not for the world, but for them which thou hast given me; for they are thine. And all mine are thine, and thine are mine; and I am glorified in them... Father, I will that they also, whom thou hast given me, be with me where I am; that they may behold my glory, which thou hast given me: for thou lovedst me before the foundation of the world.

I will come again, and receive you unto myself.—He shall come to be glorified in his saints, and to be admired in all them that believe...in that day.—We which are alive *and* remain shall be caught up together with them in the clouds, to meet the Lord in the air: and so shall we ever be with the Lord.—Thou shalt also be a crown of glory in the hand of the LORD, and a royal diadem in the hand of thy God.

Mal. 3.17; Jn. 17.6,9–10,24 § Jn. 14.3; 2 Th. 1.10; 1 Th. 4.17; Isa. 62.3

I beseech thee, shew me thy glory.

God, who commanded the light to shine out of darkness, hath shined in our hearts, to *give* the light of the knowledge of the glory of God in the face of Jesus Christ.—The Word was made flesh, and dwelt among us, (and we beheld his glory, the glory as of the only begotten of the Father,) full of grace and truth.... No man hath seen God at any time; the only begotten Son, which is in the bosom of the Father, he hath declared *him*.

My soul thirsteth for God, for the living God: when shall I come and appear before God?—*When thou saidst*, Seek ye my face; my heart said unto thee, Thy face, LORD, will I seek.

We all, with open face beholding as in a glass the glory of the Lord, are changed into the same image from glory to glory, *even* as by the Spirit of the Lord.—Father, I will that they also, whom thou hast given me, be with me where I am; that they may behold my glory, which thou hast given me: for thou lovedst me before the foundation of the world.

Ex. **33.18**; 2 Co. 4.6; Jn. 1.14,18 § Ps. 42.2; Ps. 27.8 § 2 Co. 3.18; Jn. 17.24

Upon the likeness of the throne *was* the likeness as the appearance of a man above upon it.

The man Christ Jesus.—Made in the likeness of men...found in fashion as a man.—Forasmuch...as the children are partakers of flesh and blood, he also himself likewise took part of the same; that through death he might destroy him that had the power of death.

I am he that liveth, and was dead; and, behold, I am alive for evermore.—Christ being raised from the dead dieth no more; death hath no more dominion over him. For in that he died, he died unto sin once: but in that he liveth, he liveth unto God.—*What* and if ye shall see the Son of man ascend up where he was before?—He raised him from the dead, and set *him* at his own right hand in the heavenly *places*.—In him dwelleth all the fulness of the Godhead bodily.

Though he was crucified through weakness, yet he liveth by the power of God. For we also are weak in him, but we shall live with him by the power of God.

Ezek. 1.26; 1 Tim. 2.5; Phil. 2.7,8; He. 2.14 § Rev. 1.18; Ro. 6.9–10; Jn. 6.62; Eph. 1.20; Col. 2.9 § 2 Co. 13.4

Thy word hath quickened me.

The first man Adam was made a living soul; the last Adam *was made* a quickening spirit.

As the Father hath life in himself; so hath he given to the Son to have life in himself.—I am the resurrection, and the life: he that believeth in me, though he were dead, yet shall he live: and whosoever liveth and believeth in me shall never die.

In him was life; and the life was the light of men... As many as received him, to them gave he power to become the sons of God, *even* to them that believe on his name: which were born, not of blood, nor of the will of the flesh, nor of the will of man, but of God.

It is the spirit that quickeneth; the flesh profiteth nothing: the words that I speak unto you, *they* are spirit, and *they* are life.—The word of God *is* quick, and powerful, and sharper than any twoedged sword, piercing even to the dividing asunder of soul and spirit, and of the joints and marrow, and *is* a discerner of the thoughts and intents of the heart.

Ps. 119.50;   1 Co. 15.45 § Jn. 5.26;   Jn. 11.25–26 § Jn. 1.4,12–13 § Jn. 6.63;   He. 4.12

**Suffer *it to be so* now: for thus it becometh us
to fulfil all righteousness.**

I delight to do thy will, O my God: yea, thy law *is* within my heart.

Think not that I am come to destroy the law, or the prophets: I am not come to destroy, but to fulfil. For verily I say unto you, Till heaven and earth pass, one jot or one tittle shall in no wise pass from the law, till all be fulfilled.—The LORD is well pleased for his righteousness' sake; he will magnify the law, and make *it* honourable.—Except your righteousness shall exceed *the righteousness* of the scribes and Pharisees, ye shall in no case enter into the kingdom of heaven.

What the law could not do, in that it was weak through the flesh, God sending his own Son in the likeness of sinful flesh, and for sin, condemned sin in the flesh: that the righteousness of the law might be fulfilled in us, who walk not after the flesh, but after the Spirit.—Christ *is* the end of the law for righteousness to every one that believeth.

Mt. 3.15; Ps. 40.8 § Mt. 5.17–18; Isa. 42.21; Mt. 5.20
§ Ro. 8.3–4; Ro. 10.4

I *am* thy part and thine inheritance.

Whom have I in heaven *but thee?* and *there is* none upon earth *that* I desire beside thee. My flesh and my heart faileth: *but* God *is* the strength of my heart, and my portion for ever.—The LORD *is* the portion of mine inheritance and of my cup: thou maintainest my lot. The lines are fallen unto me in pleasant *places;* yea, I have a goodly heritage.

The LORD *is* my portion, saith my soul; therefore will I hope in him.

Thy testimonies have I taken as an heritage for ever: for they *are* the rejoicing of my heart.

O God, thou *art* my God; early will I seek thee: my soul thirsteth for thee, my flesh longeth for thee in a dry and thirsty land, where no water is... Because thou hast been my help, therefore in the shadow of thy wings will I rejoice.

My beloved *is* mine, and I *am* his.

Nu. **18.20**; Ps. 73.25–26; Ps. 16.5–6 § Lam. 3.24 § Ps. 119.111 § Ps. 63.1,7 § Song 2.16

Who can say, I have made my heart clean?

The LORD looked down from heaven upon the children of men, to see if there were any that did understand, *and* seek God. They are all gone aside, they are *all* together become filthy: *there is* none that doeth good, no, not one.—They that are in the flesh cannot please God.

To will is present with me; but *how* to perform that which is good I find not. For the good that I would I do not: but the evil which I would not, that I do.—We are all as an unclean *thing,* and all our righteousnesses *are* as filthy rags; and we all do fade as a leaf; and our iniquities, like the wind, have taken us away.

The scripture hath concluded all under sin, that the promise by faith of Jesus Christ might be given to them that believe.—God was in Christ, reconciling the world unto himself, not imputing their trespasses unto them.

If we say that we have no sin, we deceive ourselves, and the truth is not in us. If we confess our sins, he is faithful and just to forgive us *our* sins, and to cleanse us from all unrighteousness.

Pro. 20.9; Ps. 14.2–3; Ro. 8.8 § Ro. 7.18–19; Isa. 64.6
§ Ga. 3.22; 2 Co. 5.19 § 1 Jn. 1.8–9

The floods lift up their waves.

The LORD on high *is* mightier than the noise of many waters, *yea, than* the mighty waves of the sea.—O LORD God of hosts, who *is* a strong LORD like unto thee? or to thy faithfulness round about thee? thou rulest the raging of the sea: when the waves thereof arise, thou stillest them.

Fear ye not me? saith the LORD: will ye not tremble at my presence, which have placed the sand *for* the bound of the sea by a perpetual decree, that it cannot pass it?

When thou passest through the waters, I *will be* with thee; and through the rivers, they shall not overflow thee.

Peter…walked on the water, to go to Jesus. But when he saw the wind boisterous, he was afraid; and beginning to sink, he cried, saying, Lord, save me. And immediately Jesus stretched forth *his* hand, and caught him, and said unto him, O thou of little faith, wherefore didst thou doubt?

What time I am afraid, I will trust in thee.

Ps. 93.3; Ps. 93.4; Ps. 89.8–9 § Jer. 5.22 § Isa.43.2 § Mt. 14.29–31 § Ps. 56.3

Thy name *is as* ointment poured forth.

Christ…hath loved us, and hath given himself for us an offering and a sacrifice to God for a sweetsmelling savour.—Unto you therefore which believe *he is* precious.—God also hath highly exalted him, and given him a name which is above every name: that at the name of Jesus every knee should bow.—In him dwelleth all the fulness of the Godhead bodily.

If ye love me, keep my commandments.—The love of God is shed abroad in our hearts by the Holy Ghost which is given unto us.—The house was filled with the odour of the ointment.—They took knowledge of them, that they had been with Jesus.

O LORD our Lord, how excellent *is* thy name in all the earth! who hast set thy glory above the heavens.—Emmanuel…God with us.—His name shall be called Wonderful, Counsellor, The mighty God, The everlasting Father, The Prince of Peace.—The name of the LORD *is* a strong tower: the righteous runneth into it, and is safe.

Song 1.3; Eph. 5.2; 1 Pe. 2.7; Phil. 2.9; Col. 2.9 § Jn. 14.15; Ro. 5.5; Jn. 12.3; Ac. 4.13 § Ps. 8.1; Mt. 1.23; Isa. 9.6; Pro. 18.10

We that are in *this* tabernacle
do groan, being burdened.

Mine iniquities are gone over mine head: as an heavy burden they are too heavy for me... Lord, all my desire is before thee; and my groaning is not hid from thee— O wretched man that I am! who shall deliver me from the body of this death?

The whole creation groaneth and travaileth in pain together until now. And not only *they*, but ourselves...which have the firstfruits of the Spirit...groan within ourselves, waiting for the adoption, *to wit*, the redemption of our body.—Now for a season, if need be, ye are in heaviness through manifold temptations.

Shortly I must put off *this* my tabernacle.—For this corruptible must put on incorruption, and this mortal *must* put on immortality. So when this corruptible shall have put on incorruption, and this mortal shall have put on immortality, then shall be brought to pass the saying that is written, Death is swallowed up in victory.

2 Co. 5.4; Ps. 38.4,9; Ro. 7.24 § Ro. 8.22–23; 1 Pe. 1.6
§ 2 Pe. 1.14; 1 Co. 15.53–54

The whole bullock shall he carry forth without the camp unto a clean place, where the ashes are poured out, and burn him on the wood with fire.

They took Jesus, and led *him* away. And he bearing his cross went forth into a place called *the place* of a skull, which is called in the Hebrew Golgotha: where they crucified him.—The bodies of those beasts, whose blood is brought into the sanctuary by the high priest for sin, are burned without the camp. Wherefore Jesus also, that he might sanctify the people with his own blood, suffered without the gate. Let us go forth therefore unto him without the camp, bearing his reproach.—The fellowship of his sufferings.

Rejoice, inasmuch as ye are partakers of Christ's sufferings; that, when his glory shall be revealed, ye may be glad also with exceeding joy.—Our light affliction, which is but for a moment, worketh for us a far more exceeding *and* eternal weight of glory.

Lev. 4.12; Jn. 19.16–18; He. 13.11–13; Phil. 3.10
§ 1 Pe. 4.13; 2 Co. 4.17

God created man in his *own* image.

Forasmuch then as we are the offspring of God, we ought not to think that the Godhead is like unto gold, or silver, or stone, graven by art and man's device.

God, who is rich in mercy, for his great love wherewith he loved us, even when we were dead in sins, hath quickened us together with Christ… We are his workmanship, created in Christ Jesus unto good works, which God hath before ordained that we should walk in them.—For whom he did foreknow, he also did predestinate *to be* conformed to the image of his Son, that he might be the firstborn among many brethren.

We know that, when he shall appear, we shall be like him; for we shall see him as he is.—I shall be satisfied, when I awake, with thy likeness.

He that overcometh shall inherit all things; and I will be his God, and he shall be my son.—If children, then heirs; heirs of God, and joint-heirs with Christ.

Ge. 1.27; Ac. 17.29 § Eph. 2.4–5,10; Ro. 8.29 § 1 Jn. 3.2; Ps. 17.15 § Rev. 21.7; Ro. 8.17

Thou *art* my hope in the day of evil.

There be many that say, Who will shew us *any* good? LORD, lift thou up the light of thy countenance upon us.—I will sing of thy power; yea, I will sing aloud of thy mercy in the morning: for thou hast been my defence and refuge in the day of my trouble.

In my prosperity I said, I shall never be moved… Thou didst hide thy face, *and* I was troubled. I cried to thee, O LORD; and unto the LORD I made supplication. What profit *is there* in my blood, when I go down to the pit? Shall the dust praise thee? shall it declare thy truth? Hear, O LORD, and have mercy upon me: LORD, be thou my helper.

For a small moment have I forsaken thee; but with great mercies will I gather thee. In a little wrath I hid my face from thee for a moment; but with everlasting kindness will I have mercy on thee, saith the LORD thy Redeemer.—Sorrow shall be turned into joy.—Weeping may endure for a night, but joy *cometh* in the morning.

Jer. 17.17; Ps. 4.6; Ps. 59.16 § Ps. 30.6,7–10 § Isa. 54.7–8; Jn. 16.20; Ps. 30.5

Adam…begat *a son* in his own likeness.

Who can bring a clean *thing* out of an unclean?—Behold, I was shapen in iniquity; and in sin did my mother conceive me.

Dead in trespasses and sins…by nature the children of wrath, even as others.—I am carnal, sold under sin. For that which I do I allow not: for what I would, that do I not; but what I hate, that do I… I know that in me (that is, in my flesh,) dwelleth no good thing.

By one man sin entered into the world…by one man's disobedience many were made sinners.—If through the offence of one many be dead, much more the grace of God, and the gift by grace, *which is* by one man, Jesus Christ, hath abounded unto many.

The law of the Spirit of life in Christ Jesus hath made me free from the law of sin and death.

Thanks *be* to God, which giveth us the victory through our Lord Jesus Christ.

Ge. 5.3; Job 14.4; Ps. 51.5 § Eph. 2.1,3; Ro. 7.14–15,18 § Ro. 5.12,19; Ro. 5.15 § Ro. 8.2 § 1 Co. 15.57

**The LORD giveth wisdom: out of his mouth
cometh knowledge and understanding.**

Trust in the LORD with all thine heart; and lean not unto thine own understanding.—If any of you lack wisdom, let him ask of God, that giveth to all *men* liberally, and upbraideth not; and it shall be given him.—The foolishness of God is wiser than men; and the weakness of God is stronger than men... But God hath chosen the foolish things of the world to confound the wise...that no flesh should glory in his presence.

The entrance of thy words giveth light; it giveth understanding unto the simple.—Thy word have I hid in my heart, that I might not sin against thee.

All bare him witness, and wondered at the gracious words which proceeded out of his mouth.—Never man spake like this man.—Of him are ye in Christ Jesus, who of God is made unto us wisdom, and righteousness, and sanctification, and redemption.

Pro. 2.6; Pro. 3.5; Jas. 1.5; 1 Co. 1.25,27,29
§ Ps. 119.130; Ps. 119.11 § Lu. 4.22; Jn. 7.46; 1 Co. 1.30

The year of my redeemed is come.

Ye shall hallow the fiftieth year, and proclaim liberty throughout *all* the land unto all the inhabitants thereof: it shall be a jubile unto you; and ye shall return every man unto his possession, and ye shall return every man unto his family.

Thy dead *men* shall live, *together with* my dead body shall they arise. Awake and sing, ye that dwell in dust: for thy dew *is as* the dew of herbs, and the earth shall cast out the dead.

The Lord himself shall descend from heaven with a shout, with the voice of the archangel, and with the trump of God: and the dead in Christ shall rise first: then we which are alive *and* remain shall be caught up together with them in the clouds, to meet the Lord in the air: and so shall we ever be with the Lord.

I will ransom them from the power of the grave; I will redeem them from death: O death, I will be thy plagues; O grave, I will be thy destruction.

Their Redeemer *is* strong; the LORD of hosts *is* his name.

Isa. 63.4; Lev. 25.10 § Isa. 26.19 § 1 Th. 4.16–17 § Hos. 13.14 § Jer. 50.34

He shall see of the travail of his soul,
***and* shall be satisfied.**

Jesus...said, It is finished: and he bowed his head, and gave up the ghost.—He hath made him *to be* sin for us, who knew no sin; that we might be made the righteousness of God in him.

This people have I formed for myself; they shall shew forth my praise.—To the intent that now unto the principalities and powers in heavenly *places* might be known by the church the manifold wisdom of God, according to the eternal purpose which he purposed in Christ Jesus our Lord.—That in the ages to come he might shew the exceeding riches of his grace in *his* kindness toward us through Christ Jesus.

After that ye believed, ye were sealed with that holy Spirit of promise, which is the earnest of our inheritance until the redemption of the purchased possession, unto the praise of his glory.—Ye *are* a chosen generation, a royal priesthood, an holy nation, a peculiar people; that ye should shew forth the praises of him who hath called you out of darkness into his marvellous light.

Isa. 53.11; Jn. 19.30; 2 Co. 5.21 § Isa. 43.21;
Eph. 3.10–11; Eph. 2.7 § Eph. 1.13–14; 1 Pe. 2.9

The day of temptation in the wilderness.

Let no man say when he is tempted, I am tempted of God: for God cannot be tempted with evil, neither tempteth he any man: but every man is tempted, when he is drawn away of his own lust, and enticed. Then when lust hath conceived, it bringeth forth sin.

They...lusted exceedingly in the wilderness, and tempted God in the desert.

Jesus being full of the Holy Ghost...was led by the Spirit into the wilderness, being forty days tempted of the devil. And in those days he did eat nothing: and when they were ended, he afterward hungered. And the devil said unto him, If thou be the Son of God, command this stone that it be made bread.

In that he himself hath suffered being tempted, he is able to succour them that are tempted.—Simon, Simon...Satan hath desired *to have* you, that he may sift *you* as wheat: but I have prayed for thee, that thy faith fail not.

He. 3.8; Jas. 1.13–15 § Ps. 106.13,14 § Lu. 4.1–3
§ He. 2.18; Lu. 22.31–32

I am the LORD which sanctify you.

I *am* the LORD your God, which have separated you from *other* people... And ye shall be holy unto me: for I the LORD *am* holy, and have severed you from *other* people, that ye should be mine.

Sanctified by God the Father.—Sanctify them through thy truth: thy word is truth.—The very God of peace sanctify you wholly; and *I pray God* your whole spirit and soul and body be preserved blameless unto the coming of our Lord Jesus Christ.

Jesus...that he might sanctify the people with his own blood, suffered without the gate.—Our Saviour Jesus Christ...gave himself for us, that he might redeem us from all iniquity, and purify unto himself a peculiar people, zealous of good works.—Both he that sanctifieth and they who are sanctified *are* all of one: for which cause he is not ashamed to call them brethren.—For their sakes I sanctify myself, that they also might be sanctified through the truth.—Through sanctification of the Spirit, unto obedience and sprinkling of the blood of Jesus Christ.

Lev. 20.8; Lev. 20.24,26 § Jude 1; Jn. 17.17;
1 Th. 5.23 § He. 13.12; Titus 2.13,14; He. 2.11;
Jn. 17.19; 1 Pe. 1.2

**Light is sown for the righteous,
and gladness for the upright in heart.**

They that sow in tears shall reap in joy. He that goeth forth and weepeth, bearing precious seed, shall doubtless come again with rejoicing, bringing his sheaves *with him.*

That which thou sowest, thou sowest not that body that shall be.

Blessed *be* the God and Father of our Lord Jesus Christ, which according to his abundant mercy hath begotten us again unto a lively hope by the resurrection of Jesus Christ from the dead... Wherein ye greatly rejoice, though now for a season, if need be, ye are in heaviness through manifold temptations: that the trial of your faith, being much more precious than of gold that perisheth, though it be tried with fire, might be found unto praise and honour and glory at the appearing of Jesus Christ.

Ps. 97.11; Ps. 126.5–6 § 1 Co. 15.37 § 1 Pe. 1.3,6–7

What man *is* he that feareth the LORD?
him shall he teach in the way *that* he shall choose.

The light of the body is the eye: if therefore thine eye be single, thy whole body shall be full of light.

Thy word *is* a lamp unto my feet, and a light unto my path.—Thine ears shall hear a word behind thee, saying, This *is* the way, walk ye in it, when ye turn to the right hand, and when ye turn to the left.—I will instruct thee and teach thee in the way which thou shalt go: I will guide thee with mine eye. Be ye not as the horse, *or* as the mule, *which* have no understanding: whose mouth must be held in with bit and bridle, lest they come near unto thee. Many sorrows *shall be* to the wicked: but he that trusteth in the LORD, mercy shall compass him about. Be glad in the LORD, and rejoice, ye righteous: and shout for joy, all *ye that are* upright in heart.

O LORD, I know that the way of man *is* not in himself: *it is* not in man that walketh to direct his steps.

Ps. 25.12; Mt. 6.22 § Ps. 119.105; Isa. 30.21;
Ps. 32.8–11 § Jer. 10.23

When thou liest down, thou shalt not be afraid: yea, thou shalt lie down, and thy sleep shall be sweet.

There arose a great storm of wind, and the waves beat into the ship, so that it was now full. And he was in the hinder part of the ship, asleep on a pillow.

Be careful for nothing; but in every thing by prayer and supplication with thanksgiving let your requests be made known unto God. And the peace of God, which passeth all understanding, shall keep your hearts and minds through Christ Jesus.

I will both lay me down in peace, and sleep: for thou, LORD, only makest me dwell in safety.—He giveth his beloved sleep.

They stoned Stephen, calling upon *God*, and saying, Lord Jesus, receive my spirit. And he kneeled down, and cried with a loud voice, Lord, lay not this sin to their charge. And when he had said this, he fell asleep.—Absent from the body…present with the Lord.

Pro. **3.24**; Mk. 4.37–38 § Phil. 4.6–7 § Ps. 4.8; Ps. 127.2 § Ac. 7.59–60; 2 Co. 5.8

**The blood of sprinkling, that speaketh
better things than *that of* Abel.**

Behold the Lamb of God, which taketh away the sin of
the world.—The Lamb slain from the foundation of the
world.—*It is* not possible that the blood of bulls and of
goats should take away sins. Wherefore when he cometh
into the world, he saith, Sacrifice and offering thou
wouldest not, but a body hast thou prepared me… By
the which will we are sanctified through the offering of
the body of Jesus Christ once *for all.*

Abel…brought of the firstlings of his flock and of
the fat thereof…the LORD had respect unto Abel and to
his offering.—Christ…hath loved us, and hath given
himself for us an offering and a sacrifice to God for a
sweetsmelling savour.

Let us draw near with a true heart in full assurance
of faith, having our hearts sprinkled from an evil conscience, and our bodies washed with pure
water.—Having…boldness to enter into the holiest by
the blood of Jesus.

He. 12.24; Jn. 1.29; Rev. 13.8; He. 10.4–5,10 § Ge. 4.4;
Eph. 5.2 § He. 10.22; He. 10.19

Who knoweth the power of thine anger?

From the sixth hour there was darkness over all the land unto the ninth hour. And about the ninth hour Jesus cried with a loud voice, saying, Eli, Eli, lama sabachthani? that is to say, My God, my God, why hast thou forsaken me?—The LORD hath laid on him the iniquity of us all.

There is therefore now no condemnation to them which are in Christ Jesus.—Being justified by faith, we have peace with God through our Lord Jesus Christ.—Christ hath redeemed us from the curse of the law, being made a curse for us.

God sent his only begotten Son into the world, that we might live through him. Herein is love, not that we loved God, but that he loved us, and sent his Son *to be* the propitiation for our sins.—That he might be just, and the justifier of him which believeth in Jesus.

Ps. 90.11; Mt. 27.45–46; Isa. 53.6 § Ro. 8.1; Ro. 5.1; Ga. 3.13 § 1 Jn. 4.9–10; Ro. 3.26

Thus saith the Lord GOD;
I will yet *for* this be enquired of.

Ye have not, because ye ask not.

Ask, and it shall be given you; seek, and ye shall find; knock, and it shall be opened unto you: for every one that asketh receiveth; and he that seeketh findeth; and to him that knocketh it shall be opened.—This is the confidence that we have in him, that, if we ask any thing according to his will, he heareth us: and if we know that he hear us, whatsoever we ask, we know that we have the petitions that we desired of him.—If any of you lack wisdom, let him ask of God, that giveth to all *men* liberally, and upbraideth not; and it shall be given him.—Open thy mouth wide, and I will fill it.—Men ought always to pray, and not to faint.

The eyes of the LORD *are* upon the righteous, and his ears *are open* unto their cry... The LORD heareth, and delivereth them out of all their troubles.—Ask, and ye shall receive, that your joy may be full... Ye shall ask in my name: and I say not unto you, that I will pray the Father for you: for the Father himself loveth you, because ye have loved me.

Ezek. 36.37; Jas. 4.2 § Mt. 7.7–8; 1 Jn. 5.14–15; Jas. 1.5; Ps. 81.10; Lu. 18.1 § Ps. 34.15,17; Jn. 16.24,26–27

**Shall we receive good at the hand of God,
and shall we not receive evil?**

I know, O LORD, that thy judgments *are* right, and *that* thou in faithfulness hast afflicted me.—O LORD, thou *art* our father; we *are* the clay, and thou our potter; and we all *are* the work of thy hand.—It *is* the LORD: let him do what seemeth him good.

Righteous *art* thou, O LORD, when I plead with thee: yet let me talk with thee of *thy* judgments.

He shall sit *as* a refiner and purifier of silver.— Whom the Lord loveth he chasteneth, and scourgeth every son whom he receiveth.—It is enough for the disciple that he be as his master, and the servant as his lord.—Though he were a Son, yet learned he obedience by the things which he suffered.

Rejoice, inasmuch as ye are partakers of Christ's sufferings; that, when his glory shall be revealed, ye may be glad also with exceeding joy.—These are they which came out of great tribulation, and have washed their robes, and made them white in the blood of the Lamb.

Job 2.10; Ps. 119.75; Isa. 64.8; 1 Sa. 3.18 § Jer. 12.1 § Mal. 3.3; He. 12.6; Mt. 10.25; He. 5.8 § 1 Pe. 4.13; Rev. 7.14

Resist the devil, and he will flee from you.

When the enemy shall come in like a flood, the Spirit of the LORD shall lift up a standard against him.—Get thee hence, Satan: for it is written, Thou shalt worship the Lord thy God, and him only shalt thou serve. Then the devil leaveth him, and, behold, angels came and ministered unto him.

Be strong in the Lord, and in the power of his might. Put on the whole armour of God, that ye may be able to stand against the wiles of the devil.—And have no fellowship with the unfruitful works of darkness, but rather reprove *them*.—Lest Satan should get an advantage of us: for we are not ignorant of his devices.—Be sober, be vigilant; because your adversary the devil, as a roaring lion, walketh about, seeking whom he may devour: whom resist stedfast in the faith, knowing that the same afflictions are accomplished in your brethren that are in the world.—This is the victory that overcometh the world, *even* our faith.

Who shall lay any thing to the charge of God's elect? *It is* God that justifieth.

Jas. 4.7; Isa. 59.19; Mt. 4.10–11 § Eph. 6.10–11; Eph. 5.11; 2 Co. 2.11; 1 Pe. 5.8–9; 1 Jn. 5.4 § Ro. 8.33

Oh that I knew where I might find him!

Who *is* among you that feareth the LORD, that obeyeth the voice of his servant, that walketh *in* darkness, and hath no light? let him trust in the name of the LORD, and stay upon his God.

Ye shall seek me, and find *me*, when ye shall search for me with all your heart.—Seek, and ye shall find; knock, and it shall be opened unto you. For every one that asketh receiveth; and he that seeketh findeth; and to him that knocketh it shall be opened.

Truly our fellowship *is* with the Father, and with his Son Jesus Christ.—Now in Christ Jesus ye who sometimes were far off are made nigh by the blood of Christ... For through him we both have access by one Spirit unto the Father.

If we say that we have fellowship with him, and walk in darkness, we lie, and do not the truth.

Lo, I am with you alway.—I will never leave thee, nor forsake thee.—I will pray the Father, and he shall give you another Comforter that he may abide with you for ever.

Job 23.3; Isa. 50.10 § Jer. 29.13; Lu. 11.9–10 § 1 Jn. 1.3; Eph. 2.13,18 § 1 Jn. 1.6 § Mt. 28.20; He. 13.5; Jn. 14.16–17

**Let us search and try our ways,
and turn again to the LORD.**

Examine me, O LORD, and prove me; try my reins and my heart.—Behold, thou desirest truth in the inward parts: and in the hidden *part* thou shalt make me to know wisdom.—I thought on my ways, and turned my feet unto thy testimonies. I made haste, and delayed not to keep thy commandments.—Let a man examine himself, and so let him eat of *that* bread, and drink of *that* cup.

If we confess our sins, he is faithful and just to forgive us *our* sins, and to cleanse us from all unrighteousness.—We have an advocate with the Father, Jesus Christ the righteous: and he is the propitiation for our sins.—Having therefore, brethren, boldness to enter into the holiest by the blood of Jesus, by a new and living way, which he hath consecrated for us, through the veil, that is to say, his flesh; and *having* an high priest over the house of God; let us draw near with a true heart in full assurance of faith, having our hearts sprinkled from an evil conscience, and our bodies washed with pure water.

Lam. 3.40; Ps. 26.2; Ps. 51.6; Ps. 119.59–60;
1 Co. 11.28 § 1 Jn. 1.9; 1 Jn. 2.1; He. 10.19–22

There was a rainbow round about the throne,
in sight like unto an emerald.

This *is* the token of the covenant which I make between me and you and every living creature that *is* with you, for perpetual generations: I do set my bow in the cloud…and I will look upon it, that I may remember the everlasting covenant between God and every living creature of all flesh that *is* upon the earth.—An everlasting covenant, ordered in all *things*, and sure.—That by two immutable things, in which *it was* impossible for God to lie, we might have a strong consolation, who have fled for refuge to lay hold upon the hope set before us.

We declare unto you glad tidings, how that the promise which was made unto the fathers, God hath fulfilled the same unto us their children, in that he hath raised up Jesus again.

Jesus Christ the same yesterday, and to day, and for ever.

Rev. 4.3; Ge. 9.12–13,16; 2 Sa. 23.5; He. 6.18
§ Ac. 13.32–33 § He. 13.8

Reckon ye also yourselves to be dead indeed unto sin, but alive unto God through Jesus Christ our Lord.

He that heareth my word, and believeth on him that sent me, hath everlasting life, and shall not come into condemnation; but is passed from death unto life.—I through the law am dead to the law, that I might live unto God. I am crucified with Christ: nevertheless I live; yet not I, but Christ liveth in me: and the life which I now live in the flesh I live by the faith of the Son of God, who loved me, and gave himself for me.

Because I live, ye shall live also.—I give unto them eternal life; and they shall never perish, neither shall any *man* pluck them out of my hand. My Father, which gave *them* me, is greater than all; and no *man* is able to pluck *them* out of my Father's hand. I and *my* Father are one.

If ye then be risen with Christ, seek those things which are above, where Christ sitteth on the right hand of God... For ye are dead, and your life is hid with Christ in God.

Ro. 6.11; Jn. 5.24; Ga. 2.19–20 § Jn. 14.19; Jn. 10.28–30 § Col. 3.1,3

God...giveth...liberally, and upbraideth not.

Woman, where are those thine accusers? hath no man condemned thee? She said, No man, Lord. And Jesus said unto her, Neither do I condemn thee: go, and sin no more.

The grace of God, and the gift by grace, *which is* by one man, Jesus Christ, hath abounded unto many... The free gift *is* of many offences unto justification.

God, who is rich in mercy, for his great love wherewith he loved us, even when we were dead in sins, hath quickened us together with Christ, (by grace ye are saved;) and hath raised *us* up together, and made *us* sit together in heavenly *places* in Christ Jesus: that in the ages to come he might shew the exceeding riches of his grace in *his* kindness toward us through Christ Jesus.

He that spared not his own Son, but delivered him up for us all, how shall he not with him also freely give us all things?

Jas. 1.5; Jn. 8.10–11 § Ro. 5.15,16 § Eph. 2.4–7 § Ro. 8.32

God so loved the world, that he gave his only begotten Son, that whosoever believeth in him should not perish, but have everlasting life.

God…hath reconciled us to himself by Jesus Christ, and hath given to us the ministry of reconciliation; to wit, that God was in Christ, reconciling the world unto himself, not imputing their trespasses unto them; and hath committed unto us the word of reconciliation. Now then we are ambassadors for Christ, as though God did beseech *you* by us: we pray *you* in Christ's stead, be ye reconciled to God. For he hath made him *to be* sin for us, who knew no sin; that we might be made the righteousness of God in him.—God is love. In this was manifested the love of God toward us, because that God sent his only begotten Son into the world, that we might live through him. Herein is love, not that we loved God, but that he loved us, and sent his Son *to be* the propitiation for our sins. Beloved, if God so loved us, we ought also to love one another.

Jn. 3.16; 2 Co. 5.18–21; 1 Jn. 4.8–11

The spirit of man *is* the candle of the LORD.

He that is without sin among you, let him first cast a stone at her... And they which heard *it,* being convicted by *their own* conscience, went out one by one, beginning at the eldest, *even* unto the last.

Who told thee that thou *wast* naked? Hast thou eaten of the tree, whereof I commanded thee that thou shouldest not eat?

To him that knoweth to do good, and doeth *it* not, to him it is sin.—If our heart condemn us, God is greater than our heart, and knoweth all things. Beloved, if our heart condemn us not, *then* have we confidence toward God.

All things indeed *are* pure; but *it is* evil for that man who eateth with offence... Happy *is* he that condemneth not himself in that thing which he alloweth.

Search me, O God, and know my heart: try me, and know my thoughts: and see if *there be any* wicked way in me, and lead me in the way everlasting.

Pro. 20.27; Jn. 8.7,9 § Ge. 3.11 § Jas. 4.17; 1 Jn. 3.20–21 § Ro. 14.20,22 § Ps. 139.23–24

**Boast not thyself of to morrow;
for thou knowest not what a day may bring forth.**

Behold, now *is* the accepted time; behold, now *is* the day of salvation.—Yet a little while is the light with you. Walk while ye have the light, lest darkness come upon you: for he that walketh in darkness knoweth not whither he goeth. While ye have light, believe in the light, that ye may be the children of light.

Whatsoever thy hand findeth to do, do *it* with thy might; for *there is* no work, nor device, nor knowledge, nor wisdom, in the grave, whither thou goest.

Soul, thou hast much goods laid up for many years; take thine ease, eat, drink, *and* be merry... *Thou* fool, this night thy soul shall be required of thee: then whose shall those things be, which thou hast provided? So *is* he that layeth up treasure for himself, and is not rich toward God.

What *is* your life? It is even a vapour, that appeareth for a little time, and then vanisheth away.—The world passeth away, and the lust thereof: but he that doeth the will of God abideth for ever.

Pro. 27.1; 2 Co. 6.2; Jn. 12.35–36 § Ec. 9.10
§ Lu. 12.19,20–21 § Jas. 4.14; 1 Jn. 2.17

Thou *art* the same, and thy years shall have no end.

Before the mountains were brought forth, or ever thou hadst formed the earth and the world, even from everlasting to everlasting, thou *art* God.

I *am* the LORD, I change not; therefore ye sons of Jacob are not consumed.—The same yesterday, and to day, and for ever.

Every good gift and every perfect gift is from above, and cometh down from the Father of lights, with whom is no variableness, neither shadow of turning.—The gifts and calling of God *are* without repentance.

God is not a man, that he should lie; neither the son of man, that he should repent.—*It is of* the LORD's mercies that we are not consumed, because his compassions fail not.

This *man*, because he continueth ever, hath an unchangeable priesthood. Wherefore he is able also to save them to the uttermost that come unto God by him, seeing he ever liveth to make intercession for them.— Fear not; I am the first and the last.

Ps. 102.27; Ps. 90.2 § Mal. 3.6; He. 13.8 § Jas. 1.17; Ro. 11.29 § Nu. 23.19; Lam. 3.22 § He. 7.24–25; Rev. 1.17

The fruit of the Spirit is love…

God is love; and he that dwelleth in love dwelleth in God, and God in him.—The love of God is shed abroad in our hearts by the Holy Ghost which is given unto us.—Unto you…which believe *he is* precious.—We love him, because he first loved us.—The love of Christ constraineth us; because we thus judge, that if one died for all, then were all dead: and *that* he died for all, that they which live should not henceforth live unto themselves, but unto him which died for them, and rose again.

Ye yourselves are taught of God to love one another.—This is my commandment, That ye love one another, as I have loved you.—Above all things have fervent charity among yourselves: for charity shall cover the multitude of sins.—Walk in love, as Christ also hath loved us, and hath given himself for us an offering and a sacrifice to God for a sweetsmelling savour.

Ga. 5.22; 1 Jn. 4.16; Ro. 5.5; 1 Pe. 2.7; 1 Jn. 4.19;
2 Co. 5.14–15 § 1 Th. 4.9; Jn. 15.12; 1 Pe. 4.8; Eph. 5.2

Jehovah-nissi. [*marg.* The Lord my banner]

If God *be* for us, who *can be* against us?—The LORD *is* on my side; I will not fear: what can man do unto me?

Thou hast given a banner to them that fear thee.— The LORD *is* my light and my salvation; whom shall I fear? the LORD *is* the strength of my life; of whom shall I be afraid?… Though an host should encamp against me, my heart shall not fear: though war should rise against me, in this *will* I *be* confident.

Behold, God himself *is* with us for *our* captain.—The LORD of hosts *is* with us; the God of Jacob *is* our refuge.

These shall make war with the Lamb, and the Lamb shall overcome them.

Why do the heathen rage, and the people imagine a vain thing?… He that sitteth in the heavens shall laugh: the Lord shall have them in derision.—Take counsel together, and it shall come to nought; speak the word, and it shall not stand: for God *is* with us.

Ex. 17.15; Ro. 8.31; Ps. 118.6 § Ps. 60.4; Ps. 27.1,3
§ 2 Chr. 13.12; Ps. 46.7 § Rev. 17.14 § Ps. 2.1,4;
Isa. 8.10

God hath caused me to be fruitful
in the land of my affliction.

Blessed *be* God, even the Father of our Lord Jesus Christ, the Father of mercies, and the God of all comfort; who comforteth us in all our tribulation, that we may be able to comfort them which are in any trouble, by the comfort wherewith we ourselves are comforted of God. For as the sufferings of Christ abound in us, so our consolation also aboundeth by Christ.

Now for a season, if need be, ye are in heaviness through manifold temptations: that the trial of your faith, being much more precious than of gold that perisheth, though it be tried with fire, might be found unto praise and honour and glory at the appearing of Jesus Christ.—The Lord stood with me, and strengthened me.

Let them that suffer according to the will of God commit the keeping of their *souls to* him in well doing, as unto a faithful Creator.

Ge. 41.52; 2 Co. 1.3–5 § 1 Pe. 1.6–7; 2 Tim. 4.17 § 1 Pe. 4.19

There remaineth therefore a rest
to the people of God.

There the wicked cease *from* troubling; and there the weary be at rest. *There* the prisoners rest together; they hear not the voice of the oppressor.

Blessed *are* the dead which die in the Lord from henceforth…they…rest from their labours; and their works do follow them.

Our friend Lazarus sleepeth… Jesus spake of his death: but they thought that he had spoken of taking of rest in sleep.

We that are in *this* tabernacle do groan, being burdened.—Ourselves also, which have the firstfruits of the Spirit, even we ourselves groan within ourselves, waiting for the adoption, *to wit*, the redemption of our body. For we are saved by hope: but hope that is seen is not hope… But if we hope for that we see not, *then* do we with patience wait for *it*.

He. 4.9; Job 3.17–18 § Rev. 14.13 § Jn. 11.11,13
§ 2 Co. 5.4; Ro. 8.23–24,25

Trust in the LORD with all thine heart; and lean not unto thine own understanding. In all thy ways acknowledge him, and he shall direct thy paths.

Trust in him at all times; ye people, pour out your heart before him: God *is* a refuge for us.

I will instruct thee and teach thee in the way which thou shalt go: I will guide thee with mine eye. Be ye not as the horse, *or* as the mule, *which* have no understanding: whose mouth must be held in with bit and bridle, lest they come near unto thee. Many sorrows *shall be* to the wicked: but he that trusteth in the LORD, mercy shall compass him about.—Thine ears shall hear a word behind thee, saying, This *is* the way, walk ye in it, when ye turn to the right hand, and when ye turn to the left.

If thy presence go not *with me*, carry us not up hence. For wherein shall it be known here that I and thy people have found grace in thy sight? *is it* not in that thou goest with us? so shall we be separated, I and thy people, from all the people that *are* upon the face of the earth.

Pro. 3.5–6; Ps. 62.8 § Ps. 32.8–10; Isa. 30.21 § Ex. 33.15–16

The prize of the high calling of God in Christ Jesus.

Thou shalt have treasure in heaven...come *and* follow me.—I *am*...thy exceeding great reward.

Well done, *thou* good and faithful servant: thou hast been faithful over a few things, I will make thee ruler over many things: enter thou into the joy of thy lord.— They shall reign for ever and ever.

Ye shall receive a crown of glory that fadeth not away.—The crown of life.—A crown of righteousness.—An incorruptible [crown].

Father, I will that they also, whom thou hast given me, be with me where I am; that they may behold my glory, which thou has given me.—So shall we ever be with the Lord.

I reckon that the sufferings of this present time *are* not worthy *to be compared* with the glory which shall be revealed in us.

Phil. 3.14; Mt. 19.21; Ge. 15.1 § Mt. 25.21; Rev. 22.5 § 1 Pe. 5.4; Jas. 1.12; 2 Tim. 4.8; 1 Co. 9.25 § Jn. 17.24; 1 Th. 4.17 § Ro. 8.18

**Set your affection on things above,
not on things on the earth.**

Love not the world, neither the things *that are* in the world. If any man love the world, the love of the Father is not in him.—Lay not up for yourselves treasures upon earth, where moth and rust doth corrupt, and where thieves break through and steal: but lay up for yourselves treasures in heaven, where neither moth nor rust doth corrupt, and where thieves do not break through nor steal: for where your treasure is, there will your heart be also.

We walk by faith, not by sight.—We faint not; but though our outward man perish, yet the inward *man* is renewed day by day. For our light affliction, which is but for a moment, worketh for us a far more exceeding *and* eternal weight of glory; while we look not at the things which are seen, but at the things which are not seen: for the things which are seen *are* temporal; but the things which are not seen *are* eternal.—An inheritance incorruptible, and undefiled, and that fadeth not away, reserved in heaven for you.

Col. 3.2; 1 Jn. 2.15; Mt. 6.19–21 §️ 2 Co. 5.7;
2 Co. 4.16–18; 1 Pe. 1.4

He...bowed his shoulder to bear.

Take, my brethren, the prophets, who have spoken in the name of the Lord, for an example of suffering affliction, and of patience.—Now all these things happened unto them for ensamples: and they are written for our admonition, upon whom the ends of the world are come.

Shall we receive good at the hand of God, and shall we not receive evil? In all this did not Job sin with his lips.—Aaron held his peace.—It *is* the LORD: let him do what seemeth him good.

Cast thy burden upon the LORD, and he shall sustain thee.—Surely he hath borne our griefs, and carried our sorrows.

Come unto me, all *ye* that labour and are heavy laden, and I will give you rest. Take my yoke upon you, and learn of me; for I am meek and lowly in heart: and ye shall find rest unto your souls. For my yoke *is* easy, and my burden is light.

Ge. 49.15; Jas. 5.10; 1 Co. 10.11 § Job 2.10; Lev. 10.3; 1 Sa. 3.18 § Ps. 55.22; Isa. 53.4 § Mt. 11.28–30

O LORD, I am oppressed; undertake for me.

Unto thee lift I up mine eyes, O thou that dwellest in the heavens. Behold, as the eyes of servants *look* unto the hand of their masters, *and* as the eyes of a maiden unto the hand of her mistress; so our eyes *wait* upon the LORD our God.—Hear my cry, O God; attend unto my prayer. From the end of the earth will I cry unto thee, when my heart is overwhelmed: lead me to the rock *that* is higher than I. For thou hast been a shelter for me, *and* a strong tower from the enemy. I will abide in thy tabernacle for ever: I will trust in the covert of thy wings.—Thou hast been a strength to the poor, a strength to the needy in his distress, a refuge from the storm.

Christ...suffered for us, leaving us an example, that ye should follow his steps: who did no sin, neither was guile found in his mouth: who, when he was reviled, reviled not again; when he suffered, he threatened not; but committed *himself* to him that judgeth righteously.

Isa. 38.14; Ps. 123.1–2; Ps. 61.1–4; Isa. 25.4
§ 1 Pe. 2.21–23

Fight the good fight of faith.

We were troubled on every side; without *were* fightings, within *were* fears.—Fear not: for they that *be* with us *are* more than they that *be* with them.—Strong in the Lord, and in the power of his might.

Thou comest to me with a sword, and with a spear, and with a shield: but I come to thee in the name of the LORD of hosts, the God of the armies of Israel, whom thou hast defied.—God *is* my strength *and* power... He teacheth my hands to war; so that a bow of steel is broken by mine arms.—Our sufficiency *is* of God.

The angel of the LORD encampeth round about them that fear him, and delivereth them.—Behold, the mountain *was* full of horses and chariots of fire round about Elisha.

The time would fail me to tell of Gedeon, and *of* Barak, and *of* Samson, and *of* Jephthae; *of* David also, and Samuel, and *of* the prophets: who through faith subdued kingdoms...out of weakness were made strong, waxed valiant in fight, turned to flight the armies of the aliens.

---

1 Tim. 6.12; 2 Co. 7.5; 2 Ki. 6.16; Eph. 6.10
§ 1 Sa. 17.45; 2 Sa. 22.33,35; 2 Co. 3.5 § Ps. 34.7;
2 Ki. 6.17 § He. 11.32,34

He...preserveth the way of his saints.

The LORD your God...went in the way before you, to
search you out a place to pitch your tents *in*, in fire by
night, to shew you by what way ye should go, and in a
cloud by day.—As an eagle stirreth up her nest, fluttereth over her young, spreadeth abroad her wings,
taketh them, beareth them on her wings: *so* the LORD
alone did lead him.—The steps of a *good* man are
ordered by the LORD: and he delighteth in his way.
Though he fall, he shall not be utterly cast down: for the
LORD upholdeth *him with* his hand.—Many *are* the
afflictions of the righteous: but the LORD delivereth him
out of them all.—For the LORD knoweth the way of the
righteous: but the way of the ungodly shall perish.—We
know that all things work together for good to them that
love God, to them who are the called according to *his*
purpose.—With us *is* the LORD our God to help us, and
to fight our battles.

The LORD thy God in the midst of thee *is* mighty; he
will save, he will rejoice over thee with joy.

Pro. 2.8; Deu. 1.32,33; Deu. 32.11,12; Ps. 37.23,24;
Ps. 34.19; Ps. 1.6; Ro. 8.28; 2 Chr. 32.8 § Zeph. 3.17

My God, my God, why hast thou forsaken me?

He *was* wounded for our transgressions, *he was* bruised for our iniquities: the chastisement of our peace *was* upon him…the LORD hath laid on him the iniquity of us all… For the transgression of my people was he stricken… It pleased the LORD to bruise him; he hath put *him* to grief.

Jesus our Lord…was delivered for our offences.—Christ also hath once suffered for sins, the just for the unjust, that he might bring us to God.—Who his own self bare our sins in his own body on the tree, that we, being dead to sins, should live unto righteousness: by whose stripes ye were healed.

He hath made him *to be* sin for us, who knew no sin; that we might be made the righteousness of God in him.

Christ hath redeemed us from the curse of the law, being made a curse for us.

Mt. 27.46; Isa. 53.5,6,8,10 § Ro. 4.24,25; 1 Pe. 3.18;
1 Pe. 2.24 § 2 Co. 5.21 § Ga. 3.13

Thy Maker *is* thine husband;
the LORD of hosts *is* his name.

This is a great mystery: but I speak concerning Christ and the church.

Thou shalt no more be termed Forsaken...but thou shalt be called Hephzibah...for the LORD delighteth in thee... And *as* the bridegroom rejoiceth over the bride, *so* shall thy God rejoice over thee.—He hath sent me...to comfort all that mourn; to appoint unto them that mourn in Zion, to give unto them beauty for ashes, the oil of joy for mourning, the garment of praise for the spirit of heaviness.

I will greatly rejoice in the LORD, my soul shall be joyful in my God; for he hath clothed me with the garments of salvation...as a bridegroom decketh *himself* with ornaments, and as a bride adorneth *herself* with her jewels.

I will betroth thee unto me for ever; yea, I will betroth thee unto me in righteousness, and in judgment, and in lovingkindness, and in mercies.

Who shall separate us from the love of Christ?

Isa. 54.5; Eph. 5.32 § Isa. 62.4,5; Isa. 61.1–3 § Isa. 61.10 § Hos. 2.19 § Ro. 8.35

My times *are* in thy hand.

All his saints *are* in thy hand.—The word of the LORD came unto him, saying, Get thee hence, and turn thee eastward, and hide thyself by the brook Cherith, that *is* before Jordan. And it shall be, *that* thou shalt drink of the brook; and I have commanded the ravens to feed thee there… And the word of the LORD came unto him, saying, Arise, get thee to Zarephath, which *belongeth* to Zidon, and dwell there: behold, I have commanded a widow woman there to sustain thee.

Take no thought for your life, what ye shall eat, or what ye shall drink; nor yet for your body, what ye shall put on… Your heavenly Father knoweth that ye have need of all these things.

Trust in the LORD with all thine heart; and lean not unto thine own understanding. In all thy ways acknowledge him, and he shall direct thy paths.—Casting all your care upon him; for he careth for you.

Ps. 31.15; Deu. 33.3; 1 Ki. 17.2–4,8–9 § Mt. 6.25,32 § Pro. 3.5–6; 1 Pe. 5.7

Thou hast cast all my sins behind thy back.

Who *is* a God like unto thee, that pardoneth iniquity, and passeth by the transgression of the remnant of his heritage? he retaineth not his anger for ever, because he delighteth *in* mercy. He will turn again, he will have compassion upon us; he will subdue our iniquities; and thou wilt cast all their sins into the depths of the sea.

For a small moment have I forsaken thee; but with great mercies will I gather thee. In a little wrath I hid my face from thee for a moment; but with everlasting kindness will I have mercy on thee, saith the LORD thy Redeemer.—I will forgive their iniquity, and I will remember their sin no more.

Blessed *is he whose* transgression *is* forgiven, *whose* sin is covered. Blessed *is* the man unto whom the LORD imputeth not iniquity, and in whose spirit *there is* no guile.—The blood of Jesus Christ his Son cleanseth us from all sin.

Isa. 38.17; Mi. 7.18–19 § Isa. 54.7–8; Jer. 31.34
§ Ps. 32.1–2; 1 Jn. 1.7

**I know whom I have believed,
and am persuaded that he is able.**

Able to do exceeding abundantly above all that we ask or think.

Able to make all grace abound toward you; that ye, always having all sufficiency in all *things*, may abound to every good work.

Able to succour them that are tempted.

Able…to save them to the uttermost that come unto God by him, seeing he ever liveth to make intercession for them.

Able to keep you from falling, and to present *you* faultless before the presence of his glory with exceeding joy.

Able to keep that which I have committed unto him against that day.

Who shall change our vile body, that it may be fashioned like unto his glorious body, according to the working whereby he is able even to subdue all things unto himself.

Believe ye that I am able to do this?… Yea, Lord… According to your faith be it unto you.

2 Tim. 1.12; Eph. 3.20 § 2 Co. 9.8 § He. 2.18 § He. 7.25 § Jude 24 § 2 Tim. 1.12 § Phil. 3.21 § Mt. 9.28,29

The living God, who giveth us richly
all things to enjoy.

Beware that thou forget not the LORD thy God, in not keeping his commandments, and his judgments, and his statutes, which I command thee this day: lest *when* thou hast eaten and art full, and hast built goodly houses, and dwelt *therein*…then thine heart be lifted up, and thou forget the LORD thy God…for *it is* he that giveth thee power to get wealth.

Except the LORD build the house, they labour in vain that build it: except the LORD keep the city, the watchman waketh *but* in vain. *It is* vain for you to rise up early, to sit up late, to eat the bread of sorrows: *for so* he giveth his beloved sleep.—They got not the land in possession by their own sword, neither did their own arm save them: but thy right hand, and thine arm, and the light of thy countenance, because thou hadst a favour unto them—*There be* many that say, Who will shew us *any* good? LORD, lift thou up the light of thy countenance upon us.

1 Tim. 6.17; Deu. 8.11–12,14,18 § Ps. 127.1–2;
Ps. 44.3; Ps. 4.6

They sung as it were a new song.

A new and living way, which he hath consecrated for us.—Not by works of righteousness which we have done, but according to his mercy he saved us, by the washing of regeneration, and renewing of the Holy Ghost; which he shed on us abundantly through Jesus Christ our Saviour.—By grace are ye saved through faith; and that not of yourselves: *it is* the gift of God: not of works, lest any man should boast.

Not unto us, O LORD, not unto us, but unto thy name give glory.—Unto him that loved us, and washed us from our sins in own blood, and hath made us kings and priests unto God and his Father; to him *be* glory and dominion for ever and ever. Amen.—Thou wast slain, and hast redeemed us to God by thy blood out of every kindred, and tongue, and people, and nation.—I beheld, and, lo, a great multitude, which no man could number…cried…saying, Salvation to our God which sitteth upon the throne, and unto the Lamb.

Rev. 14.3; He. 10.20; Titus 3.5–6; Eph. 2.8–9
§ Ps. 115.1; Rev. 1.5–6; Rev. 5.9; Rev. 7.9,10

Jehovah-jireh. [*marg.* The Lord will provide]

God will provide himself a lamb for a burnt offering.

Behold, the LORD's hand is not shortened, that it cannot save; neither his ear heavy, that it cannot hear.— There shall come out of Sion the Deliverer, and shall turn away ungodliness from Jacob.

Happy *is he* that *hath* the God of Jacob for his help, whose hope *is* in the LORD his God.—Behold, the eye of the LORD *is* upon them that fear him, upon them that hope in his mercy; to deliver their soul from death.

My God shall supply all your need according to his riches in glory by Christ Jesus.—He hath said, I will never leave thee, nor forsake thee. So that we may boldly say, The Lord *is* my helper, and I will not fear what man shall do unto me.—The LORD *is* my strength and my shield; my heart trusted in him, and I am helped: therefore my heart greatly rejoiceth; and with my song will I praise him.

Ge. 22.14; Ge. 22.8 § Isa. 59.1; Ro. 11.26 § Ps. 146.5; Ps. 33.18–19 § Phil. 4.19; He. 13.5–6; Ps. 28.7

He feedeth among the lilies.

Where two or three are gathered together in my name, there am I in the midst of them.—If a man love me, he will keep my words: and my Father will love him, and we will come unto him, and make our abode with him.

If ye keep my commandments, ye shall abide in my love; even as I have kept my Father's commandments, and abide in his love.

Let my beloved come into his garden, and eat his pleasant fruits.—I am come into my garden, my sister, *my* spouse: I have gathered my myrrh with my spice; I have eaten my honeycomb with my honey.—The fruit of the Spirit is love, joy, peace, longsuffering, gentleness, goodness, faith, meekness, temperance.

Herein is my Father glorified, that ye bear much fruit; so shall ye be my disciples.—Every *branch* that beareth fruit, he purgeth it, that it may bring forth more fruit.—Being filled with the fruits of righteousness, which are by Jesus Christ, unto the glory and praise of God.

Song 2.16; Mt. 18.20; Jn. 14.23 § Jn. 15.10
§ Song 4.16; Song 5.1; Ga. 5.22–23 § Jn. 15.8;
Jn. 15.2; Phil. 1.11

The LORD bless thee, and keep thee.

The blessing of the LORD, it maketh rich, and he addeth no sorrow with it.—Thou, LORD, wilt bless the righteous; with favour wilt thou compass him as *with* a shield.

He will not suffer thy foot to be moved: he that keepeth thee will not slumber. Behold, he that keepeth Israel shall neither slumber nor sleep. The LORD *is* thy keeper: the LORD *is* thy shade upon thy right hand... The LORD shall preserve thee from all evil: he shall preserve thy soul. The LORD shall preserve thy going out and thy coming in from this time forth, and even for evermore.—I the LORD do keep it; I will water it every moment: lest *any* hurt it, I will keep it night and day.

Holy Father, keep through thine own name those whom thou hast given me. While I was with them in the world, I kept them in thy name: those that thou gavest me I have kept.

The Lord shall deliver me from every evil work, and will preserve *me* unto his heavenly kingdom: to whom *be* glory for ever and ever. Amen.

Nu. 6.24; Pro. 10.22; Ps. 5.12 § Ps. 121.3–5,7–8;
Isa. 27.3 § Jn. 17.11,12 § 2 Tim. 4.18

Jesus wept.

A man of sorrows, and acquainted with grief.—We have not an high priest which cannot be touched with the feeling of our infirmities.—It became him, for whom *are* all things, and by whom *are* all things, in bringing many sons unto glory, to make the captain of their salvation perfect through sufferings.—Though he were a Son, yet learned he obedience by the things which he suffered.

I was not rebellious, neither turned away back. I gave my back to the smiters, and my cheeks to them that plucked off the hair: I hid not my face from shame and spitting.

Behold how he loved him!—He took not on *him the nature of* angels; but he took on *him* the seed of Abraham. Wherefore in all things it behoved him to be made like unto *his* brethren, that he might be a merciful and faithful high priest in things *pertaining* to God, to make reconciliation for the sins of the people.

Jn. 11.35; Isa. 53.3; He. 4.15; He. 2.10; He. 5.8
§ Isa. 50.5–6 § Jn. 11.36; He. 2.16–17

The LORD make his face shine upon thee,
and be gracious unto thee: the LORD lift up his
countenance upon thee, and give thee peace.

No man hath seen God at any time; the only begotten Son, which is in the bosom of the Father, he hath declared *him*.—The brightness of *his* glory, and the express image of his person.—The god of this world hath blinded the minds of them which believe not, lest the light of the glorious gospel of Christ, who is the image of God, should shine unto them.

Make thy face to shine upon thy servant: save me for thy mercies' sake. Let me not be ashamed, O LORD; for I have called upon thee.—LORD, by thy favour thou hast made my mountain to stand strong: thou didst hide thy face, *and* I was troubled.—Blessed *is* the people that know the joyful sound: they shall walk, O LORD, in the light of thy countenance.

The LORD will give strength unto his people; the LORD will bless his people with peace.

Be of good cheer; it is I; be not afraid.

Nu. 6.25,26; Jn. 1.18; He. 1.3; 2 Co. 4.4 § Ps. 31.16–17; Ps. 30.7; Ps. 89.15 § Ps. 29.11 § Mt. 14.27

Things that are pleasing in his sight.

Without faith *it is* impossible to please *him.*—So then they that are in the flesh cannot please God.—The LORD taketh pleasure in his people.

This *is* thankworthy, if a man for conscience toward God endure grief, suffering wrongfully... If, when ye do well, and suffer *for it*, ye take it patiently, this *is* acceptable with God.—*The ornament* of a meek and quiet spirit...is in the sight of God of great price.

Whoso offereth praise glorifieth me: and to him that ordereth *his* conversation *aright* will I shew the salvation of God.—I will praise the name of God with a song, and will magnify him with thanksgiving. *This* also shall please the LORD better than an ox *or* bullock that hath horns and hoofs.

I beseech you...brethren, by the mercies of God, that ye present your bodies a living sacrifice, holy, acceptable unto God, *which is* your reasonable service.

---

1 Jn. **3.22**; He. 11.6; Ro. 8.8; Ps. 149.4 § 1 Pe. 2.19,20; 1 Pe. 3.4 § Ps. 50.23; Ps. 69.30–31 § Ro. 12.1

There is one God, and one mediator
between God and men, the man Christ Jesus.

Forasmuch…as the children are partakers of flesh and blood, he also himself likewise took part of the same.

Look unto me, and be ye saved, all the ends of the earth: for I *am* God, and *there is* none else.

We have an advocate with the Father, Jesus Christ the righteous.—In Christ Jesus ye who sometimes were far off are made nigh by the blood of Christ. For he is our peace.—By his own blood he entered in once into the holy place, having obtained eternal redemption *for us*… And for this cause he is the mediator of the new testament, that by means of death, for the redemption of the transgressions *that were* under the first testament, they which are called might receive the promise of eternal inheritance.—He is able also to save them to the uttermost that come unto God by him, seeing he ever liveth to make intercession for them.

1 Tim. 2.5; He. 2.14 § Isa. 45.22 § 1 Jn. 2.1;
Eph. 2.13–14; He. 9.12,15; He. 7.25

O my God, my soul is cast down within me.

Thou wilt keep *him* in perfect peace, *whose* mind *is* stayed *on thee*: because he trusteth in thee. Trust ye in the LORD for ever: for in the LORD JEHOVAH *is* everlasting strength.

Cast thy burden upon the LORD, and he shall sustain thee.—He hath not despised nor abhorred the affliction of the afflicted; neither hath he hid his face from him; but when he cried unto him, he heard.—Is any among you afflicted? let him pray.

Let not your heart be troubled, neither let it be afraid.—Take no thought for your life, what ye shall eat, or what ye shall drink; nor yet for your body, what ye shall put on... Behold the fowls of the air: for they sow not, neither do they reap, nor gather into barns; yet your heavenly Father feedeth them. Are ye not much better than they?—Be not faithless, but believing.—Lo, I am with you alway.

Ps. 42.6; Isa. 26.3,4 § Ps. 55.22; Ps. 22.24; Jas. 5.13
§ Jn. 14.27; Mt. 6.25,26; Jn. 20.27; Mt. 28.20

Adorn the doctrine of God our Saviour
in all things.

Let your conversation be as it becometh the gospel of Christ.—Abstain from all appearance of evil.—If ye be reproached for the name of Christ, happy *are* ye... But let none of you suffer as a murderer, or *as* a thief, or *as* an evildoer, or as a busybody in other men's matters.—Be blameless and harmless, the sons of God, without rebuke, in the midst of a crooked and perverse nation, among whom ye shine as lights in the world.—Let your light so shine before men, that they may see your good works, and glorify your Father which is in heaven.

Let not mercy and truth forsake thee: bind them about thy neck; write them upon the table of thine heart: so shalt thou find favour and good understanding in the sight of God and man.—Brethren, whatsoever things are true, whatsoever things *are* honest, whatsoever things *are* just, whatsoever things *are* pure, whatsoever things *are* lovely, whatsoever things *are* of good report; if *there be* any virtue, and if *there be* any praise, think on these things.

Titus 2.10; Phil. 1.27; 1 Th. 5.22; 1 Pe. 4.14,15;
Phil. 2.15; Mt. 5.16 § Pro. 3.3–4; Phil. 4.8

**The words that I speak unto you,
they are spirit, and *they* are life.**

Of his own will begat he us with the word of truth.—
The letter killeth, but the spirit giveth life.

Christ...loved the church, and gave himself for it;
that he might sanctify and cleanse it with the washing of
water by the word, that he might present it to himself a
glorious church, not having spot, or wrinkle, or any
such thing.

Wherewithal shall a young man cleanse his way? by
taking heed *thereto* according to thy word.—Thy word
hath quickened me.—Thy word have I hid in mine
heart, that I might not sin against thee... I will not forget thy word... I trust in thy word... The law of thy
mouth *is* better unto me than thousands of gold and silver... I will never forget thy precepts: for with them
thou hast quickened me... How sweet are thy words
unto my taste! *yea, sweeter* than honey to my mouth!
Through thy precepts I get understanding: therefore I
hate every false way.

Jn. 6.63; Jas. 1.18; 2 Co. 3.6 § Eph. 5.25–27
§ Ps. 119.9; Ps. 119.50; Ps. 119.11,16,42,72,93,103–104

Perfect through sufferings.

My soul is exceeding sorrowful, even unto death: tarry ye here, and watch with me. And he went a little further, and fell on his face, and prayed, saying, O my Father, if it be possible, let this cup pass from me: nevertheless not as I will, but as thou *wilt*.—And being in an agony he prayed more earnestly: and his sweat was as it were great drops of blood falling down to the ground.

The sorrows of death compassed me, and the pains of hell gat hold upon me: I found trouble and sorrow.— Reproach hath broken my heart; and I am full of heaviness: and I looked *for some* to take pity, but *there was* none; and for comforters, but I found none.—I looked on *my* right hand, and beheld, but *there was* no man that would know me: refuge failed me; no man cared for my soul.

He is despised and rejected of men; a man of sorrows, and acquainted with grief: and we hid as it were *our* faces from him; he was despised, and we esteemed him not.

He. 2.10; Mt. 26.38–39; Lu. 22.44 § Ps. 116.3; Ps. 69.20; Ps. 142.4 § Isa. 53.3

**The LORD made heaven and earth, the sea,
and all that in them *is*.**

The heavens declare the glory of God; and the firmament sheweth his handywork.—By the word of the LORD were the heavens made; and all the host of them by the breath of his mouth... For he spake, and it was *done;* he commanded, and it stood fast.—Behold, the nations *are* as a drop of a bucket, and are counted as the small dust of the balance: behold, he taketh up the isles as a very little thing.

Through faith we understand that the worlds were framed by the word of God, so that things which are seen were not made of things which do appear.

When I consider thy heavens, the work of thy fingers, the moon and the stars, which thou hast ordained; what is man, that thou art mindful of him? and the son of man, that thou visitest him?

Ex. 20.11; Ps. 19.1; Ps. 33.6,9; Isa. 40.15 § He. 11.3 § Ps. 8.3–4

What *is* your life? It is even a vapour, that appeareth for a little time, and then vanisheth away.

My days are swifter than a post: they flee away, they see no good. They are passed away as the swift ships: as the eagle *that* hasteth to the prey.—Thou carriest them away as with a flood; they are *as* a sleep: in the morning *they are* like grass *which* groweth up. In the morning it flourisheth, and groweth up; in the evening it is cut down, and withereth.—Man *that is* born of a woman *is* of few days, and full of trouble. He cometh forth like a flower, and is cut down.

The world passeth away, and the lust thereof: but he that doeth the will of God abideth for ever.—They shall perish, but thou shalt endure: yea, all of them shall wax old like a garment; as a vesture shalt thou change them, and they shall be changed: but thou *art* the same, and thy years shall have no end.—Jesus Christ the same yesterday, and to day, and for ever.

Jas. 4.14; Job 9.25–26; Ps. 90.5–6; Job 14.1–2
§ 1 Jn. 2.17; Ps. 102.26–27; He. 13.8

**I will sing with the spirit,
and I will sing with the understanding also.**

Be filled with the Spirit; speaking to yourselves in psalms and hymns and spiritual songs, singing and making melody in your heart to the Lord.—Let the word of Christ dwell in you richly in all wisdom; teaching and admonishing one another in psalms and hymns and spiritual songs, singing with grace in your hearts to the Lord.

My mouth shall speak the praise of the LORD: and let all flesh bless his holy name for ever and ever.

Praise ye the LORD: for *it is* good to sing praises unto our God; for *it is* pleasant; *and* praise is comely... Sing unto the LORD with thanksgiving; sing praise upon the harp unto our God.

I heard a voice from heaven, as the voice of many waters, and as the voice of a great thunder: and I heard the voice of harpers harping with their harps.

---

1 Co. **14.15**; Eph. 5.18–19; Col. 3.16 § Ps. 145.21 § Ps. 147.1,7 § Rev. 14.2

**He shall put his hand upon the head of
the burnt offering; and it shall be accepted
for him to make atonement for him.**

Ye know that ye were not redeemed with corruptible things, *as* silver and gold, from your vain conversation *received* by tradition from your fathers; but with the precious blood of Christ, as of a lamb without blemish and without spot.—Who his own self bare our sins in his own body on the tree.

He hath made us accepted in the beloved.—As lively stones...built up a spiritual house, an holy priesthood, to offer up spiritual sacrifices, acceptable to God by Jesus Christ.—I beseech you therefore, brethren, by the mercies of God, that ye present your bodies a living sacrifice, holy, acceptable unto God, *which is* your reasonable service.

Now unto him that is able to keep you from falling, and to present *you* faultless before the presence of his glory with exceeding joy, to the only wise God our Saviour, *be* glory and majesty, dominion and power, both now and ever.

Lev. 1.4; 1 Pe. 1.18–19; 1 Pe. 2.24 § Eph. 1.6; 1 Pe. 2.5; Ro. 12.1 § Jude 24–25

In all points tempted like as *we are, yet* without sin.

When the woman saw that the tree *was* good for food, and that it *was* pleasant to the eyes, and a tree to be desired to make *one* wise, she took of the fruit thereof, and did eat, and gave also unto her husband with her; and he did eat.

When the tempter came to him, he said, If thou be the Son of God, command that these stones be made bread. But he answered... It is written, Man shall not live by bread alone, but by every word that proceedeth out of the mouth of God... The devil...sheweth him all the kingdoms of the world, and the glory of them... Then saith Jesus unto him, Get thee hence, Satan: for it is written, Thou shalt worship the Lord thy God, and him only shalt thou serve.

For all that *is* in the world, the lust of the flesh, and the lust of the eyes, and the pride of life, is not of the Father, but is of the world.

In that he himself hath suffered being tempted, he is able to succour them that are tempted.

Blessed *is* the man that endureth temptation.

He. 4.15;   Ge. 3.6   § Mt. 4.3–4,8,10   § 1 Jn. 2.16 § He. 2.18   § Jas. 1.12

Mine eyes fail *with looking* upward.

Have mercy upon me, O LORD; for I *am* weak: O
LORD, heal me; for my bones are vexed. My soul is also
sore vexed: but thou, O LORD, how long? Return, O
LORD, deliver my soul: oh save me for thy mercies'
sake.—My heart is sore pained within me: and the ter-
rors of death are fallen upon me. Fearfulness and
trembling are come upon me, and horror hath overwhelmed me. And I said, Oh that I had wings like a
dove! *for then* would I fly away, and be at rest.

Ye have need of patience.

While they looked stedfastly toward heaven as he
went up, behold, two men stood by them in white
apparel; which also said, Ye men of Galilee, why stand ye
gazing up into heaven? this same Jesus, which is taken
up from you into heaven, shall so come in like manner
as ye have seen him go into heaven.—Our conversation
is in heaven; from whence also we look for the Saviour,
the Lord Jesus Christ.—That blessed hope…the glorious appearing of the great God and our Saviour Jesus
Christ.

Isa. 38.14; Ps. 6.2–4; Ps. 55.4–6 § He. 10.36
§ Ac. 1.10–11; Phil. 3.20; Titus 2.13

His name *shall be* in their foreheads.

I am the good shepherd, and know my *sheep.*—The foundation of God standeth sure, having this seal, The Lord knoweth them that are his. And, Let every one that nameth the name of Christ depart from iniquity.

The LORD *is* good, a strong hold in the day of trouble; and he knoweth them that trust in him.—Hurt not the earth, neither the sea, nor the trees, till we have sealed the servants of our God in their foreheads.

After that ye believed, ye were sealed with that holy Spirit of promise, which is the earnest of our inheritance.—Now he which stablisheth us with you in Christ, and hath anointed us, *is* God; who hath also sealed us, and given the earnest of the Spirit in our hearts.

I will write upon him the name of my God, and the name of the city of my God, *which is* new Jerusalem, which cometh down out of heaven from my God: and *I will write upon him* my new name.—This *is the name* wherewith she shall be called, The LORD our righteousness.

Rev. 22.4; Jn. 10.14; 2 Tim. 2.19 § Na. 1.7; Rev. 7.3
§ Eph. 1.13–14; 2 Co. 1.21–22 § Rev. 3.12; Jer. 33.16

**God, having raised up his Son Jesus,
sent him to bless you, in turning away
every one of you from his iniquities.**

Blessed *be* the God and Father of our Lord Jesus Christ, which according to his abundant mercy hath begotten us again unto a lively hope by the resurrection of Jesus Christ from the dead.—Saved by his life.

Our Saviour Jesus Christ; who gave himself for us, that he might redeem us from all iniquity, and purify unto himself a peculiar people, zealous of good works.—As he which hath called you is holy, so be ye holy in all manner of conversation; because it is written, Be ye holy; for I am holy.

The God and Father of our Lord Jesus Christ...hath blessed us with all spiritual blessings in heavenly *places* in Christ.—In him dwelleth all the fulness of the Godhead bodily. And ye are complete in him.—Of his fulness have all we received, and grace for grace.

He that spared not his own Son, but delivered him up for us all, how shall he not with him also freely give us all things?

Ac. 3.26; 1 Pe. 1.3; Ro. 5.10 § Titus 2.13–14;
1 Pe. 1.15–16 § Eph. 1.3; Col. 2.9–10; Jn. 1.16
§ Ro. 8.32

Strengthen thou me according unto thy word.

Remember the word unto thy servant, upon which thou hast caused me to hope.—O LORD, I am oppressed; undertake for me.

Heaven and earth shall pass away: but my words shall not pass away.—Ye know in all your hearts and in all your souls, that not one thing hath failed of all the good things which the LORD your God spake concerning you; all are come to pass unto you, *and* not one thing hath failed thereof.

Fear not: peace *be* unto thee, be strong, yea, be strong. And when he had spoken unto me, I was strengthened, and said, Let my lord speak; for thou hast strengthened me.—Be strong…and work: for I *am* with you, saith the LORD of hosts.—Not by might, nor by power, but by my spirit, saith the LORD of hosts.

Be strong in the Lord, and in the power of his might.

Ps. 119.28;   Ps. 119.49;   Isa. 38.14 § Lu. 21.33;   Jos. 23.14 § Dan. 10.19;   Hag. 2.4;   Zech. 4.6 § Eph. 6.10

The entrance of thy words giveth light.

This...is the message which we have heard of him, and declare unto you, that God is light, and in him is no darkness at all.—God, who commanded the light to shine out of darkness, hath shined in our hearts, to *give* the light of the knowledge of the glory of God in the face of Jesus Christ.—The Word was God... In him was life; and the life was the light of men.—If we walk in the light, as he is in the light, we have fellowship one with another, and the blood of Jesus Christ his Son cleanseth us from all sin.

Thy word have I hid in mine heart, that I might not sin against thee.—Ye are clean through the word which I have spoken unto you.

Ye were sometimes darkness, but now *are ye* light in the Lord: walk as children of light.—Ye *are* a chosen generation, a royal priesthood, an holy nation, a peculiar people; that ye should shew forth the praises of him who hath called you out of darkness into his marvellous light.

Ps. 119.130; 1 Jn. 1.5; 2 Co. 4.6; Jn. 1.1,4; 1 Jn. 1.7
§ Ps. 119.11; Jn. 15.3 § Eph. 5.8; 1 Pe. 2.9

Noah was a just man.

The just shall live by faith.—Noah builded an altar unto the LORD; and took of every clean beast, and of every clean fowl, and offered burnt offerings on the altar. And the LORD smelled a sweet savour.—The Lamb slain from the foundation of the world.

Being justified by faith, we have peace with God through our Lord Jesus Christ.

By the deeds of the law there shall no flesh be justified in his sight: for by the law *is* the knowledge of sin. But now the righteousness of God without the law is manifested, being witnessed by the law and the prophets; even the righteousness of God *which is* by faith of Jesus Christ unto all and upon all them that believe: for there is no difference.

We...joy in God through our Lord Jesus Christ, by whom we have now received the atonement.

Who shall lay any thing to the charge of God's elect? *It is* God that justifieth.—Whom he did predestinate, them he also called: and whom he called, them he also justified.

Ge. 6.9; Ga. 3.11; Ge. 8.20–21; Rev. 13.8 § Ro. 5.1 § Ro. 3.20–22 § Ro. 5.11 § Ro. 8.33; Ro. 8.30

**Be watchful, and strengthen the things
which remain, that are ready to die.**

The end of all things is at hand: be ye therefore sober, and watch unto prayer.—Be sober, be vigilant; because your adversary the devil, as a roaring lion, walketh about, seeking whom he may devour.—Take heed to thyself, and keep thy soul diligently, lest thou forget the things which thine eyes have seen, and lest they depart from thy heart all the days of thy life.—The just shall live by faith: but if *any man* draw back, my soul shall have no pleasure in him. But we are not of them who draw back unto perdition; but of them that believe to the saving of the soul.

What I say unto you I say unto all, Watch.

Fear thou not; for I *am* with thee: be not dismayed; for I *am* thy God: I will strengthen thee; yea, I will help thee; yea, I will uphold thee with the right hand of my righteousness… I the LORD thy God will hold thy right hand.

Rev. 3.2; 1 Pe. 4.7; 1 Pe. 5.8; Deu. 4.9; He. 10.38–39
§ Mk. 13.37 § Isa. 41.10,13

Is his mercy clean gone for ever?

His mercy *endureth* for ever.—The LORD *is* longsuffering, and of great mercy.—Who *is* a God like unto thee, that pardoneth iniquity…? he retaineth not his anger for ever, because he delighteth *in* mercy. He will turn again, he will have compassion upon us; he will subdue our iniquities; and thou wilt cast all their sins into the depths of the sea.—Not by works of righteousness which we have done, but according to his mercy he saved us.

Blessed *be* God, even the Father of our Lord Jesus Christ, the Father of mercies, and the God of all comfort; who comforteth us in all our tribulation, that we may be able to comfort them which are in any trouble, by the comfort wherewith we ourselves are comforted of God.

A merciful and faithful high priest in things *pertaining* to God, to make reconciliation for the sins of the people. For in that he himself hath suffered being tempted, he is able to succour them that are tempted.

Ps. 77.8; Ps. 136.23; Nu. 14.18; Mi. 7.18–19; Titus 3.5 § 2 Co. 1.3,4 § He. 2.17–18

Lot lifted up his eyes, and beheld all the plain of Jordan, that it *was* well watered every where… *even* as the garden of the LORD… Then Lot chose him all the plain of Jordan…and pitched his tent toward Sodom. But the men of Sodom were wicked and sinners before the LORD exceedingly.

Just Lot…(that righteous man.)

Be not deceived; God is not mocked: for whatsoever a man soweth, that shall he also reap.—Remember Lot's wife.

Be ye not unequally yoked together with unbelievers: for what fellowship hath righteousness with unrighteousness? and what communion hath light with darkness? Wherefore come out from among them, and be ye separate, saith the Lord, and touch not the unclean *thing*.—Be not ye…partakers with them. For ye were sometimes darkness, but now *are ye* light in the Lord: walk as children of light…proving what is acceptable unto the Lord. And have no fellowship with the unfruitful works of darkness, but rather reprove *them*.

Ge. 13.10–13; 2 Pe. 2.7,8 § Ga. 6.7; Lu. 17.32 § 2 Co. 6.14,17; Eph. 5.7–8,10–11

**If so be the LORD *will be* with me,
then I shall be able to drive them out,
as the LORD said.**

He hath said, I will never leave thee, nor forsake thee. So that we may boldly say, The Lord *is* my helper, and I will not fear what man shall do unto me.—I will go in the strength of the Lord GOD: I will make mention of thy righteousness, *even* of thine only.

The work of righteousness shall be peace; and the effect of righteousness quietness and assurance for ever.

For we wrestle not against flesh and blood, but against principalities, against powers, against the rulers of the darkness of this world, against spiritual wickedness in high *places*. Wherefore take unto you the whole armour of God, that ye may be able to withstand in the evil day, and having done all, to stand. Stand...having your loins girt about with truth, and having on the breastplate of righteousness.—The LORD *is* with thee... Go in this thy might.

Jos. **14.12**; He. 13.5–6; Ps. 71.16 § Isa. 32.17
§ Eph. 6.12–14; Judg. 6.12,14

Holy, holy, holy, Lord God Almighty.

Thou *art* holy, *O thou* that inhabitest the praises of Israel.—Draw not nigh hither: put off thy shoes from off thy feet, for the place whereon thou standest *is* holy ground... I *am* the God of thy father, the God of Abraham, the God of Isaac, and the God of Jacob. And Moses hid his face; for he was afraid to look upon God.—To whom then will ye liken me, or shall I be equal? saith the Holy One.—I am the LORD thy God, the Holy One of Israel, thy Saviour... I, *even* I, *am* the LORD; and beside me *there is* no saviour.

As he which hath called you is holy, so be ye holy in all manner of conversation; because it is written, Be ye holy; for I am holy.—Know ye not that your body is the temple of the Holy Ghost *which is* in you, which ye have of God, and ye are not your own?—Ye are the temple of the living God; as God hath said, I will dwell in them, and walk in *them;* and I will be their God, and they shall be my people.—Can two walk together, except they be agreed?

Rev. 4.8; Ps. 22.3; Ex. 3.5,6; Isa. 40.25; Isa. 43.3,11
§ 1 Pe. 1.15–16; 1 Co. 6.19; 2 Co. 6.16; Am. 3.3

They constrained him, saying, Abide with us.

Behold, I stand at the door, and knock: if any man hear my voice, and open the door, I will come in to him, and will sup with him, and he with me.—Tell me, O thou whom my soul loveth, where thou feedest, where thou makest *thy flock* to rest at noon: for why should I be as one that turneth aside by the flocks of thy companions?—I found him whom my soul loveth: I held him, and would not let him go.

Let my beloved come into his garden, and eat his pleasant fruits.—I am come into my garden.—I said not unto the seed of Jacob, Seek ye me in vain.

Lo, I am with you alway, *even* unto the end of the world.—I will never leave thee, nor forsake thee.—Where two or three are gathered together in my name, there am I in the midst of them.—The world seeth me no more; but ye see me.

Lu. 24.29; Rev. 3.20; Song 1.7; Song 3.4 § Song 4.16; Song 5.1; Isa. 45.19 § Mt. 28.20; He. 13.5; Mt. 18.20; Jn. 14.19

[Abram] believed in the LORD;
and he counted it to him for righteousness.

He staggered not at the promise of God through unbelief; but was strong in faith, giving glory to God; and being fully persuaded that, what he had promised, he was able also to perform. And therefore it was imputed to him for righteousness. Now it was not written for his sake alone, that it was imputed to him; but for us also, to whom it shall be imputed, if we believe on him that raised up Jesus our Lord from the dead.

The promise, that he should be the heir of the world, *was* not to Abraham, or to his seed, through the law, but through the righteousness of faith.

The just shall live by faith.—Let us hold fast the profession of *our* faith without wavering; (for he *is* faithful that promised;)—Our God *is* in the heavens: he hath done whatsoever he hath pleased.—With God nothing shall be impossible… And blessed *is* she that believed: for there shall be a performance of those things which were told her from the Lord.

Ge. 15.6; Ro. 4.20–24 § Ro. 4.13 § Ro. 1.17; He. 10.23; Ps. 115.3; Lu. 1.37,45

God, who hath called you unto
his kingdom and glory.

My kingdom is not of this world: if my kingdom were of this world, then would my servants fight…but now is my kingdom not from hence.—Expecting till his enemies be made his footstool.

The kingdoms of this world are become *the kingdoms* of our Lord, and of his Christ; and he shall reign for ever and ever.—Thou…hast made us unto our God kings and priests: and we shall reign on the earth.—I saw thrones, and they sat upon them, and judgment was given unto them…and they lived and reigned with Christ a thousand years.—Then shall the righteous shine forth as the sun in the kingdom of their Father.—Fear not, little flock; for it is your Father's good pleasure to give you the kingdom.

I appoint unto you a kingdom, as my Father hath appointed unto me; that ye may eat and drink at my table in my kingdom, and sit on thrones judging the twelve tribes of Israel.

Thy kingdom come.

---

1 Th. 2.12; Jn. 18.36; He. 10.13 § Rev. 11.15;
Rev. 5.9,10; Rev. 20.4; Mt. 13.43; Lu. 12.32
§ Lu. 22.29–30 § Mt. 6.10

I will never leave thee, nor forsake thee.

So that we may boldly say, The Lord *is* my helper, and I will not fear what man shall do unto me.

Behold, I *am* with thee, and will keep thee in all *places* whither thou goest, and will bring thee again into this land; for I will not leave thee, until I have done *that* which I have spoken to thee of.—Be strong and of a good courage, fear not, nor be afraid of them: for the LORD thy God, he *it is* that doth go with thee; he will not fail thee, nor forsake thee.

Demas hath forsaken me, having loved this present world... At my first answer no man stood with me, but all *men* forsook me: *I pray God* that it may not be laid to their charge. Notwithstanding the Lord stood with me, and strengthened me.—When my father and my mother forsake me, then the LORD will take me up.

Lo, I am with you alway, *even* unto the end of the world.—*I am* he that liveth, and was dead; and, behold, I am alive for evermore.—I will not leave you comfortless: I will come to you.—My peace I give unto you.

He. 13.5; He. 13.6 § Ge. 28.15; Deu. 31.6
§ 2 Tim. 4.10,16–17; Ps. 27.10 § Mt. 28.20; Rev. 1.18;
Jn. 14.18; Jn. 14.27

**Master, we have toiled all the night,
and have taken nothing: nevertheless
at thy word I will let down the net.**

All power is given unto me in heaven and in earth. Go ye therefore, and teach all nations, baptizing them in the name of the Father, and of the Son, and of the Holy Ghost: teaching them to observe all things whatsoever I have commanded you: and, lo, I am with you alway, *even* unto the end of the world. Amen.

The kingdom of heaven is like unto a net, that was cast into the sea.

Though I preach the gospel, I have nothing to glory of: for necessity is laid upon me; yea, woe is unto me, if I preach not the gospel!… I am made all things to all *men*, that I might by all means save some.

Let us not be weary in well doing: for in due season we shall reap, if we faint not.—My word…shall not return unto me void, but it shall accomplish that which I please.—So then neither is he that planteth any thing, neither he that watereth; but God that giveth the increase.

Lu. 5.5; Mt. 28.18–20 § Mt. 13.47 § 1 Co. 9.16,22 § Ga. 6.9; Isa. 55.11; 1 Co. 3.7

The kingdom of heaven is as a man travelling into
a far country, *who* called his own servants,
and delivered unto them his goods…
to every man according to his several ability.

Know ye not, that to whom ye yield yourselves servants to obey, his servants ye are to whom ye obey…?

Now there are diversities of gifts, but the same Spirit. And there are differences of administrations, but the same Lord. And there are diversities of operations, but it is the same God which worketh all in all. But the manifestation of the Spirit is given to every man to profit withal… But all these worketh that one and the selfsame Spirit, dividing to every man severally as he will.—As every man hath received the gift, *even so* minister the same one to another, as good stewards of the manifold grace of God.—It is required in stewards, that a man be found faithful.—Unto whomsoever much is given, of him shall be much required: and to whom men have committed much, of him they will ask the more.

Who *is* sufficient for these things?—I can do all things through Christ which strengtheneth me.

Mt. 25.14,15; Ro. 6.16 § 1 Co. 12.4–7,11; 1 Pe. 4.10;
1 Co. 4.2; Lu. 12.48 § 2 Co. 2.16; Phil. 4.13

Distributing to the necessity of saints.

David said, Is there yet any that is left of the house of Saul, that I may shew him kindness for Jonathan's sake?

Come, ye blessed of my Father, inherit the kingdom prepared for you from the foundation of the world: for I was an hungred, and ye gave me meat: I was thirsty, and ye gave me drink: I was a stranger, and ye took me in: naked, and ye clothed me: I was sick, and ye visited me: I was in prison, and ye came unto me... Inasmuch as ye have done *it* unto one of the least of these my brethren, ye have done *it* unto me.—Whosoever shall give to drink unto one of these little ones a cup of cold *water* only in the name of a disciple, verily I say unto you, he shall in no wise lose his reward.

To do good and to communicate forget not: for with such sacrifices God is well pleased.—God *is* not unrighteous to forget your work and labour of love, which ye have shewed toward his name, in that ye have ministered to the saints, and do minister.

Ro. 12.13; 2 Sa. 9.1 § Mt. 25.34–36,40; Mt. 10.42
§ He. 13.16; He. 6.10

To him that soweth righteousness
shall be a sure reward.

After a long time the lord of those servants cometh, and reckoneth with them. And so he that had received five talents came and brought other five talents, saying, Lord, thou deliveredst unto me five talents: behold, I have gained beside them five talents more. His lord said unto him, Well done, *thou* good and faithful servant: thou hast been faithful over a few things, I will make thee ruler over many things; enter thou into the joy of thy lord.

We must all appear before the judgment seat of Christ; that every one may receive the things *done* in *his* body, according to that he hath done, whether *it be* good or bad.

I have fought a good fight, I have finished *my* course, I have kept the faith: henceforth there is laid up for me a crown of righteousness, which the Lord, the righteous judge, shall give me at that day: and not to me only, but unto all them also that love his appearing.

Behold, I come quickly: hold that fast which thou hast, that no man take thy crown.

Pro. 11.18; Mt. 25.19–21 § 2 Co. 5.10 § 2 Tim. 4.7–8 § Rev. 3.11

God *is* faithful.

God *is* not a man, that he should lie; neither the son of man, that he should repent: hath he said, and shall he not do *it?* or hath he spoken, and shall he not make it good?—The Lord sware and will not repent.

God, willing more abundantly to shew unto the heirs of promise the immutability of his counsel, confirmed *it* by an oath: that by two immutable things, in which *it was* impossible for God to lie, we might have a strong consolation, who have fled for refuge to lay hold upon the hope set before us.—Wherefore let them that suffer according to the will of God commit the keeping of their souls *to him* in well doing, as unto a faithful Creator.

I know whom I have believed, and am persuaded that he is able to keep that which I have committed unto him against that day—Faithful *is* he that calleth you, who also will do *it.*—All the promises of God in him *are* yea, and in him Amen, unto the glory of God by us.

---

1 Co. 10.13;   Nu. 23.19;   He. 7.21   § He. 6.17–18;
1 Pe. 4.19   § 2 Tim. 1.12;   1 Th. 5.24;   2 Co. 1.20

Be strong and of a good courage.

The LORD *is* my light and my salvation; whom shall I fear? the LORD *is* the strength of my life; of whom shall I be afraid?—He giveth power to the faint; and to *them that have* no might he increaseth strength. Even the youths shall faint and be weary, and the young men shall utterly fall: but they that wait upon the LORD shall renew *their* strength; they shall mount up with wings as eagles; they shall run, and not be weary; *and* they shall walk, and not faint.—My flesh and my heart faileth: *but* God is the strength of my heart, and my portion for ever.

If God *be* for us, who *can be* against us?—The LORD *is* on my side; I will not fear: what can man do unto me?—Through thee will we push down our enemies: through thy name will we tread them under that rise up against us.—We are more than conquerors through him that loved us.

Arise *therefore*, and be doing, and the LORD be with thee.

Jos. 1.18; Ps. 27.1; Isa. 40.29–31; Ps. 73.26 § Ro. 8.31; Ps. 118.6; Ps. 44.5; Ro. 8.37 § 1 Chr. 22.16

Our friend…sleepeth.

I would not have you to be ignorant, brethren, concerning them which are asleep, that ye sorrow not, even as others which have no hope. For if we believe that Jesus died and rose again, even so them also which sleep in Jesus will God bring with him.

If the dead rise not, then is not Christ raised: and if Christ be not raised, your faith *is* vain; ye are yet in your sins. Then they also which are fallen asleep in Christ are perished… But now is Christ risen from the dead, *and* become the firstfruits of them that slept.

It came to pass, when all the people were clean passed over Jordan, that the LORD spake unto Joshua, saying… Take you hence out of the midst of Jordan, out of the place where the priests' feet stood firm, twelve stones…and these stones shall be for a memorial unto the children of Israel for ever.—This Jesus hath God raised up, whereof we all are witnesses.—Witnesses chosen before of God…who did eat and drink with him after he rose from the dead.

Jn. 11.11; 1 Th. 4.13–14 § 1 Co. 15.16–18,20
§ Jos. 4.1,3,7; Ac. 2.32; Ac. 10.41

Come, ye blessed of my Father, inherit the kingdom prepared for you from the foundation of the world.

Fear not, little flock; for it is your Father's good pleasure to give you the kingdom.—Hath not God chosen the poor of this world rich in faith, and heirs of the kingdom which he hath promised to them that love him?—Heirs of God, and joint-heirs with Christ; if so be that we suffer with *him*, that we may be also glorified together.

The Father himself loveth you, because ye have loved me.—God is not ashamed to be called their God: for he hath prepared for them a city.

He that overcometh shall inherit all things; and I will be his God, and he shall be my son.—There is laid up for me a crown of righteousness, which the Lord, the righteous judge, shall give me at that day: and not to me only, but unto all them also that love his appearing.—He which hath begun a good work in you will perform *it* until the day of Jesus Christ.

Mt. 25.34; Lu. 12.32; Jas. 2.5; Ro. 8.17 § Jn. 16.27;
He. 11.16 § Rev. 21.7; 2 Tim. 4.8; Phil. 1.6

Riches *are* not for ever: and doth the crown *endure* to every generation?

Surely every man walketh in a vain shew: surely they are disquieted in vain: he heapeth up *riches*, and knoweth not who shall gather them.—Set your affection on things above, not on things on the earth.—Lay not up for yourselves treasures upon earth, where moth and rust doth corrupt, and where thieves break through and steal: but lay up for yourselves treasures in heaven… For where your treasure is, there will your heart be also.

They *do it* to obtain a corruptible crown; but we an incorruptible.—We look not at the things which are seen, but at the things which are not seen.—To him that soweth righteousness *shall be* a sure reward.—There is laid up for me a crown of righteousness, which the Lord, the righteous judge, shall give me at that day: and not to me only, but unto all them also that love his appearing.—A crown of glory that fadeth not away.

Pro. 27.24; Ps. 39.6; Col. 3.2; Mt. 6.19–21 § 1 Co. 9.25; 2 Co. 4.18; Pro. 11.18; 2 Tim. 4.8; 1 Pe. 5.4

Isaac went out to meditate in the field at the eventide.

Let the words of my mouth, and the meditation of my heart, be acceptable in thy sight, O LORD, my strength, and my redeemer.

When I consider thy heavens, the work of thy fingers, the moon and the stars, which thou hast ordained; what is man, that thou art mindful of him? and the son of man, that thou visitest him?—The works of the LORD *are* great, sought out of all them that have pleasure therein.

Blessed *is* the man that walketh not in the counsel of the ungodly, nor standeth in the way of sinners, nor sitteth in the seat of the scornful. But his delight *is* in the law of the LORD; and in his law doth he meditate day and night.—This book of the law shall not depart out of thy mouth; but thou shalt meditate therein day and night.—My soul shall be satisfied as *with* marrow and fatness; and my mouth shall praise *thee* with joyful lips: when I remember thee upon my bed, *and* meditate on thee in the *night* watches.

Ge. 24.63; Ps. 19.14 § Ps. 8.3–4; Ps. 111.2 § Ps. 1.1–2; Jos. 1.8; Ps. 63.5–6

How long wilt thou forget me, O LORD? for ever? how long wilt thou hide thy face from me?

Every good gift and every perfect gift is from above, and cometh down from the Father of lights, with whom is no variableness, neither shadow of turning.—But Zion said, The LORD hath forsaken me, and my Lord hath forgotten me. Can a woman forget her suckling child, that she should not have compassion on the son of her womb? yea, they may forget, yet will I not forget thee.

Thou shalt not be forgotten of me. I have blotted out, as a thick cloud, thy transgressions, and, as a cloud, thy sins.

Jesus loved Martha, and her sister, and Lazarus. When he had heard therefore that he was sick, he abode two days still in the same place where he was.—A woman…cried unto him, saying, Have mercy on me, O Lord, *thou* Son of David… But he answered her not a word.

The trial of your faith, being much more precious than of gold that perisheth.

Ps. 13.1; Jas. 1.17; Isa. 49.14–15 § Isa. 44.21–22 § Jn. 11.5–6; Mt. 15.22,23 § 1 Pe. 1.7

**My God shall supply all your need
according to his riches in glory by Christ Jesus.**

Seek ye first the kingdom of God, and his righteousness; and all these things shall be added unto you.—He that spared not his own Son, but delivered him up for us all, how shall he not with him also freely give us all things?—All things are yours; whether Paul, or Apollos, or Cephas, or the world, or life, or death, or things present, or things to come; all are yours; and ye are Christ's; and Christ *is* God's.—As having nothing, and *yet* possessing all things.

The LORD *is* my shepherd; I shall not want.—The LORD God *is* a sun and shield: the LORD will give grace and glory: no good *thing* will he withhold from them that walk uprightly.—The living God…giveth us richly all things to enjoy.—God *is* able to make all grace abound toward you; that ye, always having all sufficiency in all *things*, may abound to every good work.

Phil. 4.19;　Mt. 6.33;　Ro. 8.32;　1 Co. 3.21–23;
2 Co. 6.10 § Ps. 23.1;　Ps. 84.11;　1 Tim. 6.17;　2 Co. 9.8

What communion hath light with darkness?

Men loved darkness rather than light, because their deeds were evil.—Ye are all the children of light, and the children of the day: we are not of the night, nor of darkness.

Darkness hath blinded his eyes.—Thy word *is* a lamp unto my feet, and a light unto my path.

The dark places of the earth are full of the habitations of cruelty.—Love is of God; and every one that loveth is born of God, and knoweth God. He that loveth not knoweth not God; for God is love.

The path of the just *is* as the shining light, that shineth more and more unto the perfect day. The way of the wicked *is* as darkness: they know not at what they stumble.

I am come a light into the world, that whosoever believeth on me should not abide in darkness.

Ye were sometimes darkness, but now *are ye* light in the Lord: walk as children of light.

---

2 Co. 6.14; Jn. 3.19; 1 Th. 5.5 § 1 Jn. 2.11; Ps. 119.105
§ Ps. 74.20; 1 Jn. 4.7–8 § Pro. 4.18–19 § Jn. 12.46
§ Eph. 5.8

The fruit of the Spirit is...joy...

J oy in the Holy Ghost.—Joy unspeakable and full of glory.

Sorrowful, yet alway rejoicing...exceeding joyful in all our tribulation.—We glory in tribulations.

Jesus the author and finisher of *our* faith...for the joy that was set before him endured the cross, despising the shame.—These things have I spoken unto you, that my joy might remain in you, and *that* your joy might be full.—As the sufferings of Christ abound in us, so our consolation also aboundeth by Christ.

Rejoice in the Lord alway: *and* again I say, Rejoice.—The joy of the LORD is your strength.

In thy presence *is* fulness of joy; at thy right hand *there are* pleasures for evermore.—For the Lamb which is in the midst of the throne shall feed them, and shall lead them unto living fountains of waters: and God shall wipe away all tears from their eyes.

Ga. 5.22; Ro. 14.17; 1 Pe. 1.8 § 2 Co. 6.10, 7.4;
Ro. 5.3 § He. 12.2; Jn. 15.11; 2 Co. 1.5 § Phil. 4.4;
Ne. 8.10 § Ps. 16.11; Rev. 7.17

Jehovah-shalom. [*marg.* The Lord *send* peace]

Behold, a son shall be born to thee, who shall be a man of rest; and I will give him rest from all his enemies round about: for his name shall be Solomon, and I will give peace and quietness unto Israel in his days.

Behold, a greater than Solomon *is* here.—Unto us a child is born, unto us a son is given: and the government shall be upon his shoulder: and his name shall be called Wonderful, Counsellor, The mighty God, The everlasting Father, The Prince of Peace.—My people shall dwell in a peaceable habitation, and in sure dwellings, and in quiet resting places; when it shall hail, coming down on the forest; and the city shall be low in a low place.

He is our peace.—This *man* shall be the peace, when the Assyrian shall come into our land.

These shall make war with the Lamb, and the Lamb shall overcome them: for he is Lord of lords, and King of kings.

Peace I leave with you, my peace I give unto you.

Judg. 6.24; 1 Chr. 22.9 § Mt. 12.42; Isa. 9.6; Isa. 32.18–19 § Eph. 2.14; Mi. 5.5 § Rev. 17.14 § Jn. 14.27

If ye do return unto the LORD with all your hearts, *then* put away the strange gods and Ashtaroth from among you, and prepare your hearts unto the LORD, and serve him only.

Little children, keep yourselves from idols.—Come out from among them, and be ye separate, saith the Lord, and touch not the unclean *thing*; and I will receive you, and will be a Father unto you, and ye shall be my sons and daughters, saith the Lord Almighty.—Ye cannot serve God and mammon.

Thou shalt worship no other god: for the LORD, whose name *is* Jealous, *is* a jealous God.—Serve him with a perfect heart and with a willing mind: for the LORD searcheth all hearts, and understandeth all the imaginations of the thoughts.

Behold, thou desireth truth in the inward parts: and in the hidden *part* thou shalt make me to know wisdom.—Man looketh on the outward appearance, but the LORD looketh on the heart.—Beloved, if our heart condemn us not, *then* have we confidence toward God.

1 Sa. 7.3; 1 Jn. 5.21; 2 Co. 6.17,18; Mt. 6.24
§ Ex. 34.14; 1 Chr. 28.9 § Ps. 51.6; 1 Sa. 16.7; 1 Jn. 3.21

When the Son of man cometh,
shall he find faith on the earth?

He came unto his own, and his own received him not.—The Spirit speaketh expressly, that in the latter times some shall depart from the faith.

Preach the word; be instant in season, out of season; reprove, rebuke, exhort with all longsuffering and doctrine. For the time will come when they will not endure sound doctrine; but after their own lusts shall they heap to themselves teachers, having itching ears; and they shall turn away *their* ears from the truth, and shall be turned unto fables.

Of that day and *that* hour knoweth no man, no, not the angels which are in heaven, neither the Son, but the Father. Take ye heed, watch and pray: for ye know not when the time is.—Blessed *are* those servants, whom the lord when he cometh shall find watching.—Looking for that blessed hope, and the glorious appearing of the great God and our Saviour Jesus Christ.

Lu. 18.8; Jn. 1.11; 1 Tim. 4.1 § 2 Tim. 4.2–4 § Mk. 13.32–33; Lu. 12.37; Titus 2.13

Beloved, be not ignorant of this one thing,
that one day *is* with the Lord as a thousand years, and
a thousand years as one day. The Lord is not slack
concerning his promise, as some men count slackness.

My thoughts *are* not your thoughts, neither *are* your ways my ways, saith the LORD. For *as* the heavens are higher than the earth, so are my ways higher than your ways, and my thoughts than your thoughts. For as the rain cometh down, and the snow from heaven, and returneth not thither, but watereth the earth…so shall my word be that goeth forth out of my mouth: it shall not return unto me void, but it shall accomplish that which I please, and it shall prosper *in the thing* whereto I sent it.

God hath concluded them all in unbelief, that he might have mercy upon all. O the depth of the riches both of the wisdom and knowledge of God! how unsearchable *are* his judgments, and his ways past finding out!

2 Pe. 3.8–9; Isa. 55.8–11 § Ro. 11.32–33

Ye were as a firebrand plucked out of the burning.

The sinners in Zion are afraid; fearfulness hath surprised the hypocrites. Who among us shall dwell with the devouring fire? who among us shall dwell with everlasting burnings?—We had the sentence of death in ourselves, that we should not trust in ourselves, but in God which raiseth the dead: who delivered us from so great a death, and doth deliver: in whom we trust that he will yet deliver *us*.—The wages of sin *is* death; but the gift of God *is* eternal life through Jesus Christ our Lord.

It is a fearful thing to fall into the hands of the living God.—Knowing therefore the terror of the Lord, we persuade men.

Be instant in season, out of season.—Others save with fear, pulling *them* out of the fire.

Not by might, nor by power, but by my spirit, saith the LORD of hosts.—Who will have all men to be saved, and to come unto the knowledge of the truth.

Am. 4.11; Isa 33.14; 2 Co. 1.9–10; Ro. 6.23
§ He. 10.31; 2 Co. 5.11 § 2 Tim. 4.2; Jude 23
§ Zech. 4.6; 1 Tim. 2.4

Fear not; I am the first and the last.

Ye are not come unto the mount that might be touched, and that burned with fire, nor unto blackness, and darkness, and tempest...but ye are come unto mount Sion...to God the Judge of all, and to the spirits of just men made perfect, and to Jesus the mediator of the new covenant.—Jesus the author and finisher of *our* faith.—We have not an high priest which cannot be touched with the feeling of our infirmities; but was in all points tempted like as *we are, yet* without sin. Let us therefore come boldly unto the throne of grace, that we may obtain mercy, and find grace to help in time of need.

Thus saith the LORD the King of Israel, and his redeemer the LORD of hosts; I *am* the first, and I *am* the last; and beside me *there is* no God.—The mighty God, The everlasting Father, The Prince of Peace.

Art thou not from everlasting, O LORD my God, mine Holy One?—Who *is* God, save the LORD? and who *is* a rock, save our God?

Rev. 1.17;   He. 12.18,22–24;   He. 12.2;   He. 4.15–16
§ Isa. 44.6;   Isa. 9.6   § Hab. 1.12;   2 Sa. 22.32

Lead me to the rock *that* is higher than I.

Be careful for nothing; but in every thing by prayer and supplication with thanksgiving let your requests be made known unto God. And the peace of God, which passeth all understanding, shall keep your hearts and minds through Christ Jesus.

When my spirit was overwhelmed within me, then thou knewest my path.—He knoweth the way that I take: *when* he hath tried me, I shall come forth as gold.—LORD, thou hast been our dwelling place in all generations.—Thou hast been a strength to the poor, a strength to the needy in his distress, a refuge from the storm, a shadow from the heat.

Who *is* a rock save our God?—They shall never perish, neither shall any *man* pluck them out of my hand.—Uphold me according unto thy word, that I may live: and let me not be ashamed of my hope.—Which *hope* we have as an anchor of the soul, both sure and stedfast, and which entereth into that within the veil.

Ps. 61.2; Phil. 4.6–7 § Ps. 142.3; Job 23.10; Ps. 90.1; Isa. 25.4 § Ps.18.31; Jn. 10.28; Ps. 119.116; He. 6.19

I will not let thee go, except thou bless me.

Let him take hold of my strength, *that* he may make peace with me; *and* he shall make peace with me.

O woman, great *is* thy faith: be it unto thee even as thou wilt.—According to your faith be it unto you.—Let him ask in faith, nothing wavering. For he that wavereth is like a wave of the sea driven with the wind and tossed. For let not that man think that he shall receive any thing of the Lord.

They drew nigh unto the village, whither they went: and [Jesus] made as though he would have gone further. But they constrained him, saying, Abide with us…he vanished out of their sight. And they said one to another, Did not our heart burn within us, while he talked with us by the way, and while he opened to us the scriptures?—I pray thee, if I have found grace in thy sight, shew me now thy way, that I may know thee, that I may find grace in thy sight.—My presence shall go *with thee*, and I will give thee rest.

Ge. 32.26; Isa. 27.5 § Mt. 15.28; Mt. 9.29; Jas. 1.6–7 § Lu. 24.28–29,31–32; Ex. 33.13; Ex. 33.14

Jesus the author and finisher of *our* faith.

I am Alpha and Omega, the beginning and the ending, saith the Lord, which is, and which was, and which is to come, the Almighty.—Who hath wrought and done *it*, calling the generations from the beginning? I the LORD, the first, and with the last; I *am* he.

Sanctified by God the Father, and preserved in Jesus Christ.—The very God of peace sanctify you wholly; and *I pray God* your whole spirit and soul and body be preserved blameless unto the coming of our Lord Jesus Christ. Faithful *is* he that calleth you, who also will do *it*.—He which hath begun a good work in you will perform *it* until the day of Jesus Christ.—Are ye so foolish? having begun in the Spirit, are ye now made perfect by the flesh?—The LORD will perfect *that which* concerneth me.

It is God which worketh in you both to will and to do of *his* good pleasure.

He. 12.2; Rev. 1.8; Isa. 41.4 § Jude 1; 1 Th. 5.23–24; Phil. 1.6; Ga. 3.3; Ps. 138.8 § Phil. 2.13

He ever liveth to make intercession.

Who *is* he that condemneth? *It is* Christ that died...who also maketh intercession for us.—Christ is not entered into the holy places made with hands, *which are* the figures of the true; but into heaven itself, now to appear in the presence of God for us.

If any man sin, we have an advocate with the Father, Jesus Christ the righteous.—*There is* one God, and one mediator between God and men, the man Christ Jesus.

Seeing...that we have a great high priest, that is passed into the heavens, Jesus the Son of God, let us hold fast *our* profession. For we have not an high priest which cannot be touched with the feeling of our infirmities; but was in all points tempted like as *we are, yet* without sin. Let us therefore come boldly unto the throne of grace, that we may obtain mercy, and find grace to help in time of need.—Through him we...have access by one Spirit unto the Father.

He. 7.25; Ro. 8.34; He. 9.24 § 1 Jn. 2.1; 1 Tim. 2.5
§ He. 4.14–16; Eph. 2.18

They that know thy name will put their trust in thee.

This *is* his name whereby he shall be called, THE LORD OUR RIGHTEOUSNESS.—I will go in the strength of the Lord GOD: I will make mention of thy righteousness, *even* of thine only.

His name shall be called Wonderful, Counsellor.—O LORD, I know that the way of man *is* not in himself: *it is* not in man that walketh to direct his steps.

The mighty God, The everlasting Father.—I know whom I have believed, and am persuaded that he is able to keep that which I have committed unto him against that day.

The Prince of Peace.—He is our peace.—Being justified by faith, we have peace with God through our Lord Jesus Christ.

The name of the LORD *is* a strong tower: the righteous runneth into it, and is safe.—Woe to them that go down to Egypt for help.—As birds flying, so will the LORD of hosts defend Jerusalem; defending also he will deliver *it; and* passing over he will preserve *it.*

Ps. 9.10; Jer. 23.6; Ps. 71.16 § Isa. 9.6; Jer. 10.23
§ Isa. 9.6; 2 Tim. 1.12 § Isa. 9.6; Eph. 2.14; Ro. 5.1
§ Pro. 18.10; Isa. 31.1; Isa. 31.5

As sorrowful, yet alway rejoicing; as poor,
yet making many rich; as having nothing,
and *yet* possessing all things.

We...rejoice in hope of the glory of God. And not only *so*, but we glory in tribulations also.—I am filled with comfort, I am exceeding joyful in all our tribulation.—Believing, ye rejoice with joy unspeakable and full of glory.

In a great trial of affliction the abundance of their joy and their deep poverty abounded unto the riches of their liberality.—Unto me, who am less than the least of all saints, is this grace given, that I should preach among the Gentiles the unsearchable riches of Christ; and to make all *men* see what *is* the fellowship of the mystery, which from the beginning of the world hath been hid in God, who created all things by Jesus Christ.

Hath not God chosen the poor of this world rich in faith, and heirs of the kingdom which he hath promised to them that love him?—God *is* able to make all grace abound toward you; that ye, always having all sufficiency in all *things*, may abound to every good work.

2 Co. 6.10;　Ro. 5.2–3;　2 Co. 7.4;　1 Pe. 1.8　§ 2 Co. 8.2;
Eph. 3.8–9　§ Jas. 2.5;　2 Co. 9.8

The LORD will strengthen him upon the bed of languishing: thou wilt make all his bed in his sickness.

In all their affliction he was afflicted, and the angel of his presence saved them: in his love and in his pity he redeemed them; and he bare them, and carried them.—He whom thou lovest is sick.—My grace is sufficient for thee: for my strength is made perfect in weakness. Most gladly therefore will I rather glory in my infirmities, that the power of Christ may rest upon me.—I can do all things through Christ which strengtheneth me.

We faint not...though our outward man perish, yet the inward *man* is renewed day by day.

In him we live, and move, and have our being.—He giveth power to the faint; and to *them that have* no might he increaseth strength. Even the youths shall faint and be weary, and the young men shall utterly fall: but they that wait upon the LORD shall renew *their* strength.—The eternal God *is thy* refuge, and underneath *are* the everlasting arms.

Ps. 41.3; Isa. 63.9; Jn. 11.3; 2 Co. 12.9; Phil. 4.13
§ 2 Co. 4.16 § Ac. 17.28; Isa. 40.29–31; Deu. 33.27

In every thing ye are enriched by him.

When we were yet without strength, in due time Christ died for the ungodly.—He that spared not his own Son, but delivered him up for us all, how shall he not with him also freely give us all things?

In him dwelleth all the fulness of the Godhead bodily. And ye *are* complete in him, which is the head of all principality and power.

Abide in me, and I in you. As the branch cannot bear fruit of itself, except it abide in the vine; no more can ye, except ye abide in me. I am the vine ye *are* the branches: He that abideth in me, and I in him, the same bringeth forth much fruit: for without me ye can do nothing.— To will is present with me; but *how* to perform that which is good I find not.—Unto every one of us is given grace according to the measure of the gift of Christ.

If ye abide in me, and my words abide in you, ye shall ask what ye will, and it shall be done unto you.—Let the word of Christ dwell in you richly in all wisdom.

---

1 Co. 1.5; Ro. 5.6; Ro. 8.32 § Col. 2.9–10 § Jn. 15.4–5; Ro. 7.18; Eph. 4.7 § Jn. 15.7; Col. 3.16

They shall see his face.

I beseech thee, shew me thy glory… And he said, Thou canst not see my face: for there shall no man see me, and live.—No man hath seen God at any time; the only begotten Son, which is in the bosom of the Father, he hath declared *him*.

Every eye shall see him, and they *also* which pierced him: and all kindreds of the earth shall wail because of him.—I shall see him, but not now: I shall behold him, but not nigh.

I know *that* my redeemer liveth, and *that* he shall stand at the latter *day* upon the earth: and *though* after my skin *worms* destroy this *body*, yet in my flesh shall I see God.—I will behold thy face in righteousness: I shall be satisfied, when I awake, with thy likeness.—We shall be like him; for we shall see him as he is.—The Lord himself shall descend from heaven…the dead in Christ shall rise first: then we which are alive *and* remain shall be caught up together with them in the clouds, to meet the Lord in the air: and so shall we ever be with the Lord.

Rev. 22.4; Ex. 33.18,20; Jn. 1.18 § Rev. 1.7; Nu. 24.17 § Job 19.25–26; Ps. 17.15; 1 Jn. 3.2; 1 Th. 4.16–17

Fear not: for I have redeemed thee.

Fear not; for thou shalt not be ashamed: neither be thou confounded; for thou shalt not be put to shame: for thou shalt forget the shame of thy youth, and shalt not remember the reproach of thy widowhood any more. For thy Maker *is* thine husband; the LORD of hosts *is* his name; and thy Redeemer the Holy One of Israel.— I have blotted out, as a thick cloud, thy transgressions, and, as a cloud, thy sins: return unto me; for I have redeemed thee.—With the precious blood of Christ, as of a lamb without blemish and without spot.

Their Redeemer *is* strong; the LORD of hosts *is* his name: he shall throughly plead their cause.—My Father, which gave *them* me, is greater than all; and no *man* is able to pluck *them* out of my Father's hand.

Grace *be* to you and peace from God the Father, and *from* our Lord Jesus Christ, who gave himself for our sins, that he might deliver us from this present evil world, according to the will of God and our Father: to whom *be* glory for ever and ever. Amen.

Isa. 43.1; Isa. 54.4–5; Isa. 44.22; 1 Pe. 1.19 § Jer. 50.34; Jn. 10.29 § Ga. 1.3–5

**I will mention the lovingkindnesses of the LORD,
and the praises of the LORD, according to all that
the LORD hath bestowed on us.**

He brought me up…out of an horrible pit, out of the miry clay, and set my feet upon a rock, *and* established my goings.—The Son of God, who loved me, and gave himself for me.—He that spared not his own Son, but delivered him up for us all, how shall he not with him also freely give us all things?—God commendeth his love toward us, in that, while we were yet sinners, Christ died for us.

Who hath also sealed us, and given the earnest of the Spirit in our hearts.—Which is the earnest of our inheritance until the redemption of the purchased possession, unto the praise of his glory.

God, who is rich in mercy, for his great love wherewith he loved us, even when we were dead in sins, hath quickened us together with Christ, (by grace ye are saved;) and hath raised *us* up together, and made *us* sit together in heavenly *places* in Christ Jesus.

Isa. 63.7; Ps. 40.2; Ga. 2.20; Ro. 8.32; Ro. 5.8
§ 2 Co. 1.22; Eph. 1.14 § Eph. 2.4–6

I *am* black, but comely.

Behold, I was shapen in iniquity; and in sin did my mother conceive me.—Thy renown went forth among the heathen for thy beauty: for it *was* perfect through my comeliness, which I had put upon thee, saith the Lord GOD.

I am a sinful man, O Lord.—Behold, thou *art* fair, my love; behold, thou *art* fair.

I abhor *myself*, and repent in dust and ashes.—Thou *art* all fair, my love; *there is* no spot in thee.

When I would do good, evil is present with me.—Be of good cheer; thy sins be forgiven thee.

I know that in me (that is, in my flesh,) dwelleth no good thing.—Ye are complete in him.—Perfect in Christ Jesus.

Ye are washed…ye are sanctified…ye are justified in the name of the Lord Jesus, and by the Spirit of our God.—That ye should shew forth the praises of him who hath called you out of darkness into his marvellous light.

Song 1.5; Ps. 51.5; Ezek. 16.14 § Lu. 5.8; Song 4.1 § Job 42.6; Song 4.7 § Ro. 7.21; Mt. 9.2 § Ro. 7.18; Col. 2.10; Col. 1.28 § 1 Co. 6.11; 1 Pe. 2.9

All that will live godly in Christ Jesus shall suffer persecution.

I am come to set a man at variance against his father, and the daughter against her mother, and the daughter in law against her mother in law. And a man's foes *shall be* they of his own household.—Whosoever…will be a friend of the world is the enemy of God.—Love not the world, neither the things *that are* in the world. If any man love the world, the love of the Father is not in him. For all that *is* in the world, the lust of the flesh, and the lust of the eyes, and the pride of life, is not of the Father, but is of the world.

If the world hate you, ye know that it hated me before *it hated* you. If ye were of the world, the world would love his own: but because ye are not of the world, but I have chosen you out of the world, therefore the world hateth you… The servant is not greater than his lord.—I have given them thy word; and the world hath hated them, because they are not of the world, even as I am not of the world.

---

2 Tim. 3.12; Mt. 10.35–36; Jas. 4.4; 1 Jn. 2.15–16
§ Jn. 15.18–20; Jn. 17.14

**In the multitude of words there wanteth not sin:
but he that refraineth his lips *is* wise.**

My beloved brethren, let every man be swift to hear, slow to speak, slow to wrath.—*He that is* slow to anger *is* better than the mighty; and he that ruleth his spirit than he that taketh a city.—If any man offend not in word, the same *is* a perfect man, *and* able also to bridle the whole body.—By thy words thou shalt be justified, and by thy words thou shalt be condemned.—Set a watch, O LORD, before my mouth; keep the door of my lips.

Christ…suffered for us, leaving us an example, that ye should follow his steps: who did no sin, neither was guile found in his mouth: who, when he was reviled, reviled not again; when he suffered, he threatened not; but committed *himself* to him that judgeth righteously.—Consider him that endured such contradiction of sinners against himself, lest ye be wearied and faint in your minds.

In their mouth was found no guile: for they are without fault before the throne of God.

Pro. 10.19; Jas. 1.19; Pro. 16.32; Jas. 3.2; Mt. 12.37;
Ps. 141.3 § 1 Pe. 2.21–23; He. 12.3 § Rev. 14.5

Teach me thy way, O LORD.

I will instruct thee and teach thee in the way which thou shalt go: I will guide thee with mine eye.—Good and upright *is* the LORD: therefore will he teach sinners in the way. The meek will he guide in judgment: and the meek will he teach his way.

I am the door: by me if any man enter in, he shall be saved, and shall go in and out, and find pasture.

Jesus saith unto him, I am the way, the truth, and the life: no man cometh unto the Father, but by me.—Having...boldness to enter into the holiest by the blood of Jesus, by a new and living way, which he hath consecrated for us, through the veil, that is to say, his flesh; and *having* an high priest over the house of God; let us draw near with a true heart in full assurance of faith.

Then shall we know, *if* we follow on to know the LORD.—All the paths of the LORD *are* mercy and truth unto such as keep his covenant and his testimonies.

Ps. 27.11; Ps. 32.8; Ps. 25.8–9 § Jn. 10.9 § Jn. 14.6; He. 10.19–22 § Hos. 6.3; Ps. 25.10

> What the law could not do, in that it was
> weak through the flesh, God sending his own Son
> in the likeness of sinful flesh, and for sin,
> condemned sin in the flesh.

The law having a shadow of good things to come, *and* not the very image of the things, can never with those sacrifices which they offered year by year continually make the comers thereunto perfect. For then would they not have ceased to be offered?—By him all that believe are justified from all things, from which ye could not be justified by the law of Moses.

Forasmuch…as the children are partakers of flesh and blood, he also himself likewise took part of the same; that through death he might destroy him that had the power of death, that is, the devil; and deliver them who through fear of death were all their lifetime subject to bondage. For verily he took not on *him the nature of* angels; but he took on *him* the seed of Abraham. Wherefore in all things it behoved him to be made like unto *his* brethren.

Ro. 8.3; He. 10.1–2; Ac. 13.39 § He. 2.14–17

All have sinned, and come short of the glory of God.

There is none righteous, no, not one...there is none that doeth good, no, not one.—*There is* not a just man upon earth, that doeth good, and sinneth not.—How can he be clean *that is* born of a woman?

Let us therefore fear, lest, a promise being left *us* of entering into his rest, any of you should seem to come short of it.

I acknowledge my transgressions: and my sin *is* ever before me... Behold, I was shapen in iniquity; and in sin did my mother conceive me.

The LORD...hath put away thy sin; thou shalt not die.—Whom he justified, them he also glorified.—We all, with open face beholding as in a glass the glory of the Lord, are changed into the same image from glory to glory, *even* as by the Spirit of the Lord.—If ye continue in the faith grounded and settled, and *be* not moved away from the hope of the gospel.

Walk worthy of God, who hath called you unto his kingdom and glory.

Ro. 3.23; Ro. 3.10,12; Ec. 7.20; Job 25.4 § He. 4.1 § Ps. 51.3,5 § 2 Sa. 12.13; Ro. 8.30; 2 Co. 3.18; Col. 1.23 § 1 Th. 2.12

**Honour the LORD with thy substance,
and with the firstfruits of all thine increase.**

He which soweth sparingly shall reap also sparingly; and he which soweth bountifully shall reap also bountifully.—Upon the first *day* of the week let every one of you lay by him in store, as *God* hath prospered him.

God *is* not unrighteous to forget your work and labour of love, which ye have shewed toward his name, in that ye have ministered to the saints, and do minister.

I beseech you…brethren, by the mercies of God, that ye present your bodies a living sacrifice, holy, acceptable unto God, *which is* your reasonable service.—The love of Christ constraineth us; because we thus judge, that if one died for all, then were all dead: and *that* he died for all, that they which live should not henceforth live unto themselves, but unto him which died for them, and rose again.—Whether therefore ye eat, or drink, or whatsoever ye do, do all to the glory of God.

Pro. 3.9; 2 Co. 9.6; 1 Co. 16.2 § He. 6.10 § Ro. 12.1;
2 Co. 5.14–15; 1 Co. 10.31

There shall be no night there.

The LORD shall be unto thee an everlasting light, and thy God thy glory.

The city had no need of the sun, neither of the moon, to shine in it: for the glory of God did lighten it, and the Lamb *is* the light thereof.—They need no candle, neither light of the sun; for the Lord God giveth them light.

Ye *are* a chosen generation, a royal priesthood, an holy nation, a peculiar people; that ye should shew forth the praises of him who hath called you out of darkness into his marvellous light.—Giving thanks unto the Father, which hath made us meet to be partakers of the inheritance of the saints in light: who hath delivered us from the power of darkness, and hath translated *us* into the kingdom of his dear Son.—Ye were sometimes darkness, but now *are ye* light in the Lord: walk as children of light.

We are not of the night, nor of darkness.

The path of the just *is* as the shining light, that shineth more and more unto the perfect day.

Rev. 21.25; Isa. 60.19 § Rev. 21.23; Rev. 22.5 § 1 Pe. 2.9; Col. 1.12–13; Eph. 5.8 § 1 Th. 5.5 § Pro. 4.18

My soul shall be satisfied as *with* marrow
and fatness; and my mouth shall praise *thee* with
joyful lips: when I remember thee upon my bed,
and meditate on thee in the *night* watches.

How precious...are thy thoughts unto me, O God!
how great is the sum of them! *If* I should count them,
they are more in number than the sand: when I awake, I
am still with thee.—How sweet are thy words unto my
taste! *yea, sweeter* than honey to my mouth!—Thy love
is better than wine.

Whom have I in heaven *but thee?* and *there is* none
upon earth *that* I desire beside thee.—Thou art fairer
than the children of men.

As the apple tree among the trees of the wood, so *is*
my beloved among the sons. I sat down under his shadow with great delight, and his fruit *was* sweet to my
taste. He brought me to the banqueting house, and his
banner over me *was* love.—His countenance *is* as
Lebanon, excellent as the cedars. His mouth *is* most
sweet: yea, he *is* altogether lovely. This *is* my beloved,
and this *is* my friend.

Ps. 63.5–6; Ps. 139.17–18; Ps. 119.103; Song 1.2
§ Ps. 73.25; Ps. 45.2 § Song 2.3–4; Song 5.15–16

Restore unto me the joy of thy salvation.

I have seen his ways, and will heal him: I will lead him also, and restore comforts unto him and to his mourners.

Come now, and let us reason together, saith the LORD: though your sins be as scarlet, they shall be as white as snow; though they be red like crimson, they shall be as wool.—Return, ye backsliding children, *and* I will heal your backslidings. Behold, we come unto thee; for thou *art* the LORD our God.—I will hear what God the LORD will speak: for he will speak peace unto his people, and to his saints: but let them not turn again to folly.

Bless the LORD, O my soul, and forget not all his benefits: who forgiveth all thine iniquities; who healeth all thy diseases.—He restoreth my soul.—O LORD, I will praise thee: though thou wast angry with me, thine anger is turned away, and thou comfortedst me.

Hold thou me up, and I shall be safe.

I, *even* I, *am* he that blotteth out thy transgressions for mine own sake, and will not remember thy sins.

Ps. 51.12; Isa. 57.18 § Isa. 1.18; Jer. 3.22; Ps. 85.8
§ Ps. 103.2–3; Ps. 23.3; Isa. 12.1 § Ps. 119.117
§ Isa. 43.25

Their Redeemer *is* strong.

I know your manifold transgressions and your mighty sins.—I have laid help upon *one that is* mighty.—The LORD…thy Saviour and thy Redeemer, the mighty One of Jacob.—Mighty to save.—Able to keep you from falling.—Where sin abounded, grace did much more abound.

He that believeth on him is not condemned: but he that believeth not is condemned already, because he hath not believed in the name of the only begotten Son of God.—He is able…to save them to the uttermost that come unto God by him.

Is my hand shortened at all, that it cannot redeem?

Who shall separate us from the love of Christ?… I am persuaded, that neither death, nor life, nor angels, nor principalities, nor powers, nor things present, nor things to come, nor height, nor depth, nor any other creature, shall be able to separate us from the love of God, which is in Christ Jesus our Lord.

Jer. 50.34; Am. 5.12; Ps. 89.19; Isa. 49.26; Isa. 63.1; Jude 24; Ro. 5.20 § Jn. 3.18; He. 7.25 § Isa. 50.2 § Ro. 8.35,38–39

Seekest thou great things for thyself? seek *them* not.

Take my yoke upon you, and learn of me; for I am meek and lowly in heart: and ye shall find rest unto your souls.—Let this mind be in you, which was also in Christ Jesus: who, being in the form of God, thought it not robbery to be equal with God: but made himself of no reputation, and took upon him the form of a servant, and was made in the likeness of men: and being found in fashion as a man, he humbled himself, and became obedient unto death, even the death of the cross.

He that taketh not his cross, and followeth after me, is not worthy of me.—Christ…suffered for us, leaving us an example, that ye should follow his steps.

Godliness with contentment is great gain. For we brought nothing into *this* world, *and it is* certain we can carry nothing out. And having food and raiment let us be therewith content.

I have learned, in whatsoever state I am, *therewith* to be content.

Jer. 45.5; Mt. 11.29; Phil. 2.5–8 § Mt. 10.38; 1 Pe. 2.21 § 1 Tim. 6.6–8 § Phil. 4.11

I said in my haste, I am cut off from before thine eyes: nevertheless thou heardest the voice of my supplications when I cried unto thee.

I sink in deep mire, where *there is* no standing: I am come into deep waters, where the floods overflow me.— Waters flowed over mine head; *then* I said, I am cut off. I called upon thy name, O LORD, out of the low dungeon. Thou hast heard my voice: hide not thine ear at my breathing, at my cry. Thou drewest near in the day *that* I called upon thee: thou saidst, Fear not.

Will the Lord cast off for ever? and will he be favourable no more? Is his mercy clean gone for ever? doth *his* promise fail for evermore? Hath God forgotten to be gracious? hath he in anger shut up his tender mercies? And I said, This *is* my infirmity: *but I will remember* the years of the right hand of the most High. I will remember the works of the LORD: surely I will remember thy wonders of old.—*I had fainted*, unless I had believed to see the goodness of the LORD in the land of the living.

Ps. 31.22; Ps. 69.2; Lam. 3.54–57 § Ps. 77.7–11; Ps. 27.13

He shall call upon me, and I will answer him:
I *will be* with him in trouble; I will deliver him.

And Jabez called on the God of Israel, saying, Oh that thou wouldest bless me indeed, and enlarge my coast, and that thine hand might be with me, and that thou wouldest keep *me* from evil, that it may not grieve me! And God granted him that which he requested.—Ask what I shall give thee. And Solomon said unto God... Give me now wisdom and knowledge, that I may go out and come in before this people.—And God gave Solomon wisdom and understanding exceeding much, and largeness of heart, even as the sand that *is* on the sea shore.

Asa cried unto the LORD his God, and said, LORD, *it is* nothing with thee to help, whether with many, or with them that have no power... O LORD, thou *art* our God; let not man prevail against thee. So the LORD smote the Ethiopians before Asa.

O thou that hearest prayer, unto thee shall all flesh come.

Ps. 91.15; 1 Chr. 4.10; 2 Chr. 1.7–8,10; 1 Ki. 4.29
§ 2 Chr. 14.11–12 § Ps. 65.2

Whoso offereth praise glorifieth me.

Let the word of Christ dwell in you richly in all wisdom; teaching and admonishing one another in psalms and hymns and spiritual songs, singing with grace in your hearts to the Lord. And whatsoever ye do in word or deed, *do* all in the name of the Lord Jesus, giving thanks to God and the Father by him.—Glorify God in your body, and in your spirit, which are God's.

Ye *are*…a royal priesthood…that ye should shew forth the praises of him who hath called you out of darkness into his marvellous light.—Ye…as lively stones, are built up a spiritual house, a holy priesthood, to offer up spiritual sacrifices, acceptable to God by Jesus Christ.—By him…let us offer the sacrifice of praise to God continually, that is, the fruit of *our* lips, giving thanks to his name.

My soul shall make her boast in the LORD: the humble shall hear *thereof*, and be glad. O magnify the LORD with me, and let us exalt his name together.

Ps. 50.23; Col. 3.16–17; 1 Co. 6.20 § 1 Pe. 2.9; 1 Pe. 2.5; He. 13.15 § Ps. 34.2–3

Draw me, we will run after thee.

I have loved thee with an everlasting love: therefore with lovingkindness have I drawn thee.—I drew them with cords of a man, with bands of love.—I, if I be lifted up from the earth, will draw all *men* unto me.—Behold the Lamb of God!—As Moses lifted up the serpent in the wilderness, even so must the Son of man be lifted up: that whosoever believeth in him should not perish, but have eternal life.

Whom have I in heaven *but thee?* and *there is* none upon earth *that* I desire beside thee.—We love him, because he first loved us.

My beloved spake, and said unto me, Rise up, my love, my fair one, and come away. For, lo, the winter is past, the rain is over *and* gone; the flowers appear on the earth; the time of the singing *of birds* is come, and the voice of the turtle is heard in our land; the fig tree putteth forth her green figs, and the vines *with* the tender grape give a *good* smell. Arise, my love, my fair one, and come away.

Song 1.4; Jer. 31.3; Hos. 11.4; Jn. 12.32; Jn. 1.36; Jn. 3.14,15 § Ps. 73.25; 1 Jn. 4.19 § Song 2.10–13

I will raise them up a Prophet
from among their brethren, like unto thee.

[Moses] stood between the LORD and you at that time, to shew you the word of the LORD: for ye were afraid.—*There is* one God, and one mediator between God and men, the man Christ Jesus.

Now the man Moses *was* very meek, above all the men which *were* upon the face of the earth.—Take my yoke upon you, and learn of me; for I am meek and lowly in heart: and ye shall find rest unto your souls.— Let this mind be in you, which was also in Christ Jesus: who, being in the form of God, thought it not robbery to be equal with God: but made himself of no reputation, and took upon him the form of a servant, and was made in the likeness of men.

Moses verily *was* faithful in all his house, as a servant, for a testimony of those things which were to be spoken after; but Christ as a son over his own house; whose house are we, if we hold fast the confidence and the rejoicing of the hope firm unto the end.

Deu. 18.18; Deu. 5.5; 1 Tim. 2.5 § Nu. 12.3;
Mt. 11.29; Phil. 2.5–7 § He. 3.5–6

Everlasting consolation.

I will remember my covenant with thee in the days of thy youth, and I will establish unto thee an everlasting covenant.

By one offering he hath perfected for ever them that are sanctified.—He is able also to save them to the uttermost that come unto God by him, seeing he ever liveth to make intercession for them.—I know whom I have believed, and am persuaded that he is able to keep that which I have committed unto him against that day.

The gifts and calling of God *are* without repentance.—Who shall separate us from the love of Christ?—The Lamb which is in the midst of the throne shall feed them, and shall lead them unto living fountains of waters: and God shall wipe away all tears from their eyes.—So shall we ever be with the Lord. Wherefore comfort one another with these words.

This *is* not *your* rest.—Here have we no continuing city, but we seek one to come.

2 Th. 2.16; Ezek. 16.60 § He. 10.14; He. 7.25;
2 Tim. 1.12 § Ro. 11.29; Ro. 8.35; Rev. 7.17;
1 Th. 4.17–18 § Mi. 2.10; He. 13.14

Verily, verily, I say unto you, I am the door of the sheep.

The veil of the temple was rent in twain from the top to the bottom.—Christ...hath once suffered for sins, the just for the unjust, that he might bring us to God.— The way into the holiest of all was not yet made manifest, while as the first tabernacle was yet standing.

I am the door: by me if any man enter in, he shall be saved, and shall go in and out, and find pasture.

No man cometh unto the Father, but by me.— Through him we...have access by one Spirit unto the Father. Now therefore ye are no more strangers and for-eigners, but fellowcitizens with the saints, and of the household of God.—Having...boldness to enter into the holiest by the blood of Jesus, by a new and living way, which he hath consecrated for us, through the veil, that is to say, his flesh.—We have peace with God through our Lord Jesus Christ: by whom also we have access by faith into this grace wherein we stand, and rejoice in hope of the glory of God.

Jn. 10.7; Mt. 27.51; 1 Pe. 3.18; He. 9.8 § Jn. 10.9
§ Jn. 14.6; Eph. 2.18–19; He. 10.19–20; Ro. 5.1–2

His word was in mine heart as a burning fire
shut up in my bones, and I was weary
with forbearing, and I could not *stay*.

Necessity is laid upon me; yea, woe is unto me, if I preach not the gospel!... What is my reward then? *Verily* that, when I preach the gospel, I may make the gospel of Christ without charge, that I abuse not my power in the gospel.—They called them, and commanded them not to speak at all nor teach in the name of Jesus. But Peter and John answered and said unto them... We cannot but speak the things which we have seen and heard.— The love of Christ constraineth us.

I was afraid, and went and hid thy talent in the earth... *Thou* wicked and slothful servant...thou oughtest...to have put my money to the exchangers, and *then* at my coming I should have received mine own with usury.

Go...to thy friends, and tell them how great things the Lord hath done for thee.

Jer. 20.9; 1 Co. 9.16,18; Ac. 4.18–20; 2 Co. 5.14
§ Mt. 25.25–27 § Mk. 5.19

**There shall cleave nought of
the cursed thing to thine hand.**

Come out from among them, and be ye separate, saith the Lord, and touch not the unclean *thing*.—Dearly beloved, I beseech *you* as strangers and pilgrims, abstain from fleshly lusts, which war against the soul.—Hating even the garment spotted by the flesh.

Beloved, now are we the sons of God, and it doth not yet appear what we shall be: but we know that, when he shall appear, we shall be like him; for we shall see him as he is. And every man that hath this hope in him purifieth himself, even as he is pure.—The grace of God that bringeth salvation hath appeared to all men, teaching us that, denying ungodliness and worldly lusts, we should live soberly, righteously, and godly, in this present world; looking for that blessed hope, and the glorious appearing of the great God and our Saviour Jesus Christ; who gave himself for us, that he might redeem us from all iniquity, and purify unto himself a peculiar people, zealous of good works.

Deu. 13.17; 2 Co. 6.17; 1 Pe. 2.11; Jude 23
§ 1 Jn. 3.2–3; Titus 2.11–14

Who art thou, Lord?... I am Jesus.

It is I; be not afraid.—When thou passest through the waters, I *will be* with thee; and through the rivers, they shall not overflow thee: when thou walkest through the fire, thou shalt not be burned; neither shall the flame kindle upon thee. For I *am* the LORD thy God...thy Saviour.

Though I walk through the valley of the shadow of death, I will fear no evil: for thou *art* with me; thy rod and thy staff they comfort me.—Emmanuel...God with us.

Thou shalt call his name JESUS: for he shall save his people from their sins.—If any man sin, we have an advocate with the Father, Jesus Christ the righteous.— Who *is* he that condemneth? *It is* Christ that died, yea rather, that is risen again, who is even at the right hand of God, who also maketh intercession for us. Who shall separate us from the love of Christ? *shall* tribulation, or distress, or persecution, or famine, or nakedness, or peril, or sword?

Ac. 26.15; Mt. 14.27; Isa. 43.2–3 § Ps. 23.4; Mt. 1.23
§ Mt. 1.21; 1 Jn. 2.1; Ro. 8.34–35

Stand fast in the Lord.

My foot hath held his steps, his way have I kept, and not declined.

The LORD loveth judgment, and forsaketh not his saints; they are preserved for ever.—The LORD shall preserve thee from all evil: he shall preserve thy soul.

The just shall live by faith: but if *any man* draw back, my soul shall have no pleasure in him. But we are not of them who draw back unto perdition; but of them that believe to the saving of the soul.—If they had been of us, they would *no doubt* have continued with us: but *they went out*, that they might be made manifest that they were not all of us.

If ye continue in my word, *then* are ye my disciples indeed.—He that shall endure unto the end, the same shall be saved.—Watch ye, stand fast in the faith, quit you like men, be strong.—Hold that fast which thou hast, that no man take thy crown.—He that overcometh, the same shall be clothed in white raiment; and I will not blot out his name out of the book of life.

Phil. 4.1; Job 23.11 § Ps. 37.28; Ps. 121.7
§ He. 10.38–39; 1 Jn. 2.19 § Jn. 8.31; Mt. 24.13;
1 Co. 16.13; Rev. 3.11; Rev. 3.5

Enoch walked with God.

Can two walk together, except they be agreed?

Having made peace through the blood of his cross... You, that were sometime alienated and enemies in *your* mind by wicked works, yet now hath he reconciled in the body of his flesh through death, to present you holy and unblameable and unreproveable in his sight.—In Christ Jesus ye who sometimes were far off are made nigh by the blood of Christ.

If, when we were enemies, we were reconciled to God by the death of his Son, much more, being reconciled, we shall be saved by his life. And not only *so,* but we also joy in God through our Lord Jesus Christ.

Our fellowship *is* with the Father, and with his Son Jesus Christ.

The grace of the Lord Jesus Christ, and the love of God, and the communion of the Holy Ghost, *be* with you all. Amen.

Ge. 5.22; Am. 3.3 § Col. 1.20–22; Eph. 2.13 § Ro. 5.10–11 § 1 Jn. 1.3 § 2 Co. 13.14

If his offering *be* a burnt sacrifice of the herd,
let him offer a male without blemish: he shall offer it
of his own voluntary will... And he shall put his hand
upon the head of the burnt offering; and it shall be
accepted for him to make atonement for him.

God will provide himself a lamb for a burnt offering.—Behold the Lamb of God, which taketh away the
sin of the world.—We are sanctified through the offering of the body of Jesus Christ once *for all.*—A ransom
for many.

No man taketh it from me, but I lay it down of
myself. I have power to lay it down, and I have power to
take it again.—I will love them freely.—The Son of God,
who loved me, and gave himself for me.

He hath made him *to be* sin for us, who knew no sin;
that we might be made the righteousness of God in
him.—He hath made us accepted in the beloved.

Lev. 1.3,4; Ge. 22.8; Jn. 1.29; He. 10.10; Mt. 20.28
§ Jn. 10.18; Hos. 14.4; Ga. 2.20 § 2 Co. 5.21; Eph. 1.6

Great *is* thy mercy toward me: and thou hast delivered my soul from the lowest hell.

Fear him which is able to destroy both soul and body in hell.

Fear not: for I have redeemed thee, I have called *thee* by thy name; thou *art* mine... I, *even* I, *am* the LORD; and beside me *there is* no saviour... I, *even* I, *am* he that blotteth out thy transgressions for mine own sake, and will not remember thy sins.—They that trust in their wealth, and boast themselves in the multitude of their riches; none *of them* can by any means redeem his brother, nor give to God a ransom for him: (for the redemption of their soul *is* precious...)—I have found a ransom.—God, who is rich in mercy, for his great love wherewith he loved us, even when we were dead in sins, hath quickened us together with Christ.

Neither is there salvation in any other: for there is none other name under heaven given among men, whereby we must be saved.

Ps. 86.13; Mt. 10.28 § Isa. 43.1,11,25; Ps. 49.6–8; Job 33.24; Eph. 2.4–5 § Ac. 4.12

The LORD was my stay.

Truly in vain *is salvation hoped for* from the hills, *and from* the multitude of mountains: truly in the LORD our God *is* the salvation of Israel.—The LORD *is* my rock, and my fortress, and my deliverer; my God, my strength, in whom I will trust; my buckler, and the horn of my salvation, *and* my high tower.—Cry out and shout, thou inhabitant of Zion: for great *is* the Holy One of Israel in the midst of thee.

The angel of the LORD encampeth round about them that fear him, and delivereth them... *The righteous* cry, and the LORD heareth, and delivereth them out of all their troubles.—The eternal God *is thy* refuge, and underneath *are* the everlasting arms.—So that we may boldly say, The Lord *is* my helper, and I will not fear what man shall do unto me.—For who *is* God save the LORD? or who *is* a rock save our God? *It is* God that girdeth me with strength, and maketh my way perfect.

By the grace of God I am what I am.

Ps. **18.18**; Jer. 3.23; Ps. 18.2; Isa. 12.6 § Ps. 34.7,17; Deu. 33.27; He. 13.6; Ps. 18.31–32 § 1 Co. 15.10

All we like sheep have gone astray.

If we say that we have no sin, we deceive ourselves, and the truth is not in us.—There is none righteous, no, not one: there is none that understandeth... They are all gone out of the way, they are together become unprofitable.

Ye were as sheep going astray; but are now returned unto the Shepherd and Bishop of your souls.—I have gone astray like a lost sheep; seek thy servant; for I do not forget thy commandments.

He restoreth my soul: he leadeth me in the paths of righteousness for his name's sake.

My sheep hear my voice, and I know them, and they follow me: and I give unto them eternal life; and they shall never perish, neither shall any *man* pluck them out of my hand.

What man of you, having an hundred sheep, if he lose one of them, doth not leave the ninety and nine in the wilderness, and go after that which is lost, until he find it?

Isa. 53.6; 1 Jn. 1.8; Ro. 3.10–12 § 1 Pe. 2.25;
Ps. 119.176 § Ps. 23.3 § Jn. 10.27–28 § Lu. 15.4

**The LORD visited Sarah as he had said,
and the LORD did unto Sarah as he had spoken.**

Trust in him at all times; ye people, pour out your heart before him: God *is* a refuge for us.—David encouraged himself in the LORD his God.—God will surely visit you, and bring you out of this land unto the land which he sware to Abraham, to Isaac, and to Jacob.—I have seen, I have seen the affliction of my people which is in Egypt, and I have heard their groaning, and am come down to deliver them... He brought them out, after that he had shewed wonders and signs in the land of Egypt, and in the Red sea, and in the wilderness forty years.—There failed not ought of any good thing which the LORD had spoken unto the house of Israel; all came to pass.

He *is* faithful that promised.—Hath he said, and shall he not do *it?* or hath he spoken, and shall he not make it good?—Heaven and earth shall pass away, but my words shall not pass away.—The grass withereth, the flower fadeth: but the word of our God shall stand for ever.

Ge. 21.1;   Ps. 62.8;   1 Sa. 30.6;   Ge. 50.24;   Ac. 7.34,36;   Jos. 21.45 § He. 10.23;   Nu. 23.19;   Mt. 24.35;   Isa. 40.8

The eyes of all wait upon thee.

He giveth to all life, and breath, and all things.—The LORD *is* good to all: and his tender mercies *are* over all his works.—Behold the fowls of the air: for they sow not, neither do they reap, nor gather into barns; yet your heavenly Father feedeth them.

The same Lord over all is rich unto all that call upon him.

I will lift up mine eyes unto the hills, from whence cometh my help.—Behold, as the eyes of servants *look* unto the hand of their masters, *and* as the eyes of a maiden unto the hand of her mistress; so our eyes *wait* upon the LORD our God.

The LORD *is* a God of judgment: blessed *are* all they that wait for him.—And it shall be said in that day, Lo, this *is* our God; we have waited for him, and he will save us: this *is* the LORD; we have waited for him, we will be glad and rejoice in his salvation.—If we hope for that we see not, *then* do we with patience wait for *it*.

Ps. 145.15; Ac. 17.25; Ps. 145.9; Mt. 6.26 § Ro. 10.12 § Ps. 121.1; Ps. 123.2 § Isa. 30.18; Isa. 25.9; Ro. 8.25

**Thou shalt call his name JESUS:
for he shall save his people from their sins.**

Ye know that he was manifested to take away our sins.—That we, being dead to sins, should live unto righteousness.—He is able also to save them to the uttermost that come unto God by him.

He *was* wounded for our transgressions, *he was* bruised for our iniquities: the chastisement of our peace *was* upon him; and with his stripes we are healed… The LORD hath laid on him the iniquity of us all.—Thus it behoved Christ to suffer…that repentance and remission of sins should be preached in his name among all nations.—He appeared to put away sin by the sacrifice of himself.

Him hath God exalted with his right hand *to be* a Prince and a Saviour…to give repentance.—Through this man is preached unto you the forgiveness of sins: and by him all that believe are justified from all things, from which ye could not be justified by the law of Moses.—Your sins are forgiven you for his name's sake.

Mt. 1.21; 1 Jn. 3.5; 1 Pe. 2.24; He. 7.25 § Isa. 53.5,6; Lu. 24.46,47; He. 9.26 § Ac. 5.31; Ac. 13.38–39; 1 Jn. 2.12

**Our Lord Jesus Christ…though he was rich,
yet for your sakes…became poor,
that ye through his poverty might be rich.**

It pleased *the Father* that in him should all fulness dwell.—The brightness of *his* glory, and the express image of his person, and upholding all things by the word of his power, when he had by himself purged our sins, sat down on the right hand of the Majesty on high; being made so much better than the angels, as he hath by inheritance obtained a more excellent name than they.—Who, being in the form of God, thought it not robbery to be equal with God: but made himself of no reputation.

The foxes have holes, and the birds of the air *have* nests; but the Son of man hath not where to lay *his* head.

All things are yours; whether Paul, or Apollos, or Cephas, or the world, or life, or death, or things present, or things to come; all are yours; and ye are Christ's; and Christ *is* God's.

2 Co. 8.9; Col. 1.19; He. 1.3,4; Phil. 2.6–7 § Mt. 8.20 § 1 Co. 3.21–23

**His left hand *is* under my head,
and his right hand doth embrace me.**

Underneath *are* the everlasting arms.—When [Peter] saw the wind boisterous, he was afraid; and beginning to sink, he cried, saying, Lord, save me. And immediately Jesus stretched forth *his* hand, and caught him, and said unto him, O thou of little faith, wherefore didst thou doubt?—The steps of a *good* man are ordered by the LORD: and he delighteth in his way. Though he fall, he shall not be utterly cast down: for the LORD upholdeth *him with* his hand.

The beloved of the LORD shall dwell in safety by him; *and the LORD* shall cover him all the day long, and he shall dwell between his shoulders.—Casting all your care upon him, for he careth for you.—He that toucheth you toucheth the apple of his eye.

They shall never perish, neither shall any *man* pluck them out of my hand. My Father, which gave *them* me, is greater than all.

Song 2.6; Deu. 33.27; Mt. 14.30–31; Ps. 37.23–24
§ Deu. 33.12; 1 Pe. 5.7; Zech. 2.8 § Jn. 10.28–29

**Who *is* she *that* looketh forth as the morning,
fair as the moon, clear as the sun,
and terrible as *an army* with banners?**

The church of God, which he hath purchased with his own blood.

Christ also loved the church, and gave himself for it; that he might sanctify and cleanse it with the washing of water by the word, that he might present it to himself a glorious church, not having spot, or wrinkle, or any such thing; but that it should be holy and without blemish.

There appeared a great wonder in heaven; a woman clothed with the sun.—The marriage of the Lamb is come, and his wife hath made herself ready. And to her was granted that she should be arrayed in fine linen, clean and white: for the fine linen is the righteousness of saints.—The righteousness of God *which is* by faith of Jesus Christ unto all and upon all them that believe.

The glory which thou gavest me I have given them.

Song 6.10; Ac. 20.28 § Eph. 5.25–27 § Rev. 12.1; Rev. 19.7–8; Ro. 3.22 § Jn. 17.22

Brethren, the time is short.

Man *that is* born of a woman *is* of few days, and full of trouble. He cometh forth like a flower, and is cut down: he fleeth also as a shadow, and continueth not.—The world passeth away, and the lust thereof: but he that doeth the will of God abideth for ever.—As in Adam all die, even so in Christ shall all be made alive... Death is swallowed up in victory.—Whether we live, we live unto the Lord; and whether we die, we die unto the Lord: whether we live therefore, or die, we are the Lord's.—To live *is* Christ, and to die *is* gain.

Cast not away...your confidence, which hath great recompence of reward. For ye have need of patience, that, after ye have done the will of God, ye might receive the promise. For yet a little while, and he that shall come will come, and will not tarry.—The night is far spent, the day is at hand: let us therefore cast off the works of darkness, and let us put on the armour of light.—The end of all things is at hand: be ye therefore sober, and watch unto prayer.

1 Co. 7.29; Job 14.1–2; 1 Jn. 2.17; 1 Co. 15.22,54; Ro. 14.8; Phil. 1.21 § He. 10.35–37; Ro. 13.12; 1 Pe. 4.7

A new name.

The disciples were called Christians first in Antioch.—Let every one that nameth the name of Christ depart from iniquity.—They that are Christ's have crucified the flesh with the affections and lusts.—Ye are bought with a price: therefore glorify God in your body, and in your spirit, which are God's.

God forbid that I should glory, save in the cross of our Lord Jesus Christ, by whom the world is crucified unto me, and I unto the world. For in Christ Jesus neither circumcision availeth any thing, nor uncircumcision, but a new creature.

Be ye...followers of God, as dear children; and walk in love, as Christ also hath loved us, and hath given himself for us an offering and a sacrifice to God for a sweetsmelling savour. But fornication, and all uncleanness, or covetousness, let it not be once named among you, as becometh saints... Now *are ye* light in the Lord: walk as children of light.

Rev. 2.17; Ac. 11.26; 2 Tim. 2.19; Ga. 5.24; 1 Co. 6.20 § Ga. 6.14–15 § Eph. 5.1–3,8

Behold the Lamb of God.

It is not possible that the blood of bulls and of goats should take away sins. Wherefore when he cometh into the world, he saith, Sacrifice and offering thou wouldest not, but a body hast thou prepared me: in burnt offerings and *sacrifices* for sin thou hast had no pleasure. Then said I, Lo, I come (in the volume of the book it is written of me,) to do thy will, O God.—He was oppressed, and he was afflicted, yet he opened not his mouth: he is brought as a lamb to the slaughter, and as a sheep before her shearers is dumb, so he openeth not his mouth.

Ye were not redeemed with corruptible things, *as* silver and gold…but with the precious blood of Christ, as of a lamb without blemish and without spot…manifest in these last times for you, who by him do believe in God…that your faith and hope might be in God.

Worthy is the Lamb that was slain to receive power, and riches, and wisdom, and strength, and honour, and glory, and blessing.

Jn. 1.29; He. 10.4–7; Isa. 53.7 § 1 Pe. 1.18–21 § Rev. 5.12

I will hope continually,
and will yet praise thee more and more.

Not as though I had already attained, either were already perfect.—Leaving the principles of the doctrine of Christ, let us go on unto perfection; not laying again the foundation of repentance from dead works, and of faith toward God.—The path of the just *is* as the shining light, that shineth more and more unto the perfect day.

I love the LORD, because he hath heard my voice *and* my supplications. Because he hath inclined his ear unto me, therefore will I call upon *him* as long as I live.—I will bless the LORD at all times: his praise *shall* continually *be* in my mouth.

Praise waiteth for thee, O God, in Sion.—They rest not day and night, saying, Holy, holy, holy, Lord God Almighty.—Whoso offereth praise glorifieth me.—Rejoice evermore. Pray without ceasing. In every thing give thanks: for this is the will of God in Christ Jesus concerning you.—Rejoice in the Lord alway: *and* again I say, Rejoice.

Ps. 71.14; Phil. 3.12; He. 6.1; Pro. 4.18 § Ps. 116.1–2; Ps. 34.1 § Ps. 65.1; Rev. 4.8; Ps. 50.23; 1 Th. 5.16–18; Phil. 4.4

Consider how great *things* he hath done for you.

Thou shalt remember all the way which the LORD thy God led thee these forty years in the wilderness, to humble thee, *and* to prove thee, to know what *was* in thine heart, whether thou wouldest keep his commandments, or no… Thou shalt also consider in thine heart, that, as a man chasteneth his son, *so* the LORD thy God chasteneth thee.

Before I was afflicted I went astray: but now have I kept thy word… *It is* good for me that I have been afflicted; that I might learn thy statutes… I know, O LORD, that thy judgments *are* right, and *that* thou in faithfulness hast afflicted me.—The LORD hath chastened me sore: but he hath not given me over unto death.—He hath not dealt with us after our sins; nor rewarded us according to our iniquities. For as the heaven is high above the earth, *so* great is his mercy toward them that fear him… He knoweth our frame; he remembereth that we *are* dust.

1 Sa. 12.24;   Deu. 8.2,5   § Ps. 119.67,71,75;   Ps. 118.18;   Ps. 103.10–11,14

That blessed hope…the glorious appearing of the great God and our Saviour Jesus Christ.

Which *hope* we have as an anchor of the soul, both sure and stedfast, and which entereth into that within the veil; whither the forerunner is for us entered, *even* Jesus.—Whom the heaven must receive until the times of restitution of all things.—When he shall come to be glorified in his saints, and to be admired in all them that believe.

The whole creation groaneth and travaileth in pain together until now. And not only *they*, but ourselves also…groan within ourselves, waiting for the adoption, *to wit*, the redemption of our body.—Beloved, now are we the sons of God, and it doth not yet appear what we shall be: but we know that, when he shall appear, we shall be like him; for we shall see him as he is.—When Christ, *who is* our life, shall appear, then shall ye also appear with him in glory.

Surely I come quickly. Amen. Even so, come, Lord Jesus.

Titus 2.13; He. 6.19–20; Ac. 3.21; 2 Th. 1.10
§ Ro. 8.22–23; 1 Jn. 3.2; Col. 3.4 § Rev. 22.20

**Whoso keepeth his word,
in him verily is the love of God perfected.**

The God of peace, that brought again from the dead our Lord Jesus, that great shepherd of the sheep, through the blood of the everlasting covenant, make you perfect in every good work to do his will, working in you that which is wellpleasing in his sight, through Jesus Christ; to whom *be* glory for ever and ever. Amen.

Hereby we do know that we know him, if we keep his commandments.—If a man love me, he will keep my words: and my Father will love him, and we will come unto him, and make our abode with him.—Whosoever abideth in him sinneth not: whosoever sinneth hath not seen him, neither known him. Little children, let no man deceive you: he that doeth righteousness is righteous, even as he is righteous.—Herein is our love made perfect, that we may have boldness in the day of judgment: because as he is, so are we in this world.

1 Jn. 2.5; He. 13.20–21 § 1 Jn. 2.3; Jn. 14.23;
1 Jn. 3.6,7; 1 Jn. 4.17

He that is **slow to wrath** *is* **of great understanding.**

The LORD passed by before him, and proclaimed, The LORD, The LORD God, merciful and gracious, longsuffering.—The Lord is not slack concerning his promise, as some men count slackness; but is longsuffering to usward, not willing that any should perish, but that all should come to repentance.

Be ye…followers of God, as dear children; and walk in love.—The fruit of the Spirit is love, joy, peace, longsuffering, gentleness, goodness, faith, meekness, temperance: against such there is no law.—This *is* thankworthy, if a man for conscience toward God endure grief, suffering wrongfully… If, when ye do well, and suffer *for it*, ye take it patiently, this is acceptable with God… Christ…suffered for us, leaving us an example, that ye should follow his steps: who…when he was reviled, reviled not again; when he suffered, he threatened not; but committed *himself* to him that judgeth righteously.

Be ye angry, and sin not.

Pro. 14.29; Ex. 34.6; 2 Pe. 3.9 § Eph. 5.1; Ga. 5.22–23; 1 Pe. 2.19–21,23 § Eph. 4.26

The fruit of the Spirit is...peace...

To be spiritually minded *is* life and peace.

God hath called us to peace.—Peace I leave with you, my peace I give unto you: not as the world giveth, give I unto you. Let not your heart be troubled, neither let it be afraid.—The God of hope fill you with all joy and peace in believing, that ye may abound in hope, through the power of the Holy Ghost.

I know whom I have believed, and am persuaded that he is able to keep that which I have committed unto him against that day.—Thou wilt keep *him* in perfect peace, *whose* mind is stayed *on thee*: because he trusteth in thee.

The work of righteousness shall be peace; and the effect of righteousness quietness and assurance for ever. And my people shall dwell in a peaceable habitation, and in sure dwellings, and in quiet resting places.— Whoso hearkeneth unto me shall dwell safely, and shall be quiet from fear of evil.

Great peace have they which love thy law.

Ga. 5.22; Ro. 8.6 § 1 Co. 7.15; Jn. 14.27; Ro. 15.13
§ 2 Tim. 1.12; Isa. 26.3 § Isa. 32.17–18; Pro. 1.33
§ Ps. 119.165

The LORD *is* there. [*marg.* Jehovah-shammah]

Behold, the tabernacle of God *is* with men, and he will dwell with them, and they shall be his people, and God himself shall be with them, *and be* their God.

I saw no temple...for the Lord God Almighty and the Lamb are the temple of it. And the city had no need of the sun, neither of the moon, to shine in it: for the glory of God did lighten it, and the Lamb *is* the light thereof.

I shall be satisfied, when I awake, with thy likeness.— Whom have I in heaven *but thee?* and *there is* none upon earth *that* I desire beside thee.

Judah shall dwell for ever, and Jerusalem from generation to generation. For I will cleanse their blood *that* I have not cleansed: for the LORD dwelleth in Zion.— Sing and rejoice, O daughter of Zion: for, lo, I come, and I will dwell in the midst of thee, saith the LORD.—There shall be no more curse: but the throne of God and of the Lamb shall be in it; and his servants shall serve him.

Ezek. **48.**35; Rev. 21.3 § Rev. 21.22–23 § Ps. 17.15; Ps. 73.25 § Joel 3.20–21; Zech. 2.10; Rev. 22.3

Surely the LORD is in this place; and I knew *it* not.

Where two or three are gathered together in my name, there am I in the midst of them.—Lo, I am with you alway, *even* unto the end of the world.—My presence shall go *with thee*, and I will give thee rest.

Whither shall I go from thy spirit? or whither shall I flee from thy presence? If I ascend up into heaven, thou *art* there: if I make my bed in hell, behold, thou *art* there.—*Am* I a God at hand, saith the LORD, and not a God afar off? Can any hide himself in secret places that I shall not see him? saith the LORD. Do not I fill heaven and earth? saith the LORD.

Behold, the heaven and heaven of heavens cannot contain thee; how much less this house that I have builded?—Thus saith the high and lofty One that inhabiteth eternity, whose name *is* Holy; I dwell in the high and holy *place*, with him also *that is* of a contrite and humble spirit, to revive the spirit of the humble, and to revive the heart of the contrite ones.—Ye are the temple of the living God.

Ge. 28.16;　Mt. 18.20;　Mt. 28.20;　Ex. 33.14
§ Ps. 139.7–8;　Jer. 23.23–24　§ 1 Ki. 8.27;　Isa. 57.15;
2 Co. 6.16

Keep yourselves from idols.

My son, give me thine heart.—Set your affection on things above, not on things on the earth.

Son of man, these men have set up their idols in their heart, and put the stumblingblock of their iniquity before their face: should I be enquired of at all by them?—Mortify…your members which are upon the earth; fornication, uncleanness, inordinate affection, evil concupiscence, and covetousness, which is idolatry.—They that will be rich fall into temptation and a snare… For the love of money is the root of all evil: which while some coveted after, they have erred from the faith, and pierced themselves through with many sorrows. But thou, O man of God, flee these things.

If riches increase, set not your heart *upon them.*— My fruit *is* better than gold, yea, than fine gold; and my revenue than choice silver.

Where your treasure is, there will your heart be also.—The LORD looketh on the heart.

1 Jn. 5.21; Pro. 23.26; Col. 3.2 § Ezek. 14.3; Col. 3.5; 1 Tim. 6.9–11 § Ps. 62.10; Pro. 8.19 § Mt. 6.21; 1 Sa. 16.7

Be ye therefore perfect,
even as your Father which is in heaven is perfect.

I *am* the Almighty God; walk before me, and be thou perfect.—Ye shall be holy unto me: for I the LORD *am* holy, and have severed you from *other* people, that ye should be mine.

Ye are bought with a price: therefore glorify God in your body, and in your spirit, which are God's

Ye are complete in him, which is the head of all principality and power.—Who gave himself for us, that he might redeem us from all iniquity.—Be diligent that ye may be found of him in peace, without spot, and blameless.

Blessed *are* the undefiled in the way, who walk in the law of the LORD.—Whoso looketh into the perfect law of liberty, and continueth *therein*, he being not a forgetful hearer, but a doer of the work, this man shall be blessed in his deed.—Search me, O God, and know my heart: try me, and know my thoughts: and see if *there be any* wicked way in me, and lead me in the way everlasting.

Mt. 5.48; Ge. 17.1; Lev. 20.26 § 1 Co. 6.20 § Col. 2.10;
Titus 2.14; 2 Pe. 3.14 § Ps. 119.1; Jas. 1.25;
Ps. 139.23–24

Perfecting holiness in the fear of God.

Dearly beloved, let us cleanse ourselves from all filthiness of the flesh and spirit.

Behold, thou desirest truth in the inward parts: and in the hidden *part* thou shalt make me to know wisdom.—Teaching us that, denying ungodliness and worldly lusts, we should live soberly, righteously, and godly, in this present world.—Let your light so shine before men, that they may see your good works, and glorify your Father which is in heaven.—Not as though I had already attained, either were already perfect.

Every man that hath this hope in him purifieth himself, even as he is pure.

Now he that hath wrought us for the selfsame thing *is* God, who also hath given unto us the earnest of the Spirit.—For the perfecting of the saints, for the work of the ministry, for the edifying of the body of Christ: till we all come in the unity of the faith, and of the knowledge of the Son of God, unto a perfect man, unto the measure of the stature of the fulness of Christ.

2 Co. 7.1; 2 Co. 7.1 § Ps. 51.6; Titus 2.12; Mt. 5.16;
Phil. 3.12 § 1 Jn. 3.3 § 2 Co. 5.5; Eph. 4.12–13

**Behold, the LORD's hand is not shortened,
that it cannot save; neither his ear heavy,
that it cannot hear.**

In the day when I cried thou answeredst me, *and* strengthenedst me *with* strength in my soul.—Whiles I *was* speaking in prayer, even the man Gabriel, whom I had seen in the vision at the beginning, being caused to fly swiftly, touched me about the time of the evening oblation.

Hide not thy face *far* from me; put not thy servant away in anger: thou hast been my help; leave me not, neither forsake me, O God of my salvation.—Be not thou far from me, O LORD: O my strength, haste thee to help me.

Ah Lord GOD! behold, thou hast made the heaven and the earth by thy great power and stretched out arm, *and* there is nothing too hard for thee.—Who delivered us from so great a death, and doth deliver: in whom we trust that he will yet deliver *us*.—Shall not God avenge his own elect, which cry day and night unto him, though he bear long with them? I tell you that he will avenge them speedily.

Isa. **59.**1; Ps. 138.3; Dan. 9.21 § Ps. 27.9; Ps. 22.19
§ Jer. 32.17; 2 Co. 1.10; Lu. 18.7–8

I have glorified thee on the earth.

My meat is to do the will of him that sent me, and to finish his work.—I must work the works of him that sent me, while it is day: the night cometh, when no man can work.

Wist ye not that I must be about my Father's business? And they understood not the saying which he spake unto them.—This sickness is not unto death, but for the glory of God, that the Son of God might be glorified thereby... Said I not unto thee, that, if thou wouldest believe, thou shouldest see the glory of God?

Jesus increased in wisdom and stature, and in favour with God and man.—Thou art my beloved Son; in thee I am well pleased.—All bare him witness, and wondered at the gracious words which proceeded out of his mouth.

Thou art worthy...for thou wast slain, and hast redeemed us to God by thy blood out of every kindred, and tongue, and people, and nation; and hast made us unto our God kings and priests: and we shall reign on the earth.

Jn. 17.4; Jn. 4.34; Jn. 9.4 § Lu. 2.49–50; Jn. 11.4,40
§ Lu. 2.52; Lu. 3.22; Lu. 4.22 § Rev. 5.9–10

Take no thought, saying, What shall we eat? or, What shall we drink? or, Wherewithal shall we be clothed?...for your heavenly Father knoweth that ye have need of all these things.

O fear the LORD, ye his saints: for *there is* no want to them that fear him. The young lions do lack, and suffer hunger: but they that seek the LORD shall not want any good *thing.*—No good *thing* will he withhold from them that walk uprightly. O LORD of hosts, blessed *is* the man that trusteth in thee.

I would have you without carefulness.—Be careful for nothing; but in everything by prayer and supplication with thanksgiving let your requests be made known unto God.

Are not two sparrows sold for a farthing? and one of them shall not fall on the ground without your Father. But the very hairs of your head are all numbered. Fear ye not therefore, ye are of more value than many sparrows.—Why are ye so fearful? how is it that ye have no faith?—Have faith in God.

Mt. 6.31,32; Ps. 34.9–10; Ps. 84.11–12 § 1 Co. 7.32; Phil. 4.6 § Mt. 10.29–31; Mk. 4.40; Mk. 11.22

**He spread a cloud for a covering;
and fire to give light in the night.**

Like as a father pitieth *his* children, *so* the LORD pitieth them that fear him. For he knoweth our frame; he remembereth that we *are* dust.

The sun shall not smite thee by day, nor the moon by night.—There shall be a tabernacle for a shadow in the daytime from the heat, and for a place of refuge, and for a covert from storm and from rain.

The LORD *is* thy keeper: the LORD *is* thy shade upon thy right hand… The LORD shall preserve thy going out and thy coming in from this time forth, and even for evermore.—The LORD went before them by day in a pillar of a cloud, to lead them the way; and by night in a pillar of fire, to give them light; to go by day and night: he took not away the pillar of the cloud by day, nor the pillar of fire by night, *from* before the people.

Jesus Christ the same yesterday, and to day, and for ever.

Ps. 105.39; Ps. 103.13–14 § Ps. 121.6; Isa. 4.6 § Ps. 121.5,8; Ex. 13.21–22 § He. 13.8

Mercy and truth are met together;
righteousness and peace have kissed *each other.*

A just God and a Saviour.

The LORD is well pleased for his righteousness' sake; he will magnify the law, and make *it* honourable.

God was in Christ, reconciling the world unto himself, not imputing their trespasses unto them.—Whom God hath set forth *to be* a propitiation through faith in his blood, to declare his righteousness for the remission of sins that are past, through the forbearance of God; to declare, *I say,* at this time his righteousness: that he might be just, and the justifier of him which believeth in Jesus.—He *was* wounded for our transgressions, *he was* bruised for our iniquities: the chastisement of our peace *was* upon him; and with his stripes we are healed.— Who shall lay any thing to the charge of God's elect? *It is* God that justifieth.—To him that worketh not, but believeth on him that justifieth the ungodly, his faith is counted for righteousness.

Ps. 85.10; Isa. 45.21 § Isa. 42.21 § 2 Co. 5.19;
Ro. 3.25–26; Isa. 53.5; Ro. 8.33; Ro. 4.5

How are the dead raised up?
and with what body do they come?

Beloved, now are we the sons of God, and it doth not yet appear what we shall be: but we know that, when he shall appear, we shall be like him; for we shall see him as he is.—As we have borne the image of the earthy, we shall also bear the image of heavenly.

The Saviour, the Lord Jesus Christ: who shall change our vile body, that it may be fashioned like unto his glorious body, according to the working whereby he is able even to subdue all things unto himself.

Jesus himself stood in the midst of them, and saith unto them, Peace *be* unto you. But they were terrified and affrighted, and supposed that they had seen a spirit.—He was seen of Cephas, then of the twelve: after that, he was seen of above five hundred brethren at once.

If the Spirit of him that raised up Jesus from the dead dwell in you, he that raised up Christ from the dead shall also quicken your mortal bodies by his Spirit that dwelleth in you.

1 Co. 15.35; 1 Jn. 3.2; 1 Co. 15.49 § Phil. 3.20–21
§ Lu. 24.36–37; 1 Co. 15.5–6 § Ro. 8.11

**Ye shall hear of wars and rumours of wars:
see that ye be not troubled.**

God *is* our refuge and strength, a very present help in trouble. Therefore will not we fear, though the earth be removed, and though the mountains be carried into the midst of the sea; *though* the waters thereof roar *and* be troubled, *though* the mountains shake with the swelling thereof.—Come, my people, enter thou into thy chambers, and shut thy doors about thee: hide thyself as it were for a little moment, until the indignation be overpast. For, behold, the LORD cometh out of his place to punish the inhabitants of the earth for their iniquity.— In the shadow of thy wings will I make my refuge, until *these* calamities be overpast.—Your life is hid with Christ in God.

He shall not be afraid of evil tidings: his heart is fixed, trusting in the LORD.

These things I have spoken unto you, that in me ye might have peace. In the world ye shall have tribulation: but be of good cheer; I have overcome the world.

Mt. 24.6; Ps. 46.1–3; Isa. 26.20,21; Ps. 57.1; Col. 3.3
§ Ps. 112.7 § Jn. 16.33

They persecute *him* whom thou hast smitten.

It is impossible but that offences will come: but woe *unto him*, through whom they come!—Him, being delivered by the determinate counsel and foreknowledge of God, ye have taken, and by wicked hands have crucified and slain.—Then did they spit in his face, and buffeted him; and others smote *him* with the palms of their hands, saying, Prophesy unto us, thou Christ, Who is he that smote thee?—Likewise also the chief priests mocking *him*, with the scribes and elders, said, He saved others; himself he cannot save. If he be the King of Israel, let him now come down from the cross.—Of a truth against thy holy child Jesus, whom thou hast anointed, both Herod, and Pontius Pilate, with the Gentiles, and the people of Israel, were gathered together, for to do whatsoever thy hand and thy counsel determined before to be done.

Surely he hath borne our griefs, and carried our sorrows: yet we did esteem him stricken, smitten of God, and afflicted.

Ps. 69.26; Lu. 17.1; Ac. 2.23; Mt. 26.67–68; Mt. 27.41–42; Ac. 4.27–28 § Isa. 53.4

**It pleased the LORD to bruise him;
he hath put *him* to grief.**

Now is my soul troubled; and what shall I say? Father, save me from this hour: but for this cause came I unto this hour. Father, glorify thy name. Then came there a voice from heaven, *saying*, I have both glorified *it*, and will glorify *it* again.—Father, if thou be willing, remove this cup from me: nevertheless not my will, but thine, be done. And there appeared an angel unto him from heaven, strengthening him.

Being found in fashion as a man, he humbled himself, and became obedient unto death, even the death of the cross.—Therefore doth my Father love me, because I lay down my life, that I might take it again.—For I came down from heaven, not to do mine own will, but the will of him that sent me.—The cup which my Father hath given me, shall I not drink it?

The Father hath not left me alone; for I do always those things that please him.—My beloved Son, in whom I am well pleased.—Mine elect, *in whom* my soul delighteth.

Isa. 53.10; Jn. 12.27–28; Lu. 22.42–43 § Phil. 2.8; Jn. 10.17; Jn. 6.38; Jn. 18.11 § Jn. 8.29; Mt. 3.17; Isa. 42.1

Ye that make mention of the LORD, keep not silence.

Thou…hast made us unto our God kings and priests.—The sons of Aaron, the priests, shall blow with the trumpets; and they shall be to you for an ordinance for ever throughout your generations. And if ye go to war in your land against the enemy that oppresseth you, then ye shall blow an alarm with the trumpets; and ye shall be remembered before the LORD your God, and ye shall be saved from your enemies.

I said not unto the seed of Jacob, Seek ye me in vain.—Their voice was heard, and their prayer came *up* to his holy dwelling place, *even* unto heaven.—The eyes of the LORD *are* upon the righteous, and his ears *are open* unto their cry.—Pray one for another… The effectual fervent prayer of a righteous man availeth much.

Come, Lord Jesus.—Make no tarrying, O my God.— Looking for and hasting unto the coming of the day of God.

Isa. 62.6; Rev. 5.9,10; Nu. 10.8–9 § Isa. 45.19; 2 Chr. 30.27; Ps. 34.15; Jas. 5.16 § Rev. 22.20; Ps. 40.17; 2 Pe. 3.12

**Faith is the substance of things hoped for,
the evidence of things not seen.**

If in this life only we have hope in Christ, we are of all men most miserable.

Eye hath not seen, nor ear heard, neither have entered into the heart of man, the things which God hath prepared for them that love him. But God hath revealed *them* unto us by his Spirit.—After that ye believed, ye were sealed with that holy Spirit of promise, which is the earnest of our inheritance until the redemption of the purchased possession.

Jesus saith unto him, Thomas, because thou hast seen me, thou hast believed: blessed *are* they that have not seen, and *yet* have believed.—Whom having not seen, ye love; in whom, though now ye see *him* not, yet believing, ye rejoice with joy unspeakable and full of glory: receiving the end of your faith, *even* the salvation of *your* souls.

We walk by faith, not by sight.—Cast not away therefore your confidence, which hath great recompence of reward.

He. 11.1; 1 Co. 15.19 § 1 Co. 2.9–10; Eph. 1.13–14
§ Jn. 20.29; 1 Pe. 1.8–9 § 2 Co. 5.7; He. 10.35

It is I; be not afraid.

When I saw him, I fell at his feet as dead. And he laid his right hand upon me, saying unto me, Fear not; I am the first and the last: *I am* he that liveth, and was dead; and, behold, I am alive for evermore, Amen; and have the keys of hell and of death.—I, *even* I, *am* he that blotteth out thy transgressions for mine own sake, and will not remember thy sins.

Woe *is* me! for I am undone…mine eyes have seen the King, the LORD of hosts. Then flew one of the seraphims unto me, having a live coal in his hand, *which* he had taken with the tongs from off the altar: and he laid *it* upon my mouth, and said, Lo, this hath touched thy lips; and thine iniquity is taken away, and thy sin purged.—I have blotted out, as a thick cloud, thy transgressions, and, as a cloud, thy sins: return unto me; for I have redeemed thee.

If any man sin, we have an advocate with the Father, Jesus Christ the righteous.

Jn. 6.20; Rev. 1.17–18; Isa. 43.25 § Isa. 6.5–7;
Isa. 44.22 § 1 Jn. 2.1

**For this purpose the Son of God was manifested,
that he might destroy the works of the devil.**

We wrestle not against flesh and blood, but against principalities, against powers, against the rulers of the darkness of this world, against spiritual wickedness in high *places*.—Forasmuch…as the children are partakers of flesh and blood, he also himself likewise took part of the same; that through death he might destroy him that had the power of death, that is, the devil.—*And* having spoiled principalities and powers, he made a shew of them openly, triumphing over them.—I heard a loud voice saying in heaven, Now is come salvation, and strength, and the kingdom of our God, and the power of his Christ: for the accuser of our brethren is cast down, which accused them before our God day and night. And they overcame him by the blood of the Lamb, and by the word of their testimony; and they loved not their lives unto the death.

Thanks *be* to God, which giveth us the victory through our Lord Jesus Christ.

1 Jn. 3.8; Eph. 6.12; He. 2.14; Col. 2.15; Rev. 12.10–11
§ 1 Co. 15.57

Vanity of vanities; all *is* vanity.

We spend our years as a tale *that is told*. The days of our years *are* threescore years and ten; and if by reason of strength *they be* fourscore years, yet *is* their strength labour and sorrow; for it is soon cut off, and we fly away.

If in this life only we have hope in Christ, we are of all men most miserable.—Here have we no continuing city, but we seek one to come.—I *am* the LORD, I change not.—Our conversation is in heaven; from whence also we look for the Saviour, the Lord Jesus Christ: who shall change our vile body, that it may be fashioned like unto his glorious body, according to the working whereby he is able even to subdue all things unto himself.—The creature was made subject to vanity, not willingly, but by reason of him who hath subjected *the same* in hope.

Jesus Christ the same yesterday, and to day, and for ever.—Holy, holy, holy, Lord God Almighty, which was, and is, and is to come.

Ec. 1.2; Ps. 90.9–10 § 1 Co. 15.19; He. 13.14; Mal. 3.6; Phil. 3.20–21; Ro. 8.20 § He. 13.8; Rev. 4.8

Awake to righteousness,
and sin not.

Ye are all the children of light, and the children of the day… Therefore let us not sleep, as *do* others; but let us watch and be sober.

It is high time to awake out of sleep: for now *is* our salvation nearer than when we believed. The night is far spent, the day is at hand: let us therefore cast off the works of darkness, and let us put on the armour of light.—Wherefore take unto you the whole armour of God, that ye may be able to withstand in the evil day, and having done all, to stand.—Cast away from you all your transgressions, whereby ye have transgressed; and make you a new heart and a new spirit.—Lay apart all filthiness and superfluity of naughtiness, and receive with meekness the engrafted word, which is able to save your souls.—Little children, abide in him; that, when he shall appear, we may have confidence, and not be ashamed before him at his coming. If ye know that he is righteous, ye know that every one that doeth righteousness is born of him.

1 Co. 15.34; 1 Th. 5.5,6 § Ro. 13.11–12; Eph. 6.13;
Ezek. 18.31; Jas. 1.21; 1 Jn. 2.28–29

My sheep hear my voice.

Behold, I stand at the door, and knock: if any man hear my voice, and open the door, I will come in to him, and will sup with him, and he with me.

I sleep, but my heart waketh: *it is* the voice of my beloved that knocketh, *saying*, Open to me, my sister, my love, my dove, my undefiled... I opened to my beloved; but my beloved had withdrawn himself, *and* was gone: my soul failed when he spake: I sought him, but I could not find him; I called him, but he gave me no answer.

Speak; for thy servant heareth.—When Jesus came to the place, he looked up, and saw him, and said unto him, Zacchaeus, make haste, and come down; for to day I must abide at thy house. And he made haste, and came down, and received him joyfully.—I will hear what God the LORD will speak: for he will speak peace unto his people, and to his saints: but let them not turn again to folly.

Jn. **10.27**; Rev. **3.20** § Song 5.2,6 § 1 Sa. 3.10; Lu. 19.5–6; Ps. 85.8

Beloved, let us love one another:
for love is of God; and every one that loveth
is born of God, and knoweth God.

The love of God is shed abroad in our hearts by the Holy Ghost which is given unto us.—Ye have not received the spirit of bondage again to fear; but ye have received the Spirit of adoption, whereby we cry, Abba, Father. The Spirit itself beareth witness with our spirit, that we are the children of God.—He that believeth on the Son of God hath the witness in himself.

In this was manifested the love of God toward us, because that God sent his only begotten Son into the world, that we might live through him.—In whom we have redemption through his blood, the forgiveness of sins, according to the riches of his grace.—That in the ages to come he might shew the exceeding riches of his grace in *his* kindness toward us through Christ Jesus.

Beloved, if God so loved us, we ought also to love one another.

---

1 Jn. 4.7; Ro. 5.5; Ro. 8.15–16; 1 Jn. 5.10 § 1 Jn. 4.9;
Eph. 1.7; Eph. 2.7 § 1 Jn. 4.11

Reproach hath broken my heart.

Is not this the carpenter's son?—Can there any good thing come out of Nazareth?—Say we not well that thou art a Samaritan, and hast a devil?—He casteth out devils through the prince of the devils.—We know that this man is a sinner.—He deceiveth the people.—This *man* blasphemeth.—Behold a man gluttonous, and a winebibber, a friend of publicans and sinners.

It is enough for the disciple that he be as his master, and the servant as his lord.—This *is* thankworthy, if a man for conscience toward God endure grief, suffering wrongfully... For even hereunto were ye called: because Christ also suffered for us, leaving us an example, that ye should follow his steps: who did no sin, neither was guile found in his mouth: who, when he was reviled, reviled not again; when he suffered, he threatened not; but committed *himself* to him that judgeth righteously.—If ye be reproached for the name of Christ, happy *are ye.*

Ps. 69.20; Mt. 13.55; Jn. 1.46; Jn. 8.48; Mt. 9.34; Jn. 9.24; Jn. 7.12; Mt. 9.3; Mt. 11.19 § Mt. 10.25; 1 Pe. 2.19,21–23; 1 Pe. 4.14

**Pray every where, lifting up holy hands,
without wrath and doubting.**

The true worshippers shall worship the Father in spirit and in truth: for the Father seeketh such to worship him. God *is* a Spirit: and they that worship him must worship *him* in spirit and in truth.—Then shalt thou call, and the LORD shall answer; thou shalt cry, and he shall say, Here I *am.*—When ye stand praying, forgive, if ye have ought against any.

Without faith *it is* impossible to please *him:* for he that cometh to God must believe that he is, and *that* he is a rewarder of them that diligently seek him.—Let him ask in faith, nothing wavering. For he that wavereth is like a wave of the sea driven with the wind and tossed. For let not that man think that he shall receive any thing of the LORD.

If I regard iniquity in my heart, the LORD will not hear *me.*—My little children, these things write I unto you, that ye sin not. And if any man sin, we have an advocate with the Father, Jesus Christ the righteous: and he is the propitiation for our sins.

1 Tim. 2.8;   Jn. 4.23–24;   Isa. 58.9;   Mk. 11.25
§ He. 11.6;   Jas. 1.6–7   § Ps. 66.18;   1 Jn. 2.1–2

My heart panteth,
my strength faileth me.

Hear my cry, O God; attend unto my prayer. From the end of the earth will I cry unto thee, when my heart is overwhelmed: lead me to the rock *that* is higher than I.

He said unto me, My grace is sufficient for thee: for my strength is made perfect in weakness. Most gladly therefore will I rather glory in my infirmities, that the power of Christ may rest upon me...for when I am weak, then am I strong.

When [Peter] saw the wind boisterous, he was afraid; and beginning to sink, he cried, saying, Lord, save me. And immediately Jesus stretched forth *his* hand, and caught him, and said unto him, O thou of little faith, wherefore didst thou doubt?—*If* thou faint in the day of adversity, thy strength *is* small.—He giveth power to the faint; and to *them that have* no might he increaseth strength.—The eternal God *is thy* refuge, and underneath *are* the everlasting arms.—Strengthened with all might, according to his glorious power.

Ps. 38.10; Ps. 61.1–2 § 2 Co. 12.9,10 § Mt. 14.30–31;
Pro. 24.10; Isa. 40.29; Deu. 33.27; Col. 1.11

The fellowship of his sufferings.

It is enough for the disciple that he be as his master, and the servant as his lord.

He is despised and rejected of men; a man of sorrows, and acquainted with grief: and we hid as it were *our* faces from him; he was despised, and we esteemed him not.—In the world ye shall have tribulation.—Because ye are not of the world, but I have chosen you out of the world, therefore the world hateth you.

I looked *for some* to take pity, but *there was* none.—At my first answer no man stood with me, but all *men* forsook me.

The foxes have holes, and the birds of the air *have* nests; but the Son of man hath not where to lay *his* head.—Here have we no continuing city, but we seek one to come.

Let us run with patience the race that is set before us, looking unto Jesus the author and finisher of *our* faith; who for the joy that was set before him endured the cross, despising the shame, and is set down at the right hand of the throne of God.

Phil. 3.10; Mt. 10.25 § Isa. 53.3; Jn. 16.33; Jn. 15.19 § Ps. 69.20; 2 Tim. 4.16 § Mt. 8.20; He. 13.14 § He. 12.1–2

They overcame...
by the blood of the Lamb.

Who shall lay any thing to the charge of God's elect? *It is* God that justifieth. Who *is* he that condemneth? *It is* Christ that died.—It *is* the blood *that* maketh an atonement for the soul.—I *am* the LORD. And the blood shall be to you for a token upon the houses where ye *are:* and when I see the blood, I will pass over you.

*There is...*no condemnation to them which are in Christ Jesus.

What are these which are arrayed in white robes? and whence came they?... These are they which came out of great tribulation, and have washed their robes, and made them white in the blood of the Lamb.

Unto him that loved us, and washed us from our sins in his own blood, and hath made us kings and priests unto God and his Father; to him *be* glory and dominion for ever and ever. Amen.

Rev. 12.11; Ro. 8.33–34; Lev. 17.11; Ex. 12.12–13
§ Ro. 8.1 § Rev. 7.13,14 § Rev. 1.5–6

God shall wipe away all tears…
there shall be no more death, neither sorrow…
for the former things are passed away.

He will swallow up death in victory; and the Lord GOD will wipe away tears from off all faces; and the rebuke of his people shall he take away from off all the earth: for the LORD hath spoken *it.*—Thy sun shall no more go down; neither shall thy moon withdraw itself: for the LORD shall be thine everlasting light, and the days of thy mourning shall be ended.—The inhabitant shall not say, I am sick: the people that dwell therein *shall be* forgiven *their* iniquity.—The voice of weeping shall be no more heard in her, nor the voice of crying.—Sorrow and sighing shall flee away.

I will ransom them from the power of the grave; I will redeem them from death: O death, I will be thy plagues; O grave, I will be thy destruction.—The last enemy *that* shall be destroyed *is* death… Then shall be brought to pass the saying that is written, Death is swallowed up in victory.

The things which are not seen *are* eternal.

Rev. 21.4; Isa. 25.8; Isa. 60.20; Isa. 33.24; Isa. 65.19;
Isa. 35.10 § Hos. 13.14; 1 Co. 15.26,54 § 2 Co. 4.18

Together in heavenly *places*
in Christ Jesus.

Fear not… I *am* he that liveth.—Father, I will that they also, whom thou hast given me, be with me where I am.

We are members of his body, of his flesh, and of his bones.—He is the head of the body, the church: who is the beginning, the firstborn from the dead.—Ye are complete in him, which is the head.

Forasmuch…as the children are partakers of flesh and blood, he also himself likewise took part of the same; that through death he might destroy him that had the power of death, that is, the devil; and deliver them who through fear of death were all their lifetime subject to bondage.

This corruptible must put on incorruption, and this mortal *must* put on immortality. So when this corruptible shall have put on incorruption, and this mortal shall have put on immortality, then shall be brought to pass the saying that is written, Death is swallowed up in victory.

Eph. 2.6; Rev. 1.17,18; Jn. 17.24 § Eph. 5.30; Col. 1.18; Col. 2.10 § He. 2.14–15 § 1 Co. 15.53–54

A servant of Jesus Christ.

Ye call me Master and Lord: and ye say well; for *so* I am.—If any man serve me, let him follow me; and where I am, there shall also my servant be: if any man serve me, him will *my* Father honour.—Take my yoke upon you, and learn of me; for I am meek and lowly in heart: and ye shall find rest unto your souls. For my yoke *is* easy, and my burden is light.

What things were gain to me, those I counted loss for Christ.—Being made free from sin, and become servants to God, ye have your fruit unto holiness, and the end everlasting life.

Henceforth I call you not servants; for the servant knoweth not what his lord doeth: but I have called you friends; for all things that I have heard of my Father I have made known unto you.—Thou art no more a servant, but a son.

Stand fast therefore in the liberty wherewith Christ hath made us free, and be not entangled again with the yoke of bondage... For, brethren, ye have been called unto liberty; only *use* not liberty for an occasion to the flesh.

Ro. 1.1; Jn. 13.13; Jn. 12.26; Mt. 11.29–30 § Phil. 3.7; Ro. 6.22 § Jn. 15.15; Ga. 4.7 § Ga. 5.1,13

I will bless the LORD,
who hath given me counsel.

His name shall be called Wonderful, Counsellor.—Counsel *is* mine, and sound wisdom: I *am* understanding; I have strength.—Thy word *is* a lamp unto my feet, and a light unto my path.—Trust in the LORD with all thine heart; and lean not unto thine own understanding. In all thy ways acknowledge him, and he shall direct thy paths.

O LORD, I know that the way of man *is* not in himself: *it is* not in man that walketh to direct his steps.—Thine ears shall hear a word behind thee, saying, This *is* the way, walk ye in it, when ye turn to the right hand, and when ye turn to the left.—Commit thy works unto the LORD, and thy thoughts shall be established.—He knoweth the way that I take.—Man's goings *are* of the LORD; how can a man then understand his own way?

Thou shalt guide me with thy counsel, and afterward receive me *to* glory.—This God *is* our God for ever and ever: he will be our guide *even* unto death.

Ps. 16.7; Isa. 9.6; Pro. 8.14; Ps. 119.105; Pro. 3.5–6
§ Jer. 10.23; Isa. 30.21; Pro. 16.3; Job 23.10; Pro. 20.24
§ Ps. 73.24; Ps. 48.14

**I *am* the LORD your God; walk in my statutes,
and keep my judgments, and do them.**

As he which hath called you is holy, so be ye holy in all manner of conversation.—He that saith he abideth in him ought himself also so to walk, even as he walked… If ye know that he is righteous, ye know that every one that doeth righteousness is born of him.—Circumcision is nothing, and uncircumcision is nothing, but the keeping of the commandments of God.—Whosoever shall keep the whole law, and yet offend in one *point*, he is guilty of all.

Not that we are sufficient of ourselves to think any thing as of ourselves; but our sufficiency *is* of God.— Teach me, O LORD, the way of thy statutes.

Work out your own salvation with fear and trembling. For it is God which worketh in you both to will and to do of *his* good pleasure.—The God of peace…make you perfect in every good work to do his will, working in you that which is wellpleasing in his sight, through Jesus Christ.

Ezek. 20.19;   1 Pe. 1.15;   1 Jn. 2.6,29;   1 Co. 7.19;
Jas. 2.10 § 2 Co. 3.5;   Ps. 119.33 § Phil. 2.12–13;
He. 13.20,21

I have exalted *one*
chosen out of the people.

Verily he took not on *him the nature of* angels; but he took on *him* the seed of Abraham... In all things it behoved him to be made like unto *his* brethren.—Upon the likeness of the throne *was* the likeness as the appearance of a man above upon it.—The Son of man which is in heaven.—Behold my hands and my feet, that it is I myself: handle me, and see; for a spirit hath not flesh and bones, as ye see me have.

Who...made himself of no reputation, and took upon him the form of a servant, and was made in the likeness of men: and being found in fashion as a man, he humbled himself, and became obedient unto death, even the death of the cross. Wherefore God also hath highly exalted him, and given him a name which is above every name: that at the name of Jesus every knee should bow.—Be watchful, and strengthen the things which remain, that are ready to die: for I have not found thy works perfect before God.

Ps. 89.19; He. 2.16,17; Ezek. 1.26; Jn. 3.13; Lu. 24.39
§ Phil. 2.6–10; Rev. 3.2

As the Father hath life in himself;
so hath he given to the Son to have life in himself.

Our Saviour Jesus Christ...hath abolished death, and hath brought life and immortality to light through the gospel.—I am the resurrection, and the life.—Because I live, ye shall live also.—We are made partakers of Christ.—Partakers of the Holy Ghost.—Partakers of the divine nature.—The first man Adam was made a living soul; the last Adam *was made* a quickening spirit.—Behold, I shew you a mystery; We shall not all sleep, but we shall all be changed, in a moment, in the twinkling of an eye, at the last trump: for the trumpet shall sound, and the dead shall be raised incorruptible, and we shall be changed.

Holy, holy, holy, Lord God Almighty, which was, and is, and is to come.—Who liveth for ever and ever.—The blessed and only Potentate, the King of kings, and Lord of lords; who only hath immortality.—Unto the King eternal, immortal...*be* honour and glory for ever and ever. Amen.

Jn. 5.26; 2 Tim. 1.10; Jn. 11.25; Jn. 14.19; He. 3.14;
He. 6.4; 2 Pe. 1.4; 1 Co. 15.45; 1 Co. 15.51–52
§ Rev. 4.8; Rev. 4.9; 1 Tim. 6.15–16; 1 Tim. 1.17

Let us not be desirous of vain glory.

Gideon said unto them, I would desire a request of you, that ye would give me every man the earrings of his prey. (For they had golden earrings, because they *were* Ishmaelites.) And they answered, We will willingly give *them*. And they spread a garment, and did cast therein every man the earrings of his prey… And Gideon made an ephod thereof, and put it in his city, *even* in Ophrah: and all Israel went thither a whoring after it: which thing became a snare unto Gideon, and to his house.

Seekest thou great things for thyself? seek *them* not.—Lest I should be exalted above measure through the abundance of the revelations, there was given to me a thorn in the flesh.

Let nothing *be done*, through strife or vainglory; but in lowliness of mind let each esteem other better than themselves.—Charity envieth not; charity vaunteth not itself, is not puffed up, doth not behave itself unseemly, seeketh not her own.

Take my yoke upon you, and learn of me.

Ga. 5.26; Judg. 8.24–25,27 § Jer. 45.5; 2 Co. 12.7
§ Phil. 2.3; 1 Co. 13.4–5 § Mt. 11.29

Wash me throughly from mine iniquity.

I will cleanse them from all their iniquity, whereby they have sinned against me; and I will pardon all their iniquities, whereby they have sinned, and whereby they have transgressed against me.—Then will I sprinkle clean water upon you, and ye shall be clean: from all your filthiness, and from all your idols, will I cleanse you.

Except a man be born of water and *of* the Spirit, he cannot enter into the kingdom of God.—If the blood of bulls and of goats, and the ashes of an heifer sprinkling the unclean, sanctifieth to the purifying of the flesh: how much more shall the blood of Christ, who through the eternal Spirit offered himself without spot to God, purge your conscience from dead works to serve the living God?

He saved them for his name's sake, that he might make his mighty power to be known.—Not unto us, O LORD, not unto us, but unto thy name give glory, for thy mercy, *and* for thy truth's sake.

Ps. 51.2; Jer. 33.8; Ezek. 36.25 § Jn. 3.5; He. 9.13–14 § Ps. 106.8; Ps. 115.1

Fellowship in the gospel.

As the body is one, and hath many members, and all the members of that one body, being many, are one body: so also *is* Christ. For by one Spirit are we all baptized into one body, whether *we be* Jews or Gentiles, whether *we be* bond or free; and have been all made to drink into one Spirit.

God *is* faithful, by whom ye were called unto the fellowship of his Son Jesus Christ our Lord.—That which we have seen and heard declare we unto you, that ye also may have fellowship with us: and truly our fellowship *is* with the Father, and with his Son Jesus Christ.

If we walk in the light, as he is in the light, we have fellowship one with another, and the blood of Jesus Christ his Son cleanseth us from all sin.—These words spake Jesus... Neither pray I for these alone, but for them also which shall believe on me through their word; that they all may be one; as thou, Father, *art* in me, and I in thee, that they also may be one in us.

Phil. 1.5; 1 Co. 12.12–13 § 1 Co. 1.9; 1 Jn. 1.3 § 1 Jn. 1.7; Jn. 17.1,20–21

Take heed unto thyself.

Every man that striveth for the mastery is temperate in all things. Now they *do it* to obtain a corruptible crown; but we an incorruptible. I therefore so run, not as uncertainly; so fight I, not as one that beateth the air: but I keep under my body, and bring *it* into subjection: lest that by any means, when I have preached to others, I myself should be a castaway.—Put on the whole armour of God, that ye may be able to stand against the wiles of the devil. For we wrestle not against flesh and blood, but against principalities, against powers, against the rulers of the darkness of this world, against spiritual wickedness in high *places*.

They that are Christ's have crucified the flesh with the affections and lusts. If we live in the Spirit, let us also walk in the Spirit.—For as many as are led by the Spirit of God, they are the sons of God.—Meditate upon these things; give thyself wholly to them; that thy profiting may appear to all.

1 Tim. 4.16; 1 Co. 9.25–27; Eph. 6.11–12
§ Ga. 5.24–25; Ro. 8.14; 1 Tim. 4.15

Jesus saith unto her, Mary.

Fear not: for I have redeemed thee, I have called *thee* by thy name; thou *art* mine.—The sheep hear his voice: and he calleth his own sheep by name...and the sheep follow him: for they know his voice.

Behold, I have graven thee upon the palms of *my* hands; thy walls *are* continually before me.

The foundation of God standeth sure, having this seal, The Lord knoweth them that are his.—We have a great high priest, that is passed into the heavens, Jesus the Son of God.

Thou shalt take two onyx stones, and grave on them the names of the children of Israel... And Aaron shall bear their names before the LORD upon his two shoulders for a memorial... And thou shalt make the breastplate of judgment... And thou shalt set in it settings of stones... And the stones shall be with the names of the children of Israel... And Aaron shall bear the names of the children of Israel in the breastplate of judgment upon his heart, when he goeth in unto the holy *place*, for a memorial before the LORD continually.

Jn. 20.16; Isa. 43.1; Jn. 10.3,4 § Isa. 49.16
§ 2 Tim. 2.19; He. 4.14 § Ex. 28.9,12,15,17,21,29

**My brethren, be strong in the Lord,
and in the power of his might.**

My grace is sufficient for thee: for my strength is made perfect in weakness. Most gladly therefore will I rather glory in my infirmities, that the power of Christ may rest upon me. Therefore I take pleasure in infirmities, in reproaches, in necessities, in persecutions, in distresses for Christ's sake: for when I am weak, then am I strong.—I will go in the strength of the Lord GOD: I will make mention of thy righteousness, *even* of thine only.—The gospel of Christ…is the power of God unto salvation.

I can do all things through Christ which strengtheneth me.—I also labour, striving according to his working, which worketh in me mightily.—We have this treasure in earthen vessels, that the excellency of the power may be of God, and not of us.

The joy of the LORD is your strength.—Strengthened with all might, according to his glorious power, unto all patience and longsuffering with joyfulness.

Eph. 6.10; 2 Co. 12.9–10; Ps. 71.16; Ro. 1.16
§ Phil. 4.13; Col. 1.29; 2 Co. 4.7 § Ne. 8.10; Col. 1.11

Jesus Christ our Lord.

JESUS: for he shall save his people from their sins.—He humbled himself, and became obedient unto death, even the death of the cross. Wherefore God also hath highly exalted him, and given him a name which is above every name: that at the name of Jesus every knee should bow, of *things* in heaven, and *things* in earth, and *things* under the earth.

Messias...which is called Christ.—The LORD hath anointed me to preach good tidings unto the meek; he hath sent me to bind up the brokenhearted, to proclaim liberty to the captives.

The last Adam *was made* a quickening spirit... The second man *is* the Lord from heaven.—My Lord and my God.—Ye call me Master and Lord: and ye say well; for *so* I am. If I then, *your* Lord and Master, have washed your feet; ye also ought to wash one another's feet. For I have given you an example, that ye should do as I have done to you.

1 Co. 1.9; Mt. 1.21; Phil. 2.8–10 § Jn. 4.25; Isa. 61.1 § 1 Co. 15.45,47; Jn. 20.28; Jn. 13.13–15

**Peace I leave with you, my peace I give unto you:
not as the world giveth, give I unto you.**

The world passeth away, and the lust thereof.—Surely
every man walketh in a vain shew: surely they are disquieted in vain: he heapeth up *riches*, and knoweth not
who shall gather them.—What fruit had ye then in
those things whereof ye are now ashamed? for the end
of those things *is* death.

Martha, Martha, thou are careful and troubled about
many things: but one thing is needful: and Mary hath
chosen that good part, which shall not be taken away
from her.—I would have you without carefulness.

These things I have spoken unto you, that in me ye
might have peace. In the world ye shall have tribulation:
but be of good cheer; I have overcome the world.—The
Lord of peace himself give you peace always by all
means.—The LORD bless thee, and keep thee: the LORD
make his face shine upon thee, and be gracious unto
thee: the LORD lift up his countenance upon thee, and
give thee peace.

Jn. 14.27; 1 Jn. 2.17; Ps. 39.6; Ro. 6.21 § Lu. 10.41–42;
1 Co. 7.32 § Jn. 16.33; 2 Th. 3.16; Nu. 6.24–26

The Spirit also helpeth our infirmities.

The Comforter, *which is* the Holy Ghost.—What? know ye not that your body is the temple of the Holy Ghost *which is* in you, which ye have of God?—It is God which worketh in you.

We know not what we should pray for as we ought: but the Spirit itself maketh intercession for us with groanings which cannot be uttered. And he that searcheth the hearts knoweth what *is* the mind of the Spirit, because he maketh intercession for the saints according to *the will of* God.

He knoweth our frame; he remembereth that we *are* dust.—A bruised reed shall he not break, and the smoking flax shall he not quench.

The spirit indeed *is* willing, but the flesh *is* weak.

The LORD *is* my shepherd; I shall not want. He maketh me to lie down in green pastures: he leadeth me beside the still waters.

Ro. 8.26; Jn. 14.26; 1 Co. 6.19; Phil. 2.13
§ Ro. 8.26–27 § Ps. 103.14; Isa. 42.3 § Mt. 26.41
§ Ps. 23.1–2

Thou shalt put the two stones upon
the shoulders of the ephod *for* stones of
memorial unto the children of Israel: and Aaron
shall bear their names before the LORD.

 B ut this *man*, because he continueth ever, hath an unchangeable priesthood. Wherefore he is able also to save them to the uttermost that come unto God by him, seeing he ever liveth to make intercession for them.— Now unto him that is able to keep you from falling, and to present *you* faultless before the presence of his glory with exceeding joy, to the only wise God our Saviour, *be* glory and majesty, dominion and power, both now and ever. Amen.

Seeing…that we have a great high priest, that is passed into the heavens, Jesus the Son of God, let us hold fast *our* profession. For we have not an high priest which cannot be touched with the feeling of our infirmities; but was in all points tempted like as *we are, yet* without sin. Let us therefore come boldly unto the throne of grace.

The beloved of the LORD shall dwell in safety by him; *and the LORD* shall cover him all the day long, and he shall dwell between his shoulders.

Ex. 28.12; He. 7.24–25; Jude 24 § He. 4.14–16
§ Deu. 33.12

On that night could not the king sleep.

Thou holdest mine eyes waking.—Who *is* like unto the LORD our God…who humbleth *himself* to behold *the things that are* in heaven, and in the earth!

He doeth according to his will in the army of heaven, and *among* the inhabitants of the earth.—Thy way *is* in the sea, and thy path in the great waters, and thy footsteps are not known.—Surely the wrath of man shall praise thee: the remainder of wrath shalt thou restrain.

The eyes of the LORD run to and fro throughout the whole earth, to shew himself strong in the behalf of *them* whose heart *is* perfect toward him.—We know that all things work together for good to them that love God.

Are not two sparrows sold for a farthing? and one of them shall not fall on the ground without your Father. But the very hairs of your head are all numbered.

Est. 6.1; Ps. 77.4; Ps. 113.5,6 § Dan. 4.35; Ps. 77.19; Ps. 76.10 § 2 Chr. 16.9; Ro. 8.28 § Mt. 10.29–30

Grieve not the holy Spirit of God, whereby ye are sealed unto the day of redemption.

The love of the Spirit.—The Comforter, *which is* the Holy Ghost.—In all their affliction he was afflicted, and the angel of his presence saved them: in his love and in his pity he redeemed them; and he bare them, and carried them all the days of old. But they rebelled, and vexed his holy Spirit: therefore he was turned to be their enemy, *and* he fought against them.

Hereby know we that we dwell in him, and he in us, because he hath given us of his Spirit.—After that ye believed, ye were sealed with that holy Spirit of promise, which is the earnest of our inheritance until the redemption of the purchased possession.—*This* I say then, Walk in the Spirit, and ye shall not fulfil the lust of the flesh. For the flesh lusteth against the Spirit, and the Spirit against the flesh: and these are contrary the one to the other: so that ye cannot do the things that ye would.

The Spirit also helpeth our infirmities.

Eph. 4.30; Ro. 15.30; Jn. 14.26; Isa. 63.9–10
§ 1 Jn. 4.13; Eph. 1.13–14; Ga. 5.16–17 § Ro. 8.26

I will go *and* return to my place, till they acknowledge their offence, and seek my face.

Your iniquities have separated between you and your God, and your sins have hid *his* face from you.—My beloved had withdrawn himself, *and* was gone... I sought him, but I could not find him; I called him, but he gave me no answer.—I hid me, and was wroth, and he went on frowardly in the way of his heart. I have seen his ways, and will heal him.—Hast thou not procured this unto thyself, in that thou hast forsaken the LORD thy God, when he led thee by the way?

He arose, and came to his father. But when he was yet a great way off, his father saw him, and had compassion, and ran, and fell on his neck, and kissed him.—I will heal their backsliding, I will love them freely: for mine anger is turned away.

If we confess our sins, he is faithful and just to forgive us *our* sins, and to cleanse us from all unrighteousness.

Hos. 5.15; Isa. 59.2; Song 5.6; Isa. 57.17–18; Jer. 2.17 § Lu. 15.20; Hos. 14.4 § 1 Jn. 1.9

Oh how great *is* thy goodness, which thou hast laid up
for them that fear thee; *which* thou hast wrought for
them that trust in thee before the sons of men!

Since the beginning of the world *men* have not heard,
nor perceived by the ear, neither hath the eye seen, O
God, beside thee, *what* he hath prepared for him that
waiteth for him.—Eye hath not seen, nor ear heard, neither have entered into the heart of man, the things
which God hath prepared for them that love him. But
God hath revealed *them* unto us by his Spirit.—Thou
wilt shew me the path of life: in thy presence *is* fulness
of joy; at thy right hand *there are* pleasures for evermore.

How excellent *is* thy lovingkindness, O God! therefore the children of men put their trust under the
shadow of thy wings. They shall be abundantly satisfied
with the fatness of thy house; and thou shalt make them
drink of the river of thy pleasures. For with thee *is* the
fountain of life: in thy light shall we see light.

Godliness is profitable unto all things, having promise of the life that now is, and of that which is to come.

Ps. 31.19; Isa. 64.4; 1 Co. 2.9–10; Ps. 16.11
§ Ps. 36.7–9 § 1 Tim. 4.8

The Son of God...
hath his eyes like unto a flame of fire.

The heart *is* deceitful above all *things*, and desperately wicked: who can know it? I the LORD search the heart, *I* try the reins, even to give every man according to his ways, *and* according to the fruit of his doings.—Thou hast set our iniquities before thee, our secret *sins* in the light of thy countenance.—The Lord turned, and looked upon Peter... And Peter went out, and wept bitterly.

Jesus did not commit himself unto them, because he knew all *men*, and needed not that any should testify of man: for he knew what was in man.—He knoweth our frame; he remembereth that we *are* dust.—A bruised reed shall he not break, and the smoking flax shall he not quench.

The Lord knoweth them that are his.—I am the good shepherd, and know my *sheep*... My sheep hear my voice, and I know them, and they follow me: and I give unto them eternal life; and they shall never perish, neither shall any *man* pluck them out of my hand.

Rev. 2.18; Jer. 17.9–10; Ps. 90.8; Lu. 22.61,62 § Jn. 2.24–25; Ps. 103.14; Isa. 42.3 § 2 Tim. 2.19; Jn. 10.14,27–28

Our Lord Jesus,
that great shepherd of the sheep.

The chief Shepherd.—I am the good shepherd, and know my *sheep*, and am known of mine... My sheep hear my voice, and I know them, and they follow me: and I give unto them eternal life; and they shall never perish, neither shall any *man* pluck them out of my hand.

The LORD *is* my shepherd; I shall not want. He maketh me to lie down in green pastures: he leadeth me beside the still waters. He restoreth my soul: he leadeth me in the paths of righteousness for his name's sake.

All we like sheep have gone astray; we have turned every one to his own way; and the LORD hath laid on him the iniquity us all.—I am the good shepherd: the good shepherd giveth his life for the sheep.—I will seek that which was lost, and bring again that which was driven away, and will bind up *that which was* broken, and will strengthen that which was sick.—Ye were as sheep going astray; but are now returned unto the Shepherd and Bishop of your souls.

He. 13.20; 1 Pe. 5.4; Jn. 10.14,27–28 § Ps. 23.1–3
§ Isa. 53.6; Jn. 10.11; Ezek. 34.16; 1 Pe. 2.25

**The city had no need of the sun, neither of the moon,
to shine in it: for the glory of God did lighten it,
and the Lamb *is* the light thereof.**

I saw in the way a light from heaven, above the brightness of the sun, shining round about me…and I said, Who art thou, Lord? And he said, I am Jesus whom thou persecutest.—Jesus taketh Peter, James, and John his brother, and bringeth them up into an high mountain apart, and was transfigured before them: and his face did shine as the sun, and his raiment was white as the light.—The sun shall be no more thy light by day; neither for brightness shall the moon give light unto thee: but the LORD shall be unto thee an everlasting light, and thy God thy glory. Thy sun shall no more go down; neither shall thy moon withdraw itself: for the LORD shall be thine everlasting light, and the days of thy mourning shall be ended.

The God of all grace…hath called us unto his eternal glory by Christ Jesus.

Rev. 21.23; Ac. 26.13,15; Mt. 17.1–2; Isa. 60.19–20
§ 1 Pe. 5.10

The LORD *is* good, a strong hold in the day of trouble;
and he knoweth them that trust in him.

Praise the LORD of hosts: for the LORD *is* good; for his
mercy *endureth* for ever.—God *is* our refuge and
strength, a very present help in trouble.—I will say of
the LORD, *He is* my refuge and my fortress: my God; in
him will I trust.—Who *is* like unto thee, O people saved
by the LORD, the shield of thy help, and who *is* the sword
of thy excellency!—*As for* God, his way *is* perfect; the
word of the LORD *is* tried: he is a buckler to all them that
trust in him. For who *is* God, save the LORD? and who *is*
a rock, save our God?

If any man love God, the same is known of him.—
The foundation of God standeth sure, having this seal,
The Lord knoweth them that are his. And, Let every one
that nameth the name of Christ depart from iniquity.—
The LORD knoweth the way of the righteous: but the
way of the ungodly shall perish.—Thou hast found
grace in my sight, and I know thee by name.

Na. 1.7; Jer. 33.11; Ps. 46.1; Ps. 91.2; Deu. 33.29;
2 Sa. 22.31–32 § 1 Co. 8.3; 2 Tim. 2.19; Ps. 1.6;
Ex. 33.17

I would have you without carefulness.

He careth for you.—The eyes of the LORD run to and fro throughout the whole earth, to shew himself strong in the behalf of *them* whose heart *is* perfect toward him.

O taste and see that the LORD *is* good: blessed *is* the man *that* trusteth in him… The young lions do lack, and suffer hunger: but they that seek the LORD shall not want any good *thing.*—Therefore I say unto you, Take no thought for your life, what ye shall eat, or what ye shall drink; nor yet for your body, what ye shall put on. Is not the life more than meat, and the body than raiment? Behold the fowls of the air: for they sow not, neither do they reap, nor gather into barns; yet your heavenly Father feedeth them. Are ye not much better than they?—Be careful for nothing; but in every thing by prayer and supplication with thanksgiving let your requests be made known unto God. And the peace of God, which passeth all understanding, shall keep your hearts and minds through Christ Jesus.

1 Co. 7.32; 1 Pe. 5.7; 2 Chr. 16.9 § Ps. 34.8,10; Mt. 6.25–26; Phil. 4.6–7

We look for the Saviour.

The grace of God that bringeth salvation hath appeared to all men, teaching us that, denying ungodliness and worldly lusts, we should live soberly, righteously, and godly, in this present world; looking for that blessed hope, and the glorious appearing of the great God and our Saviour Jesus Christ; who gave himself for us, that he might redeem us from all iniquity, and purify unto himself a peculiar people, zealous of good works.—We, according to his promise, look for new heavens and a new earth, wherein dwelleth righteousness. Wherefore, beloved, seeing that ye look for such things, be diligent that ye may be found of him in peace, without spot, and blameless.

Christ was once offered to bear the sins of many; and unto them that look for him shall he appear the second time without sin unto salvation.—And it shall be said in that day, Lo, this *is* our God; we have waited for him, and he will save us: this *is* the LORD; we have waited for him, we will be glad and rejoice in his salvation.

Phil. 3.20; Titus 2.11–14; 2 Pe. 3.13–14 § He. 9.28; Isa. 25.9

So run, that ye may obtain.

The slothful *man* saith, *There is* a lion without.—Let us lay aside every weight, and the sin which doth so easily beset *us*, and let us run with patience the race that is set before us, looking unto Jesus the author and finisher of *our* faith.

Let us cleanse ourselves from all filthiness of the flesh and spirit, perfecting holiness in the fear of God.

I press toward the mark.—I…so run, not as uncertainly… I keep under my body, and bring *it* into subjection: lest that by any means…I myself should be a castaway.

The fashion of this world passeth away.

Nevertheless we, according to his promise, look for new heavens and a new earth, wherein dwelleth righteousness. Wherefore, beloved, seeing that ye look for such things, be diligent.—Gird up the loins of your mind, be sober, and hope to the end for the grace that is to be brought unto you at the revelation of Jesus Christ.

1 Co. 9.24; Pro. 22.13; He. 12.1–2 § 2 Co. 7.1
§ Phil. 3.14; 1 Co. 9.26,27 § 1 Co. 7.31 § 2 Pe. 3.13–14;
1 Pe. 1.13

The life of the flesh *is* in the blood:
and I have given it to you upon the altar to make
an atonement for your souls: for it *is* the blood
that maketh an atonement for the soul.

Behold the Lamb of God, which taketh away the sin of the world.—The blood of the Lamb.—The precious blood of Christ, as of a lamb without blemish and without spot.—Without shedding of blood is no remission.—The blood of Jesus Christ his Son cleanseth us from all sin.

By his own blood he entered in once into the holy place, having obtained eternal redemption *for us.*—Having therefore, brethren, boldness to enter into the holiest by the blood of Jesus, by a new and living way, which he hath consecrated for us, through the veil, that is to say, his flesh… Let us draw near with a true heart in full assurance of faith.

Ye are bought with a price: therefore glorify God in your body, and in your spirit, which are God's.

Lev. 17.11; Jn. 1.29; Rev. 7.14; 1 Pe. 1.19; He. 9.22;
1 Jn. 1.7 § He. 9.12; He. 10.19–20,22 § 1 Co. 6.20

Oh that I had wings like a dove!
for then **would I fly away, and be at rest.**

It came to pass, when the sun did arise, that God pre-pared a vehement east wind; and the sun beat upon the head of Jonah, that he fainted, and wished in himself to die, and said, *It is* better for me to die than to live.

Job spake, and said... Wherefore is light given to him that is in misery, and life unto the bitter *in* soul; which long for death, but it *cometh* not; and dig for it more than for hid treasures?—Many *are* the afflictions of the righteous: but the LORD delivereth him out of them all.

Now is my soul troubled; and what shall I say? Father, save me from this hour.—In all things it behoved him to be made like unto *his* brethren, that he might be a merciful and faithful high priest in things *pertaining* to God, to make reconciliation for the sins of the people. For in that he himself hath suffered being tempted, he is able to succour them that are tempted.

Ps. 55.6; Jon. 4.8 § Job 3.2,20–21; Ps. 34.19
§ Jn. 12.27; He. 2.17–18

Let us labour therefore to enter into that rest.

Enter ye in at the strait gate: for wide *is* the gate, and broad *is* the way, that leadeth to destruction…strait *is* the gate, and narrow *is* the way, which leadeth unto life, and few there be that find it.—The kingdom of heaven suffereth violence, and the violent take it by force.— Labour not for the meat which perisheth, but for that meat which endureth unto everlasting life, which the Son of man shall give unto you.—Give diligence to make your calling and election sure…for so an entrance shall be ministered unto you abundantly into the ever-lasting kingdom of our Lord and Saviour Jesus Christ.—So run, that ye may obtain. And every man that striveth for the mastery is temperate in all things. Now they *do it* to obtain a corruptible crown; but we an incorruptible.

For he that is entered into his rest, he also hath ceased from his own works, as God *did* from his.—The LORD shall be unto thee an everlasting light, and thy God thy glory.

He. 4.11; Mt. 7.13,14; Mt. 11.12; Jn. 6.27;
2 Pe. 1.10,11; 1 Co. 9.24–25 § He. 4.10; Isa. 60.19

Thou hearest me always.

Jesus lifted up *his* eyes, and said, Father, I thank thee that thou hast heard me.—Father, glorify thy name. Then came there a voice from heaven, *saying*, I have both glorified *it*, and will glorify *it* again.—Lo, I come...to do thy will, O God.—Not my will, but thine, be done.

As he is, so are we in this world.—This is the confidence that we have in him, that, if we ask any thing according to his will, he heareth us.

Whatsoever we ask, we receive of him, because we keep his commandments, and do those things that are pleasing in his sight.

Without faith *it is* impossible to please *him*: for he that cometh to God must believe that he is, and *that* he is a rewarder of them that diligently seek him.

He ever liveth to make intercession for them.—We have an advocate with the Father, Jesus Christ the righteous.

Jn. 11.42; Jn. 11.41; Jn. 12.28; He. 10.7; Lu. 22.42
§ 1 Jn. 4.17; 1 Jn. 5.14 § 1 Jn. 3.22 § He. 11.6
§ He. 7.25; 1 Jn. 2.1

Thy name shall be called...Israel:
for as a prince hast thou power with God
and with men, and hast prevailed.

By his strength he had power with God: yea, he had power over the angel, and prevailed: he wept, and made supplication unto him.—He staggered not at the promise of God through unbelief; but was strong in faith, giving glory to God.

Have faith in God. For verily I say unto you, That whosoever shall say unto this mountain, Be thou removed, and be thou cast into the sea; and shall not doubt in his heart, but shall believe that those things which he saith shall come to pass; he shall have whatsoever he saith. Therefore I say unto you, What things soever ye desire, when ye pray, believe that ye receive *them*, and ye shall have *them*.—If thou canst believe, all things *are* possible to him that believeth.—Blessed *is* she that believed: for there shall be a performance of those things which were told her from the Lord.

Lord, Increase our faith.

Ge. 32.28; Hos. 12.3,4; Ro. 4.20 § Mk. 11.22–24;
Mk. 9.23; Lu. 1.45 § Lu. 17.5

Little children, abide in him.

He that wavereth is like a wave of the sea driven with the wind and tossed. For let not that man think that he shall receive any thing of the Lord. A double minded man *is* unstable in all his ways.

I marvel that ye are so soon removed from him that called you into the grace of Christ unto another gospel: which is not another...though we, or an angel from heaven, preach any other gospel unto you than that which we have preached unto you, let him be accursed.

Christ is become of no effect unto you, whosoever of you are justified by the law; ye are fallen from grace... Ye did run well; who did hinder you?

As the branch cannot bear fruit of itself, except it abide in the vine; no more can ye, except ye abide in me... If ye abide in me, and my words abide in you, ye shall ask what ye will, and it shall be done unto you.— For all the promises of God in him *are* yea, and in him Amen, unto the glory of God by us.

1 Jn. 2.28; Jas. 1.6–8 § Ga. 1.6–8 § Ga. 5.4,7
§ Jn. 15.4,7; 2 Co. 1.20

The fruit of the Spirit is…
longsuffering, gentleness…

The LORD, the LORD God, merciful and gracious, long-suffering, and abundant in goodness and truth.

Walk worthy of the vocation wherewith ye are called, with all lowliness and meekness, with longsuffering, forbearing one another in love.——Be ye kind one to another, tenderhearted, forgiving one another, even as God for Christ's sake hath forgiven you.——The wisdom that is from above is first pure, then peaceable, gentle, *and* easy to be intreated, full of mercy and good fruits, without partiality, and without hypocrisy.——Charity suffereth long, *and* is kind.

In due season we shall reap, if we faint not.——Be patient therefore, brethren, unto the coming of the Lord. Behold, the husbandman waiteth for the precious fruit of the earth, and hath long patience for it, until he receive the early and latter rain. Be ye also patient; stablish your hearts: for the coming of the Lord draweth nigh.

Ga. 5.22; Ex. 34.6 § Eph. 4.1–2; Eph. 4.32; Jas. 3.17; 1 Co. 13.4 § Ga. 6.9; Jas. 5.7–8

Emmanuel...God with us.

Will God in very deed dwell with men on the earth? behold, heaven and the heaven of heavens cannot contain thee.—The Word was made flesh, and dwelt among us, (and we beheld his glory, the glory as of the only begotten of the Father,) full of grace and truth.— Great is the mystery of godliness: God was manifest in the flesh.

God...hath in these last days spoken unto us by *his* Son, whom he hath appointed heir of all things, by whom also he made the worlds.

The first *day* of the week, when the doors were shut where the disciples were assembled...came Jesus and stood in the midst... Then were the disciples glad, when they saw the Lord... After eight days again his disciples were within, and Thomas with them... Then saith [Jesus] to Thomas, Reach hither thy finger, and behold my hands; and reach hither thy hand, and thrust *it* into my side: and be not faithless, but believing. And Thomas answered and said... My Lord and my God.—Unto us a son is given... The mighty God.

Mt. 1.23; 2 Chr. 6.18; Jn. 1.14; 1 Tim. 3.16 § He. 1.1,2 § Jn. 20.19,20,26–28; Isa. 9.6

Thus shall ye eat it;
with **your loins girded...**
and ye shall eat it in haste:
it *is* **the LORD's passover.**

Arise ye, and depart; for this *is* not *your* rest.—Here have we no continuing city, but we seek one to come.—There remaineth therefore a rest to the people of God.

Let your loins be girded about, and *your* lights burning; and ye yourselves like unto men that wait for their lord, when he will return from the wedding; that when he cometh and knocketh, they may open unto him immediately. Blessed *are* those servants, whom the lord when he cometh shall find watching.—Gird up the loins of your mind, be sober, and hope to the end for the grace that is to be brought unto you at the revelation of Jesus Christ.—*This* one thing *I do*, forgetting those things which are behind... I press toward the mark for the prize of the high calling of God in Christ Jesus. Let us therefore, as many as be perfect, be thus minded.

Ex. 12.11; Mi. 2.10; He. 13.14; He. 4.9 § Lu. 12.35–37; 1 Pe. 1.13; Phil. 3.13–15

The LORD *is* the portion
of mine inheritance and of my cup.

Heirs of God, and joint-heirs with Christ.—All things are yours.—My beloved *is* mine.—The Son of God, who loved me, and gave himself for me.

The LORD spake unto Aaron, Thou shalt have no inheritance in their land, neither shalt thou have any part among them: I *am* thy part and thine inheritance among the children of Israel.

Whom have I in heaven *but thee?* and *there is* none upon earth *that* I desire beside thee. My flesh and my heart faileth: *but* God *is* the strength of my heart, and my portion for ever.

Though I walk through the valley of the shadow of death, I will fear no evil: for thou *art* with me; thy rod and thy staff they comfort me.—I know whom I have believed, and am persuaded that he is able to keep that which I have committed unto him against that day.

O God, thou *art* my God; early will I seek thee: my soul thirsteth for thee, my flesh longeth for thee in a dry and thirsty land.

Ps. 16.5; Ro. 8.17; 1 Co. 3.21; Song 2.16; Ga. 2.20
§ Nu. 18.20 § Ps. 73.25–26 § Ps. 23.4; 2 Tim. 1.12
§ Ps. 63.1

**Watch therefore,
for ye know neither the day nor the hour
wherein the Son of man cometh.**

Take heed to yourselves, lest at any time your hearts be overcharged with surfeiting, and drunkenness, and cares of this life, and *so* that day come upon you unawares. For as a snare shall it come on all them that dwell on the face of the whole earth. Watch ye therefore, and pray always, that ye may be accounted worthy to escape all these things that shall come to pass, and to stand before the Son of man.

The day of the Lord so cometh as a thief in the night. For when they shall say, Peace and safety; then sudden destruction cometh upon them, as travail upon a woman with child; and they shall not escape. But ye, brethren, are not in darkness, that that day should overtake you as a thief. Ye are all the children of light, and the children of the day: we are not of the night, nor of darkness. Therefore let us not sleep, as *do* others; but let us watch and be sober.

Mt. 25.13; Lu. 21.34–36 § 1 Th. 5.2–6

I *am* the Almighty God;
walk before me, and be thou perfect.

Not as though I had already attained, either were already perfect... I count not myself to have apprehended: but *this* one thing *I do*, forgetting those things which are behind, and reaching forth unto those things which are before, I press toward the mark for the prize of the high calling of God in Christ Jesus.

Enoch walked with God: and he *was* not; for God took him.

Grow in grace, and *in* the knowledge of our Lord and Saviour Jesus Christ.—We all, with open face beholding as in a glass the glory of the Lord, are changed into the same image from glory to glory, *even* as by the Spirit of the Lord.

These words spake Jesus... I pray not that thou shouldest take them out of the world, but that thou shouldest keep them from the evil... I in them, and thou in me, that they may be made perfect in one.

Ge. 17.1; Phil. 3.12,13–14 § Ge. 5.24 § 2 Pe. 3.18; 2 Co. 3.18 § Jn. 17.1,15,23

The glory of this latter house shall be greater than of the former…and in this place will I give peace.

The house *that is* to be builded for the LORD *must be* exceeding magnifical, of fame and of glory throughout all countries.—The glory of the LORD…filled the LORD's house.

Destroy this temple, and in three days I will raise it up… He spake of the temple of his body.—That which was made glorious had no glory in this respect, by reason of the glory that excelleth.—The Word was made flesh, and dwelt among us, (and we beheld his glory, the glory as of the only begotten of the Father,) full of grace and truth.—God…hath in these last days spoken unto us by *his* Son, whom he hath appointed heir of all things, by whom also he made the worlds.

Glory to God in the highest, and on earth peace, good will toward men.—The Prince of Peace.—He is our peace.—The peace of God, which passeth all understanding, shall keep your hearts and minds through Christ Jesus.

Hag. 2.9; 1 Chr. 22.5; 2 Chr. 7.2 § Jn. 2.19,21;
2 Co. 3.10; Jn. 1.14; He. 1.1,2 § Lu. 2.14; Isa. 9.6;
Eph. 2.14; Phil. 4.7

Let us put on
the armour of light.

Put...on the Lord Jesus Christ.—That I may win Christ, and be found in him, not having mine own righteousness, which is of the law, but that which is through the faith of Christ, the righteousness which is of God by faith.—The righteousness of God *which is* by faith of Jesus Christ unto all and upon all them that believe.

He hath covered me with the robe of righteousness.—I will go in the strength of the Lord GOD: I will make mention of thy righteousness, *even* of thine only.

Ye were sometimes darkness, but now *are ye* light in the Lord: walk as children of light... And have no fellowship with the unfruitful works of darkness, but rather reprove *them*... But all things that are reproved are made manifest by the light: for whatsoever doth make manifest is light... Awake thou that sleepest, and arise from the dead, and Christ shall give thee light. See then that ye walk circumspectly.

Ro. 13.12; Ro. 13.14; Phil. 3.8–9; Ro. 3.22 § Isa. 61.10; Ps. 71.16 § Eph. 5.8,11,13,14–15

When ye shall have done all those things
which are commanded you, say,
We are unprofitable servants.

Where *is* boasting then? It Is excluded. By what law? of works? Nay: but by the law of faith.—What hast thou that thou didst not receive? now if thou didst receive *it*, why dost thou glory, as if thou hadst not received *it*?— By grace are ye saved through faith; and that not of yourselves: *it is* the gift of God: not of works, lest any man should boast. For we are his workmanship, created in Christ Jesus unto good works, which God hath before ordained that we should walk in them.

By the grace of God I am what I am: and his grace which *was bestowed* upon me was not in vain; but I laboured more abundantly than they all: yet not I, but the grace of God which was with me.—For of him, and through him, and to him, *are* all things.—All things *come* of thee, and of thine own have we given thee.

Enter not into judgment with thy servant: for in thy sight shall no man living be justified.

Lu. 17.10; Ro. 3.27; 1 Co. 4.7; Eph. 2.8–10
  1 Co. 15.10; Ro. 11.36; 1 Chr. 29.14 § Ps. 143.2

He knoweth our frame;
he remembereth that we are dust.

The LORD God formed man *of* the dust of the ground, and breathed into his nostrils the breath of life; and man became a living soul.

I will praise thee; for I am fearfully *and* wonderfully made: marvellous *are* thy works; and *that* my soul knoweth right well. My substance was not hid from thee, when I was made in secret... Thine eyes did see my substance, yet being unperfect; and in thy book all *my members* were written, *which* in continuance were fashioned, when *as yet there was* none of them.

Have we not all one father? hath not one God created us?—In him we live, and move, and have our being.—Like as a father pitieth *his* children, *so* the LORD pitieth them that fear him.

He, *being* full of compassion, forgave *their* iniquity, and destroyed *them* not: yea, many a time turned he his anger away, and did not stir up all his wrath. For he remembered that they *were but* flesh; a wind that passeth away, and cometh not again.

Ps. 103.14; Ge. 2.7 § Ps. 139.14–15,16 § Mal. 2.10; Ac. 17.28; Ps. 103.13 § Ps. 78.38–39

He will rest in his love.

The LORD did not set his love upon you, nor choose you, because ye were more in number than any people; for ye *were* the fewest of all people: but because the LORD loved you.—We love him, because he first loved us.—You…hath he reconciled in the body of his flesh through death, to present you holy and unblameable and unreproveable in his sight.

Herein is love, not that we loved God, but that he loved us, and sent his Son *to be* the propitiation for our sins.—God commendeth his love toward us, in that, while we were yet sinners, Christ died for us.

Lo a voice from heaven, saying, This is my beloved Son, in whom I am well pleased.—Therefore doth my Father love me, because I lay down my life, that I might take it again.—*His* Son…who being the brightness of *his* glory, and the express image of his person, and upholding all things by the word of his power, when he had by himself purged our sins, sat down on the right hand of the Majesty on high.

Zeph. 3.17; Deu. 7.7–8; 1 Jn. 4.19; Col. 1.21–22
§ 1 Jn. 4.10; Ro. 5.8 § Mt. 3.17; Jn. 10.17; He. 1.2,3

A new and living way.

C ain went out from the presence of the LORD.—
Your iniquities have separated between you and your
God, and your sins have hid *his* face from you.—
Follow...holiness, without which no man shall see
the Lord.

I am the way, the truth, and the life: no man cometh
unto the Father, but by me.—Our Saviour Jesus
Christ...hath abolished death, and hath brought life and
immortality to light through the gospel.

The way into the holiest of all was not yet made
manifest, while as the first tabernacle was yet standing.—He is our peace, who hath made both one, and
hath broken down the middle wall of partition *between
us*.—The veil of the temple was rent in twain from the
top to the bottom.

Strait *is* the gate, and narrow *is* the way, which leadeth unto life, and few there be that find it.—Thou wilt
shew me the path of life: in thy presence *is* fulness of joy;
at thy right hand *there are* pleasures for evermore.

He. 10.20; Ge. 4.16; Isa. 59.2; He. 12.14 § Jn. 14.6;
2 Tim. 1.10 § He. 9.8; Eph. 2.14; Mt. 27.51 § Mt. 7.14;
Ps. 16.11

Men ought always to pray, and not to faint.

Which of you shall have a friend, and shall go unto him at midnight, and say unto him, Friend, lend me three loaves; for a friend of mine in his journey is come to me, and I have nothing to set before him? And he from within shall answer and say, Trouble me not: the door is now shut, and my children are with me in bed; I cannot rise and give thee. I say unto you, Though he will not rise and give him, because he is his friend, yet because of his importunity he will rise and give him as many as he needeth.—Praying always with all prayer and supplication in the Spirit, and watching thereunto with all perseverance and supplication for all saints.

I will not let thee go, except thou bless me... As a prince hast thou power with God and with men.—Continue in prayer, and watch in the same with thanksgiving.

[Jesus] went out into a mountain to pray, and continued all night in prayer to God.

Lu. 18.1; Lu. 11.5–8; Eph. 6.18 § Ge. 32.26,28; Col. 4.2 § Lu. 6.12

Forgive all my sins.

Come now, and let us reason together, saith the LORD: though your sins be as scarlet, they shall be as white as snow; though they be red like crimson, they shall be as wool.

Be of good cheer; thy sins be forgiven thee.—I, *even* I, *am* he that blotteth out thy transgressions for mine own sake, and will not remember thy sins.

The Son of man hath power on earth to forgive sins.—In whom we have redemption through his blood, the forgiveness of sins, according to the riches of his grace.—Not by works of righteousness which we have done, but according to his mercy he saved us, by the washing of regeneration, and renewing of the Holy Ghost; which he shed on us abundantly through Jesus Christ our Saviour.—Having forgiven you all trespasses; blotting out the handwriting of ordinances that was against us, which was contrary to us, and took it out of the way, nailing it to his cross.

Bless the LORD, O my soul...who forgiveth all thine iniquities.

Ps. 25.18; Isa. 1.18 § Mt. 9.2; Isa. 43.25 § Mt. 9.6; Eph. 1.7; Titus 3.5–6; Col. 2.13–14 § Ps. 103.2,3

The LORD made all that he did
to prosper in his hand.

Blessed *is* every one that feareth the LORD; that walketh in his ways. For thou shalt eat the labour of thine hands: happy *shalt* thou *be*, and *it shall be* well with thee.—Trust in the LORD, and do good; *so* shalt thou dwell in the land, and verily thou shalt be fed. Delight thyself also in the LORD; and he shall give thee the desires of thine heart.—Be not afraid, neither be thou dismayed: for the LORD thy God *is* with thee whithersoever thou goest.

Seek ye first the kingdom of God, and his righteousness; and all these things shall be added unto you.

As long as he sought the LORD, God made him to prosper.—Beware that thou forget not the LORD thy God, in not keeping his commandments, and his judgments, and his statutes, which I command thee this day...and thou say in thine heart, My power and the might of *mine* hand hath gotten me this wealth.

Is not the LORD your God with you? and hath he *not* given you rest on every side?

Ge. 39.3; Ps. 128.1–2; Ps. 37.3–4; Jos. 1.9 § Mt. 6.33 § 2 Chr. 26.5; Deu. 8.11,17 § 1 Chr. 22.18

Why reason ye these things
in your hearts?

Being not weak in faith, [Abraham] considered not his own body now dead, when he was about an hundred years old, neither yet the deadness of Sara's womb: he staggered not at the promise of God through unbelief; but was strong in faith, giving glory to God.

Is it easier to say to the sick of the palsy, *Thy* sins be forgiven thee; or to say, Arise, and take up thy bed, and walk?—If thou canst believe, all things *are* possible to him that believeth.

All power is given unto me in heaven and in earth.—Why are ye so fearful? how is it that ye have no faith?—Behold the fowls of the air…your heavenly Father feedeth them. Are ye not much better than they?—Why reason ye among yourselves, because ye have brought no bread? Do ye not…remember the five loaves of the five thousand?

My God shall supply all your need according to his riches in glory by Christ Jesus.

Mk. 2.8; Ro. 4.19–20 § Mk. 2.9; Mk. 9.23 § Mt. 28.18;
Mk. 4.40; Mt. 6.26; Mt. 16.8–9 § Phil. 4.19

Never man spake like this man.

Thou art fairer than the children of men: grace is poured into thy lips: therefore God hath blessed thee for ever.—The Lord GOD hath given me the tongue of the learned, that I should know how to speak a word in season to *him that is* weary.—His mouth *is* most sweet: yea, he *is* altogether lovely. This *is* my beloved, and this *is* my friend.

All bare him witness, and wondered at the gracious words which proceeded out of his mouth.—He taught them as *one* having authority, and not as the scribes.

Let the word of Christ dwell in you richly in all wisdom.—The sword of the Spirit...is the word of God.—The word of God *is* quick, and powerful, and sharper than any twoedged sword.—(For the weapons of our warfare *are* not carnal, but mighty through God to the pulling down of strong holds;) casting down imaginations, and every high thing that exalteth itself against the knowledge of God, and bringing into captivity every thought to the obedience of Christ.

Jn. 7.46; Ps. 45.2; Isa. 50.4; Song 5.16 § Lu. 4.22; Mt. 7.29 § Col. 3.16; Eph. 6.17; He. 4.12; 2 Co. 10.4–5

The triumphing of the wicked *is* short.

Thou shalt bruise his heel.—This is your hour, and the power of darkness.—As the children are partakers of flesh and blood, he also himself likewise took part of the same; that through death he might destroy him that had the power of death, that is, the devil.—Having spoiled principalities and powers, he made a shew of them openly, triumphing over them in it.

Be sober, be vigilant; because your adversary the devil, as a roaring lion, walketh about, seeking whom he may devour: whom resist stedfast in the faith.—Resist the devil, and he will flee from you.

The wicked plotteth against the just, and gnasheth upon him with his teeth. The Lord shall laugh at him: for he seeth that his day is coming.—The God of peace shall bruise Satan under your feet shortly.—The devil...was cast into the lake of fire and brimstone...and shall be tormented day and night for ever and ever.

Job 20.5; Ge. 3.15; Lu. 22.53; He. 2.14; Col. 2.15
§ 1 Pe. 5.8–9; Jas. 4.7 § Ps. 37.12–13; Ro. 16.20;
Rev. 20.10

**The younger son gathered all together,
and took his journey into a far country, and there
wasted his substance with riotous living.**

Such were some of you: but ye are washed, but ye are sanctified, but ye are justified in the name of the Lord Jesus, and by the Spirit of our God.—We…were by nature the children of wrath, even as others. But God, who is rich in mercy, for his great love wherewith he loved us, even when we were dead in sins, hath quickened us together with Christ, (by grace ye are saved;) and hath raised *us* up together, and made *us* sit together in heavenly *places* in Christ Jesus.

Herein is love, not that we loved God, but that he loved us, and sent his Son *to be* the propitiation for our sins.

God commendeth his love toward us, in that, while we were yet sinners, Christ died for us… If, when we were enemies, we were reconciled to God by the death of his Son, much more, being reconciled, we shall be saved by his life.

Lu. 15.13; 1 Co. 6.11; Eph. 2.3–6 § 1 Jn. 4.10
§ Ro. 5.8,10

As Christ forgave you, so also *do* ye.

There was a certain creditor which had two debtors: the one owed five hundred pence, and the other fifty. And when they had nothing to pay, he frankly forgave them both.—I forgave thee all that debt...shouldest not thou also have had compassion on thy fellowservant, even as I had pity on thee?

When ye stand praying, forgive, if ye have ought against any: that your Father also which is in heaven may forgive you your trespasses. But if ye do not forgive, neither will your Father which is in heaven forgive your trespasses.—Put on therefore, as the elect of God, holy and beloved, bowels of mercies, kindness, humbleness of mind, meekness, longsuffering; forbearing one another, and forgiving one another, if any man have a quarrel against any.

How oft shall my brother sin against me, and I forgive him? till seven times? Jesus saith unto him, I say not unto thee, Until seven times: but, Until seventy times seven.

Charity...is the bond of perfectness.

Col. **3.13**; Lu. 7.41–42; Mt.18.32,33 § Mk. 11.25–26; Col. 3.12–13 § Mt. 18.21–22 § Col. 3.14

He arose, and came to his father.
But when he was yet a great way off,
his father saw him, and had compassion, and ran,
and fell on his neck, and kissed him.

The LORD *is* merciful and gracious, slow to anger, and plenteous in mercy. He will not always chide: neither will he keep *his anger* for ever. He hath not dealt with us after our sins; nor rewarded us according to our iniquities. For as the heaven is high above the earth, *so* great is his mercy toward them that fear him. As far as the east is from the west, *so* far hath he removed our transgressions from us. Like as a father pitieth *his* children, *so* the LORD pitieth them that fear him.

Ye have received the Spirit of adoption, whereby we cry, Abba, Father. The Spirit itself beareth witness with our spirit, that we are the children of God.—Ye who sometimes were far off are made nigh by the blood of Christ.—Now therefore ye are no more strangers and foreigners, but fellowcitizens with the saints, and of the household of God.

Lu. 15.20; Ps. 103.8–13 § Ro. 8.15–16; Eph. 2.13;
Eph. 2.19

Behold, I make all things new.

Except a man be born again, he cannot see the kingdom of God.—If any man *be* in Christ, *he is* a new creature: old things are passed away; behold, all things are become new.

A new heart also will I give you, and a new spirit will I put within you: and I will take away the stony heart out of your flesh, and I will give you an heart of flesh.— Purge out therefore the old leaven, that ye may be a new lump.—The new man, which after God is created in righteousness and true holiness.

Thou shalt be called by a new name, which the mouth of the LORD shall name.

Behold, I create new heavens and a new earth: and the former shall not be remembered, nor come into mind.—*Seeing…that* all these things shall be dissolved, what manner *of persons* ought ye to be in *all* holy conversation and godliness…?

Rev. 21.5; Jn. 3.3; 2 Co. 5.17 § Ezek. 36.26; 1 Co. 5.7; Eph. 4.24 § Isa. 62.2 § Isa. 65.17; 2 Pe. 3.11

> Every thing that may abide the fire,
> ye shall make *it* go through the fire,
> and it shall be clean.

The LORD your God proveth you, to know whether ye love the LORD your God with all your heart and with all your soul.—He shall sit *as* a refiner and purifier of silver: and he shall purify the sons of Levi, and purge them as gold and silver, that they may offer unto the LORD an offering in righteousness.—Every man's work shall be made manifest: for the day shall declare it, because it shall be revealed by fire; and the fire shall try every man's work of what sort it is.

I will turn my hand upon thee, and purely purge away thy dross, and take away all thy tin.—I will melt them, and try them.

Thou, O God, hast proved us: thou hast tried us, as silver is tried... We went through fire and through water: but thou broughtest us out into a wealthy *place*.

When thou walkest through the fire, thou shalt not be burned; neither shall the flame kindle upon thee.

Nu. 31.23; Deu. 13.3; Mal. 3.3; 1 Co. 3.13 § Isa. 1.25; Jer. 9.7 § Ps. 66.10,12 § Isa. 43.2

**We, being dead to sins,
should live unto righteousness.**

Put off concerning the former conversation the old man, which is corrupt according to the deceitful lusts; and be renewed in the spirit of your mind; and…put on the new man, which after God is created in righteousness and true holiness.

Ye are dead, and your life is hid with Christ in God.—As Christ was raised up from the dead by the glory of the Father, even so we also should walk in newness of life…knowing this, that our old man is crucified with *him*, that the body of sin might be destroyed, that henceforth we should not serve sin. For he that is dead is freed from sin… Likewise reckon ye also yourselves to be dead indeed unto sin, but alive unto God through Jesus Christ our Lord. Let not sin therefore reign in your mortal body, that ye should obey it in the lusts thereof…but yield yourselves unto God, as those that are alive from the dead, and your members *as* instruments of righteousness unto God.

1 Pe. 2.24; Eph. 4.22–24 § Col. 3.3; Ro. 6.4,6–7,11–13

Abide in me, and I in you.

I am crucified with Christ: nevertheless I live; yet not I, but Christ liveth in me: and the life which I now live in the flesh I live by the faith of the Son of God, who loved me, and gave himself for me.

I know that in me (that is, in my flesh,) dwelleth no good thing: for to will is present with me; but *how* to perform that which is good I find not... O wretched man that I am! who shall deliver me from the body of this death? I thank God through Jesus Christ our Lord.—If Christ *be* in you, the body *is* dead because of sin; but the Spirit *is* life because of righteousness.—If ye continue in the faith grounded and settled, and *be* not moved away from the hope of the gospel, which ye have heard.

Little children, abide in him; that, when he shall appear, we may have confidence, and not be ashamed before him at his coming.—He that saith he abideth in him ought himself also so to walk, even as he walked.

Jn. 15.4; Ga. 2.20 § Ro. 7.18,24–25; Ro. 8.10; Col. 1.23
§ 1 Jn. 2.28; 1 Jn. 2.6

Dost thou believe on the Son of God?

W̲ho is he, Lord, that I might believe on him?

The brightness of *his* glory, and the express image of his person.—The blessed and only Potentate, the King of kings, and Lord of lords; who only hath immortality, dwelling in the light which no man can approach unto; whom no man hath seen, nor can see: to whom *be* honour and power everlasting. Amen.—I am Alpha and Omega, the beginning and the ending, saith the Lord, which is, and which was, and which is to come, the Almighty.

Lord, I believe.—I know whom I have believed, and am persuaded that he is able to keep that which I have committed unto him against that day.

Behold, I lay in Sion a chief corner stone, elect, precious: and he that believeth on him shall not be confounded. Unto you therefore which believe *he is* precious.

Jn. 9.35; Jn. 9.36 § He. 1.3; 1 Tim. 6.15–16; Rev. 1.8 § Jn. 9.38; 2 Tim. 1.12 § 1 Pe. 2.6–7

**As the sufferings of Christ abound in us,
so our consolation also aboundeth by Christ.**

The fellowship of his sufferings.—Rejoice, inasmuch as ye are partakers of Christ's sufferings; that, when his glory shall be revealed, ye may be glad also with exceeding joy.—For if we be dead with *him*, we shall also live with *him*.—If children, then heirs; heirs of God, and joint-heirs with Christ; if so be that we suffer with *him*, that we may be also glorified together.

God, willing more abundantly to shew unto the heirs of promise the immutability of his counsel, confirmed *it* by an oath: that by two immutable things, in which *it was* impossible for God to lie, we might have a strong consolation, who have fled for refuge to lay hold upon the hope set before us.—Our Lord Jesus Christ Himself, and God, even our Father, which hath loved us, and hath given *us* everlasting consolation and good hope through grace, comfort your hearts, and stablish you in every good word and work.

---

2 Co. 1.5; Phil. 3.10; 1 Pe. 4.13; 2 Tim. 2.11; Ro. 8.17
§ He. 6.17–18; 2 Th. 2.16–17

Martha, Martha, thou art careful and troubled about many things.

Consider the ravens: for they neither sow nor reap... Consider the lilies how they grow: they toil not, they spin not... Seek not ye what ye shall eat, or what ye shall drink, neither be ye of doubtful mind... Your Father knoweth that ye have need of these things.

Having food and raiment let us be therewith content... They that will be rich fall into temptation and a snare, and *into* many foolish and hurtful lusts, which drown men in destruction and perdition. For the love of money is the root of all evil: which while some coveted after, they have erred from the faith, and pierced themselves through with many sorrows.

The cares of this world, and the deceitfulness of riches, and the lusts of other things entering in, choke the word, and it becometh unfruitful.

Let us lay aside every weight, and the sin which doth so easily beset *us*, and let us run with patience the race that is set before us.

Lu. 10.41; Lu. 12.24,27,29,30 § 1 Tim. 6.8,9–10 § Mk. 4.19 § He. 12.1

The secret *things belong* unto the LORD our God:
but those *things which are* revealed *belong* unto us.

LORD, my heart is not haughty, nor mine eyes lofty:
neither do I exercise myself in great matters, or in things
too high for me. Surely I have behaved and quieted
myself, as a child that is weaned of his mother: my soul
is even as a weaned child.

The secret of the LORD *is* with them that fear him;
and he will shew them his covenant.—There is a God in
heaven that revealeth secrets.—Lo, these *are* parts of his
ways: but how little a portion is heard of him?

Henceforth I call you not servants; for the servant
knoweth not what his lord doeth: but I have called you
friends; for all things that I have heard of my Father I
have made known unto you.—If ye love me, keep my
commandments. And I will pray the Father, and he shall
give you another Comforter, that he may abide with you
for ever; *even* the Spirit of truth.

Deu. 29.29; Ps. 131.1–2 § Ps. 25.14; Dan. 2.28;
Job 26.14 § Jn. 15.15; Jn. 14.15–17

The Spirit...
maketh intercession for the saints
according to *the will* of God.

Verily, verily, I say unto you, Whatsoever ye shall ask the Father in my name, he will give *it* you. Hitherto have ye asked nothing in my name: ask, and ye shall receive, that your joy may be full.—Praying always with all prayer and supplication in the Spirit.

This is the confidence that we have in him, that, if we ask any thing according to his will, he heareth us: and if we know that he hear us, whatsoever we ask, we know that we have the petitions that we desired of him.—This is the will of God, *even* your sanctification.

God hath...called us...unto holiness...who hath also given unto us his holy Spirit.

Rejoice evermore. Pray without ceasing. In every thing give thanks: for this is the will of God in Christ Jesus concerning you. Quench not the Spirit.

Ro. 8.27; Jn. 16.23–24; Eph. 6.18 § 1 Jn. 5.14–15; 1 Th. 4.3 § 1 Th. 4.7,8 § 1 Th. 5.16–19

**See then that ye walk circumspectly,
not as fools, but as wise, redeeming the time,
because the days are evil.**

Take diligent heed to do the commandment and the law...to love the LORD your God, and to walk in all his ways, and to keep his commandments, and to cleave unto him, and to serve him with all your heart and with all your soul.—Walk in wisdom toward them that are without, redeeming the time. Let your speech *be* alway with grace, seasoned with salt, that ye may know how ye ought to answer every man.—Abstain from all appearance of evil.

While the bridegroom tarried, they all slumbered and slept. And at midnight there was a cry made, Behold, the bridegroom cometh; go ye out to meet him.—Watch therefore, for ye know neither the day nor the hour wherein the Son of man cometh.

Brethren, give diligence to make your calling and election sure: for if ye do these things, ye shall never fall.—Blessed *are* those servants, whom the lord when he cometh shall find watching.

Eph. 5.15–16;   Jos. 22.5;   Col. 4.5–6;   1 Th. 5.22
§ Mt. 25.5–6;   Mt. 25.13   § 2 Pe. 1.10;   Lu. 12.37

Hold that fast which thou hast,
that no man take thy crown.

If I may but touch his garment, I shall be whole.—Lord, if thou wilt, thou canst make me clean... I will; be thou clean.—Faith as a grain of mustard seed.

Cast not away...your confidence, which hath great recompence of reward.—Work out your own salvation with fear and trembling. For it is God which worketh in you both to will and to do of *his* good pleasure.

First the blade, then the ear, after that the full corn in the ear.—Then shall we know, *if* we follow on to know the LORD.—The kingdom of heaven suffereth violence, and the violent take it by force.—So run, that ye may obtain.

I have fought a good fight, I have finished *my* course, I have kept the faith: henceforth there is laid up for me a crown of righteousness, which the Lord, the righteous judge, shall give me at that day.

Rev. 3.11; Mt. 9.21; Mt. 8.2,3; Mt. 17.20 § He. 10.35; Phil. 2.12–13 § Mk. 4.28; Hos. 6.3; Mt. 11.12; 1 Co. 9.24 § 2 Tim. 4.7–8

**In every thing by prayer and supplication
with thanksgiving let your requests
be made known unto God.**

I love the LORD, because he hath heard my voice *and* my supplications. Because he hath inclined his ear unto me, therefore will I call upon *him* as long as I live.

When ye pray, use not vain repetitions, as the heathen *do*: for they think that they shall be heard for their much speaking.—The Spirit...helpeth our infirmities: for we know not what we should pray for as we ought: but the Spirit itself maketh intercession for us with groanings which cannot be uttered.

I will therefore that men pray every where, lifting up holy hands, without wrath and doubting.—Praying always with all prayer and supplication in the Spirit, and watching thereunto with all perseverance and supplication for all saints.

If two of you shall agree on earth as touching any thing that they shall ask, it shall be done for them of my Father which is in heaven.

Phil. 4.6; Ps. 116.1–2 § Mt. 6.7; Ro. 8.26 § 1 Tim. 2.8; Eph. 6.18 § Mt. 18.19

**All thy works shall praise thee, O LORD;
and thy saints shall bless thee.**

Bless the LORD, O my soul: and all that is within me, *bless* his holy name. Bless the LORD, O my soul, and forget not all his benefits.—I will bless the LORD at all times: his praise *shall* continually *be* in my mouth.—Every day will I bless thee; and I will praise thy name for ever and ever.

Because thy lovingkindness *is* better than life, my lips shall praise thee. Thus will I bless thee while I live: I will lift up my hands in thy name. My soul shall be satisfied as *with* marrow and fatness; and my mouth shall praise *thee* with joyful lips.

My soul doth magnify the Lord, and my spirit hath rejoiced in God my Saviour.

Thou art worthy, O Lord, to receive glory and honour and power: for thou hast created all things, and for thy pleasure they are and were created.

Ps. 145.10; Ps. 103.1–2; Ps. 34.1; Ps. 145.2
§ Ps. 63.3–5 § Lu. 1.46–47 § Rev. 4.11

**Thou shalt put the mercy seat above
upon the ark...and there I will meet with thee.**

The way into the holiest of all was not yet made manifest.—Jesus, when he had cried again with a loud voice, yielded up the ghost. And, behold, the veil of the temple was rent in twain from the top to the bottom.

Having...brethren, boldness to enter into the holiest by the blood of Jesus, by a new and living way, which he hath consecrated for us, through the veil, that is to say, his flesh...let us draw near with a true heart in full assurance of faith, having our hearts sprinkled from an evil conscience, and our bodies washed with pure water.—Let us therefore come boldly unto the throne of grace, that we may obtain mercy, and find grace to help in time of need.

Christ Jesus: whom God hath set forth *to be* a propitiation through faith in his blood, to declare his righteousness for the remission of sins that are past, through the forbearance of God.—Through him we both have access by one Spirit unto the Father.

Ex. 25.21,22; He. 9.8; Mt. 27.50–51
§ He. 10.19–20,22; He. 4.16 § Ro. 3.24–25; Eph. 2.18

Faith as a grain of mustard seed.

Barak said unto [Deborah], If thou wilt go with me, then I will go: but if thou wilt not go with me, *then* I will not go... God subdued on that day Jabin the king of Canaan.—And Gideon said unto God, If thou wilt save Israel by mine hand, as thou hast said...let me prove, I pray thee... And God did so.

Thou hast a little strength, and hast kept my word, and hast not denied my name.—Who hath despised the day of small things?

We are bound to thank God always for you, brethren, as it is meet, because that your faith groweth exceedingly.—Lord, Increase our faith.—I will be as the dew unto Israel: he shall grow as the lily, and cast forth his roots as Lebanon. His branches shall spread, and his beauty shall be as the olive tree, and his smell as Lebanon.

Mt. 17.20; Judg. 4.8,23; Judg. 6.36,39,40 § Rev. 3.8; Zech. 4.10 § 2 Th. 1.3; Lu. 17.5; Hos. 14.5–6

Holiness, without which no man shall see the Lord.

Except a man be born again, he cannot see the kingdom of God.—There shall in no wise enter into it any thing that defileth.—*There is* no spot in thee.

Ye shall be holy: for I the LORD your God *am* holy.—As obedient children, not fashioning yourselves according to the former lusts in your ignorance: but as he which hath called you is holy, so be ye holy in all manner of conversation; because it is written, Be ye holy; for I am holy. And if ye call on the Father, who without respect of persons judgeth according to every man's work, pass the time of your sojourning *here* in fear.—Put off concerning the former conversation the old man, which is corrupt according to the deceitful lusts; and be renewed in the spirit of your mind; and…put on the new man, which after God is created in righteousness and true holiness.—He hath chosen us in him before the foundation of the world, that we should be holy and without blame before him in love.

He. 12.14; Jn. 3.3; Rev. 21.27; Song 4.7 § Lev. 19.2;
1 Pe. 1.14–17; Eph. 4.22–24; Eph. 1.4

Gold tried in the fire.

There is no man that hath left house, or brethren, or sisters, or father, or mother, or wife, or children, or lands, for my sake, and the gospel's, but he shall receive an hundredfold now in this time, houses, and brethren, and sisters, and mothers, and children, and lands, with persecutions; and in the world to come eternal life.

Beloved, think it not strange concerning the fiery trial which is to try you, as though some strange thing happened unto you.—Now for a season, if need be, ye are in heaviness through manifold temptations: that the trial of your faith, being much more precious than of gold that perisheth, though it be tried with fire, might be found unto praise and honour and glory at the appearing of Jesus Christ.

The God of all grace, who hath called us unto his eternal glory by Christ Jesus, after that ye have suffered a while, make you perfect, stablish, strengthen, settle *you.*—In the world ye shall have tribulation: but be of good cheer; I have overcome the world.

Rev. 3.18; Mk. 10.29–30 § 1 Pe. 4.12; 1 Pe. 1.6–7 § 1 Pe. 5.10; Jn. 16.33

Take this child away, and nurse it for me, and I will give *thee* thy wages.

Go ye...into the vineyard, and whatsoever is right I will give you.—Whosoever shall give you a cup of water to drink in my name, because ye belong to Christ, verily I say unto you, he shall not lose his reward.—The liberal soul shall be made fat: and he that watereth shall be watered also himself.—God *is* not unrighteous to forget your work and labour of love...in that ye have ministered to the saints, and do minister.

Every man shall receive his own reward according to his own labour.

Lord, when saw we thee an hungred, and fed *thee*? or thirsty, and gave *thee* drink? When saw we thee a stranger, and took *thee* in? or naked, and clothed *thee*?... And the King shall answer and say unto them... Inasmuch as ye have done *it* unto one of the least of these my brethren, ye have done *it* unto me.—Come, ye blessed of my Father, inherit the kingdom prepared for you from the foundation of the world.

Ex. 2.9; Mt. 20.4; Mk. 9.41; Pro. 11.25; He. 6.10
§ 1 Co. 3.8 § Mt. 25.37–38,40; Mt. 25.34

Thou compassest my path
and my lying down.

Jacob awaked out of his sleep, and he said, Surely the LORD is in this place; and I knew *it* not. And he was afraid, and said, How dreadful *is* this place! this *is* none other but the house of God, and this *is* the gate of heaven.

The eyes of the LORD run to and fro throughout the whole earth, to shew himself strong in the behalf of *them* whose heart *is* perfect toward him.

I will both lay me down in peace, and sleep: for thou, LORD, only makest me dwell in safety.

Because thou hast made the LORD, *which is* my refuge, *even* the most High, thy habitation; there shall no evil befall thee, neither shall any plague come nigh thy dwelling. For he shall give his angels charge over thee, to keep thee in all thy ways.—When thou liest down, thou shalt not be afraid: yea, thou shalt lie down, and thy sleep shall be sweet.—So he giveth his beloved sleep.

Ps. 139.3; Ge. 28.16–17 § 2 Chr. 16.9 § Ps. 4.8 § Ps. 91.9–11; Pro. 3.24; Ps. 127.2

**Christ also suffered for us, leaving us an example,
that ye should follow his steps.**

Even the Son of man came not to be ministered unto,
but to minister.—Whosoever of you will be the chiefest,
shall be servant of all.

Jesus of Nazareth...went about doing good.—Bear
ye one another's burdens, and so fulfil the law of Christ.

The meekness and gentleness of Christ.—In lowliness of mind let each esteem other better than
themselves.

Father, forgive them; for they know not what they
do.—Be ye kind one to another, tenderhearted, forgiving one another, even as God for Christ's sake hath
forgiven you.

He that saith he abideth in him ought himself also so
to walk, even as he walked.—Looking unto Jesus the
author and finisher of *our* faith; who for the joy that was
set before him endured the cross, despising the shame,
and is set down at the right hand of the throne of God.

1 Pe. 2.21; Mk. 10.45; Mk. 10.44 § Ac. 10.38; Ga. 6.2
§ 2 Co. 10.1; Phil. 2.3 § Lu. 23.34; Eph. 4.32
§ 1 Jn. 2.6; He. 12.2

I sought him, but I could not find him; I called him, but he gave me no answer.

O Lord, what shall I say, when Israel turneth their backs before their enemies!…and the Lord said unto Joshua, Get thee up; wherefore liest thou thus upon thy face? Israel hath sinned…for they have even taken of the accursed thing…and they have put *it* even among their own stuff.

Behold, the Lord's hand is not shortened, that it cannot save; neither his ear heavy, that it cannot hear: but your iniquities have separated between you and your God, and your sins have hid *his* face from you, that he will not hear.

If I regard iniquity in my heart, the Lord will not hear *me*.

Beloved, if our heart condemn us not, *then* have we confidence toward God. And whatsoever we ask, we receive of him, because we keep his commandments, and do those things that are pleasing in his sight.

Song 5.6; Jos. 7.8,10–11 § Isa. 59.1–2 § Ps. 66.18 § 1 Jn. 3.21–22

Ye are dead, and your life is hid with Christ in God.

How shall we, that are dead to sin, live any longer therein?—I am crucified with Christ: nevertheless I live; yet not I, but Christ liveth in me: and the life which I now live in the flesh I live by the faith of the Son of God, who loved me, and gave himself for me.—He died for all, that they which live should not henceforth live unto themselves, but unto him which died for them, and rose again.—If any man *be* in Christ, *he is* a new creature: old things are passed away; behold, all things are become new.

We are in him that is true, *even* in his Son Jesus Christ.—As thou, Father, *art* in me, and I in thee, that they also may be one in us.—Ye are the body of Christ, and members in particular.—Because I live, ye shall live also.

To him that overcometh will I give to eat of the hidden manna, and will give him a white stone, and in the stone a new name written, which no man knoweth saving he that receiveth *it*.

Col. 3.3; Ro. 6.2; Ga. 2.20; 2 Co. 5.15; 2 Co. 5.17
§ 1 Jn. 5.20; Jn. 17.21; 1 Co. 12.27; Jn. 14.19 § Rev. 2.17

Behold how he loved.

He died for all.—Greater love hath no man than this, that a man lay down his life for his friends.

He...liveth to make intercession for them.—I go to prepare a place for you.

I will come again, and receive you unto myself; that where I am, *there* ye may be also.—Father, I will that they also, whom thou hast given me, be with me where I am.—Having loved his own which were in the world, he loved them unto the end.

We love him, because he first loved us.—The love of Christ constraineth us; because we thus judge, that if one died for all, then were all dead: and *that* he died for all, that they which live should not henceforth live unto themselves, but unto him which died for them, and rose again.

If ye keep my commandments, ye shall abide in my love; even as I have kept my Father's commandments, and abide in his love.

Jn. 11.36; 2 Co. 5.15; Jn. 15.13 § He. 7.25; Jn. 14.2
§ Jn. 14.3; Jn. 17.24; Jn. 13.1 § 1 Jn. 4.19;
2 Co. 5.14–15 § Jn. 15.10

I will pray the Father, and he shall give you another Comforter...*even* the Spirit of truth.

It is expedient for you that I go away: for if I go not away, the Comforter will not come unto you; but if I depart, I will send him unto you.

The Spirit itself beareth witness with our spirit, that we are the children of God.—Ye have not received the spirit of bondage again to fear; but ye have received the Spirit of adoption, whereby we cry, Abba, Father.—The Spirit...helpeth our infirmities: for we know not what we should pray for as we ought: but the Spirit itself maketh intercession for us with groanings which cannot be uttered.

The God of hope fill you with all joy and peace in believing, that ye may abound in hope, through the power of the Holy Ghost.—Hope maketh not ashamed; because the love of God is shed abroad in our hearts by the Holy Ghost which is given unto us.

Hereby know we that we dwell in him, and he in us, because he hath given us of his Spirit.

Jn. 14.16,17; Jn. 16.7 § Ro. 8.16; Ro. 8.15; Ro. 8.26 § Ro. 15.13; Ro. 5.5 § 1 Jn. 4.13

Shall I not seek rest for thee,
that it may be well with thee?

There remaineth…a rest to the people of God.—My people shall dwell in a peaceable habitation, and in sure dwellings, and in quiet resting places.—There the wicked cease *from* troubling; and there the weary be at rest.—They…rest from their labours.

The forerunner is for us entered, *even* Jesus, made an high priest for ever after the order of Melchisedec.

Come unto me, all *ye* that labour and are heavy laden, and I will give you rest. Take my yoke upon you, and learn of me; for I am meek and lowly in heart: and ye shall find rest unto your souls. For my yoke *is* easy, and my burden is light.—In returning and rest shall ye be saved; in quietness and in confidence shall be your strength.

The LORD *is* my shepherd; I shall not want. He maketh me to lie down in green pastures: he leadeth me beside the still waters.

Ru. 3.1; He. 4.9; Isa. 32.18; Job 3.17; Rev. 14.13
§ He. 6.20 § Mt. 11.28–30; Isa. 30.15 § Ps. 23.1–2

**The ark of the covenant of the LORD
went before them…
to search out a resting place for them.**

My times *are* in thy hand.—He shall choose our inheritance for us.—Lead me, O LORD, in thy righteousness …make thy way straight before my face.

Commit thy way unto the LORD; trust also in him; and he shalt bring *it* to pass.—In all thy ways acknowledge him, and he shall direct thy paths.—Thine ears shall hear a word behind thee, saying, This *is* the way, walk ye in it, when ye turn to the right hand, and when ye turn to the left.

The LORD *is* my shepherd; I shall not want. He maketh me to lie down in green pastures: he leadeth me beside the still waters.—Like as a father pitieth *his* children, *so* the LORD pitieth them that fear him. For he knoweth our frame; he remembereth that we *are* dust.—Your heavenly Father knoweth that ye have need of all these things.—Casting all your care upon him; for he careth for you.

Nu. 10.33; Ps. 31.15; Ps. 47.4; Ps. 5.8 § Ps. 37.5;
Pro. 3.6; Isa. 30.21 § Ps. 23.1–2; Ps. 103.13–14;
Mt. 6.32; 1 Pe. 5.7

Rabbi (which is to say…Master,)
where dwellest thou?
He saith unto them, Come and see.

In my Father's house are many mansions: *if it were* not *so*, I would have told you. I go to prepare a place for you. And if I go and prepare a place for you, I will come again, and receive you unto myself; that where I am, *there* ye may be also.—To him that overcometh will I grant to sit with me in my throne.

Thus saith the high and lofty One that inhabiteth eternity, whose name *is* Holy; I dwell in the high and holy *place*, with him also *that is* of a contrite and humble spirit, to revive the spirit of the humble, and to revive the heart of the contrite ones.

Behold, I stand at the door, and knock: if any man hear my voice, and open the door, I will come in to him, and will sup with him, and he with me.

Lo, I am with you alway, *even* unto the end of the world.—How excellent *is* thy lovingkindness, O God! therefore the children of men put their trust under the shadow of thy wings.

Jn. 1.38–39; Jn. 14.2–3; Rev. 3.21 § Isa. 57.15 § Rev. 3.20 § Mt. 28.20; Ps. 36.7

**When he shall appear, we shall be like him;
for we shall see him as he is.**

As many as received him, to them gave he power to become the sons of God, *even* to them that believe on his name.—Whereby are given unto us exceeding great and precious promises: that by these ye might be partakers of the divine nature, having escaped the corruption that is in the world through lust.

Since the beginning of the world *men* have not heard, nor perceived by the ear, neither hath the eye seen, O God, beside thee, *what* he hath prepared for him that waiteth for him.

Now we see through a glass, darkly; but then face to face: now I know in part; but then shall I know even as also I am known.—Christ…shall change our vile body, that it may be fashioned like unto his glorious body, according to the working whereby he is able even to subdue all things unto himself.—As for me, I will behold thy face in righteousness: I shall be satisfied, when I awake, with thy likeness.

1 Jn. 3.2; Jn. 1.12; 2 Pe. 1.4 § Isa. 64.4 § 1 Co. 13.12; Phil. 3.20,21; Ps. 17.15

**The man *that is* my fellow,
saith the LORD of hosts.**

In him dwelleth all the fulness of the Godhead bodily.—I have laid help upon *one that is* mighty; I have exalted *one* chosen out of the people.—I have trodden the winepress alone; and of the people *there was* none with me.

Great is the mystery of godliness: God was manifest in the flesh.—Unto us a child is born, unto us a son is given: and the government shall be upon his shoulder: and his name shall be called Wonderful, Counsellor, The mighty God, The everlasting Father, The Prince of Peace.

The brightness of *his* glory, and the express image of his person, and upholding all things by the word of his power, when he had by himself purged our sins, sat down on the right hand of the Majesty on high.—Unto the Son *he saith*, Thy throne, O God, *is* for ever and ever.

Let all the angels of God worship him.

KING OF KINGS, AND LORD OF LORDS.

Zech. 13.7; Col. 2.9; Ps. 89.19; Isa. 63.3 § 1 Tim. 3.16;
Isa. 9.6 § He. 1.3; He. 1.8 § He. 1.6 § Rev. 19.16

**Oh that thou wouldest bless me indeed...
and that thou wouldest keep *me* from evil...
And God granted him that which he requested.**

The blessing of the LORD, it maketh rich, and he addeth no sorrow with it.—When he giveth quietness, who then can make trouble? and when he hideth *his* face, who then can behold him?

Salvation *belongeth* unto the LORD: thy blessing *is* upon thy people.—How great *is* thy goodness, which thou hast laid up for them that fear thee; *which* thou hast wrought for them that trust in thee before the sons of men!—I pray not that thou shouldest take them out of the world, but that thou shouldest keep them from the evil.

Ask, and it shall be given you; seek, and ye shall find; knock, and it shall be opened unto you: for every one that asketh receiveth; and he that seeketh findeth; and to him that knocketh it shall be opened.—The LORD redeemeth the soul of his servants: and none of them that trust in him shall be desolate.

---

1 Chr. 4.10; Pro. 10.22; Job 34.29 § Ps. 3.8; Ps. 31.19; Jn. 17.15 § Mt. 7.7–8; Ps. 34.22

It *is* a night to be much observed unto the LORD for bringing them out from the land of Egypt.

The Lord Jesus the *same* night in which he was betrayed took bread: and when he had given thanks, he brake *it*, and said, Take, eat: this is my body, which is broken for you: this do in remembrance of me. After the same manner also *he took* the cup, when he had supped, saying, This cup is the new testament in my blood: this do ye, as oft as ye drink *it*, in remembrance of me.

He...kneeled down, and prayed... And being in an agony he prayed more earnestly: and his sweat was as it were great drops of blood falling down to the ground.

It was the preparation of the passover, and about the sixth hour...they took Jesus, and led *him* away...into a place called... Golgotha: where they crucified him.

Christ our passover is sacrificed for us: therefore let us keep the feast.

Ex. 12.42; 1 Co. 11.23–25 § Lu. 22.41,44
§ Jn. 19.14,16,17–18 § 1 Co. 5.7–8

Who shall be able to stand?

Who may abide the day of his coming? and who shall stand when he appeareth? for he *is* like a refiner's fire, and like fullers' soap.

I beheld, and, lo, a great multitude, which no man could number, of all nations, and kindreds, and people, and tongues, stood before the throne, and before the Lamb, clothed with white robes, and palms in their hands... These are they which came out of great tribulation, and have washed their robes, and made them white in the blood of the Lamb... They shall hunger no more, neither thirst any more; neither shall the sun light on them, nor any heat. For the Lamb which is in the midst of the throne shall feed them, and shall lead them unto living fountains of waters: and God shall wipe away all tears from their eyes.

There is therefore now no condemnation to them which are in Christ Jesus, who walk not after the flesh, but after the Spirit.—Stand fast therefore in the liberty wherewith Christ hath made us free.

Rev. 6.17; Mal. 3.2 § Rev. 7.9,14,16–17 § Ro. 8.1; Ga. 5.1

**Enter not into judgment with thy servant:
for in thy sight shall no man living be justified.**

Come now, and let us reason together, saith the LORD: though your sins be as scarlet, they shall be as white as snow; though they be red like crimson, they shall be as wool.

Let him take hold of my strength, *that* he may make peace with me; *and* he shall make peace with me.— Acquaint now thyself with him, and be at peace.

Being justified by faith, we have peace with God through our Lord Jesus Christ.—A man is not justified by the works of the law, but by the faith of Jesus Christ.—By the deeds of the law there shall no flesh be justified in his sight.

By him all that believe are justified from all things, from which ye could not be justified by the law of Moses.

Thanks *be* to God, which giveth us the victory through our Lord Jesus Christ.

Ps. 143.2; Isa. 1.18 § Isa. 27.5; Job 22.21 § Ro. 5.1; Ga. 2.16; Ro. 3.20 § Ac. 13.39 § 1 Co. 15.57

I know *that* my redeemer liveth.

If, when we were enemies, we were reconciled to God by the death of his Son, much more, being reconciled, we shall be saved by his life.—This *man*, because he continueth ever, hath an unchangeable priesthood. Wherefore he is able also to save them to the uttermost that come unto God by him, seeing he ever liveth to make intercession for them.

Because I live, ye shall live also.—If in this life only we have hope in Christ, we are of all men most miserable. But now is Christ risen from the dead, *and* become the firstfruits of them that slept.

The Redeemer shall come to Zion, and unto them that turn from transgression in Jacob, saith the LORD.— We have redemption through his blood, the forgiveness of sins, according to the riches of his grace.—Ye were not redeemed with corruptible things, *as* silver and gold, from your vain conversation *received* by tradition from your fathers; but with the precious blood of Christ, as of a lamb without blemish and without spot.

Job 19.25; Ro. 5.10; He. 7.24–25 § Jn. 14.19;
1 Co. 15.19–20 § Isa. 59.20; Eph. 1.7; 1 Pe. 1.18–19

Remember not
the sins of my youth,
nor my transgressions.

I have blotted out, as a thick cloud, thy transgressions, and, as a cloud, thy sins.—I, *even* I, *am* he that blotteth out thy transgressions for mine own sake, and will not remember thy sins.—Come now, and let us reason together, saith the LORD: though your sins be as scarlet, they shall be as white as snow; though they be red like crimson, they shall be as wool.—I will forgive their iniquity, and I will remember their sin no more.—Thou wilt cast all their sins into the depths of the sea.

Thou hast in love to my soul *delivered it* from the pit of corruption: for thou hast cast all my sins behind thy back.—Who *is* a God like unto thee, that pardoneth iniquity?…he retaineth not his anger for ever, because he delighteth *in* mercy.—Unto him that loved us, and washed us from our sins in his own blood…to him *be* glory and dominion for ever and ever. Amen.

Ps. 25.7; Isa. 44.22; Isa. 43.25; Isa. 1.18; Jer. 31.34;
Mi. 7.19 § Isa. 38.17; Mi. 7.18; Rev. 1.5,6

As many as I love,
I rebuke and chasten.

My son, despise not thou the chastening of the Lord, nor faint when thou art rebuked of him: for whom the Lord loveth he chasteneth, and scourgeth every son whom he receiveth.—Even as a father the son *in whom* he delighteth.—He maketh sore, and bindeth up: he woundeth, and his hands make whole.—Humble yourselves therefore under the mighty hand of God, that he may exalt you in due time.—I have chosen thee in the furnace of affliction.

He doth not afflict willingly nor grieve the children of men.—He hath not dealt with us after our sins; nor rewarded us according to our iniquities. For as the heaven is high above the earth, *so* great is his mercy toward them that fear him. As far as the east is from the west, *so* far hath he removed our transgressions from us. Like as a father pitieth *his* children, *so* the LORD pitieth them that fear him. For he knoweth our frame; he remembereth that we *are* dust.

Rev. 3.19; He. 12.5–6; Pro. 3.12; Job 5.18; 1 Pe. 5.6; Isa. 48.10 § Lam. 3.33; Ps. 103.10–14

God *is* in heaven, and thou upon earth:
therefore let thy words be few.

When ye pray, use not vain repetitions, as the heathen *do:* for they think that they shall be heard for their much speaking. Be not ye therefore like unto them: for your Father knoweth what things ye have need of, before ye ask him.

They...called on the name of Baal from morning even until noon, saying, O Baal, hear us.

Two men went up into the temple to pray; the one a Pharisee, and the other a publican. The Pharisee stood and prayed thus with himself, God, I thank thee, that I am not as other men *are*, extortioners, unjust, adulterers, or even as this publican... And the publican, standing afar off, would not lift up so much as *his* eyes unto heaven, but smote upon his breast, saying, God be merciful to me a sinner. I tell you, this man went down to his house justified *rather* than the other.

Lord, teach us to pray.

Ec. 5.2; Mt. 6.7–8 § 1 Ki. 18.26 § Lu. 18.10–11,13–14 § Lu. 11.1

The fruit of the Spirit is...goodness.

Be ye...followers of God, as dear children.—Love your enemies, bless them that curse you, do good to them that hate you, and pray for them which despitefully use you, and persecute you; that ye may be the children of your Father which is in heaven: for he maketh his sun to rise on the evil and on the good, and sendeth rain on the just and on the unjust.—Be ye therefore merciful, as your Father also is merciful.

The fruit of the Spirit *is* in all goodness and righteousness and truth.

After that the kindness and love of God our Saviour toward man appeared, not by works of righteousness which we have done, but according to his mercy he saved us, by the washing of regeneration, and renewing of the Holy Ghost; which he shed on us abundantly through Jesus Christ our Saviour.—The LORD *is* good to all: and his tender mercies *are* over all his works.—He that spared not his own Son, but delivered him up for us all, how shall he not with him also freely give us all things?

Ga. 5.22; Eph. 5.1; Mt. 5.44–45; Lu. 6.36 § Eph. 5.9 § Titus 3.4–6; Ps. 145.9; Ro. 8.32

Ebenezer...
Hitherto hath the LORD helped us.

I was brought low, and he helped me.—Blessed *be* the LORD, because he hath heard the voice of my supplications. The LORD *is* my strength and my shield; my heart trusted in him, and I am helped: therefore my heart greatly rejoiceth; and with my song will I praise him.

It is better to trust in the LORD than to put confidence in man. *It is* better to trust in the LORD than to put confidence in princes.—Happy *is he* that *hath* the God of Jacob for his help, whose hope *is* in the LORD his God.—He led them forth by the right way, that they might go to a city of habitation.—There failed not ought of any good thing which the LORD had spoken unto the house of Israel; all came to pass.

When I sent you without purse, and scrip, and shoes, lacked ye any thing? And they said, Nothing.—Because thou hast been my help, therefore in the shadow of thy wings will I rejoice.

---

1 Sa. 7.12; Ps. 116.6; Ps. 28.6–7 § Ps. 118.8–9; Ps. 146.5; Ps. 107.7; Jos. 21.45 § Lu. 22.35; Ps. 63.7

This *is* the ordinance of the passover: There shall no stranger eat thereof.

We have an altar, whereof they have no right to eat which serve the tabernacle.—Except a man be born again, he cannot see the kingdom of God.—At that time ye were without Christ, being aliens from the commonwealth of Israel, and strangers from the covenants of promise... But now in Christ Jesus ye who sometimes were far off are made nigh by the blood of Christ.

For he is our peace, who hath made both one...having abolished in his flesh the enmity, *even* the law of commandments *contained* in ordinances; for to make in himself of twain one new man, *so* making peace.

Now therefore ye are no more strangers and foreigners, but fellowcitizens with the saints, and of the household of God.

If any man hear my voice, and open the door, I will come in to him, and will sup with him, and he with me.

Ex. 12.43; He. 13.10; Jn. 3.3; Eph. 2.12,13
§ Eph. 2.14,15 § Eph. 2.19 § Rev. 3.20

[Jesus] prayed the third time, saying the same words.

Who in the days of his flesh…offered up prayers and supplications with strong crying and tears unto him that was able to save him from death.

Then shall we know, *if* we follow on to know the LORD.—Continuing instant in prayer.—Praying always with all prayer and supplication in the Spirit, and watching thereunto with all perseverance and supplication.—By prayer and supplication with thanksgiving let your requests be made known unto God. And the peace of God, which passeth all understanding, shall keep your hearts and minds through Christ Jesus.

Nevertheless not as I will, but as thou *wilt.*—This is the confidence that we have in him, that, if we ask any thing according to his will, he heareth us.

Delight thyself…in the LORD; and he shall give thee the desires of thine heart. Commit thy way unto the LORD; trust also in him; and he shall bring *it* to pass.

Mt. 26.44; He. 5.7 § Hos. 6.3; Ro. 12.12; Eph. 6.18;
Phil. 4.6–7 § Mt. 26.39; 1 Jn. 5.14 § Ps. 37.4–5

**If children, then heirs; heirs of God,
and joint-heirs with Christ.**

If ye *be* Christ's, then are ye Abraham's seed, and heirs according to the promise.

Behold, what manner of love the Father hath bestowed upon us, that we should be called the sons of God.—Thou art no more a servant, but a son; and if a son, then an heir of God through Christ.—Having predestinated us unto the adoption of children by Jesus Christ to himself, according to the good pleasure of his will.

Father, I will that they also, whom thou hast given me, be with me where I am; that they may behold my glory, which thou hast given me.

He that overcometh, and keepeth my works unto the end, to him will I give power over the nations.—To him that overcometh will I grant to sit with me in my throne, even as I also overcame, and am set down with my Father in his throne.

Ro. 8.17; Ga. 3.29 § 1 Jn. 3.1; Ga. 4.7; Eph. 1.5
§ Jn. 17.24 § Rev. 2.26; Rev. 3.21

Things which are despised, hath God chosen.

Behold, are not all these which speak Galilæans?

Jesus…saw two brethren…casting a net into the sea: for they were fishers. And he saith unto them, Follow me.—Now when they saw the boldness of Peter and John, and perceived that they were unlearned and ignorant men, they marvelled; and they took knowledge of them, that they had been with Jesus.

My speech and my preaching *was* not with enticing words of man's wisdom, but in demonstration of the Spirit and of power: that your faith should not stand in the wisdom of men, but in the power of God.

Ye have not chosen me, but I have chosen you, and ordained you, that ye should go and bring forth fruit.— He that abideth in me, and I in him, the same bringeth forth much fruit: for without me ye can do nothing.— We have this treasure in earthen vessels, that the excellency of the power may be of God.

1 Co. 1.28; Ac. 2.7 § Mt. 4.18–19; Ac. 4.13
§ 1 Co. 2.4–5 § Jn. 15.16; Jn. 15.5; 2 Co. 4.7

Leaning on Jesus' bosom.

As one whom his mother comforteth, so will I comfort you.—They brought young children to him, that he should touch them… And he took them up in his arms, put *his* hands upon them, and blessed them.—Jesus called his disciples *unto him*, and said, I have compassion on the multitude, because they continue with me now three days, and have nothing to eat: and I will not send them away fasting, lest they faint in the way.—An high priest…touched with the feeling of our infirmities.—In his love and in his pity he redeemed them.

I will not leave you comfortless [*marg.* orphans]: I will come to you.—Can a woman forget her sucking child, that she should not have compassion on the son of her womb? yea, they may forget, yet will I not forget thee.

The Lamb which is in the midst of the throne shall feed them, and shall lead them unto living fountains of waters: and God shall wipe away all tears from their eyes.

Jn. 13.23; Isa. 66.13; Mk. 10.13,16; Mt. 15.32; He. 4.15; Isa. 63.9 § Jn. 14.18; Isa. 49.15 § Rev. 7.17

Jesus Christ the righteous...
the propitiation for our sins.

Toward the mercy seat shall the faces of the cherubims be. And thou shalt put the mercy seat above upon the ark; and in the ark thou shalt put the testimony that I shall give thee. And there I will meet with thee, and I will commune with thee from above the mercy seat.

Surely his salvation *is* nigh them that fear him... Mercy and truth are met together; righteousness and peace have kissed *each other*.

If thou, LORD, shouldest mark iniquities, O Lord, who shall stand? But *there is* forgiveness with thee, that thou mayest be feared... Let Israel hope in the LORD: for with the LORD *there is* mercy, and with him *is* plenteous redemption. And he shall redeem Israel from all his iniquities.—All have sinned, and come short of the glory of God; being justified freely by his grace through the redemption that is in Christ Jesus: whom God hath set forth *to be* a propitiation through faith in his blood, to declare his righteousness for the remission of sins.

1 Jn. 2.1,2; Ex. 25.20–22 § Ps. 85.9,10 § Ps. 130.3–4,7–8; Ro. 3.23–25

We have known and believed
the love that God hath to us.

God, who is rich in mercy, for his great love where-with he loved us, even when we were dead in sins, hath quickened us together with Christ, (by grace ye are saved;) and hath raised *us* up together, and made *us* sit together in heavenly *places* in Christ Jesus: that in the ages to come he might shew the exceeding riches of his grace in *his* kindness toward us through Christ Jesus.

God so loved the world, that he gave his only begotten Son, that whosoever believeth in him should not perish, but have everlasting life.—He that spared not his own Son, but delivered him up for us all, how shall he not with him also freely give us all things?—The LORD *is* good to all: and his tender mercies *are* over all his works.

We love him, because he first loved us.

Blessed *is* she that believed: for there shall be a performance of those things which were told her from the Lord.

---

1 Jn. 4.16; Eph. 2.4–7 § Jn. 3.16; Ro. 8.32; Ps. 145.9
§ 1 Jn. 4.19 § Lu. 1.45

Mind not high things,
but condescend to men of low estate.

M̲y brethren, have not the faith of our Lord Jesus Christ, *the Lord* of glory, with respect of persons... Hath not God chosen the poor of this world rich in faith, and heirs of the kingdom which he hath promised to them that love him?

Let no man seek his own, but every man another's *wealth.*—Having food and raiment let us be therewith content. But they that will be rich fall into temptation and a snare, and *into* many foolish and hurtful lusts, which drown men in destruction and perdition.

God hath chosen the foolish things of the world to confound the wise; and God hath chosen the weak things of the world to confound the things which are mighty; and base things of the world, and things which are despised, hath God chosen, *yea*, and things which are not, to bring to nought things that are: that no flesh should glory in his presence.

LORD, my heart is not haughty, nor mine eyes lofty.

Ro. 12.16; Jas. 2.1,5 § 1 Co. 10.24; 1 Tim. 6.8–9
§ 1 Co. 1.27–29 § Ps. 131.1

Let your speech *be*
alway with grace.

A word fitly spoken *is like* apples of gold in pictures of silver. *As* an earring of gold, and an ornament of fine gold, *so is* a wise reprover upon an obedient ear.—Let no corrupt communication proceed out of your mouth, but that which is good to the use of edifying, that it may minister grace unto the hearers.—A good man out of the good treasure of the heart bringeth forth good things: and an evil man out of the evil treasure bringeth forth evil things.—By thy words thou shalt be justified.—The tongue of the wise *is* health.

They that feared the LORD spake often one to another: and the LORD hearkened, and heard *it*, and a book of remembrance was written before him for them that feared the LORD, and that thought upon his name.

If thou take forth the precious from the vile, thou shalt be as my mouth.—Therefore, as ye abound in every *thing, in* faith, and utterance, and knowledge, and *in* all diligence…*see* that ye abound in this grace also.

Col. 4.6; Pro. 25.11–12; Eph. 4.29; Mt. 12.35;
Mt. 12.37; Pro. 12.18 § Mal. 3.16 § Jer. 15.19; 2 Co. 8.7

Thy lovingkindness *is* before mine eyes.

The LORD *is* gracious, and full of compassion; slow to anger, and of great mercy.—Your Father which is in heaven...maketh his sun to rise on the evil and on the good, and sendeth rain on the just and on the unjust.

Be ye...followers of God, as dear children; and walk in love, as Christ also hath loved us, and hath given himself for us an offering and a sacrifice to God for a sweetsmelling savour.—Be ye kind to one another, tenderhearted, forgiving one another, even as God for Christ's sake hath forgiven you.—Seeing ye have purified your souls in obeying the truth through the Spirit unto unfeigned love of the brethren, *see that ye* love one another with a pure heart fervently.—The love of Christ constraineth us.

Love ye your enemies, and do good, and lend, hoping for nothing again; and your reward shall be great, and ye shall be the children of the Highest: for he is kind unto the unthankful and *to* the evil. Be ye therefore merciful, as your Father also is merciful.

Ps. 26.3; Ps. 145.8; Mt. 5.45 § Eph. 5.1–2; Eph. 4.32;
1 Pe. 1.22; 2 Co. 5.14 § Lu. 6.35–36

Then was Jesus led up of the Spirit into the wilderness to be tempted of the devil.

In the days of his flesh, when he had offered up prayers and supplications with strong crying and tears unto him that was able to save him from death, and was heard in that he feared; though he were a Son, yet learned he obedience by the things which he suffered; and being made perfect, he became the author of eternal salvation unto all them that obey him.—We have not an high priest which cannot be touched with the feeling of our infirmities; but was in all points tempted like as *we are, yet* without sin.

There hath no temptation taken you but such as is common to man: but God *is* faithful, who will not suffer you to be tempted above that ye are able; but will with the temptation also make a way to escape, that ye may be able to bear *it*.—My grace is sufficient for thee: for my strength is made perfect in weakness.

Mt. 4.1; He. 5.7–9; He. 4.15 § 1 Co. 10.13; 2 Co. 12.9

**The Son of man came...
to give his life a ransom for many.**

If the blood of bulls and of goats, and the ashes of an heifer sprinkling the unclean, sanctifieth to the purifying of the flesh: how much more shall the blood of Christ, who through the eternal Spirit offered himself without spot to God, purge your conscience from dead works to serve the living God?

He is brought as a lamb to the slaughter.—I lay down my life for the sheep... No man taketh it from me, but I lay it down of myself. I have power to lay it down, and I have power to take it again.

The life of the flesh *is* in the blood: and I have given it to you upon the altar to make an atonement for your souls: for it *is* the blood *that* maketh an atonement for the soul.—Without shedding of blood is no remission.

While we were yet sinners, Christ died for us. Much more then, being now justified by his blood, we shall be saved from wrath through him.

Mt. 20.28; He. 9.13–14 § Isa. 53.7; Jn. 10.15,18
§ Lev. 17.11; He. 9.22 § Ro. 5.8–9

If we confess our sins,
he is faithful and just to forgive us *our* sins,
and to cleanse us from all unrighteousness.

I acknowledge my transgressions: and my sin *is* ever before me. Against thee, thee only, have I sinned, and done *this* evil in thy sight.

And he arose, and came to his father. But when he was yet a great way off, his father saw him, and had compassion, and ran, and fell on his neck, and kissed him.—I have blotted out, as a thick cloud, thy transgressions, and, as a cloud, thy sins: return unto me; for I have redeemed thee.—Your sins are forgiven you for his name's sake.—God for Christ's sake hath forgiven you.—That he might be just, and the justifier of him which believeth in Jesus.

Then will I sprinkle clean water upon you, and ye shall be clean.—They shall walk with me in white: for they are worthy.

This is he that came by water and blood, *even* Jesus Christ; not by water only, but by water and blood.

---

1 Jn. 1.9; Ps. 51.3–4 § Lu. 15.20; Isa. 44.22; 1 Jn. 2.12; Eph. 4.32; Ro. 3.26 § Ezek. 36.25; Rev. 3.4 § 1 Jn. 5.6

Shall the throne of iniquity
have fellowship with thee?

Truly our fellowship *is* with the Father, and with his Son Jesus Christ.—Beloved, now are we the sons of God, and it doth not yet appear what we shall be: but we know that, when he shall appear, we shall be like him; for we shall see him as he is. And every man that hath this hope in him purifieth himself, even as he is pure.

The prince of this world cometh, and hath nothing in me.—An high priest…holy, harmless, undefiled.

We wrestle not against flesh and blood, but against principalities, against powers, against the rulers of the darkness of this world, against spiritual wickedness in high *places.*—The prince of the power of the air, the spirit that now worketh in the children of disobedience.

Whosoever is born of God sinneth not; but he that is begotten of God keepeth himself, and that wicked one toucheth him not. *And* we know that we are of God, and the whole world lieth in wickedness.

Ps. 94.20;   1 Jn. 1.3;   1 Jn. 3.2–3   § Jn. 14.30;   He. 7.26
§ Eph. 6.12;   Eph. 2.2   § 1 Jn. 5.18–19

**I have caused thine iniquity to pass from thee,
and I will clothe thee with change of raiment.**

Blessed *is he whose* transgression *is* forgiven, *whose* sin *is* covered.—We are all as an unclean *thing.*—I know that in me (that is, in my flesh,) dwelleth no good thing: for to will is present with me; but *how* to perform that which is good I find not.

As many of you as have been baptized into Christ have put on Christ.—Ye have put off the old man with his deeds; and have put on the new *man*, which is renewed in knowledge after the image of him that created him.—Not having mine own righteousness, which is of the law, but…the righteousness which is of God by faith.

Bring forth the best robe, and put *it* on him.—The fine linen is the righteousness of saints.—I will greatly rejoice in the LORD, my soul shall be joyful in my God; for he hath clothed me with the garments of salvation, he hath covered me with the robe of righteousness.

Zech. 3.4; Ps. 32.1; Isa. 64.6; Ro. 7.18 § Ga. 3.27; Col. 3.9–10; Phil. 3.9 § Lu. 15.22; Rev. 19.8; Isa. 61.10

The day shall declare it.

Judge nothing before the time, until the Lord come, who both will bring to light the hidden things of darkness, and will make manifest the counsels of the hearts: and then shall every man have praise of God.

Why dost thou judge thy brother? or why dost thou set at nought thy brother? for we shall all stand before the judgment seat of Christ... So then every one of us shall give account of himself to God. Let us not therefore judge one another any more.

God shall judge the secrets of men by Jesus Christ.— The Father judgeth no man, but hath committed all judgment unto the Son...and hath given him authority to execute judgment also, because he is the Son of man.

The Great, the Mighty God, the LORD of hosts, *is* his name, great in counsel, and mighty in work: for thine eyes *are* open upon all the ways of the sons of men: to give every one according to his ways, and according to the fruit of his doings.

---

1 Co. 3.13; 1 Co. 4.5 § Ro. 14.10,12–13 § Ro. 2.16; Jn. 5.22,27 § Jer. 32.18–19

The disciple is not above *his* master.

Ye call me Master and Lord: and ye say well; for *so* I am.

It is enough for the disciple that he be as his master, and the servant as his lord.——If they have persecuted me, they will also persecute you; if they have kept my saying, they will keep yours also.——I have given them thy word; and the world hath hated them, because they are not of the world, even as I am not of the world.

Consider him that endured such contradiction of sinners against himself, lest ye be wearied and faint in your minds. Ye have not yet resisted unto blood, striving against sin.

Let us run with patience the race that is set before us, looking unto Jesus the author and finisher of *our* faith; who for the joy that was set before him endured the cross, despising the shame, and is set down at the right hand of the throne of God.——Forasmuch…as Christ hath suffered for us in the flesh, arm yourselves likewise with the same mind.

Mt. 10.24; Jn. 13.13 § Mt. 10.25; Jn. 15.20; Jn. 17.14 § He. 12.3,4 § He. 12.1–2; 1 Pe. 4.1

My son, give me thine heart.

O that there were such an heart in them, that they would fear me, and keep all my commandments always, that it might be well with them, and with their children for ever!

Thy heart is not right in the sight of God.—Because the carnal mind is enmity against God: for it is not subject to the law of God, neither indeed can be. So then they that are in the flesh cannot please God.

They…first gave their own selves to the Lord.—And thus did Hezekiah throughout all Judah, and wrought *that which was* good and right and truth before the LORD his God. And in every work that he began in the service of the house of God, and in the law, and in the commandments, to seek his God, he did *it* with all his heart, and prospered.

Keep thy heart with all diligence; for out of it *are* the issues of life.

Whatsoever ye do, do *it* heartily, as to the Lord.—As the servants of Christ, doing the will of God from the heart; with good will doing service, as to the Lord, and not to men.

I will run the way of thy commandments, when thou shalt enlarge my heart.

Pro. 23.26;   Deu. 5.29 § Ac. 8.21;   Ro. 8.7–8 § 2 Co. 8.5;   2 Chr. 31.20–21 § Pro. 4.23 § Col. 3.23; Eph. 6.6–7 § Ps. 119.32

I *am* with thee to save thee.

Shall the prey be taken from the mighty, or the lawful captive delivered? But thus saith the LORD, Even the captives of the mighty shall be taken away, and the prey of the terrible shall be delivered: for I will contend with him that contendeth with thee…and all flesh shall know that I the LORD *am* thy Saviour and thy Redeemer, the mighty One of Jacob.—Fear thou not; for I *am* with thee: be not dismayed; for I *am* thy God: I will strengthen thee; yea, I will help thee; yea, I will uphold thee with the right hand of my righteousness.

We have not an high priest which cannot be touched with the feeling of our infirmities; but was in all points tempted like as *we are, yet* without sin.—In that he himself hath suffered being tempted, he is able to succour them that are tempted.—The steps of a *good* man are ordered by the LORD: and he delighteth in his way. Though he fall, he shall not be utterly cast down: for the LORD upholdeth *him with* his hand.

Jer. 15.20; Isa. 49.24–26; Isa. 41.10 § He. 4.15; He. 2.18; Ps. 37.23–24

**He satisfieth the longing soul,
and filleth the hungry soul with goodness.**

Ye have tasted that the Lord *is* gracious.

O God, thou *art* my God; early will I seek thee: my soul thirsteth for thee, my flesh longeth for thee in a dry and thirsty land, where no water is; to see thy power and thy glory.—My soul longeth, yea, even fainteth for the courts of the LORD: my heart and my flesh crieth out for the living God.—Having a desire to depart, and to be with Christ; which is far better.

I shall be satisfied, when I awake, with thy likeness.— They shall hunger no more, neither thirst any more; neither shall the sun light on them, nor any heat. For the Lamb which is in the midst of the throne shall feed them, and shall lead them unto living fountains of waters: and God shall wipe away all tears from their eyes.—They shall be abundantly satisfied with the fatness of thy house; and thou shalt make them drink of the river of thy pleasures.—My people shall be satisfied with my goodness, saith the LORD.

Ps. 107.9; 1 Pe. 2.3 § Ps. 63.1–2; Ps. 84.2; Phil. 1.23 § Ps. 17.15; Rev. 7.16–17; Ps. 36.8; Jer. 31.14

**My presence shall go *with thee,*
and I will give thee rest.**

Be strong and of a good courage, fear not, nor be afraid of them: for the LORD thy God, he *it is* that doth go with thee; he will not fail thee, nor forsake thee... The LORD, he *it is* that doth go before thee; he will be with thee, he will not fail thee, neither forsake thee: fear not, neither be dismayed.—Have not I commanded thee? Be strong and of a good courage; be not afraid, neither be thou dismayed: for the LORD thy God *is* with thee whithersoever thou goest.—In all thy ways acknowledge him, and he shall direct thy paths.

He hath said, I will never leave thee, nor forsake thee. So that we may boldly say, The Lord *is* my helper, and I will not fear what man shall do unto me.—Our sufficiency *is* of God.

Lead us not into temptation.—O LORD, I know that the way of man *is* not in himself: *it is* not in man that walketh to direct his steps.—My times *are* in thy hand.

Ex. 33.14; Deu. 31.6,8; Jos. 1.9; Pro. 3.6 § He. 13.5–6; 2 Co. 3.5 § Mt. 6.13; Jer. 10.23; Ps. 31.15

**Let us consider one another
to provoke unto love and to good works.**

How forcible are right words!—I stir up your pure minds by way of remembrance.

They that feared the LORD spake often one to another: and the LORD hearkened, and heard *it*, and a book of remembrance was written before him for them that feared the LORD, and that thought upon his name.—If two of you shall agree on earth as touching any thing that they shall ask, it shall be done for them of my Father which is in heaven.

The LORD God said, *it is* not good that the man should be alone.—Two *are* better than one; because they have a good reward for their labour. For if they fall, the one will lift up his fellow: but woe to him *that is* alone when he falleth; for *he hath* not another to help him up.

Let...no man put a stumblingblock or an occasion to fall in *his* brother's way.—Brethren, if a man be overtaken in a fault, ye which are spiritual, restore such an one in the spirit of meekness; considering thyself, lest thou also be tempted. Bear ye one another's burdens, and so fulfil the law of Christ.

He. 10.24; Job 6.25; 2 Pe. 3.1 § Mal. 3.16; Mt. 18.19 § Ge. 2.18; Ec. 4.9–10 § Ro. 14.13; Ga. 6.1–2

I *am* my beloved's,
and his desire *is* toward me.

I know whom I have believed, and am persuaded that he is able to keep that which I have committed unto him against that day.—I am persuaded, that neither death, nor life, nor angels, nor principalities, nor powers, nor things present, nor things to come, nor height, nor depth, nor any other creature, shall be able to separate us from the love of God, which is in Christ Jesus our Lord.—Those that thou gavest me I have kept, and none of them is lost.

The LORD taketh pleasure in his people.—My delights *were* with the sons of men.—His great love wherewith he loved us.—Greater love hath no man than this, that a man lay down his life for his friends.

Ye are bought with a price: therefore glorify God in your body, and in your spirit, which are God's.— Whether we live, we live unto the Lord; and whether we die, we die unto the Lord: whether we live therefore, or die, we are the Lord's.

Song 7.10; 2 Tim. 1.12; Ro. 8.38–39; Jn. 17.12
§ Ps. 149.4; Pro. 8.31; Eph. 2.4; Jn. 15.13 § 1 Co. 6.20;
Ro. 14.8

Seek ye out of
the book of the LORD.

Therefore shall ye lay up these my words in your heart and in your soul, and bind them for a sign upon your hand, that they may be as frontlets between your eyes.— This book of the law shall not depart out of thy mouth; but thou shalt meditate therein day and night, that thou mayest observe to do according to all that is written therein: for then thou shalt make thy way prosperous, and then thou shalt have good success.

The law of his God *is* in his heart; none of his steps shall slide.—By the word of thy lips I have kept *me from* the paths of the destroyer.—Thy word have I hid in mine heart, that I might not sin against thee.

We have…a more sure word of prophecy; whereunto ye do well that ye take heed, as unto a light that shineth in a dark place, until the day dawn, and the day star arise in your hearts.—That we through patience and comfort of the scriptures might have hope.

Isa. 34.16; Deu. 11.18; Jos. 1.8 § Ps. 37.31; Ps. 17.4; Ps. 119.11 § 2 Pe. 1.19; Ro. 15.4

Out of the abundance of the heart
the mouth speaketh.

Let the word of Christ dwell in you richly in all wisdom.

Keep thy heart with all diligence; for out of it *are* the issues of life.—Death and life *are* in the power of the tongue.—The mouth of the righteous speaketh wisdom, and his tongue talketh of judgment. The law of his God *is* in his heart; none of his steps shall slide.—Let no corrupt communication proceed out of your mouth, but that which is good to the use of edifying, that it may minister grace unto the hearers.

We cannot but speak the things which we have seen and heard.—I believed, therefore have I spoken.

Whosoever...shall confess me before men, him will I confess also before my Father which is in heaven.— With the heart man believeth unto righteousness; and with the mouth confession is made unto salvation.

Mt. 12.34; Col. 3.16 § Pro. 4.23; Pro. 18.21;
Ps. 37.30–31; Eph. 4.29 § Ac. 4.20; Ps. 116.10
§ Mt. 10.32; Ro. 10.10

**I trust I shall shortly see thee,
and we shall speak face to face.**

Oh that thou wouldest rend the heavens, that thou wouldest come down—As the hart panteth after the water brooks, so panteth my soul after thee, O God. My soul thirsteth for God, for the living God: when shall I come and appear before God?—Make haste, my beloved, and be thou like to a roe or to a young hart upon the mountains of spices.

Our conversation is in heaven; from whence also we look for the Saviour, the Lord Jesus Christ.—Looking for that blessed hope, and the glorious appearing of the great God and our Saviour Jesus Christ.—God our Saviour, and Lord Jesus Christ, *which is* our hope.—Whom having not seen, ye love.

He which testifieth these things saith, Surely I come quickly. Amen. Even so, come, Lord Jesus.—It shall be said in that day, Lo, this *is* our God; we have waited for him, and he will save us: this *is* the LORD; we have waited for him, we will be glad and rejoice in his salvation.

2 Jn. 14; Isa. 64.1; Ps. 42.1–2; Song 8.14 § Phil. 3.20;
Titus 2.13; 1 Tim. 1.1; 1 Pe. 1.8 § Rev. 22.20; Isa. 25.9

Thy will be done in earth,
as *it is* in heaven.

Bless the LORD, ye his angels, that excel in strength, that do his commandments, hearkening unto the voice of his word. Bless ye the LORD, all *ye* his hosts; *ye* ministers of his, that do his pleasure.

I came down from heaven, not to do mine own will, but the will of him that sent me.—I delight to do thy will, O my God: yea, thy law *is* within my heart.—O my Father, if this cup may not pass away from me, except I drink it, thy will be done.

Not every one that saith unto me, Lord, Lord, shall enter into the kingdom of heaven; but he that doeth the will of my Father which is in heaven.—(Not the hearers of the law *are* just before God, but the doers of the law shall be justified…)—If ye know these things, happy are ye if ye do them.—To him that knoweth to do good, and doeth *it* not, to him it is sin.

Be not conformed to this world: but be ye transformed by the renewing of your mind.

Mt. 6.10; Ps. 103.20–21 § Jn. 6.38; Ps. 40.8; Mt. 26.42 § Mt. 7.21; Ro. 2.13; Jn. 13.17; Jas. 4.17 § Ro. 12.2

**The ear trieth words,
as the mouth tasteth meat.**

Beloved, believe not every spirit, but try the spirits whether they are of God: because many false prophets are gone out into the world.—Judge not according to the appearance, but judge righteous judgment.—I speak as to wise men; judge ye what I say.—Let the word of Christ dwell in you richly in all wisdom.

He that hath an ear, let him hear what the Spirit saith.—He that is spiritual judgeth all things.

Take heed what ye hear.—I know thy works...and how...thou hast tried them which say they are apostles, and are not, and hast found them liars.—Prove all things; hold fast that which is good.

He calleth his own sheep by name, and leadeth them out. And when he putteth forth his own sheep, he goeth before them, and the sheep follow him: for they know his voice. And a stranger will they not follow, but will flee from him: for they know not the voice of strangers.

Job 34.3; 1 Jn. 4.1; Jn. 7.24; 1 Co. 10.15; Col. 3.16
§ Rev. 2.29; 1 Co. 2.15 § Mk. 4.24; Rev. 2.2; 1 Th. 5.21
§ Jn. 10.3–5

Ye shall be unto me a kingdom of priests, and an holy nation.

Thou wast slain, and hast redeemed us to God by thy blood out of every kindred, and tongue, and people, and nation; and hast made us unto our God kings and priests.—Ye *are* a chosen generation, a royal priesthood, an holy nation, a peculiar people; that ye should shew forth the praises of him who hath called you out of darkness into his marvellous light.

Ye shall be named the Priests of the LORD: *men* shall call you the Ministers of our God.—Priests of God and of Christ.

Wherefore, holy brethren, partakers of the heavenly calling, consider the Apostle and High Priest of our profession, Christ Jesus.—By him therefore let us offer the sacrifice of praise to God continually, that is, the fruit of *our* lips giving thanks to his name.

For we are his workmanship, created in Christ Jesus unto good works, which God hath before ordained that we should walk in them.—The temple of God is holy, which *temple* ye are.

Ex. 19.6;   Rev. 5.9–10;   1 Pe. 2.9   § Isa. 61.6;   Rev. 20.6 § He. 3.1;   He. 13.15   § Eph. 2.10;   1 Co. 3.17

**We made our prayer unto our God,
and set a watch against them.**

Watch and pray, that ye enter not into temptation.—
Continue in prayer, and watch in the same with
thanksgiving.—Casting all your care upon him; for he
careth for you. Be sober, be vigilant; because your adversary the devil, as a roaring lion, walketh about, seeking
whom he may devour: whom resist stedfast in the faith.

Why call ye me, Lord, Lord, and do not the things
which I say?—Be ye doers of the word, and not hearers
only, deceiving your own selves.

Wherefore criest thou unto me? speak unto the children of Israel, that they go forward.

Be careful for nothing; but in every thing by prayer
and supplication with thanksgiving let your requests be
made known unto God. And the peace of God, which
passeth all understanding, shall keep your hearts and
minds through Christ Jesus.

Ne. 4.9; Mt. 26.41; Col. 4.2; 1 Pe. 5.7–9 § Lu. 6.46;
Jas. 1.22 § Ex. 14.15 § Phil. 4.6–7

**Thou *art* a gracious God, and merciful,
slow to anger, and of great kindness,
and repentest thee of the evil.**

I beseech thee, let the power of my Lord be great, according as thou hast spoken, saying, The LORD *is* longsuffering, and of great mercy, forgiving iniquity and transgression, and by no means clearing *the guilty,* visiting the iniquity of the fathers upon the children unto the third and fourth *generation.*

O remember not against us former iniquities: let thy tender mercies speedily prevent us… Help us, O God of our salvation, for the glory of thy name: and deliver us, and purge away our sins, for thy name's sake.—LORD, though our iniquities testify against us, do thou *it* for thy name's sake: for our backslidings are many; we have sinned against thee.—We acknowledge, O LORD, our wickedness, *and* the iniquity of our fathers: for we have sinned against thee.

If thou, LORD, shouldest mark iniquities, O Lord, who shall stand? But *there is* forgiveness with thee, that thou mayest be feared.

Jon. 4.2; Nu. 14.17–18 § Ps. 79.8,9; Jer. 14.7; Jer. 14.20 § Ps. 130.3–4

Sanctification of the Spirit.

Awake, O north wind; and come, thou south; blow upon my garden, *that* the spices thereof may flow out.

Behold this selfsame thing, that ye sorrowed after a godly sort, what carefulness it wrought in you, yea, *what* clearing of yourselves, yea, *what* indignation, yea, *what* fear, yea, *what* vehement desire, yea, *what* zeal, yea, *what* revenge!—(For the fruit of the Spirit *is* in all goodness and righteousness and truth;) proving what is acceptable unto the Lord.

The Comforter...*is* the Holy Ghost.—The love of God is shed abroad in our hearts by the Holy Ghost which is given unto us.

The fruit of the Spirit is love, joy, peace.

In a great trial of affliction the abundance of their joy and their deep poverty abounded unto the riches of their liberality.

All these worketh that one and the selfsame Spirit, dividing to every man severally as he will.

---

2 Th. 2.13; Song 4.16 § 2 Co. 7.11; Eph. 5.9,10
§ Jn. 14.26; Ro. 5.5 § Ga. 5.22 § 2 Co. 8.2 § 1 Co. 12.11

He calleth his own sheep by name, and leadeth them out.

The foundation of God standeth sure, having this seal, The Lord knoweth them that are his. And, Let every one that nameth the name of Christ depart from iniquity.—Many will say to me in that day, Lord, Lord, have we not prophesied in thy name? and in thy name have cast out devils? and in thy name done many wonderful works? And then will I profess unto them, I never knew you: depart from me, ye that work iniquity.—The LORD knoweth the way of the righteous: but the way of the ungodly shall perish.

Behold, I have graven thee upon the palms of *my* hands; thy walls *are* continually before me.—Set me as a seal upon thine heart, as a seal upon thine arm.—The LORD *is* good, a strong hold in the day of trouble; and he knoweth them that trust in him.

I go to prepare a place for you. And if I go and prepare a place for you, I will come again, and receive you unto myself; that where I am, *there* ye may be also.

Jn. 10.3;   2 Tim. 2.19;   Mt. 7.22–23;   Ps. 1.6   § Isa. 49.16; Song 8.6;   Na. 1.7   § Jn. 14.2–3

She hath done what she could.

This poor widow hath cast in more than they all.—Whosoever shall give you a cup of water to drink in my name, because ye belong to Christ, verily I say unto you, he shall not lose his reward.—If there be first a willing mind, *it is* accepted according to that a man hath, *and* not according to that he hath not.

Let us not love in word, neither in tongue; but in deed and in truth.—If a brother or sister be naked, and destitute of daily food, and one of you say unto them, Depart in peace, be *ye* warmed and filled; notwithstanding ye give them not those things which are needful to the body; what *doth it* profit?—He which soweth bountifully shall reap also bountifully. Every man according as he purposeth in his heart, *so let him give;* not grudgingly, or of necessity: for God loveth a cheerful giver.

When ye shall have done all those things which are commanded you, say, We are unprofitable servants: we have done that which was our duty to do.

Mk. 14.8; Lu. 21.3; Mk. 9.41; 2 Co. 8.12 § 1 Jn. 3.18; Jas. 2.15–16; 2 Co. 9.6–7 § Lu. 17.10

He that is mighty
hath done to me great things;
and holy *is* his name.

Who *is* like unto thee, O LORD, among the gods? who *is* like thee, glorious in holiness, fearful *in* praises, doing wonders?—Among the gods *there is* none like unto thee, O Lord; neither *are there any works* like unto thy works.—Who shall not fear thee, O Lord, and glorify thy name? for *thou* only *art* holy.—Hallowed be thy name.

Blessed *be* the Lord God of Israel; for he hath visited and redeemed his people.

Who *is* this that cometh from Edom, with dyed garments from Bozrah? this *that is* glorious in his apparel, travelling in the greatness of his strength? I that speak in righteousness, mighty to save.—I have laid help upon *one that is* mighty; I have exalted *one* chosen out of the people.

Now unto him that is able to do exceeding abundantly above all that we ask or think, according to the power that worketh in us...*be* glory.

Lu. 1.49; Ex. 15.11; Ps. 86.8; Rev. 15.4; Mt. 6.9
§ Lu. 1.68 § Isa. 63.1; Ps. 89.19 § Eph. 3.20–21

The dew of Hermon.

Mount Sion, which *is* Hermon.—There the LORD commanded the blessing, *even* life for evermore.—I will be as the dew unto Israel: he shall grow as the lily, and cast forth his roots as Lebanon.

My doctrine shall drop as the rain, my speech shall distil as the dew, as the small rain upon the tender herb, and as the showers upon the grass.—As the rain cometh down, and the snow from heaven, and returneth not thither, but watereth the earth, and maketh it bring forth and bud, that it may give seed to the sower, and bread to the eater: so shall my word be that goeth forth out of my mouth: it shall not return unto me void, but it shall accomplish that which I please, and it shall prosper *in the thing* whereto I sent it.

God giveth not the Spirit by measure *unto him.*—And of his fulness have all we received, and grace for grace.—*It is* like the precious ointment upon the head…*even* Aaron's…that went down to the skirts of his garments.

Ps. 133.3;   Deu. 4.48;   Ps. 133.3;   Hos. 14.5   § Deu. 32.2; Isa. 55.10–11   § Jn. 3.34; Jn. 1.16; Ps. 133.2

They are not of the world,
even as I am not of the world.

He is despised and rejected of men; a man of sorrows, and acquainted with grief.—In the world ye shall have tribulation: but be of good cheer; I have overcome the world.

Such an high priest became us, *who is* holy, harmless, undefiled, separate from sinners.—That ye may be blameless and harmless, the sons of God, without rebuke, in the midst of a crooked and perverse nation.

Jesus of Nazareth…went about doing good, and healing all that were oppressed of the devil; for God was with him.—As we have therefore opportunity, let us do good unto all *men*, especially unto them who are of the household of faith.

That was the true Light, which lighteth every man that cometh into the world.—Ye are the light of the world. A city that is set on an hill cannot be hid… Let your light so shine before men, that they may see your good works, and glorify your Father which is in heaven.

Jn. 17.16; Isa. 53.3; Jn. 16.33 § He. 7.26; Phil. 2.15
§ Ac. 10.38; Ga. 6.10 § Jn. 1.9; Mt. 5.14,16

He that is of a merry heart *hath* a continual feast.

The joy of the LORD is your strength.—The kingdom of God is not meat and drink; but righteousness, and peace, and joy in the Holy Ghost.—Be filled with the Spirit; speaking to yourselves in psalms and hymns and spiritual songs, singing and making melody in your heart to the Lord; giving thanks always for all things unto God and the Father in the name of our Lord Jesus Christ.

By him...let us offer the sacrifice of praise to God continually, that is, the fruit of *our* lips giving thanks to his name.

Although the fig tree shall not blossom, neither *shall* fruit *be* in the vines; the labour of the olive shall fail, and the fields shall yield no meat; the flock shall be cut off from the fold, and *there shall be* no herd in the stalls: yet I will rejoice in the LORD, I will joy in the God of my salvation.—Sorrowful, yet alway rejoicing.—We glory in tribulations also.

Pro. 15.15; Ne. 8.10; Ro. 14.17; Eph. 5.18–20
§ He. 13.15 § Hab. 3.17–18; 2 Co. 6.10; Ro. 5.3

What profit *is there* of circumcision?

Much every way.—Circumcise yourselves to the
LORD, and take away the foreskins of your heart.—
If...their uncircumcised hearts be humbled, and they
then accept of the punishment of their iniquity: then
will I remember my covenant with Jacob, and also my
covenant with Isaac, and also my covenant with
Abraham will I remember.

Jesus Christ was a minister of the circumcision for
the truth of God, to confirm the promises *made* unto
the fathers.—In whom also ye are circumcised with the
circumcision made without hands, in putting off the
body of the sins of the flesh by the circumcision of
Christ.—You, being dead in your sins and the uncircumcision of your flesh, hath he quickened together
with him, having forgiven you all trespasses.

Put off concerning the former conversation the old
man, which is corrupt according to the deceitful lusts;
and be renewed in the spirit of your mind; and...put on
the new man, which after God is created in righteousness.

Ro. 3.1; Ro. 3.2; Jer. 4.4; Lev. 26.41–42 § Ro. 15.8;
Col. 2.11; Col. 2.13 § Eph. 4.22–23,24

The veil of the temple was rent in twain
from the top to the bottom.

The Lord Jesus the *same* night in which he was betrayed took bread: and when he had given thanks, he brake *it*, and said, Take, eat: this is my body, which is broken for you: this do in remembrance of me.—The bread that I will give is my flesh, which I will give for the life of the world.

Except ye eat the flesh of the Son of man, and drink his blood, ye have no life in you. Whoso eateth my flesh, and drinketh my blood, hath eternal life... He that eateth my flesh, and drinketh my blood, dwelleth in me, and I in him. As the living Father hath sent me, and I live by the Father: so he that eateth me, even he shall live by me... Doth this offend you? *What* and if ye shall see the Son of man ascend up where he was before? It is the spirit that quickeneth; the flesh profiteth nothing.

A new and living way, which he hath consecrated for us, through the veil, that is to say, his flesh...let us draw near.

Mt. 27.51; 1 Co. 11.23–24; Jn. 6.51
§ Jn. 6.53–54,56–57,61–63 § He. 10.20,22

**In that he died, he died unto sin once:
but in that he liveth, he liveth unto God.**

He was numbered with the transgressors.—Christ was once offered to bear the sins of many.—Who his own self bare our sins in his own body on the tree, that we, being dead to sins, should live unto righteousness: by whose stripes ye were healed.—By one offering he hath perfected for ever them that are sanctified.

This *man*, because he continueth ever, hath an unchangeable priesthood. Wherefore he is able also to save them to the uttermost that come unto God by him, seeing he ever liveth to make intercession for them.— While we were yet sinners, Christ died for us. Much more then, being now justified by his blood, we shall be saved from wrath through him.

Forasmuch…as Christ hath suffered for us in the flesh, arm yourselves likewise with the same mind: for he that hath suffered in the flesh hath ceased from sin; that he no longer should live the rest of *his* time in the flesh to the lusts of men, but to the will of God.

Ro. 6.10;   Isa. 53.12;   He. 9.28;   1 Pe. 2.24;   He. 10.14
§ He. 7.24–25;   Ro. 5.8–9 § 1 Pe. 4.1–2

Keep yourselves in the love of God.

Abide in me, and I in you. As the branch cannot bear fruit of itself, except it abide in the vine; no more can ye, except ye abide in me. I am the vine, ye *are* the branches: He that abideth in me, and I in him, the same bringeth forth much fruit: for without me ye can do nothing.

The fruit of the Spirit is love.

Herein is my Father glorified, that ye bear much fruit; so shall ye be my disciples. As the Father hath loved me, so have I loved you: continue ye in my love. If ye keep my commandments, ye shall abide in my love; even as I have kept my Father's commandments, and abide in his love.—Whoso keepeth his word, in him verily is the love of God perfected.

This is my commandment, That ye love one another, as I have loved you.—God commendeth his love toward us, in that, while we were yet sinners, Christ died for us.—God is love; and he that dwelleth in love dwelleth in God, and God in him.

Jude 21; Jn. 15.4–5 § Ga. 5.22 § Jn. 15.8–10; 1 Jn. 2.5 § Jn. 15.12; Ro. 5.8; 1 Jn. 4.16

Then *cometh* the end.

Of that day and *that* hour knoweth no man, no, not the angels which are in heaven, neither the Son, but the Father. Take ye heed, watch and pray: for ye know not when the time is… And what I say unto you I say unto all, Watch.—The Lord is not slack concerning his promise, as some men count slackness; but is longsuffering to us-ward, not willing that any should perish, but that all should come to repentance.—The coming of the Lord draweth nigh… The judge standeth before the door.—Surely I come quickly.

Seeing…that all these things shall be dissolved, what manner *of persons* ought ye to be in *all* holy conversation and godliness?

The end of all things is at hand: be ye therefore sober, and watch unto prayer.—Let your loins be girded about, and *your* lights burning; and ye yourselves like unto men that wait for their lord, when he will return from the wedding; that when he cometh and knocketh, they may open unto him immediately.

1 Co. 15.24; Mk. 13.32–33,37; 2 Pe. 3.9; Jas. 5.8,9; Rev. 22.20 § 2 Pe. 3.11 § 1 Pe. 4.7; Lu. 12.35–36

Brethren, pray for us.

Is any sick among you? let him call for the elders of the church; and let them pray over him… And the prayer of faith shall save the sick, and the Lord shall raise him up… Pray one for another, that ye may be healed. The effectual fervent prayer of a righteous man availeth much. Elias was a man subject to like passions as we are, and he prayed earnestly that it might not rain: and it rained not on the earth by the space of three years and six months. And he prayed again, and the heaven gave rain, and the earth brought forth her fruit.

Praying always with all prayer and supplication in the Spirit, and watching thereunto with all perseverance and supplication for all saints.

Without ceasing I make mention of you always in my prayers.—Always labouring fervently for you in prayers, that ye may stand perfect and complete in all the will of God.

1 Th. 5.25; Jas. 5.14,15,16–18 § Eph. 6.18 § Ro. 1.9; Col. 4.12

Patient in tribulation.

It *is* the LORD: let him do what seemeth him good.—
Whom, though I were righteous, *yet* would I not answer,
but I would make supplication to my judge.—The LORD
gave, and the LORD hath taken away; blessed be the
name of the LORD.—What? shall we receive good at the
hand of God, and shall we not receive evil?

Jesus wept.—A man of sorrows, and acquainted with
grief… Surely he hath borne our griefs, and carried our
sorrows.

Whom the Lord loveth he chasteneth, and scourgeth
every son whom he receiveth… Now no chastening for
the present seemeth to be joyous, but grievous: nevertheless afterward it yieldeth the peaceable fruit of
righteousness unto them which are exercised thereby.—
Strengthened with all might, according to his glorious
power, unto all patience and longsuffering with joyfulness.—In the world ye shall have tribulation: but be of
good cheer; I have overcome the world.

Ro. 12.12;　1 Sa. 3.18;　Job 9.15;　Job 1.21;　Job 2.10
§ Jn. 11.35;　Isa. 53.3,4　§ He. 12.6,11;　Col. 1.11;
Jn. 16.33

He staggered not
at the promise of God through unbelief.

Have faith in God…whosoever shall say unto this mountain, Be thou removed, and be thou cast into the sea; and shall not doubt in his heart, but shall believe that those things which he saith shall come to pass; he shall have whatsoever he saith. Therefore I say unto you, What things soever ye desire, when ye pray, believe that ye receive *them*, and ye shall have *them*.—Without faith *it is* impossible to please *him:* for he that cometh to God must believe that he is, and *that* he is a rewarder of them that diligently seek him.

He that had received the promises offered up his only begotten *son*, of whom it was said, That in Isaac shall thy seed be called: accounting that God *was* able to raise *him* up, even from the dead.—Being fully persuaded that, what he had promised, he was able also to perform.

Is any thing too hard for the LORD?—With God all things are possible.—Lord, Increase our faith.

Ro. 4.20; Mk. 11.22,23–24; He. 11.6 § He. 11.17–19; Ro. 4.21 § Ge. 18.14; Mt. 19.26; Lu. 17.5

We know that we have passed from death unto life.

He that heareth my word, and believeth on him that sent me, hath everlasting life, and shall not come into condemnation; but is passed from death unto life.—He that hath the Son hath life; *and* he that hath not the Son of God hath not life.

He which stablisheth us with you in Christ, and hath anointed us, *is* God; who hath also sealed us, and given the earnest of the Spirit in our hearts.—Hereby we know that we are of the truth, and shall assure our hearts before him. Beloved, if our heart condemn us not, *then* have we confidence toward God.—We know that we are of God, and the whole world lieth in wickedness.

You *hath he quickened*, who were dead in trespasses and sins.—Quickened...together with Christ.—Who hath delivered us from the power of darkness, and hath translated *us* into the kingdom his dear Son.

---

1 Jn. 3.14; Jn. 5.24; 1 Jn. 5.12 § 2 Co. 1.21–22;
1 Jn. 3.19,21; 1 Jn. 5.19 § Eph. 2.1; Eph. 2.5; Col. 1.13

Thou wilt shew me the path of life.

Thus saith the LORD; Behold, I set before you the way of life, and the way of death.—I will teach you the good and the right way.—I am the way, the truth, and the life: no man cometh unto the Father, but by me.— Follow me.

There is a way which seemeth right unto a man, but the end thereof *are* the ways of death.—Wide *is* the gate, and broad *is* the way, that leadeth to destruction, and many there be which go in thereat: because strait *is* the gate, and narrow *is* the way, which leadeth unto life, and few there be that find it.

An highway shall be there, and a way, and it shall be called The way of holiness; the unclean shall not pass over it; but it *shall be* for those: the wayfaring men, though fools, shall not err *therein.*—Then shall we know, *if* we follow on to know the LORD.

In my Father's house are many mansions: if *it were* not *so,* I would have told you. I go to prepare a place for you.

Ps. 16.11; Jer. 21.8; 1 Sa. 12.23; Jn. 14.6; Mt. 4.19
§ Pro. 14.12; Mt. 7.13–14 § Isa. 35.8; Hos. 6.3
§ Jn. 14.2

By faith Abraham…
called to go out into a place which he should
after receive for an inheritance, obeyed.

He shall choose our inheritance for us.—He led him about, he instructed him, he kept him as the apple of his eye. As an eagle stirreth up her nest, fluttereth over her young, spreadeth abroad her wings, taketh them, beareth them on her wings: *so* the LORD alone did lead him, and *there was* no strange god with him.

I *am* the LORD thy God which teacheth thee to profit, which leadeth thee by the way *that* thou shouldest go.—Who teacheth like him?

We walk by faith, not by sight.—Here have we no continuing city, but we seek one to come.—Dearly beloved, I beseech *you* as strangers and pilgrims, abstain from fleshly lusts, which war against the soul.—Arise ye, and depart; for this *is* not *your* rest: because it is polluted, it shall destroy *you*, even with a sore destruction.

He. 11.8; Ps. 47.4; Deu. 32.10–12 § Isa. 48.17; Job 36.22 § 2 Co. 5.7; He. 13.14; 1 Pe. 2.11; Mi. 2.10

Give thanks at the remembrance of his holiness.

The heavens are not clean in his sight. How much more abominable and filthy *is* man, which drinketh iniquity like water?—Yea, the stars are not pure in his sight. How much less man, *that is* a worm?

Who *is* like unto thee, O LORD, among the gods? who *is* like thee, glorious in holiness?—Holy, holy, holy, *is* the LORD of hosts.

As he which hath called you is holy, so be ye holy in all manner of conversation; because it is written, Be ye holy; for I am holy.—Partakers of his holiness.

The temple of God is holy, which *temple* ye are.— What manner *of persons* ought ye to be in *all* holy conversation and godliness…without spot, and blameless?

Let no corrupt communication proceed out of your mouth, but that which is good to the use of edifying… And grieve not the holy Spirit of God, whereby ye are sealed unto the day of redemption.

Ps. 97.12; Job 15.15–16; Job 25.5–6 § Ex. 15.11; Isa. 6.3 § 1 Pe. 1.15,16; He. 12.10 § 1 Co. 3.17; 2 Pe. 3.11,14 § Eph. 4.29,30

Christel, who is the image of God.

The glory of the LORD shall be revealed, and all flesh shall see *it* together.—And the Word was made flesh, and dwelt among us, (and we beheld his glory, the glory as of the only begotten of the Father,) full of grace and truth... No man hath seen God at any time; the only begotten Son, which is in the bosom of the Father, he hath declared *him*.—He that hath seen me hath seen the Father.—The brightness of *his* glory, and the express image of his person.—God was manifest in the flesh.

In whom we have redemption through his blood, *even* the forgiveness of sins: who is the image of the invisible God, the firstborn of every creature.—Whom he did foreknow, he also did predestinate *to be* conformed to the image of his Son, that he might be the firstborn among many brethren.

As we have borne the image of the earthy, we shall also bear the image of the heavenly.

---

2 Co. 4.4; Isa. 40.5; Jn. 1.14,18; Jn. 14.9; He. 1.3;
1 Tim. 3.16 § Col. 1.14–15; Ro. 8.29 § 1 Co. 15.49

Thou hast girded me with strength unto the battle.

When I am weak, then am I strong.

Asa cried unto the LORD his God, and said, LORD, *it is* nothing with thee to help, whether with many, or with them that have no power: help us, O LORD our God; for we rest on thee, and in thy name we go against this multitude. O LORD, thou *art* our God; let not man prevail against thee.—Jehoshaphat cried out, and the LORD helped him.

It is better to trust in the LORD than to put confidence in man. *It is* better to trust in the LORD than to put confidence in princes.—There is no king saved by the multitude of an host: a mighty man is not delivered by much strength. An horse *is* a vain thing for safety: neither shall he deliver *any* by his great strength.

We wrestle not against flesh and blood, but against principalities, against powers, against the rulers of the darkness of this world, against spiritual wickedness in high *places*. Wherefore take unto you the whole armour of God.

Ps. 18.39; 2 Co. 12.10 § 2 Chr. 14.11; 2 Chr. 18.31 § Ps. 118.8–9; Ps. 33.16–17 § Eph. 6.12–13

Walk in love.

A new commandment I give unto you, That ye love one another; as I have loved you, that ye also love one another.—Above all things have fervent charity among yourselves: for charity shall cover the multitude of sins.—Love covereth all sins.

When ye stand praying, forgive, if ye have ought against any: that your Father also which is in heaven may forgive you your trespasses.—Love ye your enemies, and do good, and lend, hoping for nothing again.—Rejoice not when thine enemy falleth, and let not thine heart be glad when he stumbleth.—Not rendering evil for evil, or railing for railing: but contrariwise blessing; knowing that ye are thereunto called, that ye should inherit a blessing.—If it be possible, as much as lieth in you, live peaceably with all men.—Be ye kind one to another, tenderhearted, forgiving one another, even as God for Christ's sake hath forgiven you.

My little children, let us not love in word, neither in tongue; but in deed and in truth.

Eph. 5.2; Jn. 13.34; 1 Pe. 4.8; Pro. 10.12 § Mk. 11.25; Lu. 6.35; Pro. 24.17; 1 Pe. 3.9; Ro. 12.18; Eph. 4.32 § 1 Jn. 3.18

Let your requests be
made known unto God.

Abba, Father, all things *are* possible unto thee; take away this cup from me: nevertheless not what I will, but what thou wilt.—There was given to me a thorn in the flesh... For this thing I besought the Lord thrice, that it might depart from me. And he said unto me, My grace is sufficient for thee: for my strength is made perfect in weakness. Most gladly therefore will I rather glory in my infirmities.

I poured out my complaint before him; I shewed before him my trouble.—Hannah...*was* in bitterness of soul, and prayed unto the LORD, and wept sore. And she vowed a vow, and said, O LORD of hosts, if thou wilt indeed look on the affliction of thine handmaid, and...wilt give unto thine handmaid a man child, then I will give him unto the LORD all the days of his life... The LORD remembered her.

We know not what we should pray for as we ought.—He shall choose our inheritance for us.

Phil. 4.6; Mk. 14.36; 2 Co. 12.7,8–9 § Ps. 142.2;
1 Sa. 1.9,10–11,19 § Ro. 8.26; Ps. 47.4

**Oh that thou wouldest rend the heavens,
that thou wouldest come down.**

Make haste, my beloved, and be thou like to a roe or to a young hart upon the mountains of spices.—We ourselves groan within ourselves, waiting for the adoption, *to wit*, the redemption of our body.—Bow thy heavens, O LORD, and come down: touch the mountains, and they shall smoke.

This same Jesus, which is taken up from you into heaven, shall so come in like manner as ye have seen him go into heaven.—Unto them that look for him shall he appear the second time without sin unto salvation.—It shall be said in that day, Lo, this *is* our God; we have waited for him, and he will save us: this *is* the LORD; we have waited for him, we will be glad and rejoice in his salvation.

He which testifieth these things saith, Surely I come quickly. Amen. Even so, come, Lord Jesus.—That blessed hope, and the glorious appearing of the great God and our Saviour Jesus Christ.—Our conversation is in heaven.

Isa. 64.1; Song 8.14; Ro. 8.23; Ps. 144.5 § Ac. 1.11; He. 9.28; Isa. 25.9 § Rev. 22.20; Titus 2.13; Phil. 3.20

**Thou hast given *me* the heritage
of those that fear thy name.**

No weapon that is formed against thee shall prosper; and every tongue *that* shall rise against thee in judgment thou shalt condemn. This *is* the heritage of the servants of the LORD, and their righteousness *is* of me, saith the LORD.—The angel of the LORD encampeth round about them that fear him, and delivereth them. O taste and see that the LORD *is* good: blessed *is* the man *that* trusteth in him. O fear the LORD, ye his saints: for *there is* no want to them that fear him. The young lions do lack, and suffer hunger: but they that seek the LORD shall not want any good *thing*.—The lines are fallen unto me in pleasant *places*; yea, I have a goodly heritage.

Unto you that fear my name shall the Sun of righteousness arise with healing in his wings; and ye shall go forth, and grow up as calves of the stall.—He that spared not his own Son, but delivered him up for us all, how shall he not with him also freely give us all things?

Ps. 61.5; Isa. 54.17; Ps. 34.7–10; Ps. 16.6 § Mal. 4.2; Ro. 8.32

**Seek those things which are above,
where Christ sitteth on the right hand of God.**

Get wisdom, get understanding.—The wisdom that is from above.—The depth saith, It *is* not in me: and the sea saith, *It is* not with me.—We are buried with him by baptism into death: that like as Christ was raised up from the dead by the glory of the Father, even so we also should walk in newness of life. For if we have been planted together in the likeness of his death, we shall be also *in the likeness* of *his* resurrection.

Let us lay aside every weight, and the sin which doth so easily beset *us,* and let us run with patience the race that is set before us.—But God...hath quickened us together with Christ...and hath raised *us* up together, and made *us* sit together in heavenly *places* in Christ Jesus.

They that say such things declare plainly that they seek a country.—Seek ye the LORD, all ye meek of the earth, which have wrought his judgment; seek righteousness, seek meekness.

Col. 3.1; Pro. 4.5; Jas. 3.17; Job 28.14; Ro. 6.4–5
§ He. 12.1; Eph. 2.4,5,6 § He. 11.14; Zeph. 2.3

Nicodemus…
(he that came to Jesus by night).

Peter followed him afar off.—Among the chief rulers also many believed on him; but because of the Pharisees they did not confess *him*, lest they should be put out of the synagogue: for they loved the praise of men more than the praise of God.—The fear of man bringeth a snare: but whoso putteth his trust in the LORD shall be safe.

Him that cometh to me I will in no wise cast out.—A bruised reed shall he not break, and the smoking flax shall he not quench.—Faith as a grain of mustard seed.

God hath not given us the spirit of fear; but of power, and of love, and of a sound mind. Be not thou therefore ashamed of the testimony of our Lord.—Little children, abide in him; that, when he shall appear, we may have confidence, and not be ashamed before him at his coming.—Whosoever…shall confess me before men, him will I confess also before my Father which is in heaven.

Jn. 7.50; Mt. 26.58; Jn. 12.42–43; Pro. 29.25 § Jn. 6.37;
Isa. 42.3; Mt. 17.20 § 2 Tim. 1.7–8; 1 Jn. 2.28;
Mt. 10.32

Endure hardness,
as a good soldier of Jesus Christ.

I have given him *for* a witness to the people, a leader and a commander to the people.—It became him, for whom *are* all things, and by whom *are* all things, in bringing many sons unto glory, to make the captain of their salvation perfect through sufferings.—We must through much tribulation enter into the kingdom of God.

We wrestle not against flesh and blood, but against principalities, against powers, against the rulers of the darkness of this world, against spiritual wickedness in high *places*. Wherefore take unto you the whole armour of God.—We do not war after the flesh: (for the weapons of our warfare *are* not carnal, but mighty through God to the pulling down of strong holds)…

The God of all grace, who hath called us unto his eternal glory by Christ Jesus, after that ye have suffered a while, make you perfect, stablish, strengthen, settle *you*.

---

2 **Tim**. 2.3; Isa. 55.4; He. 2.10; Ac. 14.22
§ Eph. 6.12–13; 2 Co. 10.3–4 § 1 Pe. 5.10

The unity of the Spirit.

There is one body, and one Spirit.—Through him we both have access by one Spirit unto the Father. Now therefore ye are no more strangers and foreigners, but fellowcitizens with the saints, and of the household of God; and are built upon the foundation of the apostles and prophets, Jesus Christ himself being the chief corner *stone*; in whom all the building fitly framed together groweth unto an holy temple in the Lord: in whom ye also are builded together for an habitation of God through the Spirit.

Behold, how good and how pleasant *it is* for brethren to dwell together in unity! *It is* like the precious ointment upon the head, that ran down upon the beard, *even* Aaron's beard: that went down to the skirts of his garments.

Seeing ye have purified your souls in obeying the truth through the Spirit unto unfeigned love of the brethren, *see that ye* love one another with a pure heart fervently.

Eph. 4.3; Eph. 4.4; Eph. 2.18–22 § Ps. 133.1–2 § 1 Pe. 1.22

The fruit of the Spirit is…faith.

By grace are ye saved through faith; and that not of yourselves: *it is* the gift of God.—Without faith *it is* impossible to please *him*.—He that believeth on him is not condemned: but he that believeth not is condemned already, because he hath not believed in the name of the only begotten Son of God.—Lord, I believe; help thou mine unbelief.

Whoso keepeth his word, in him verily is the love of God perfected: hereby know we that we are in him.—Faith…worketh by love.—Faith without works is dead.

We walk by faith, not by sight.—I am crucified with Christ: nevertheless I live; yet not I, but Christ liveth in me: and the life which I now live in the flesh I live by the faith of the Son of God, who loved me, and gave himself for me.—Whom having not seen, ye love; in whom, though now ye see *him* not, yet believing, ye rejoice with joy unspeakable and full of glory: receiving the end of your faith, *even* the salvation of *your* souls.

Ga. 5.22; Eph. 2.8; He. 11.6; Jn. 3.18; Mk. 9.24
§ 1 Jn. 2.5; Ga. 5.6; Jas. 2.20 § 2 Co. 5.7; Ga. 2.20;
1 Pe. 1.8–9

The Lord is very pitiful, and of tender mercy.

Like as a father pitieth *his* children, *so* the LORD pitieth them that fear him.—The LORD *is* gracious and full of compassion…he will ever be mindful of his covenant.

He that keepeth thee will not slumber. Behold, he that keepeth Israel shall neither slumber nor sleep.—As an eagle stirreth up her nest, fluttereth over her young, spreadeth abroad her wings, taketh them, beareth them on her wings: *so* the LORD alone did lead him, and *there was* no strange god with him.

His compassions fail not. *They are* new every morning: great *is* thy faithfulness.

Jesus went forth, and saw a great multitude, and was moved with compassion toward them, and he healed their sick.—The same yesterday, and to day, and for ever.

Are not two sparrows sold for a farthing? and one of them shall not fall on the ground without your Father. But the very hairs of your head are all numbered. Fear ye not therefore, ye are of more value than many sparrows

Jas. 5.11; Ps. 103.13; Ps. 111.4,5 § Ps. 121.3–4;
Deu. 32.11–12 § Lam. 3.22–23 § Mt. 14.14; He. 13.8
§ Mt. 10.29–31

The Lamb slain from
the foundation of the world.

Your lamb shall be without blemish…and the whole assembly of the congregation of Israel shall kill it in the evening. And they shall take of the blood, and strike *it* on the two side posts and on the upper door post of the houses, wherein they shall eat it…and when I see the blood, I will pass over you.——The blood of sprinkling.——Christ our passover is sacrificed for us.——Being delivered by the determinate counsel and foreknowledge of God.——According to his own purpose and grace, which was given us in Christ Jesus before the world began.

We have redemption through his blood, the forgiveness of sins.

Forasmuch then as Christ hath suffered for us in the flesh, arm yourselves likewise with the same mind: for he that hath suffered in the flesh hath ceased from sin; that he no longer should live the rest of *his* time in the flesh to the lusts of men, but to the will of God.

Rev. 13.8; Ex. 12.5,6–7,13; He. 12.24; 1 Co. 5.7; Ac. 2.23; 2 Tim. 1.9 § Eph. 1.7 § 1 Pe. 4.1–2

I have trodden the winepress alone.

Who *is* like unto thee, O LORD, among the gods? who *is* like thee, glorious in holiness, fearful *in* praises, doing wonders?—He saw that *there was* no man, and wondered that *there was* no intercessor: therefore his arm brought salvation unto him; and his righteousness, it sustained him.—Who his own self bare our sins in his own body on the tree.—Being made a curse for us.

O sing unto the LORD a new song; for he hath done marvellous things: his right hand, and his holy arm, hath gotten him the victory.—Having spoiled principalities and powers, he made a shew of them openly, triumphing over them in it.—He shall see of the travail of his soul, *and* shall be satisfied: by his knowledge shall my righteous servant justify many; for he shall bear their iniquities.

O my soul, thou hast trodden down strength.—We are more than conquerors through him that loved us.—They overcame…by the blood of the Lamb, and by the word of their testimony.

Isa. 63.3; Ex. 15.11; Isa. 59.16; 1 Pe. 2.24; Ga. 3.13 § Ps. 98.1; Col. 2.15; Isa. 53.11 § Judg. 5.21; Ro. 8.37; Rev. 12.11

His mercy *is* on them that fear Him.

Oh how great *is* thy goodness, which thou hast laid up for them that fear thee; *which* thou hast wrought for them that trust in thee before the sons of men! Thou shalt hide them in the secret of thy presence from the pride of man: thou shalt keep them secretly in a pavilion from the strife of tongues.

If ye call on the Father, who without respect of persons judgeth according to every man's work, pass the time of your sojourning *here* in fear.—The LORD *is* nigh unto all them that call upon him, to all that call upon him in truth. He will fulfil the desire of them that fear him: he also will hear their cry, and will save them.

Because thine heart was tender, and thou hast humbled thyself before the LORD...and hast rent thy clothes, and wept before me; I also have heard *thee*, saith the LORD.—To this *man* will I look, *even* to *him that is* poor and of a contrite spirit, and trembleth at my word.—The LORD *is* nigh unto them that are of a broken heart; and saveth such as be of a contrite spirit.

Lu. 1.50; Ps. 31.19–20 § 1 Pe. 1.17; Ps. 145.18–19
§ 2 Ki. 22.19; Isa. 66.2; Ps. 34.18

Them that honour me
I will honour.

Whosoever...shall confess me before men, him will I confess also before my Father which is in heaven.—He that loveth father or mother more than me is not worthy of me: and he that loveth son or daughter more than me is not worthy of me. And he that taketh not his cross, and followeth after me, is not worthy of me. He that findeth his life shall lose it: and he that loseth his life for my sake shall find it.

Blessed *is* the man that endureth temptation: for when he is tried, he shall receive the crown of life, which the Lord hath promised to them that love him.

Fear none of those things which thou shalt suffer...be thou faithful unto death, and I will give thee a crown of life.

Our light affliction, which is but for a moment, worketh for us a far more exceeding *and* eternal weight of glory.—Praise and honour and glory at the appearing of Jesus Christ.

1 Sa. 2.30; Mt. 10.32; Mt. 10.37–39 § Jas. 1.12
§ Rev. 2.10 § 2 Co. 4.17; 1 Pe. 1.7

It is finished:
and he bowed his head, and gave up the ghost.

Jesus the author and finisher of *our* faith.—I have glorified thee on the earth: I have finished the work which thou gavest me to do.—We are sanctified through the offering of the body of Jesus Christ once *for all*. And every priest standeth daily ministering and offering oftentimes the same sacrifices, which can never take away sins: but this man, after he had offered one sacrifice for sins for ever, sat down on the right hand of God; from henceforth expecting till his enemies be made his footstool. For by one offering he hath perfected for ever them that are sanctified.—Blotting out the handwriting of ordinances that was against us, which was contrary to us, and took it out of the way, nailing it to his cross.

I lay down my life, that I might take it again. No man taketh it from me, but I lay it down of myself. I have power to lay it down, and I have power to take it again.—Greater love hath no man than this, that a man lay down his life for his friends.

Jn. 19.30; He. 12.2; Jn. 17.4; He. 10.10–14; Col. 2.14
§ Jn. 10.17–18; Jn. 15.13

**He sent from above, he took me,
he drew me out of many waters.**

He brought me up…out of an horrible pit, out of the miry clay, and set my feet upon a rock, *and* established my goings.—You *hath he quickened*, who were dead in trespasses and sins; wherein in time past ye walked according to the course of this world…among whom also we all had our conversation in times past in the lusts of our flesh.

Hear my cry, O God; attend unto my prayer. From the end of the earth will I cry unto thee, when my heart is overwhelmed: lead me to the rock *that* is higher than I.—Out of the belly of hell cried I, *and* thou heardest my voice. For thou hadst cast me into the deep, in the midst of the seas; and the floods compassed me about: all thy billows and thy waves passed over me.—We went through fire and through water: but thou broughtest us out into a wealthy *place*.

When thou passest through the waters, I *will be* with thee; and through the rivers, they shall not overflow thee.

Ps. 18.16; Ps. 40.2; Eph. 2.1–2,3 § Ps. 61.1–2;
Jon. 2.2–3; Ps. 66.12 § Isa. 43.2

Walk in newness of life.

As ye have yielded your members servants to uncleanness and to iniquity unto iniquity; even so now yield your members servants to righteousness unto holiness.—I beseech you…brethren, by the mercies of God, that ye present your bodies a living sacrifice, holy, acceptable unto God, *which is* your reasonable service. And be not conformed to this world: but be ye transformed by the renewing of your mind.

If any man *be* in Christ, *he is* a new creature: old things are passed away; behold, all things are become new.—In Christ Jesus neither circumcision availeth any thing, nor uncircumcision, but a new creature. And as many as walk according to this rule, peace *be* on them, and mercy.—This I say therefore, and testify in the Lord, that ye henceforth walk not as other Gentiles walk, in the vanity of their mind.—Ye have not so learned Christ; if so be that ye have heard him, and have been taught by him, as the truth is in Jesus…that ye put on the new man, which after God is created in righteousness and true holiness.

Ro. 6.4; Ro. 6.19; Ro. 12.1–2 § 2 Co. 5.17;
Ga. 6.15–16; Eph. 4.17; Eph. 4.20–21,24

Thy will be done.

O LORD, I know that the way of man *is* not in himself: *it is* not in man that walketh to direct his steps.—Not as I will, but as thou *wilt.*—Surely I have behaved and quieted myself, as a child that is weaned of his mother: my soul *is* even as a weaned child.

We know not what we should pray for as we ought: but the Spirit itself maketh intercession for us with groanings which cannot be uttered. And he that searcheth the hearts knoweth what *is* the mind of the Spirit, because he maketh intercession for the saints according to *the will of* God.

Ye know not what ye ask.—He gave them their request; but sent leanness into their soul.—These things were our examples, to the intent we should not lust after evil things, as they also lusted.

I would have you without carefulness.—Thou wilt keep *him* in perfect peace, *whose* mind *is* stayed *on thee:* because he trusteth in thee.

Mt. 26.42; Jer. 10.23; Mt. 26.39; Ps. 131.2
§ Ro. 8.26–27 § Mt. 20.22; Ps. 106.15; 1 Co. 10.6
§ 1 Co. 7.32; Isa. 26.3

Whom the LORD loveth he correcteth.

See now that I, *even* I, *am* he, and *there is* no god with me: I kill, and I make alive; I wound, and I heal: neither *is there any* that can deliver out of my hand.——I know the thoughts that I think toward you, saith the LORD, thoughts of peace, and not of evil, to give you an expected end.——My thoughts *are* not your thoughts, neither *are* your ways my ways, saith the LORD.

I will allure her, and bring her into the wilderness, and speak comfortably unto her.——As a man chasteneth his son, *so* the LORD thy God chasteneth thee.——Now no chastening for the present seemeth to be joyous, but grievous: nevertheless afterward it yieldeth the peaceable fruit of righteousness unto them which are exercised thereby.——Humble yourselves therefore under the mighty hand of God, that he may exalt you in due time.

I know, O LORD, that thy judgments *are* right, and *that* thou in faithfulness hast afflicted me.

Pro. 3.12; Deu. 32.39; Jer. 29.11; Isa. 55.8 § Hos. 2.14; Deu. 8.5; He. 12.11; 1 Pe. 5.6 § Ps. 119.75

**The earth *is* the LORD's,
and the fulness thereof.**

She did not know that I gave her corn, and wine, and oil, and multiplied her silver and gold... Therefore will I return, and take away my corn in the time thereof, and my wine in the season thereof, and will recover my wool and my flax.

All things *come* of thee, and of thine own have we given thee. For we *are* strangers before thee, and sojourners, as *were* all our fathers: our days on the earth *are* as a shadow, and *there is* none abiding. O LORD our God, all this store...*cometh* of thine hand, and *is* all thine own.—Of him, and through him, and to him, *are* all things: to whom *be* glory for ever. Amen.

The living God...giveth us richly all things to enjoy.—Every creature of God *is* good, and nothing to be refused, if it be received with thanksgiving: for it is sanctified by the word of God and prayer.

My God shall supply all your need according to his riches in glory by Christ Jesus.

Ps. 24.1; Hos. 2.8,9 § 1 Chr. 29.14–16; Ro. 11.36
§ 1 Tim. 6.17; 1 Tim. 4.4–5 § Phil. 4.19

The Comforter, *which is* the Holy Ghost, whom the Father will send in my name.

If thou knewest the gift of God, and who it is that saith to thee, Give me to drink; thou wouldest have asked of him, and he would have given thee living water.—If ye…being evil, know how to give good gifts unto your children: how much more shall *your* heavenly Father give the Holy Spirit to them that ask him?—Verily, verily, I say unto you, Whatsoever ye shall ask the Father in my name, he will give *it* you. Hitherto have ye asked nothing in my name: ask, and ye shall receive, that your joy may be full.—Ye have not, because ye ask not.

Howbeit when he, the Spirit of truth, is come, he will guide you into all truth: for he shall not speak of himself; but whatsoever he shall hear, *that* shall he speak: and he will shew you things to come. He shall glorify me: for he shall receive of mine, and shall shew *it* unto you.

They rebelled, and vexed his holy Spirit: therefore he was turned to be their enemy, *and* he fought against them.

Jn. 14.26; Jn. 4.10; Lu. 11.13; Jn. 16.23,24; Jas. 4.2
§ Jn. 16.13–14 § Isa. 63.10

What think ye of Christ?

Lift up your heads, O ye gates; even lift *them* up, ye everlasting doors; and the King of glory shall come in. Who is this King of glory? The LORD of hosts, he *is* the King of glory.—He hath on *his* vesture and on his thigh a name written, KING OF KINGS, AND LORD OF LORDS.

Unto you…which believe *he is* precious: but unto them which be disobedient, the stone which the builders disallowed, the same is made the head of the corner.—Christ crucified, unto the Jews a stumblingblock, and unto the Greeks foolishness; but unto them which are called, both Jews and Greeks, Christ the power of God, and the wisdom of God.

I count all things *but* loss for the excellency of the knowledge of Christ Jesus my Lord: for whom I have suffered the loss of all things, and do count them *but* dung, that I may win Christ.—Lord, thou knowest all things; thou knowest that I love thee.

Mt. 22.42; Ps. 24.9–10; Rev. 19.16 § 1 Pe. 2.7;
1 Co. 1.23–24 § Phil. 3.8; Jn. 21.17

**The path of the just *is* as the shining light,
that shineth more and more unto the perfect day.**

Not as though I had already attained, either were already perfect: but I follow after, if that I may apprehend that for which also I am apprehended of Christ Jesus.—Then shall we know, *if* we follow on to know the LORD.

Then shall the righteous shine forth as the sun in the kingdom of their Father.—We all, with open face beholding as in a glass the glory of the Lord, are changed into the same image from glory to glory, *even* as by the Spirit of the Lord.—When that which is perfect is come, then that which is in part shall be done away... For now we see through a glass, darkly; but then face to face: now I know in part; but then shall I know even as also I am known.—Beloved, now are we the sons of God, and it doth not yet appear what we shall be: but we know that, when he shall appear, we shall be like him; for we shall see him as he is. And every man that hath this hope in him purifieth himself, even as he is pure.

Pro. 4.18; Phil. 3.12; Hos. 6.3 § Mt. 13.43; 2 Co. 3.18;
1 Co. 13.10,12; 1 Jn. 3.2–3

Whosoever shall call upon
the name of the Lord shall be saved.

Him that cometh to me I will in no wise cast out.— Lord, remember me when thou comest into thy kingdom. And Jesus said unto him, Verily I say unto thee, To day shalt thou be with me in paradise.—What will ye that I shall do unto you? They say unto him, Lord, that our eyes may be opened. So Jesus had compassion *on them*, and touched their eyes: and immediately their eyes received sight, and they followed him.

If ye then, being evil, know how to give good gifts unto your children: how much more shall *your* heavenly Father give the Holy Spirit to them that ask him?—I will put my spirit within you... Thus saith the Lord GOD; I will yet *for* this be enquired of.

This is the confidence that we have in him, that, if we ask any thing according to his will, he heareth us: and if we know that he hear us, whatsoever we ask, we know that we have the petitions that we desired of him.

Ro. 10.13; Jn. 6.37; Lu. 23.42–43; Mt. 20.32–34
§ Lu. 11.13; Ezek. 36.27,37 § 1 Jn. 5.14–15

**Thou *art* all fair, my love;
there is no spot in thee.**

The whole head is sick, and the whole heart faint. From the sole of the foot even unto the head *there is* no soundness in it; *but* wounds, and bruises, and putrifying sores: they have not been closed, neither bound up, neither mollified with ointment.—We are all as an unclean *thing*, and all our righteousnesses *are* as filthy rags.—I know that in me (that is, in my flesh,) dwelleth no good thing.

Ye are washed…ye are sanctified…ye are justified in the name of the Lord Jesus, and by the Spirit of our God.—The king's daughter *is* all glorious within.—Perfect through my comeliness, which I had put upon thee, saith the Lord GOD.

Let the beauty of the LORD our God be upon us.

These are they which…have washed their robes, and made them white in the blood of the Lamb.—A glorious church, not having spot, or wrinkle, or any such thing; but…holy and without blemish.—Ye are complete in him.

Song 4.7; Isa. 1.5–6; Isa. 64.6; Ro. 7.18 § 1 Co. 6.11; Ps. 45.13; Ezek. 16.14 § Ps. 90.17 § Rev. 7.14; Eph. 5.27; Col. 2.10

Broken cisterns, that can hold no water.

Eve...bare Cain, and said, I have gotten a man from the LORD.

Go to, let us build us a city and a tower, whose top *may reach* unto heaven... The LORD scattered them.— Lot chose him all the plain of Jordan.—It *was* well watered every where...even as the garden of the LORD... But the men of Sodom *were* wicked and sinners before the LORD exceedingly.

I gave my heart to know wisdom, and to know madness and folly: I perceived that this also is vexation of spirit. For in much wisdom *is* much grief: and he that increaseth knowledge increaseth sorrow.—I made me great works; I builded me houses; I planted me vineyards...I gathered me also silver and gold... Then I looked on all that my hands had wrought...and, behold, all *was* vanity and vexation of spirit.

If any man thirst, let him come unto me, and drink.—He satisfieth the longing soul, and filleth the hungry soul with goodness.

Set your affection on things above, not on things on the earth.

Jer. 2.13;   Ge. 4.1   § Ge. 11.4,8;   Ge. 13.11;   Ge. 13.10,13 § Ec. 1.17–18;   Ec. 2.4,8,11   § Jn. 7.37;   Ps. 107.9 § Col. 3.2

**I pray not that thou shouldest take them
out of the world, but that thou shouldest
keep them from the evil.**

Blameless and harmless, the sons of God, without
rebuke, in the midst of a crooked and perverse nation,
among whom ye shine as lights in the world.—Ye are
the salt of the earth…the light of the world.—Let your
light so shine before men, that they may see your good
works, and glorify your Father which is heaven.

I also withheld thee from sinning against me.

The Lord is faithful, who shall stablish you, and keep
you from evil.—So did not I, because of the fear of
God.—Who gave himself for our sins, that he might
deliver us from this present evil world, according to the
will of God and our Father.—Now unto him that is able
to keep you from falling, and to present *you* faultless
before the presence of his glory with exceeding joy, to
the only wise God our Saviour, *be* glory and majesty,
dominion and power, both now and ever. Amen.

Jn. 17.15; Phil. 2.15; Mt. 5.13,14; Mt. 5.16 § Ge. 20.6
§ 2 Th. 3.3; Ne. 5.15; Ga. 1.4; Jude 24–25

Whoso putteth his trust in the LORD shall be safe. [*marg.* set on high]

The LORD is exalted; for he dwelleth on high.—The LORD *is* high above all nations, *and* his glory above the heavens... He raiseth up the poor out of the dust, *and* lifteth the needy out of the dunghill; that he may set *him* with princes.

God, who is rich in mercy, for his great love wherewith he loved us, even when we were dead in sins, hath quickened us together with Christ, (by grace ye are saved;) and hath raised *us* up together, and made *us* sit together in heavenly *places* in Christ Jesus.

He that spared not his own Son, but delivered him up for us all, how shall he not with him also freely give us all things?... For I am persuaded, that neither death, nor life, nor angels, nor principalities, nor powers, nor things present, nor things to come, nor height, nor depth, nor any other creature, shall be able to separate us from the love of God, which is in Christ Jesus our Lord.

Pro. 29.25; Isa. 33.5; Ps. 113.4,7–8 § Eph. 2.4–6 § Ro. 8.32,38–39

That through death he might destroy him that had the power of death.

Our Saviour Jesus Christ…hath abolished death, and hath brought life and immortality to light through the gospel.—He will swallow up death in victory; and the Lord GOD will wipe away tears from off all faces; and the rebuke of his people shall he take away from off all the earth: for the LORD hath spoken *it*.—When this corruptible shall have put on incorruption, and this mortal shall have put on immortality, then shall be brought to pass the saying that is written, Death is swallowed up in victory. O death, where *is* thy sting? O grave, where *is* thy victory? The sting of death *is* sin; and the strength of sin *is* the law. But thanks *be* to God, which giveth us the victory through our Lord Jesus Christ.

God hath not given us the spirit of fear; but of power, and of love, and of a sound mind.—Yea, though I walk through the valley of the shadow of death, I will fear no evil: for thou *art* with me; thy rod and thy staff they comfort me.

He. 2.14;   2 Tim. 1.10;   Isa. 25.8;   1 Co. 15.54–57
§ 2 Tim. 1.7;   Ps. 23.4

Where *is* the way *where* light dwelleth?

God is light, and in him is no darkness at all.—As long as I am in the world, I am the light of the world.

If we say that we have fellowship with him, and walk in darkness, we lie, and do not the truth: but if we walk in the light, as he is in the light, we have fellowship one with another, and the blood of Jesus Christ his Son cleanseth us from all sin.—The Father…hath made us meet to be partakers of the inheritance of the saints in light: who hath delivered us from the power of darkness, and hath translated *us* into the kingdom of his dear Son: in whom we have redemption through his blood, *even* the forgiveness of sins.

Ye are all the children of light, and the children of the day: we are not of the night, nor of darkness.—Ye are the light of the world. A city that is set on an hill cannot be hid… Let your light so shine before men, that they may see your good works, and glorify your Father which is in heaven.

Job 38.19; 1 Jn. 1.5; Jn. 9.5 § 1 Jn. 1.6–7; Col. 1.12–14 § 1 Th. 5.5; Mt. 5.14,16

The Lord will not cast off for ever:
but though he cause grief,
yet will he have compassion.

Fear thou not...saith the LORD: for I *am* with thee...I will not make a full end of thee, but correct thee in measure.—For a small moment have I forsaken thee; but with great mercies will I gather thee. In a little wrath I hid my face from thee for a moment; but with everlasting kindness will I have mercy on thee, saith the LORD thy Redeemer... For the mountains shall depart, and the hills be removed; but my kindness shall not depart from thee, neither shall the covenant of my peace be removed, saith the LORD that hath mercy on thee. O thou afflicted, tossed with tempest, *and* not comforted, behold, I will lay thy stones with fair colours, and lay thy foundations with sapphires.

I will bear the indignation of the LORD, because I have sinned against him, until he plead my cause, and execute judgment for me: he will bring me forth to the light, *and* I shall behold his righteousness.

Lam. 3.31–32; Jer. 46.28; Isa. 54.7–8,10–11 § Mi. 7.9

**God hath chosen the weak things of the world
to confound the things which are mighty.**

When the children of Israel cried unto the LORD, the LORD raised them up a deliverer, Ehud…a man left-handed… After him was Shamgar…which slew of the Philistines six hundred men with an ox goad: and he also delivered Israel.

The LORD looked upon [Gideon], and said, Go in this thy might…have not I sent thee? And he said unto him, Oh my Lord, wherewith shall I save Israel? behold, my family *is* poor in Manasseh, and I *am* the least in my father's house.

The LORD said unto Gideon, The people that *are* with thee *are* too many for me…lest Israel vaunt themselves against me, saying, Mine own hand hath saved me.

Not by might, nor by power, but by my spirit, saith the LORD of hosts.—My brethren, be strong in the Lord, and in the power of his might.

1 Co. 1.27; Judg. 3.15,31 § Judg. 6.14–15 § Judg. 7.2 § Zech. 4.6; Eph. 6.10

He hath prepared for them a city.

If I go and prepare a place for you, I will come again, and receive you unto myself; that where I am, *there* ye may be also.—An inheritance incorruptible, and undefiled, and that fadeth not away, reserved in heaven for you.—Here have we no continuing city, but we seek one to come.

This same Jesus, which is taken up from you into heaven, shall so come in like manner as ye have seen him go into heaven.—Be patient therefore, brethren, unto the coming of the Lord. Behold, the husbandman waiteth for the precious fruit of the earth, and hath long patience for it, until he receive the early and latter rain. Be ye also patient; stablish your hearts: for the coming of the Lord draweth nigh.—Yet a little while, and he that shall come will come, and will not tarry.

We which are alive *and* remain shall be caught up together with them in the clouds, to meet the Lord in the air: and so shall we ever be with the Lord. Wherefore comfort one another with these words.

He. 11.16; Jn. 14.3; 1 Pe. 1.4 § He. 13.14; Ac. 1.11; Jas. 5.7–8; He. 10.37 § 1 Th. 4.17–18

Base things of the world…
hath God chosen.

Be not deceived: neither fornicators, nor idolators, nor adulterers, nor effeminate, nor abusers of themselves with mankind, nor thieves, nor covetous, nor drunkards, nor revilers, nor extortioners, shall inherit the kingdom of God. And such were some of you: but ye are washed, but ye are sanctified, but ye are justified in the name of the Lord Jesus, and by the Spirit of our God.

You *hath he quickened*, who were dead in trespasses and sins; wherein in time past ye walked according to the course of this world…among whom also we all had our conversation in times past in the lusts of our flesh, fulfilling the desires of the flesh and of the mind.

According to his mercy he saved us, by the washing of regeneration, and renewing of the Holy Ghost; which he shed on us abundantly through Jesus Christ our Saviour.

My thoughts *are* not your thoughts, neither *are* your ways my ways, saith the LORD.

---

1 Co. 1.28; 1 Co. 6.9–11 § Eph. 2.1–2,3 § Titus 3.5–6 § Isa. 55.8

The joy of the LORD
is your strength.

Sing, O heavens; and be joyful, O earth; and break forth into singing, O mountains: for the LORD hath comforted his people, and will have mercy upon his afflicted.—Behold, God *is* my salvation; I will trust, and not be afraid: for the LORD JEHOVAH *is* my strength and *my* song; he also is become my salvation.—The LORD *is* my strength and my shield; my heart trusted in him, and I am helped: therefore my heart greatly rejoiceth; and with my song will I praise him.—My soul shall be joyful in my God; for he hath clothed me with the garments of salvation, he hath covered me with the robe of righteousness, as a bridegroom decketh *himself* with ornaments, and as a bride adorneth *herself* with her jewels.

I have therefore whereof I may glory through Jesus Christ in those things which pertain to God.—We…joy in God through our Lord Jesus Christ, by whom we have now received the atonement.—I will joy in the God of my salvation.

Ne. 8.10; Isa. 49.13; Isa.12.2; Ps. 28.7; Isa. 61.10
§ Ro. 15.17; Ro. 5.11; Hab. 3.18

He hath made with me an everlasting covenant, ordered in all *things*, and sure.

I know whom I have believed, and am persuaded that he able to keep that which I have committed unto him against that day.

Blessed *be* the God and Father of our Lord Jesus Christ, who hath blessed us with all spiritual blessings in heavenly *places* in Christ: according as he hath chosen us in him before the foundation of the world, that we should be holy and without blame before him in love: having predestinated us unto the adoption of children by Jesus Christ to himself, according to the good pleasure of his will.

We know that all things work together for good to them that love God, to them who are the called according to *his* purpose. For whom he did foreknow, he also did predestinate *to be* conformed to the image of his Son... Moreover whom be did predestinate, them he also called: and whom he called, them he also justified: and whom he justified, them he also glorified.

2 Sa. 23.5; 2 Tim. 1.12 § Eph. 1.3–5 § Ro. 8.28–29,30

The God of peace…
make you perfect in every good work
to do his will.

Be perfect, be of good comfort, be of one mind, live in peace; and the God of love and peace shall be with you.

By grace are ye saved through faith; and that not of yourselves: *it is* the gift of God: not of works, lest any man should boast.—Every good gift and every perfect gift is from above, and cometh down from the Father of lights, with whom is no variableness neither shadow of turning.

Work out your own salvation with fear and trembling. For it is God which worketh in you both to will and to do of *his* good pleasure.—Be ye transformed by the renewing of your mind, that ye may prove what *is* that good, and acceptable, and perfect, will of God.— Being filled with the fruits of righteousness, which are by Jesus Christ, unto the glory and praise of God.

Not that we are sufficient of ourselves to think any thing as of ourselves; but our sufficiency *is* of God.

He. 13.20,21;   2 Co. 13.11   § Eph. 2.8–9;   Jas. 1.17
§ Phil. 2.12–13;   Ro. 12.2;   Phil. 1.11 § 2 Co. 3.5

**I will allure her,
and bring her into the wilderness,
and speak comfortably unto her.**

Come out from among them, and be ye separate, saith the Lord, and touch not the unclean *thing;* and I will receive you, and will be a Father unto you, and ye shall be my sons and daughters, saith the Lord Almighty.— Having therefore these promises, dearly beloved, let us cleanse ourselves from all filthiness of the flesh and spirit, perfecting holiness in the fear of God.

Jesus…that he might sanctify the people with his own blood, suffered without the gate. Let us go forth therefore unto him without the camp, bearing his reproach.

And [Jesus] said…Come ye yourselves apart into a desert place, and rest a while.—The LORD *is* my shepherd; I shall not want. He maketh me to lie down in green pastures: he leadeth me beside the still waters. He restoreth my soul: he leadeth me in the paths of righteousness for his name's sake.

Hos. 2.14; 2 Co. 6.17–18; 2 Co. 7.1 § He. 13.12–13
§ Mk. 6.31; Ps. 23.1–3

**The house *that is* to be builded for the LORD
must be exceeding magnifical.**

Ye…as lively stones, are built up a spiritual house.—
Know ye not that ye are the temple of God, and *that* the
Spirit of God dwelleth in you? If any man defile the temple of God, him shall God destroy; for the temple of
God is holy, which *temple* ye are.—Know ye not that
your body is the temple of the Holy Ghost *which is* in
you, which ye have of God, and ye are not your own? For
ye are bought with a price: therefore glorify God in your
body, and in your spirit, which are God's.—What agreement hath the temple of God with idols? for ye are the
temple of the living God; as God hath said, I will dwell
in them, and walk in *them;* and I will be their God, and
they shall be my people.—Ye…are built upon the foundation of the apostles and prophets, Jesus Christ himself
being the chief corner *stone;* in whom all the building
fitly framed together groweth unto an holy temple in
the Lord: in whom ye also are builded together for an
habitation of God through the Spirit.

1 Chr. 22.5; 1 Pe. 2.5; 1 Co. 3.16–17; 1 Co. 6.19–20;
2 Co. 6.16; Eph. 2.19,20–22

He is before all things.

The Amen...the beginning of the creation of God.—
The beginning, the firstborn from the dead; that in all
things he might have the preeminence.

The LORD possessed me in the beginning of his way,
before his works of old. I was set up from everlasting,
from the beginning, or ever the earth was... When he
prepared the heavens, I *was* there: when he set a compass upon the face of the depth: when he established the
clouds above: when he strengthened the fountains of the
deep: when he gave to the sea his decree, that the waters
should not pass his commandment... I was daily *his*
delight, rejoicing always before him.—Yea, before the
day *was* I am *he.*

The Lamb slain from the foundation of the world.—
The author and finisher of *our* faith; who for the joy that
was set before him endured the cross, despising the
shame, and is set down at the right hand of the throne
of God.

Col. 1.17; Rev. 3.14; Col. 1.18 § Pro. 8.22–23,27–29,30;
Isa. 43.13 § Rev. 13.8; He. 12.2

**Pray one for another,
that ye may be healed.**

Abraham answered and said, Behold now, I have
taken upon me to speak unto the Lord, which *am but*
dust and ashes: peradventure there shall lack five of the
fifty righteous: wilt thou destroy all the city for *lack of*
five? And he said, If I find there forty and five, I will not
destroy it.

Father, forgive them; for they know not what they
do.—Pray for them which despitefully use you, and persecute you.

I pray for them: I pray not for the world, but for
them which thou hast given me; for they are thine…
Neither pray I for these alone, but for them also which
shall believe on me through their word.—Bear ye one
another's burdens, and so fulfil the law of Christ.

The effectual fervent prayer of a righteous man
availeth much. Elias was a man subject to like passions
as we are, and he prayed earnestly that it might not rain:
and it rained not on the earth by the space of three years
and six months.

Jas. 5.16; Ge. 18.27–28 § Lu. 23.34; Mt. 5.44
§ Jn. 17.9,20; Ga. 6.2 § Jas. 5.16–17

As for man, his days are as grass:
as a flower of the field, so he flourisheth.
For the wind passeth over it, and it is gone; and
the place thereof shall know it no more.

So teach *us* to number our days, that we may apply *our* hearts *unto* wisdom.—What shall it profit a man, if he shall gain the whole world, and lose his own soul?

Surely the people *is* grass. The grass withereth, the flower fadeth: but the word of our God shall stand for ever.—The world passeth away, and the lust thereof: but he that doeth the will of God abideth for ever.

Behold, now *is* the accepted time; behold, now *is* the day of salvation.—Use this world, as not abusing *it:* for the fashion of this world passeth away.—Let us consider one another to provoke unto love and to good works: not forsaking the assembling of ourselves together, as the manner of some *is;* but exhorting *one another:* and so much the more, as ye see the day approaching.

Ps. 103.15–16; Ps. 90.12; Mk. 8.36 § Isa. 40.7–8;
1 Jn. 2.17 § 2 Co. 6.2; 1 Co. 7.31; He. 10.24–25

**What God *is there* in heaven or in earth,
that can do according to thy works,
and according to thy might?**

Who in the heaven can be compared unto the LORD? *who* among the sons of the mighty can be likened unto the LORD?... O LORD God of hosts, who *is* a strong LORD like unto thee? or to thy faithfulness round about thee?—Among the gods *there is* none like unto thee, O Lord; neither *are there any works* like unto thy works.—For thy word's sake, and according to thine own heart, hast thou done all these great things, to make thy servant know *them*. Wherefore thou art great, O LORD God: for *there is* none like thee, neither *is there any* God beside thee, according to all that we have heard with our ears.

Eye hath not seen, nor ear heard, neither have entered into the heart of man, the things which God hath prepared for them that love him. But God hath revealed *them* unto us by his Spirit.—The secret *things belong* unto the LORD our God: but those *things which are* revealed *belong* unto us and to our children.

Deu. 3.24; Ps. 89.6,8; Ps. 86.8; 2 Sa. 7.21–22
§ 1 Co. 2.9–10; Deu. 29.29

He that glorieth, let him glory in the Lord.

Let not the wise *man* glory in his wisdom, neither let the mighty *man* glory in his might, let not the rich *man* glory in his riches: but let him that glorieth glory in this, that he understandeth and knoweth me, that I *am* the LORD.

I count all things *but* loss for the excellency of the knowledge of Christ Jesus my Lord: for whom I have suffered the loss of all things, and do count them *but* dung, that I may win Christ.—I am not ashamed of the gospel of Christ: for it is the power of God unto salvation to every one that believeth.—I have…whereof I may glory through Jesus Christ in those things which pertain to God.

Whom have I in heaven *but thee*? and *there is* none upon earth *that* I desire beside thee.—My heart rejoiceth in the LORD…I rejoice in thy salvation.

Not unto us, O LORD, not unto us, but unto thy name give glory, for thy mercy, *and* for thy truth's sake.

---

1 Co. 1.31; Jer. 9.23–24 § Phil. 3.8; Ro. 1.16; Ro. 15.17
§ Ps. 73.25; 1 Sa. 2.1 § Ps. 115.1

**As he which hath called you is holy,
so be ye holy in all manner of conversation.**

Ye know how we exhorted…and charged every one of you… That ye would walk worthy of God, who hath called you unto his kingdom and glory.—An holy nation…that ye should shew forth the praises of him who hath called you out of darkness into his marvellous light.

Ye were sometimes darkness, but now *are ye* light in the Lord: walk as children of light: (for the fruit of the Spirit *is* in all goodness and righteousness and truth;) proving what is acceptable unto the Lord. And have no fellowship with the unfruitful works of darkness, but rather reprove *them*.—Being filled with the fruits of righteousness, which are by Jesus Christ, unto the glory and praise of God.

Let your light so shine before men, that they may see your good works, and glorify your Father which is in heaven.—Whether therefore ye eat, or drink, or whatsoever ye do, do all to the glory of God.

1 Pe. 1.15;　1 Th. 2.11,12;　1 Pe. 2.9　§ Eph. 5.8–11;
Phil. 1.11　§ Mt. 5.16;　1 Co. 10.31

**Ask me of things to come
concerning my sons, and concerning the work
of my hands command ye me.**

A new heart…will I give you, and a new spirit will I put within you: and I will take away the stony heart out of your flesh, and I will give you an heart of flesh. And I will put my spirit within you, and cause you to walk in my statutes… Thus saith the Lord GOD; I will yet *for* this be enquired of by the house of Israel, to do *it* for them.

If two of you shall agree on earth as touching any thing that they shall ask, it shall be done for them of my Father which is in heaven. For where two or three are gathered together in my name, there am I in the midst of them.

Have faith in God. For verily I say unto you, That whosoever shall say unto this mountain, Be thou removed, and be thou cast into the sea; and shall not doubt in his heart, but shall believe that those things which he saith shall come to pass; he shall have whatsoever he saith.

Isa. 45.11; Ezek. 36.26–27,37 § Mt. 18.19–20
§ Mk. 11.22–23

**God *is* not a man, that he should lie;
neither the son of man, that he should repent.**

The Father of lights, with whom is no variableness, neither shadow of turning.—Jesus Christ the same yesterday, and to day, and for ever.

His truth *shall be thy* shield and buckler.

God, willing more abundantly to shew unto the heirs of promise the immutability of his counsel, confirmed *it* by an oath: that by two immutable things, in which *it was* impossible for God to lie, we might have a strong consolation, who have fled for refuge to lay hold upon the hope set before us.

The faithful God, which keepeth covenant and mercy with them that love him and keep his commandments to a thousand generations.—All the paths of the LORD *are* mercy and truth unto such as keep his covenant and his testimonies.—Happy *is he* that *hath* the God of Jacob for his help, whose hope *is* in the LORD his God...which keepeth truth for ever.

Nu. 23.19; Jas. 1.17; He. 13.8 § Ps. 91.4 § He. 6.17–18 § Deu. 7.9; Ps. 25.10; Ps. 146.5,6

If thou faint in the day of adversity, thy strength is small.

He giveth power to the faint; and to *them that have* no might he increaseth strength.—My grace is sufficient for thee: for my strength is made perfect in weakness.—He shall call upon me, and I will answer him: I *will be* with him in trouble; I will deliver him.—The eternal God *is thy* refuge, and underneath *are* the everlasting arms: and he shall thrust out the enemy from before thee.

I looked *for some* to take pity, but *there was* none; and for comforters, but I found none.

Every high priest taken from among men is ordained for men in things *pertaining* to God…who can have compassion on the ignorant, and on them that are out of the way…so also Christ…though he were a Son, yet learned he obedience by the things which he suffered; and being made perfect, he became the author of eternal salvation unto all them that obey him.—Surely he hath borne our griefs, and carried our sorrows.

Pro. 24.10; Isa. 40.29; 2 Co. 12.9; Ps. 91.15; Deu. 33.27 § Ps. 69.20 § He. 5.1,2,5,8–9; Isa. 53.4

Thou art my portion, O LORD.

All things are yours…and ye are Christ's; and Christ *is* God's.—Our Saviour Jesus Christ…gave himself for us.—The God of our Lord Jesus Christ, the Father of glory…gave him *to be* the head over all *things* to the church.—Christ also loved the church, and gave himself for it… That he might present it to himself a glorious church, not having spot, or wrinkle, or any such thing; but that it should be holy and without blemish.

My soul shall make her boast in the LORD.—I will greatly rejoice in the LORD, my soul shall be joyful in my God; for he hath clothed me with the garments of salvation, he hath covered me with the robe of righteousness.

Whom have I in heaven *but thee?* and *there is* none upon earth *that* I desire beside thee. My flesh and my heart faileth: *but* God *is* the strength of my heart, and my portion for ever.—O *my soul,* thou hast said unto the LORD, Thou *art* my Lord… The LORD *is* the portion of mine inheritance and of my cup: thou maintainest my lot. The lines are fallen unto me in pleasant *places*; yea, I have a goodly heritage.

Ps. 119.57; 1 Co. 3.21,23; Titus 2.13,14; Eph. 1.17,22; Eph. 5.25,27 § Ps. 34.2; Isa. 61.10 § Ps. 73.25–26; Ps. 16.2,5–6

**There is a way which seemeth right unto a man,
but the end thereof are the ways of death.**

He that trusteth in his own heart is a fool.

Thy word *is* a lamp unto my feet, and a light unto my path.—Concerning the works of men, by the word of thy lips I have kept *me from* the paths of the destroyer.

If there arise among you a prophet, or a dreamer of dreams…saying, Let us go after other gods, which thou hast not known, and let us serve them; thou shalt not hearken unto the words of that prophet, or that dreamer of dreams: for the LORD your God proveth you, to know whether ye love the LORD your God with all your heart and with all your soul. Ye shall walk after the LORD your God, and fear him, and keep his commandments, and obey his voice, and ye shall serve him, and cleave unto him.

I will instruct thee and teach thee in the way which thou shalt go: I will guide thee with mine eye.

Pro. 14.12; Pro. 28.26 § Ps. 119.105; Ps. 17.4
§ Deu. 13.1,2–4 § Ps. 32.8

**None of us liveth to himself,
and no man dieth to himself.**

Whether we live, we live unto the Lord; and whether we die, we die unto the Lord: whether we live therefore, or die, we are the Lord's.—Let no man seek his own, but every man another's *wealth*.—Ye are bought with a price: therefore glorify God in your body, and in your spirit, which are God's.

Christ shall be magnified in my body, whether *it be* by life, or by death. For to me to live *is* Christ, and to die *is* gain. But if I live in the flesh, this *is* the fruit of my labour: yet what I shall choose I wot not. For I am in a strait betwixt two, having a desire to depart, and to be with Christ; which is far better.

I through the law am dead to the law, that I might live unto God. I am crucified with Christ: nevertheless I live; yet not I, but Christ liveth in me: and the life which I now live in the flesh I live by the faith of the Son of God, who loved me, and gave himself for me.

Ro. 14.7; Ro. 14.8; 1 Co. 10.24; 1 Co. 6.20
§ Phil. 1.20–23 § Ga. 2.19–20

**God gave Solomon...largeness of heart,
even as the sand that *is* on the sea shore.**

Behold, a greater than Solomon *is* here.—The Prince
of Peace.

Scarcely for a righteous man will one die: yet peradventure for a good man some would even dare to die.
But God commendeth his love toward us, in that, while
we were yet sinners, Christ died for us.—Who, being in
the form of God, thought it not robbery to be equal
with God: but made himself of no reputation, and took
upon him the form of a servant, and was made in the
likeness of men: and being found in fashion as a man, he
humbled himself, and became obedient unto death,
even the death of the cross.—The love of Christ, which
passeth knowledge.

Christ the power of God, and the wisdom of God.—
In whom are hid all the treasures of wisdom and
knowledge.—The unsearchable riches of Christ.—Of
him are ye in Christ Jesus, who of God is made unto us
wisdom, and righteousness, and sanctification, and
redemption.

---

1 Ki. 4.29; Mt. 12.42; Isa. 9.6 § Ro. 5.7–8; Phil. 2.6–8;
Eph. 3.19 § 1 Co. 1.24; Col. 2.3; Eph. 3.8; 1 Co. 1.30

I have loved thee with an everlasting love: therefore with lovingkindness have I drawn thee.

We are bound to give thanks alway to God for you, brethren beloved of the Lord, because God hath from the beginning chosen you to salvation through sanctification of the Spirit and belief of the truth: whereunto he called you by our gospel, to the obtaining of the glory of our Lord Jesus Christ.—God...hath saved us, and called *us* with an holy calling, not according to our works, but according to his own purpose and grace, which was given us in Christ Jesus before the world began.—Thine eyes did see my substance, yet being unperfect; and in thy book all *my members* were written, *which* in continuance were fashioned, when *as yet there was* none of them.

God so loved the world, that he gave his only begotten Son, that whosoever believeth in him should not perish, but have everlasting life.

Herein is love, not that we loved God, but that he loved us, and sent his Son *to be* the propitiation for our sins.

Jer. 31.3; 2 Th. 2.13–14; 2 Tim. 1.8,9; Ps. 139.16
§ Jn. 3.16 § 1 Jn. 4.10

I have made, and I will bear.

Thus saith the LORD that created thee, O Jacob, and he that formed thee, O Israel, Fear not: for I have redeemed thee, I have called *thee* by thy name; thou *art* mine. When thou passest through the waters, I *will be* with thee; and through the rivers, they shall not overflow thee.—*Even* to *your* old age I *am* he; and *even* to hoar hairs will I carry *you*.

As an eagle stirreth up her nest, fluttereth over her young, spreadeth abroad her wings, taketh them, beareth them on her wings: *so* the LORD alone did lead him.—He bare them, and carried them all the days of old.

Jesus Christ the same yesterday, and to day, and for ever.—For I am persuaded, that neither…height, nor depth, nor any other creature, shall be able to separate us from the love of God, which is in Christ Jesus our Lord.

Can a woman forget her sucking child, that she should not have compassion on the son of her womb? yea, they may forget, yet will I not forget thee.

Isa. 46.4; Isa. 43.1–2; Isa. 46.4 § Deu. 32.11–12; Isa. 63.9 § He. 13.8; Ro. 8.38,39 § Isa. 49.15

I know their sorrows.

A man of sorrows, and acquainted with grief.—
Touched with the feeling of our infirmities.

Himself took our infirmities, and bare *our* sicknesses.—Jesus...being wearied with *his* journey, sat thus on
the well.

When Jesus...saw her weeping, and the Jews also
weeping which came with her, he groaned in the spirit,
and was troubled, and said, Where have ye laid him?
They said unto him, Lord, come and see. Jesus wept.—
For in that he himself hath suffered being tempted, he is
able to succour them that are tempted.

He hath looked down from the height of his sanctuary; from heaven did the LORD behold the earth; to hear
the groaning of the prisoner; to loose those that are
appointed to death.—He knoweth the way that I take:
when he hath tried me, I shall come forth as gold.—
When my spirit was overwhelmed within me, then thou
knewest my path.

He that toucheth you toucheth the apple of his
eye.—In all their affliction he was afflicted, and the
angel of his presence saved them.

Ex. 3.7; Isa. 53.3; He. 4.15 § Mt. 8.17; Jn. 4.6
§ Jn. 11.33–35; He. 2.18 § Ps. 102.19–20; Job 23.10;
Ps. 142.3 § Zech. 2.8; Isa. 63.9

I must work the works of him that sent me, while it is day.

The soul of the sluggard desireth, and *hath* nothing: but the soul of the diligent shall be made fat.—He that watereth shall be watered.

My meat is to do the will of him that sent me, and to finish his work. Say not ye, There are yet four months, and *then* cometh harvest? behold, I say unto you, Lift up your eyes, and look on the fields; for they are white already to harvest. And he that reapeth receiveth wages, and gathereth fruit unto life eternal: that both he that soweth and he that reapeth may rejoice together.—The kingdom of heaven is like unto a man *that is* an householder, which went out early in the morning to hire labourers into his vineyard. And when he had agreed with the labourers for a penny a day, he sent them into his vineyard.

Preach the word; be instant in season, out of season.—Occupy till I come.

I laboured more abundantly than they all: yet not I, but the grace of God which was with me.

Jn. 9.4; Pro. 13.4; Pro. 11.25 § Jn. 4.34–36; Mt. 20.1,2 § 2 Tim. 4.2; Lu. 19.13 § 1 Co. 15.10

**Look unto the rock *whence* ye are hewn,
and to the hole of the pit *whence* ye are digged.**

Behold, I was shapen in iniquity.—None eye pitied thee…but thou wast cast out in the open field, to the lothing of thy person, in the day that thou wast born. And when I passed by thee, and saw thee polluted in thine own blood, I said unto thee…Live.

He brought me up…out of an horrible pit, out of the miry clay, and set my feet upon a rock, *and* established my goings. And he hath put a new song in my mouth, *even* praise unto our God.

When we were yet without strength, in due time Christ died for the ungodly. For scarcely for a righteous man will one die: yet peradventure for a good man some would even dare to die. But God commendeth his love toward us, in that, while we were yet sinners, Christ died for us.—God, who is rich in mercy, for his great love wherewith he loved us, even when we were dead in sins, hath quickened us together with Christ.

Isa. 51.1; Ps. 51.5; Ezek. 16.5–6 § Ps. 40.2–3
§ Ro. 5.6–8; Eph. 2.4–5

**I will greatly rejoice in the LORD,
my soul shall be joyful in my God.**

I will bless the LORD at all times: his praise *shall* continually *be* in my mouth. My soul shall make her boast in the LORD: the humble shall hear *thereof*, and be glad. O magnify the LORD with me, and let us exalt his name together.—The LORD will give grace and glory: no good *thing* will he withhold from them that walk uprightly. O LORD of hosts, blessed *is* the man that trusteth in thee.—Bless the LORD, O my soul: and all that is within me, *bless* his holy name.

Is any merry? let him sing psalms.—Be filled with the Spirit; speaking to yourselves in psalms and hymns and spiritual songs, singing and making melody in your heart to the Lord; giving thanks always for all things.—Singing with grace in your hearts to the Lord.

At midnight Paul and Silas prayed, and sang praises unto God: and the prisoners heard them.—Rejoice in the Lord alway: *and* again I say, Rejoice.

Isa. 61.10; Ps. 34.1–3; Ps. 84.11–12; Ps. 103.1 § Jas. 5.13; Eph. 5.18–20; Col. 3.16 § Ac. 16.25; Phil. 4.4

**Thou shalt make a plate *of* pure gold,
and grave upon it, *like* the engravings of a signet,
HOLINESS TO THE LORD.**

Holiness, without which no man shall see the Lord.—
God *is* a Spirit: and they that worship him must worship
him in spirit and in truth.—But we are all as an unclean
thing, and all our righteousnesses *are* as filthy rags.—I
will be sanctified in them that come nigh me, and before
all the people I will be glorified.

This *is* the law of the house; Upon the top of the
mountain the whole limit thereof round about *shall be*
most holy.—Holiness becometh thine house, O LORD,
for ever.

For their sakes I sanctify myself, that they also might
be sanctified through the truth.—Seeing…that we have
a great high priest, that is passed into the heavens, Jesus
the Son of God, let us hold fast *our* profession… Let
us…come boldly unto the throne of grace, that we may
obtain mercy, and find grace to help in time of need.

Ex. 28.36; He. 12.14; Jn. 4.24; Isa. 64.6; Lev. 10.3
§ Ezek. 43.12; Ps. 93.5 § Jn. 17.19; He. 4.14,16

My cup runneth over.

O taste and see that the LORD *is* good: blessed *is* the man *that* trusteth in him. O fear the LORD, ye his saints: for *there is* no want to them that fear him. The young lions do lack, and suffer hunger: but they that seek the LORD shall not want any good *thing.*—His compassions fail not. *They are* new every morning: great *is* thy faithfulness.

The LORD *is* the portion of mine inheritance and of my cup: thou maintainest my lot. The lines are fallen unto me in pleasant *places;* yea, I have a goodly heritage.—Whether...the world, or life, or death, or things present, or things to come; all are yours.—Blessed *be* the God and Father of our Lord Jesus Christ, who hath blessed us with all spiritual blessings in heavenly *places* in Christ.

I have learned, in whatsoever state I am, *therewith* to be content.—Godliness with contentment is great gain.—My God shall supply all your need according to his riches in glory by Christ Jesus.

Ps. 23.5; Ps. 34.8–10; Lam. 3.22–23 § Ps. 16.5–6; 1 Co. 3.22; Eph. 1.3 § Phil. 4.11; 1 Tim. 6.6; Phil. 4.19

Thy word *is* a lamp unto my feet, and a light unto my path.

By the word of thy lips I have kept *me from* the paths of the destroyer. Hold up my goings in thy paths, *that* my footsteps slip not.—When thou goest, it shall lead thee; when thou sleepest, it shall keep thee; and *when* thou awakest, it shall talk with thee. For the commandment *is* a lamp; and the law *is* light; and reproofs of instruction *are* the way of life.—Thine ears shall hear a word behind thee, saying, This *is* the way, walk ye in it, when ye turn to the right hand, and when ye turn to the left.

I am the light of the world: he that followeth me shall not walk in darkness, but shall have the light of life.—We have also a more sure word of prophecy; whereunto ye do well that ye take heed, as unto a light that shineth in a dark place.—Now we see through a glass, darkly; but then face to face: now I know in part; but then shall I know even as also I am known.—They need no candle, neither light of the sun; for the Lord God giveth them light: and they shall reign for ever and ever.

Ps. 119.105;   Ps. 17.4–5;   Pro. 6.22–23;   Isa. 30.21
§ Jn. 8.12;   2 Pe. 1.19;   1 Co. 13.12;   Rev. 22.5

What meanest thou, O sleeper? arise.

This *is* not *your* rest...it is polluted, it shall destroy *you*.—Set your affection on things above, not on things on the earth.—If riches increase, set not your heart *upon them*.—Set your heart and your soul to seek the LORD your God; arise therefore.

Why sleep ye? rise and pray, lest ye enter into temptation.—Take heed to yourselves, lest at any time your hearts be overcharged with surfeiting, and drunkenness, and cares of this life, and *so* that day come upon you unawares.

While the bridegroom tarried, they all slumbered and slept.—Yet a little while, and he that shall come will come, and will not tarry.—Now *it is* high time to awake out of sleep: for now *is* our salvation nearer than when we believed.—Watch ye therefore: for ye know not when the master of the house cometh, at even, or at midnight, or at the cockcrowing, or in the morning: lest coming suddenly he find you sleeping.

Jon. 1.6; Mi. 2.10; Col. 3.2; Ps. 62.10; 1 Chr. 22.19 § Lu. 22.46; Lu. 21.34 § Mt. 25.5; He. 10.37; Ro. 13.11; Mk. 13.35–36

**The accuser of our brethren is cast down,
which accused them before our God day and night.**

They overcame him by the blood of the Lamb, and by the word of their testimony.—Who shall lay any thing to the charge of God's elect? *It is* God that justifieth. Who *is* he that condemneth? *It is* Christ that died, yea rather, that is risen again, who is even at the right hand of God, who also maketh intercession for us.

Having spoiled principalities and powers, he made a shew of them openly.—That through death he might destroy him that had the power of death, that is, the devil; and deliver them who through fear of death were all their lifetime subject to bondage.—In all these things we are more than conquerors through him that loved us.—Put on the whole armour of God, that ye may be able to stand against the wiles of the devil... And take...the sword of the Spirit, which is the word of God.—Thanks *be* to God, which giveth us the victory through our Lord Jesus Christ.

Rev. 12.10; Rev. 12.11; Ro. 8.33–34 § Col. 2.15;
He. 2.14–15; Ro. 8.37; Eph. 6.11,17; 1 Co. 15.57

The tree of life.

God hath given to us eternal life, and this life is in his Son.—He gave his only begotten Son, that whosoever believeth in him should not perish, but have everlasting life.—As the Father raiseth up the dead, and quickeneth *them;* even so the Son quickeneth whom he will... As the Father hath life in himself; so hath he given to the Son to have life in himself.

To him that overcometh will I give to eat of the tree of life, which is in the midst of the paradise of God.—In the midst of the street of it, and on either side of the river, *was there* the tree of life, which bare twelve *manner of* fruits, *and* yielded her fruit every month: and the leaves of the tree *were* for the healing of the nations.

Happy *is* the man *that* findeth wisdom... Length of days *is* in her right hand... She *is* a tree of life to them that lay hold upon her: and happy *is every one* that retaineth her.—Christ Jesus...is made unto us wisdom.

Ge. 2.9; 1 Jn. 5.11; Jn. 3.16; Jn. 5.21,26 § Rev. 2.7; Rev. 22.2 § Pro. 3.13,16,18; 1 Co. 1.30

Whoso trusteth in the LORD,
happy *is* he.

[A braham] staggered not at the promise of God through unbelief; but was strong in faith, giving glory to God; and being fully persuaded that, what he had promised, he was able also to perform.—The children of Judah prevailed, because they relied upon the LORD God of their fathers.

God *is* our refuge and strength, a very present help in trouble. Therefore will not we fear, though the earth be removed, and though the mountains be carried into the midst of the sea.—*It is* better to trust in the LORD than to put confidence in man. *It is* better to trust in the LORD than to put confidence in princes.—The steps of a *good* man are ordered by the LORD: and he delighteth in his way. Though he fall, he shall not be utterly cast down: for the LORD upholdeth *him with* his hand.

O taste and see that the LORD *is* good: blessed *is* the man *that* trusteth in him. O fear the LORD, ye his saints: for *there is* no want to them that fear him.

Pro. 16.20; Ro. 4.20–21; 2 Chr. 13.18 § Ps. 46.1–2; Ps. 118.8–9; Ps. 37.23–24 § Ps. 34.8–9

**I will both lay me down in peace, and sleep:
for thou, LORD, only
makest me dwell in safety.**

Even as a hen gathereth her chickens under *her* wings.—He shall cover thee with his feathers, and under his wings shalt thou trust: his truth *shall be thy* shield and buckler. Thou shalt not be afraid for the terror by night.—He will not suffer thy foot to be moved: he that keepeth thee will not slumber. Behold, he that keepeth Israel shall neither slumber nor sleep. The LORD *is* thy keeper: the LORD *is* thy shade upon thy right hand.

I will abide in thy tabernacle for ever: I will trust in the covert of thy wings.—The darkness hideth not from thee; but the night shineth as the day: the darkness and the light *are* both alike *to thee.*

He that spared not his own Son, but delivered him up for us all, how shall he not with him also freely give us all things?—Ye are Christ's; and Christ *is* God's.—I will trust, and not be afraid.

Ps. 4.8; Mt. 23.37; Ps. 91.4–5; Ps. 121.3–5 § Ps. 61.4;
Ps. 139.12 § Ro. 8.32; 1 Co. 3.23; Isa. 12.2

**The king held out...the golden sceptre...
So Esther drew near,
and touched the top of the sceptre.**

It shall come to pass, when he crieth unto me, that I will hear; for I *am* gracious.

We have known and believed the love that God hath to us. God is love; and he that dwelleth in love dwelleth in God, and God in him. Herein is our love made perfect, that we may have boldness in the day of judgment: because as he is, so are we in this world. There is no fear in love; but perfect love casteth out fear: because fear hath torment. He that feareth is not made perfect in love. We love him, because he first loved us.

Let us draw near with a true heart in full assurance of faith, having our hearts sprinkled from an evil conscience, and our bodies washed with pure water.—For through him we...have access by one Spirit unto the Father.—We have boldness and access with confidence by the faith of him.—Let us therefore come boldly unto the throne of grace, that we may obtain mercy, and find grace to help in time of need.

Est. 5.2; Ex. 22.27 § 1 Jn. 4.16–19 § He. 10.22;
Eph. 2.18; Eph. 3.12; He. 4.16

They said... It *is* manna:
for they wist not what it *was*.

Without controversy great is the mystery of godliness: God was manifest in the flesh.—The bread of God is he which cometh down from heaven, and giveth life unto the world.

Your fathers did eat manna in the wilderness, and are dead... If any man eat of this bread, he shall live for ever: and the bread that I will give is my flesh, which I will give for the life of the world... My flesh is meat indeed, and my blood is drink indeed.

The children of Israel...gathered, some more, some less... He that gathered much had nothing over, and he that gathered little had no lack... They gathered it every morning, every man according to his eating.

Take no thought, saying, What shall we eat? or, What shall we drink?... Your heavenly Father knoweth that ye have need of all these things. But seek ye first the kingdom of God, and his righteousness; and all these things shall be added unto you.

Ex. 16.15; 1 Tim. 3.16; Jn. 6.33 § Jn. 6.49,51,55
§ Ex. 16.17,18,21 § Mt. 6.31,32–33

The free gift *is* of many offences
unto justification.

Though your sins be as scarlet, they shall be as white as snow; though they be red like crimson, they shall be as wool.—I, *even* I, *am* he that blotteth out thy transgressions for mine own sake, and will not remember thy sins. Put me in remembrance: let us plead together: declare thou, that thou mayest be justified.—I have blotted out, as a thick cloud, thy transgressions, and, as a cloud, thy sins: return unto me; for I have redeemed thee.

God so loved the world, that he gave his only begotten Son, that whosoever believeth in him should not perish, but have everlasting life.—Not as the offence, so also *is* the free gift. For if through the offence of one many be dead, much more the grace of God, and the gift by grace, *which is* by one man, Jesus Christ, hath abounded unto many.—And such were some of you: but ye are washed, but ye are sanctified, but ye are justified in the name of the Lord Jesus, and by the Spirit of our God.

Ro. 5.16; Isa. 1.18; Isa. 43.25–26; Isa. 44.22 § Jn. 3.16; Ro. 5.15; 1 Co. 6.11

Occupy till I come.

For the Son of man is as a man taking a far journey, who left his house, and gave authority to his servants, and to every man his work, and commanded the porter to watch.—Unto one he gave five talents, to another two, and to another one; to every man according to his several ability; and straightway took his journey.

I must work the works of him that sent me, while it is day: the night cometh, when no man can work.—Wist ye not that I must be about my Father's business?— Leaving us an example, that ye should follow his steps.

Preach the word; be instant in season, out of season; reprove, rebuke, exhort with all longsuffering and doctrine.—Every man's work shall be made manifest: for the day shall declare it.—Therefore, my beloved brethren, be ye stedfast, unmoveable, always abounding in the work of the Lord, forasmuch as ye know that your labour is not in vain in the Lord.

Lu. 19.13; Mk. 13.34; Mt. 25.15 § Jn. 9.4; Lu. 2.49; 1 Pe. 2.21 § 2 Tim. 4.2; 1 Co. 3.13; 1 Co. 15.58

The fruit of the spirit is...meekness.

The meek...shall increase *their* joy in the LORD, and the poor among men shall rejoice in the Holy One of Israel.—Except ye be converted, and become as little children, ye shall not enter into the kingdom of heaven. Whosoever therefore shall humble himself as this little child, the same is greatest in the kingdom of heaven.— *The ornament* of a meek and quiet spirit...is in the sight of God of great price.—Charity vaunteth not itself, is not puffed up.

Follow after...meekness.—Take my yoke upon you, and learn of me; for I am meek and lowly in heart.—He was oppressed, and he was afflicted, yet he opened not his mouth: he is brought as a lamb to the slaughter, and as a sheep before her shearers is dumb, so he openeth not his mouth.—Christ also suffered for us, leaving us an example, that ye should follow his steps: who did no sin, neither was guile found in his mouth: who, when he was reviled, reviled not again...but committed *himself* to him that judgeth righteously.

Ga. 5.22,23; Isa. 29.19; Mt. 18.3,4; 1 Pe. 3.4;
1 Co. 13.4 § 1 Tim. 6.11; Mt. 11.29; Isa. 53.7;
1 Pe. 2.21–23

If any *man* will come after me, let him deny himself, and take up his cross daily, and follow me.

By honour and dishonour, by evil report and good report.—All that will live godly in Christ Jesus shall suffer persecution.—The offence of the cross.

If I yet pleased men, I should not be the servant of Christ.

If ye be reproached for the name of Christ, happy *are ye*...but let none of you suffer as a murderer, or *as* a thief, or *as* an evildoer, or as a busybody in other men's matters. Yet if *any man suffer* as a Christian, let him not be ashamed; but let him glorify God on this behalf.

Unto you it is given in the behalf of Christ, not only to believe on him, but also to suffer for his sake.—If one died for all, then were all dead: and *that* he died for all, that they which live should not henceforth live unto themselves, but unto him which died for them, and rose again.—If we suffer, we shall also reign with *him*.

Lu. 9.23; 2 Co. 6.8; 2 Tim. 3.12; Ga. 5.11 § Ga. 1.10 § 1 Pe. 4.14,15–16 § Phil. 1.29; 2 Co. 5.14–15; 2 Tim. 2.12

**Wait on the LORD: be of good courage,
and he shall strengthen thine heart.**

Hast thou not known? hast thou not heard, *that* the everlasting God, the LORD, the Creator of the ends of the earth, fainteth not, neither is weary?... He giveth power to the faint; and to *them that have* no might he increaseth strength.—Fear thou not; for I *am* with thee: be not dismayed; for I *am* thy God: I will strengthen thee; yea, I will help thee; yea, I will uphold thee with the right hand of my righteousness.—Thou hast been a strength to the poor, a strength to the needy in his distress, a refuge from the storm, a shadow from the heat, when the blast of the terrible ones *is* as a storm *against* the wall.

The trying of your faith worketh patience. But let patience have *her* perfect work, that ye may be perfect and entire, wanting nothing.—Cast not away therefore your confidence, which hath great recompence of reward. For ye have need of patience, that, after ye have done the will of God, ye might receive the promise.

Ps. 27.14; Isa. 40.28,29; Isa. 41.10; Isa. 25.4
§ Jas. 1.3,4; He. 10.35–36

He maketh me to lie down
in green pastures.

The wicked *are* like the troubled sea, when it cannot rest, whose waters cast up mire and dirt. *There is* no peace, saith my God, to the wicked.

Come unto me, all *ye* that labour and are heavy laden, and I will give you rest.—Rest in the LORD.—He that is entered into his rest, he also hath ceased from his own works.

Be not carried about with divers and strange doctrines. For *it is* a good thing that the heart be established with grace.—That we *henceforth* be no more children, tossed to and fro, and carried about with every wind of doctrine, by the sleight of men, *and* cunning craftiness, whereby they lie in wait to deceive; but speaking the truth in love, may grow up into him in all things, which is the head, *even* Christ.

I sat down under his shadow with great delight, and his fruit *was* sweet to my taste. He brought me to the banqueting house, and his banner over me *was* love.

Ps. 23.2; Isa. 57.20–21 § Mt. 11.28; Ps.37.7; He. 4.10 § He. 13.9; Eph. 4.14–15 § Song 2.3–4

Neither shall there be leaven seen with thee in all thy quarters.

The fear of the LORD *is* to hate evil.—Abhor that which is evil.—Abstain from all appearance of evil.—Looking diligently lest any man fail of the grace of God; lest any root of bitterness springing up trouble *you*, and thereby many be defiled.

If I regard iniquity in my heart, the Lord will not hear *me*.

Know ye not that a little leaven leaveneth the whole lump? Purge out therefore the old leaven, that ye may be a new lump, as ye are unleavened. For even Christ our passover is sacrificed for us: therefore let us keep the feast, not with old leaven, neither with the leaven of malice and wickedness; but with the unleavened *bread* of sincerity and truth.—Let a man examine himself, and so let him eat of *that* bread, and drink of *that* cup.

Let every one that nameth the name of Christ depart from iniquity.—Such an high priest became us, *who is* holy, harmless, undefiled, separate from sinners.—In him is no sin.

Ex. 13.7; Pro. 8.13; Ro. 12.9; 1 Th. 5.22; He. 12.15 § Ps. 66.18 § 1 Co. 5.6–8; 1 Co. 11.28 § 2 Tim. 2.19; He. 7.26; 1 Jn. 3.5

**The serpent said unto the woman,
Ye shall not surely die…your eyes shall be opened,
and ye shall be as gods, knowing good and evil.**

I fear, lest by any means, as the serpent beguiled Eve through his subtilty, so your minds should be corrupted from the simplicity that is in Christ.

My brethren, be strong in the Lord, and in the power of his might. Put on the whole armour of God, that ye may be able to stand against the wiles of the devil… Wherefore take unto you the whole armour of God, that ye may be able to withstand in the evil day, and having done all, to stand. Stand therefore, having your loins girt about with truth, and having on the breastplate of righteousness; and your feet shod with the preparation of the gospel of peace; above all, taking the shield of faith, wherewith ye shall be able to quench all the fiery darts of the wicked. And take the helmet of salvation, and the sword of the Spirit, which is the word of God.—Lest Satan should get an advantage of us: for we are not ignorant of his devices.

Ge. 3.4,5; 2 Co. 11.3 § Eph. 6.10–11,13–17; 2 Co. 2.11

Sit still, my daughter.

Take heed, and be quiet; fear not, neither be faint-hearted.—Be still, and know that I *am* God.—Said I not unto thee, that, if thou wouldest believe, thou shouldest see the glory of God?—The loftiness of man shall be bowed down, and the haughtiness of men shall be made low: and the LORD alone shall be exalted in that day.

Mary...sat at Jesus' feet, and heard his word.—Mary hath chosen that good part, which shall not be taken away from her.—In returning and rest shall ye be saved; in quietness and in confidence shall be your strength.—Commune with your own heart upon your bed, and be still.

Rest in the LORD, and wait patiently for him: fret not thyself because of him who prospereth in his way, because of the man who bringeth wicked devices to pass.

He shall not be afraid of evil tidings: his heart is fixed, trusting in the LORD. His heart *is* established.

He that believeth shall not make haste.

Ru. 3.18; Isa. 7.4; Ps. 46.10; Jn. 11.40; Isa. 2.17
§ Lu. 10.39; Lu. 10.42; Isa. 30.15; Ps. 4.4 § Ps. 37.7
§ Ps. 112.7–8 § Isa. 28.16

**What I do thou knowest not now;
but thou shalt know hereafter.**

Thou shalt remember all the way which the LORD thy God led thee these forty years in the wilderness, to humble thee, *and* to prove thee, to know what *was* in thine heart, whether thou wouldest keep his commandments, or no.

When I passed by thee, and looked upon thee, behold, thy time *was* the time of love...yea, I sware unto thee, and entered into a covenant with thee, saith the Lord GOD, and thou becamest mine.—Whom the Lord loveth he chasteneth.

Beloved, think it not strange concerning the fiery trial which is to try you, as though some strange thing happened unto you: but rejoice, inasmuch as ye are partakers of Christ's sufferings; that, when his glory shall be revealed, ye may be glad also with exceeding joy.—Our light affliction, which is but for a moment, worketh for us a far more exceeding *and* eternal weight of glory; while we look not at the things which are seen, but at the things which are not seen.

Jn. 13.7;   Deu. 8.2   § Ezek. 16.8;   He. 12.6
§ 1 Pe. 4.12–13;   2 Co. 4.17–18

**As the body is one, and hath many members...
so also *is* Christ.**

He is the head of the body, the church.—The head over all *things* to the church, which is his body, the fulness of him that filleth all in all.—We are members of his body, of his flesh, and of his bones.

A body hast thou prepared me.—Thine eyes did see my substance, yet being unperfect; and in thy book all *my members* were written, *which* in continuance were fashioned, when *as yet there was* none of them.

Thine they were, and thou gavest them me.—He hath chosen us in him before the foundation of the world.—Whom he did foreknow, he also did predestinate *to be* conformed to the image of his Son.

That we...may grow up into him in all things, which is the head, *even* Christ: from whom the whole body fitly joined together and compacted by that which every joint supplieth...maketh increase of the body unto the edifying of itself in love.

---

1 Co. 12.12; Col. 1.18; Eph. 1.22–23; Eph. 5.30
§ He. 10.5; Ps. 139.16 § Jn. 17.6; Eph. 1.4; Ro. 8.29
§ Eph. 4.14,15,16

The fountain of living waters.

How excellent *is* thy lovingkindness, O God! therefore the children of men put their trust under the shadow of thy wings. They shall be abundantly satisfied with the fatness of thy house; and thou shalt make them drink of the river of thy pleasures. For with thee *is* the fountain of life.

Thus saith the Lord GOD, Behold, my servants shall eat, but ye shall be hungry: behold, my servants shall drink, but ye shall be thirsty.—Whosoever drinketh of the water that I shall give him shall never thirst; but the water that I shall give him shall be in him a well of water springing up into everlasting life.—This spake he of the Spirit, which they that believe on him should receive.

Ho, every one that thirsteth, come ye to the waters.—The Spirit and the bride say, Come. And let him that heareth say, Come. And let him that is athirst come. And whosoever will, let him take the water of life freely.

Jer. 2.13; Ps. 36.7–9 § Isa. 65.13; Jn. 4.14; Jn. 7.39
§ Isa. 55.1; Rev. 22.17

Let us lift up our heart with *our* hands
unto God in the heavens.

Who *is* like unto the LORD our God, who dwelleth on high, who humbleth *himself* to behold *the things that are* in heaven, and in the earth!—Unto thee, O LORD, do I lift up my soul.—I stretch forth my hands unto thee: my soul *thirsteth* after thee, as a thirsty land…hide not thy face from me, lest I be like unto them that go down into the pit. Cause me to hear thy lovingkindness in the morning; for in thee do I trust: cause me to know the way wherein I should walk; for I lift up my soul unto thee.

Because thy lovingkindness *is* better than life, my lips shall praise thee. Thus will I bless thee while I live: I will lift up my hands in thy name.—Rejoice the soul of thy servant: for unto thee, O Lord, do I lift up my soul. For thou, Lord, *art* good, and ready to forgive; and plenteous in mercy unto all them that call upon thee.

Whatsoever ye shall ask in my name, that will I do.

Lam. 3.41; Ps. 113.5–6; Ps. 25.1; Ps. 143.6–8
§ Ps. 63.3–4; Ps. 86.4–5 § Jn. 14.13

Watchman, what of the night?

It is high time to awake out of sleep: for now *is* our salvation nearer than when we believed. The night is far spent, the day is at hand: let us therefore cast off the works of darkness, and let us put on the armour of light.

Learn a parable of the fig tree; When his branch is yet tender, and putteth forth leaves, ye know that summer *is* nigh: so likewise ye, when ye shall see all these things, know that it is near, *even* at the doors... Heaven and earth shall pass away, but my words shall not pass away.

I wait for the LORD, my soul doth wait, and in his word do I hope. My soul *waiteth* for the Lord more than they that watch for the morning: *I say, more than* they that watch for the morning.

He which testifieth these things saith, Surely I come quickly. Amen. Even so, come, Lord Jesus.

Watch therefore, for ye know neither the day nor the hour wherein the Son of man cometh.

Isa. **21.11**; Ro. 13.11–12 § Mt. 24.32–33,35 § Ps. 130.5–6 § Rev. 22.20 § Mt. 25.13

Rejoicing in hope.

The hope which is laid up for you in heaven.—If in this life only we have hope in Christ, we are of all men most miserable.—We must through much tribulation enter into the kingdom of God.—Whosoever doth not bear his cross, and come after me, cannot be my disciple.—No man should be moved by these afflictions: for yourselves know that we are appointed thereunto.

Rejoice in the Lord alway: *and* again I say, Rejoice.— The God of hope fill you with all joy and peace in believing, that ye may abound in hope, through the power of the Holy Ghost.—Blessed *be* the God and Father of our Lord Jesus Christ, which according to his abundant mercy hath begotten us again unto a lively hope by the resurrection of Jesus Christ from the dead.—Whom having not seen, ye love; in whom, though now ye see *him* not, yet believing, ye rejoice with joy unspeakable and full of glory.—By whom also we have access by faith into this grace wherein we stand, and rejoice in hope of the glory of God.

Ro. 12.12; Col. 1.5; 1 Co. 15.19; Ac. 14.22; Lu. 14.27; 1 Th. 3.3 § Phil. 4.4; Ro. 15.13; 1 Pe. 1.3; 1 Pe. 1.8; Ro. 5.2

I am poor and needy;
yet the Lord thinketh upon me.

I know the thoughts that I think toward you, saith the LORD, thoughts of peace, and not of evil.—My thoughts *are* not your thoughts, neither *are* your ways my ways, saith the LORD. For *as* the heavens are higher than the earth, so are my ways higher than your ways, and my thoughts than your thoughts.

How precious...are thy thoughts unto me, O God! how great is the sum of them! If I should count them, they are more in number than the sand: when I awake, I am still with thee.—LORD, how great are thy works! and thy thoughts are very deep.—Many, O LORD my God, are thy wonderful works which thou hast done, and thy thoughts which are to us-ward.

Not many mighty, not many noble, are called.—Hath not God chosen the poor of this world rich in faith, and heirs of the kingdom?—Having nothing, and yet possessing all things.—The unsearchable riches of Christ.

Ps. 40.17; Jer. 29.11; Isa. 55.8–9 § Ps. 139.17–18; Ps. 92.5; Ps. 40.5 § 1 Co. 1.26; Jas. 2.5; 2 Co. 6.10; Eph. 3.8

Thou art weighed in the balances, and art found wanting.

The LORD *is* a God of knowledge, and by him actions are weighed.—That which is highly esteemed among men is abomination in the sight of God.—*The LORD seeth* not as man seeth; for man looketh on the outward appearance, but the LORD looketh on the heart.—Be not deceived; God is not mocked: for whatsoever a man soweth, that shall he also reap. For he that soweth to his flesh shall of the flesh reap corruption; but he that soweth to the Spirit shall of the Spirit reap life everlasting.

What is a man profited, if he shall gain the whole world, and lose his own soul? or what shall a man give in exchange for his soul?—What things were gain to me, those I counted loss for Christ.

Behold, thou desirest truth in the inward parts.—Thou hast proved mine heart; thou hast visited *me* in the night; thou hast tried me, *and* shalt find nothing.

Dan. 5.27;   1 Sa. 2.3;   Lu. 16.15;   1 Sa. 16.7;   Ga. 6.7–8 § Mt. 16.26;   Phil. 3.7   § Ps. 51.6;   Ps. 17.3

Christic the firstfruits.

Except a corn of wheat fall into the ground and die, it abideth alone: but if it die, it bringeth forth much fruit.—If the firstfruit *be* holy, the lump *is* also *holy:* and if the root *be* holy, so *are* the branches.—Now is Christ risen from the dead, *and* become the firstfruits of them that slept.—If we have been planted together in the likeness of his death, we shall be also *in the likeness* of *his* resurrection.—The Lord Jesus Christ...shall change our vile body, that it may be fashioned like unto his glorious body, according to the working whereby he is able even to subdue all things unto himself.

The firstborn from the dead.—If the Spirit of him that raised up Jesus from the dead dwell in you, he that raised up Christ from the dead shall also quicken your mortal bodies by his Spirit that dwelleth in you.

I am the resurrection, and the life: he that believeth in me, though he were dead, yet shall he live.

---

1 Co. 15.23; Jn. 12.24; Ro. 11.16; 1 Co. 15.20; Ro. 6.5; Phil. 3.20,21 § Col. 1.18; Ro. 8.11 § Jn. 11.25

**He hath filled the hungry with good things;
and the rich he hath sent empty away.**

Thou sayest, I am rich, and increased with goods, and have need of nothing; and knowest not that thou art wretched, and miserable, and poor, and blind, and naked: I counsel thee to buy of me gold tried in the fire, that thou mayest be rich... As many as I love, I rebuke and chasten: be zealous therefore, and repent.

Blessed *are* they which do hunger and thirst after righteousness: for they shall be filled.—*When* the poor and needy seek water, and *there* is none, *and* their tongue faileth for thirst, I the LORD will hear them, *I* the God of Israel will not forsake them.—I *am* the LORD thy God...open thy mouth wide, and I will fill it.

Wherefore do ye spend money for *that which is* not bread? and your labour for *that which* satisfieth not? hearken diligently unto me, and eat ye *that which is* good, and let your soul delight itself in fatness.—I am the bread of life: he that cometh to me shall never hunger; and he that believeth on me shall never thirst.

Lu. 1.53; Rev. 3.17–18,19 § Mt. 5.6; Isa. 41.17;
Ps. 81.10 § Isa. 55.2; Jn. 6.35

**My feet were almost gone;
my steps had well nigh slipped.**

When I said, My foot slippeth; thy mercy, O LORD, held me up.

The Lord said, Simon, Simon, behold, Satan hath desired *to have* you, that he may sift *you* as wheat: but I have prayed for thee, that thy faith fail not.

A just *man* falleth seven times, and riseth up again.—Though he fall, he shall not be utterly cast down: for the LORD upholdeth *him with* his hand.

Rejoice not against me, O mine enemy: when I fall, I shall arise; when I sit in darkness, the LORD *shall be* a light unto me.—He shall deliver thee in six troubles: yea, in seven there shall no evil touch thee.

If any man sin, we have an advocate with the Father, Jesus Christ the righteous.—Wherefore he is able also to save them to the uttermost that come unto God by him, seeing he ever liveth to make intercession for them.

Ps. 73.2; Ps. 94.18 § Lu. 22.31–32 § Pro. 24.16; Ps. 37.24 § Mi. 7.8; Job 5.19 § 1 Jn. 2.1; He. 7.25

I will give them one heart, and one way,
that they may fear me for ever,
for the good of them,
and of their children after them.

A new heart...will I give you, and a new spirit will I put within you.—Good and upright *is* the LORD: therefore will he teach sinners in the way. The meek will he guide in judgment: and the meek will he teach his way. All the paths of the LORD *are* mercy and truth unto such as keep his covenant and his testimonies.

That they all may be one; as thou, Father, *art* in me, and I in thee, that they also may be one in us: that the world may believe that thou hast sent me.

I...beseech you that ye walk worthy of the vocation wherewith ye are called, with all lowliness and meekness...endeavouring to keep the unity of the Spirit in the bond of peace. *There is* one body, and one Spirit, even as ye are called in one hope of your calling; one Lord, one faith, one baptism, one God and Father of all, who *is* above all, and through all, and in you all.

Jer. 32.39; Ezek. 36.26; Ps. 25.8–10 § Jn. 17.21 § Eph. 4.1–2,3–6

**They that wait upon the LORD
shall renew *their* strength.**

When I am weak, then am I strong.—God shall be my strength.—He said unto me, My grace is sufficient for thee: for my strength is made perfect in weakness. Most gladly therefore will I rather glory in my infirmities, that the power of Christ may rest upon me.—Let him take hold of my strength.

Cast thy burden upon the LORD, and he shall sustain thee.—The arms of his hands were made strong by the hands of the mighty *God* of Jacob.

I will not let thee go, except thou bless me.

Thou comest to me with a sword, and with a spear, and with a shield: but I come to thee in the name of the LORD of hosts, the God of the armies of Israel, whom thou hast defied.—Plead *my cause*, O LORD, with them that strive with me: fight against them that fight against me. Take hold of shield and buckler, and stand up for mine help.

Isa. 40.31; 2 Co. 12.10; Isa. 49.5; 2 Co. 12.9; Isa. 27.5 § Ps. 55.22; Ge. 49.24 § Ge. 32.26 § 1 Sa. 17.45; Ps. 35.1–2

**Be not conformed to this world: but be ye trans-
formed by the renewing of your mind.**

Thou shalt not follow a multitude to *do* evil.—If sinners entice thee, consent thou not

Know ye not that the friendship of the world is
enmity with God? whosoever therefore will be a friend
of the world is the enemy of God.

What fellowship hath righteousness with unrighteousness? and what communion hath light with
darkness? And what concord hath Christ with Belial? or
what part hath he that believeth with an infidel? And
what agreement hath the temple of God with idols?—
Love not the world, neither the things *that are* in the
world. If any man love the world, the love of the Father
is not in him... The world passeth away, and the lust
thereof: but he that doeth the will of God abideth for
ever.

In time past ye walked according to the course of this
world, according to the prince of the power of the air,
the spirit that now worketh in the children of disobedience.—Ye have not so learned Christ; if so be that ye
have heard him...as the truth is in Jesus.

Ro. 12.2; Ex. 23.2; Pro. 1.10 § Jas. 4.4 § 2 Co. 6.14–16;
1 Jn. 2.15,17 § Eph. 2.2; Eph. 4.20,21

**Man goeth forth unto his work
and to his labour until the evening.**

In the sweat of thy face shalt thou eat bread, till thou return unto the ground.—We commanded you, that if any would not work, neither should he eat.—Study to be quiet, and to do your own business, and to work with your own hands.

Whatsoever thy hand findeth to do, do *it* with thy might; for *there is* no work, nor device, nor knowledge, nor wisdom, in the grave, whither thou goest.—The night cometh, when no man can work.

Let us not be weary in well doing: for in due season we shall reap, if we faint not.—Always abounding in the work of the Lord, forasmuch as ye know that your labour is not in vain in the Lord.

There remaineth…a rest to the people of God.— Unto us, which have borne the burden and heat of the day.—This *is* the rest *wherewith* ye may cause the weary to rest; and this *is* the refreshing.

Ps. 104.23; Ge. 3.19; 2 Th. 3.10; 1 Th. 4.11
§ Ec. 9.10; Jn. 9.4 § Ga. 6.9; 1 Co. 15.58 § He. 4.9;
Mt. 20.12; Isa. 28.12

I have seen his ways, and will heal him.

I *am* the LORD that healeth thee.

O LORD, thou hast searched me, and known *me*. Thou knowest my downsitting and mine uprising, thou understandest my thought afar off. Thou compassest my path and my lying down, and art acquainted *with* all my ways.—Thou hast set our iniquities before thee, our secret *sins* in the light of thy countenance.—All things *are* naked and opened unto the eyes of him with whom we have to do.

Come now, and let us reason together, saith the LORD: though your sins be as scarlet, they shall be as white as snow; though they be red like crimson, they shall be as wool.—He is gracious unto him, and saith, Deliver him from going down to the pit: I have found a ransom.—He *was* wounded for our transgressions, *he was* bruised for our iniquities: the chastisement of our peace *was* upon him; and with his stripes we are healed.—He hath sent me to bind up the brokenhearted.—Thy faith hath made thee whole; go in peace, and be whole of thy plague.

Isa. 57.18; Ex. 15.26 § Ps. 139.1–3; Ps. 90.8; He. 4.13 § Isa. 1.18; Job 33.24; Isa. 53.5; Isa. 61.1; Mk. 5.34

The LORD taketh my part.

The LORD hear thee in the day of trouble; the name of the God of Jacob defend thee; send thee help from the sanctuary, and strengthen thee out of Zion... We will rejoice in thy salvation, and in the name of our God we will set up *our* banners... Some *trust* in chariots, and some in horses: but we will remember the name of the LORD our God. They are brought down and fallen: but we are risen, and stand upright.

When the enemy shall come in like a flood, the Spirit of the LORD shall lift up a standard against him.—There hath no temptation taken you but such as is common to man: but God *is* faithful, who will not suffer you to be tempted above that ye are able; but will with the temptation also make a way to escape, that ye may be able to bear *it*.

If God *be* for us, who *can be* against us?—The LORD *is* on my side; I will not fear.

Our God whom we serve is able to deliver us...and he will deliver *us*.

Ps. 118.7; Ps. 20.1–2,5,7–8 § Isa. 59.19; 1 Co. 10.13
§ Ro. 8.31; Ps. 118.6 § Dan. 3.17

If any man thirst,
let him come unto me,
and drink.

My soul longeth, yea, even fainteth for the courts of the LORD: my heart and my flesh crieth out for the living God.—O God, thou *art* my God; early will I seek thee: my soul thirsteth for thee, my flesh longeth for thee in a dry and thirsty land, where no water is; to see thy power and thy glory, so *as* I have seen thee in the sanctuary.

Ho, every one that thirsteth, come ye to the waters, and he that hath no money; come ye, buy, and eat; yea, come, buy wine and milk without money and without price.—The Spirit and the bride say, Come. And let him that heareth say, Come. And let him that is athirst come. And whosoever will, let him take the water of life freely.—Whosoever drinketh of the water that I shall give him shall never thirst; but the water that I shall give him shall be in him a well of water springing up into everlasting life.—My blood is drink indeed.

Eat, O friends; drink, yea, drink abundantly, O beloved.

Jn. 7.37;   Ps. 84.2;   Ps. 63.1–2   § Isa. 55.1;   Rev. 22.17; Jn. 4.14;   Jn. 6.55   § Song 5.1

Ye are the salt of the earth.

That which is not corruptible.—Being born again, not of corruptible seed, but of incorruptible, by the word of God, which liveth and abideth for ever.—He that believeth in me, though he were dead, yet shall he live.— The children of God, being the children of the resurrection.—The uncorruptible God.

If any man have not the Spirit of Christ, he is none of his. And if Christ *be* in you, the body *is* dead because of sin; but the Spirit *is* life because of righteousness. But if the Spirit of him that raised up Jesus from the dead dwell in you, he that raised up Christ from the dead shall also quicken your mortal bodies by his Spirit that dwelleth in you.—It is sown in corruption; it is raised in incorruption.

Have salt in yourselves, and have peace one with another.—Let no corrupt communication proceed out of your mouth, but that which is good to the use of edifying, that it may minister grace unto the hearers.

Mt. 5.13; 1 Pe. 3.4; 1 Pe. 1.23; Jn. 11.25; Lu. 20.36;
Ro. 1.23 § Ro. 8.9–11; 1 Co. 15.42 § Mk. 9.50;
Eph. 4.29

I, *even* I, *am* he that comforteth you.

Blessed *be* God, even the Father of our Lord Jesus Christ, the Father of mercies, and the God of all comfort; who comforteth us in all our tribulation, that we may be able to comfort them which are in any trouble, by the comfort wherewith we ourselves are comforted of God.—Like as a father pitieth *his* children, *so* the LORD pitieth them that fear him. For he knoweth our frame; he remembereth that we *are* dust.—As one whom his mother comforteth, so will I comfort you.—Casting all your care upon him; for he careth for you.

Thou, O Lord, *art* a God full of compassion, and gracious, longsuffering, and plenteous in mercy and truth.

Another Comforter…*even* the Spirit of truth.—The Spirit…helpeth our infirmities.

God shall wipe away all tears from their eyes; and there shall be no more death, neither sorrow, nor crying, neither shall there be any more pain: for the former things are passed away.

Isa. 51.12; 2 Co. 1.3,4; Ps. 103.13–14; Isa. 66.13;
1 Pe. 5.7 § Ps. 86.15 § Jn. 14.16,17; Ro. 8.26
§ Rev. 21.4

Ye were called unto
the fellowship of his Son.

He received from God the Father honour and glory, when there came such a voice to him from the excellent glory, This is my beloved Son, in whom I am well pleased.—Behold, what manner of love the Father hath bestowed upon us, that we should be called the sons of God.

Be ye...followers of God, as dear children.—If children, then heirs; heirs of God, and joint-heirs with Christ.

The brightness of *his* glory, and the express image of his person.—Let your light so shine before men, that they may see your good works, and glorify your Father which is in heaven.

Jesus the author and finisher of *our* faith; who for the joy that was set before him endured the cross, despising the shame.—These things I speak in the world, that they might have my joy fulfilled in themselves.—As the sufferings of Christ abound in us, so our consolation also aboundeth by Christ.

1 Co. 1.9; 2 Pe. 1.17; 1 Jn. 3.1 § Eph. 5.1; Ro. 8.17
§ He. 1.3; Mt. 5.16 § He. 12.2; Jn. 17.13; 2 Co. 1.5

**Sin shall not have dominion over you:
for ye are not under the law,
but under grace.**

W hat then? shall we sin, because we are not under the law, but under grace? God forbid.—My brethren, ye...are become dead to the law by the body of Christ; that ye should be married to another, *even* to him who is raised from the dead, that we should bring forth fruit unto God.—Being not without law to God, but under the law to Christ.—The sting of death *is* sin; and the strength of sin *is* the law. But thanks *be* to God, which giveth us the victory through our Lord Jesus Christ.

The law of the Spirit of life in Christ Jesus hath made me free from the law of sin and death.—Whosoever committeth sin is the servant of sin.—If the Son...shall make you free, ye shall be free indeed.

Stand fast therefore in the liberty wherewith Christ hath made us free, and be not entangled again with the yoke of bondage.

Ro. 6.14; Ro. 6.15; Ro. 7.4; 1 Co. 9.21; 1 Co. 15.56–57
§ Ro. 8.2; Jn. 8.34; Jn. 8.36 § Ga. 5.1

A double minded man
is unstable in all his ways.

No man, having put his hand to the plough, and looking back, is fit for the kingdom of God.

He that cometh to God must believe that he is, and *that* he is a rewarder of them that diligently seek him.—Let him ask in faith, nothing wavering. For he that wavereth is like a wave of the sea driven with the wind and tossed. For let not that man think that he shall receive any thing of the Lord.—What things soever ye desire, when ye pray, believe that ye receive *them*, and ye shall have *them*.

Be no more children, tossed to and fro, and carried about with every wind of doctrine, by the sleight of men, *and* cunning craftiness, whereby they lie in wait to deceive; but speaking the truth in love…grow up into him in all things, which is the head, *even* Christ.

Abide in me.—Be ye stedfast, unmoveable, always abounding in the work of the Lord, forasmuch as ye know that your labour is not in vain in the Lord.

Jas. 1.8; Lu. 9.62 § He. 11.6; Jas. 1.6,7; Mk. 11.24
§ Eph. 4.14–15 § Jn. 15.4; 1 Co. 15.58

The LORD pondereth the hearts.

The LORD knoweth the way of the righteous: but the way of the ungodly shall perish.—The LORD will shew who *are* his, and *who is* holy.—Thy Father which seeth in secret himself shall reward thee openly.

Search me, O God, and know my heart: try me, and know my thoughts: and see if *there be any* wicked way in me, and lead me in the way everlasting.—There is no fear in love; but perfect love casteth out fear.

Lord, all my desire *is* before thee; and my groaning is not hid from thee.—When my spirit was overwhelmed within me, then thou knewest my path.—He that searcheth the hearts knoweth what *is* the mind of the Spirit, because he maketh intercession for the saints according to *the will of* God.

The foundation of God standeth sure, having this seal, The Lord knoweth them that are his. And, Let every one that nameth the name of Christ depart from iniquity.

Pro. 21.2; Ps. 1.6; Nu. 16.5; Mt. 6.4 § Ps. 139.23–24; 1 Jn. 4.18 § Ps. 38.9; Ps. 142.3; Ro. 8.27 § 2 Tim. 2.19

Weeping may endure for a night,
but joy *cometh* in the morning.

No man should be moved by these afflictions: for yourselves know that we are appointed thereunto. For verily, when we were with you, we told you before that we should suffer tribulation.—In me ye…have peace. In the world ye shall have tribulation: but be of good cheer; I have overcome the world.

I shall be satisfied, when I awake, with thy likeness.— The night is far spent, the day is at hand.—*He shall be* as the light of the morning, *when* the sun riseth, *even* a morning without clouds; *as* the tender grass *springing* out of the earth by clear shining after rain.

He will swallow up death in victory; and the Lord GOD will wipe away tears from off all faces.—There shall be no more death, neither sorrow, nor crying, neither shall there be any more pain: for the former things are passed away.—We which are alive *and* remain shall be caught up together with them in the clouds, to meet the Lord in the air… Wherefore comfort one another with these words.

Ps. 30.5; 1 Th. 3.3,4; Jn. 16.33 § Ps. 17.15; Ro. 13.12; 2 Sa. 23.4 § Isa. 25.8; Rev. 21.4; 1 Th. 4.17,18

A bruised reed shall he not break.

The sacrifices of God *are* a broken spirit: a broken and a contrite heart, O God, thou wilt not despise.—He healeth the broken in heart, and bindeth up their wounds.—Thus saith the high and lofty One that inhabiteth eternity, whose name *is* Holy; I dwell in the high and holy *place*, with him also *that is* of a contrite and humble spirit, to revive the spirit of the humble, and to revive the heart of the contrite ones. For I will not contend for ever, neither will I be always wroth: for the spirit should fail before me, and the souls *which* I have made.

I will seek that which was lost, and bring again that which was driven away, and will bind up *that which was* broken, and will strengthen that which was sick.—Wherefore lift up the hands which hang down, and the feeble knees; and make straight paths for your feet, lest that which is lame be turned out of the way; but let it rather be healed.—Behold, your God…will come and save you.

Mt. 12.20; Ps. 51.17; Ps. 147.3; Isa. 57.15–16
§ Ezek. 34.16; He. 12.12–13; Isa. 35.4

**O taste and see that the LORD *is* good:
blessed *is* the man *that* trusteth in him.**

When the ruler of the feast had tasted the water that was made wine, and knew not whence it was…[he] saith…Every man at the beginning doth set forth good wine; and when men have well drunk, then that which is worse: *but* thou hast kept the good wine until now.

The ear trieth words, as the mouth tasteth meat.—I believed, and therefore have I spoken.—I know whom I have believed.—I sat down under his shadow with great delight, and his fruit *was* sweet to my taste.

The goodness of God.—He that spared not his own Son, but delivered him up for us all, how shall he not with him also freely give us all things?

As newborn babes, desire the sincere milk of the word, that ye may grow thereby: if so be ye have tasted that the Lord *is* gracious.

Let all those that put their trust in thee rejoice: let them ever shout for joy.

Ps. 34.8; Jn. 2.9,10 § Job 34.3; 2 Co. 4.13; 2 Tim. 1.12; Song 2.3 § Ro. 2.4; Ro. 8.32 § 1 Pe. 2.2–3 § Ps. 5.11

Open thou mine eyes,
that I may behold
wondrous things out of thy law.

Then opened he their understanding, that they might understand the scriptures.—It is given unto you to know the mysteries of the kingdom of heaven, but to them it is not given.—I thank thee, O Father, Lord of heaven and earth, because thou hast hid these things from the wise and prudent, and hast revealed them unto babes. Even so, Father: for so it seemed good in thy sight.—We have received, not the spirit of the world, but the spirit which is of God; that we might know the things that are freely given to us of God.—How precious also are thy thoughts unto me, O God! how great is the sum of them! *If* I should count them, they are more in number than the sand.—O the depth of the riches both of the wisdom and knowledge of God! how unsearchable *are* his judgments, and his ways past finding out! For who hath known the mind of the Lord? or who hath been his counsellor?... For of him, and through him, and to him, are all things: to whom *be* glory for ever. Amen.

Ps. 119.18; Lu. 24.45; Mt. 13.11; Mt. 11.25–26; 1 Co. 2.12; Ps. 139.17–18; Ro. 11.33–34,36

En-hakkore.
[*marg.* The well of him that called, *or*, cried]

If thou knewest the gift of God, and who it is that saith to thee, Give me to drink; thou wouldest have asked of him, and he would have given thee living water.—If any man thirst, let him come unto me, and drink… (But this spake he of the Spirit, which they that believe on him should receive.)

Prove me now herewith, saith the LORD of hosts, if I will not open you the windows of heaven, and pour you out a blessing, that *there shall* not *be room* enough *to receive it.*—If ye…being evil, know how to give good gifts unto your children: how much more shall *your* heavenly Father give the Holy Spirit to them that ask him?—Ask, and it shall be given you; seek, and ye shall find.

Because ye are sons, God hath sent forth the Spirit of his Son into your hearts, crying, Abba, Father.—Ye have not received the spirit of bondage again to fear; but ye have received the Spirit of adoption, whereby we cry, Abba, Father.

Judg. 15.19; Jn. 4.10; Jn. 7.37,39 § Mal. 3.10; Lu. 11.13; Lu. 11.9 § Ga. 4.6; Ro. 8.15

The God of all grace.

I will proclaim the name of the LORD before thee; and will be gracious to whom I will be gracious.—He is gracious unto him, and saith, Deliver him from going down to the pit: I have found a ransom.—Being justified freely by his grace through the redemption that is in Christ Jesus: whom God hath set forth *to be* a propitiation through faith in his blood, to declare his righteousness for the remission of sins that are past, through the forbearance of God.—Grace and truth came by Jesus Christ.

By grace are ye saved through faith; and that not of yourselves: *it is* the gift of God.—Grace, mercy, *and* peace, from God our Father and Jesus Christ our Lord.—Unto every one of us is given grace according to the measure of the gift of Christ.—As every man hath received the gift, *even so* minister the same one to another, as good stewards of the manifold grace of God.—He giveth more grace.

Grow in grace, and *in* the knowledge of our Lord and Saviour Jesus Christ. To him *be* glory both now and for ever.

---

1 Pe. 5.10; Ex. 33.19; Job 33.24; Ro. 3.24–25; Jn. 1.17
§ Eph. 2.8; 1 Tim. 1.2; Eph. 4.7; 1 Pe. 4.10; Jas. 4.6
§ 2 Pe. 3.18

**I will lift up mine eyes unto the hills,
from whence cometh my help.
My help cometh from the LORD.**

*A*s the mountains *are* round about Jerusalem, so the LORD *is* round about his people from henceforth even for ever.

Unto thee lift I up mine eyes, O thou that dwellest in the heavens. Behold, as the eyes of servants *look* unto the hand of their masters, *and* as the eyes of a maiden unto the hand of her mistress; so our eyes *wait* upon the LORD our God, until that he have mercy upon us.— Because thou hast been my help, therefore in the shadow of thy wings will I rejoice.

O our God, wilt thou not judge them? for we have no might against this great company that cometh against us; neither know we what to do: but our eyes *are* upon thee.—Mine eyes *are* ever toward the LORD; for he shall pluck my feet out of the net.—Our help *is* in the name of the LORD, who made heaven and earth.

Ps. 121.1–2; Ps. 125.2 § Ps. 123.1–2; Ps. 63.7
§ 2 Chr. 20.12; Ps. 25.15; Ps. 124.8

Happy *is* the man *that* findeth wisdom, and the man *that* getteth understanding.

Whoso findeth me findeth life, and shall obtain favour of the LORD.

Thus saith the LORD, Let not the wise *man* glory in his wisdom, neither let the mighty *man* glory in his might...but let him that glorieth glory in this, that he understandeth and knoweth me, that I *am* the LORD.— The fear of the LORD *is* the beginning of wisdom.

What things were gain to me, those I counted loss for Christ. Yea doubtless, and I count all things *but* loss for the excellency of the knowledge of Christ Jesus my Lord: for whom I have suffered the loss of all things, and do count them *but* dung, that I may win Christ.—In whom are hid all the treasures of wisdom and knowledge.— Counsel *is* mine, and sound wisdom: I *am* understanding; I have strength.

Christ Jesus...is made unto us wisdom, and righteousness, and sanctification, and redemption.

He that winneth souls *is* wise.

Pro. 3.13; Pro. 8.35 § Jer. 9.23,24; Pro. 9.10
§ Phil. 3.7–8; Col. 2.3; Pro. 8.14 § 1 Co. 1.30
§ Pro. 11.30

Poor, yet making
many rich.

Ye know the grace of our Lord Jesus Christ, that, though he was rich, yet for your sakes he became poor, that ye through his poverty might be rich.—Of his fulness have all we received, and grace for grace.—My God shall supply all your need according to his riches in glory by Christ Jesus.—God *is* able to make all grace abound toward you; that ye, always having all sufficiency in all *things*, may abound to every good work.

Hath not God chosen the poor of this world rich in faith, and heirs of the kingdom which he hath promised to them that love him?—Not many wise men after the flesh, not many mighty, not many noble, *are called:* but God hath chosen the foolish things of the world to confound the wise; and God hath chosen the weak things of the world to confound the things which are mighty.

We have this treasure in earthen vessels, that the excellency of the power may be of God, and not of us.

2 Co. 6.10; 2 Co. 8.9; Jn. 1.16; Phil. 4.19; 2 Co. 9.8
§ Jas. 2.5; 1 Co. 1.26–27 § 2 Co. 4.7

We know that all things work together
for good to them that love God.

Surely the wrath of man shall praise thee: the remainder of wrath shalt thou restrain.—Ye thought evil against me; *but* God meant it unto good.

All things are yours; whether…the world, or life, or death, or things present, or things to come; all are yours; and ye are Christ's; and Christ *is* God's.—All things *are* for your sakes, that the abundant grace might through the thanksgiving of many redound to the glory of God. For which cause we faint not; but though our outward man perish, yet the inward *man* is renewed day by day. For our light affliction, which is but for a moment, worketh for us a far more exceeding *and* eternal weight of glory.

My brethren, count it all joy when ye fall into divers temptations; knowing *this*, that the trying of your faith worketh patience. But let patience have *her* perfect work, that ye may be perfect and entire, wanting nothing.

Ro. 8.28; Ps. 76.10; Ge. 50.20 § 1 Co. 3.21–23;
2 Co. 4.15–17 § Jas. 1.2–4

The communion of the Holy Ghost,
be with you all.

I will pray the Father, and he shall give you another Comforter, that he may abide with you for ever; *even* the Spirit of truth; whom the world cannot receive, because it seeth him not, neither knoweth him: but ye know him; for he dwelleth with you, and shall be in you.—He shall not speak of himself… He shall glorify me: for he shall receive of mine, and shall shew *it* unto you.

The love of God is shed abroad in our hearts by the Holy Ghost which is given unto us.

He that is joined unto the Lord is one spirit.—Know ye not that your body is the temple of the Holy Ghost *which is* in you, which ye have of God, and ye are not your own?

Grieve not the holy Spirit of God, whereby ye are sealed unto the day of redemption.—The Spirit also helpeth our infirmities: for we know not what we should pray for as we ought: but the Spirit itself maketh intercession for us with groanings which cannot be uttered.

2 Co. 13.14;   Jn. 14.16–17;   Jn. 16.13,14   § Ro. 5.5
§ 1 Co. 6.17;   1 Co. 6.19   § Eph. 4.30;   Ro. 8.26

My meditation of him shall be sweet:
I will be glad in the LORD.

As the apple tree among the trees of the wood, so *is* my beloved among the sons. I sat down under his shadow with great delight, and his fruit *was* sweet to my taste.—For who in the heaven can be compared unto the LORD? *who* among the sons of the mighty can be likened unto the LORD?

My beloved *is* white and ruddy, the chiefest among ten thousand.—One pearl of great price.—The prince of the kings of the earth.

His head *is as* the most fine gold, his locks *are* bushy, *and* black as a raven.—The head over all *things.*—He is the head of the body, the church.

His cheeks *are* as a bed of spices, *as* sweet flowers.— He could not be hid.

His lips *like* lilies, dropping sweet smelling myrrh.— Never man spake like this man.

His countenance *is* as Lebanon, excellent as the cedars.—Make thy face to shine upon thy servant.— LORD, lift thou up the light of thy countenance upon us.

Ps. 104.34; Song 2.3; Ps. 89.6 § Song 5.10; Mt. 13.46; Rev. 1.5 § Song 5.11; Eph. 1.22; Col. 1.18 § Song 5.13; Mk. 7.24 § Song 5.13; Jn. 7.46 § Song 5.15; Ps. 31.16; Ps. 4.6

**O my Father, if it be possible,
let this cup pass from me: nevertheless
not as I will, but as thou wilt.**

Now is my soul troubled; and what shall I say? Father, save me from this hour: but for this cause came I unto this hour.

I came down from heaven, not to do mine own will, but the will of him that sent me.—He…became obedient unto death, even the death of the cross.—In the days of his flesh, when he had offered up prayers and supplications with strong crying and tears unto him that was able to save him from death, and was heard in that he feared; though he were a Son, yet learned he obedience by the things which he suffered.

Thinkest thou that I cannot now pray to my Father, and he shall presently give me more than twelve legions of angels?—Thus it is written, and thus it behoved Christ to suffer, and to rise from the dead the third day: and that repentance and remission of sins should be preached in his name among all nations, beginning at Jerusalem.

Mt. 26.39; Jn. 12.27 § Jn. 6.38; Phil. 2.8; He. 5.7–8
§ Mt. 26.53; Lu. 24.46–47

Our God hath not forsaken us.

Beloved, think it not strange concerning the fiery trial which is to try you, as though some strange thing happened unto you.—If ye endure chastening, God dealeth with you as with sons; for what son is he whom the father chasteneth not? But if ye be without chastisement, whereof all are partakers, then are ye bastards, and not sons.

The LORD your God proveth you, to know whether ye love the LORD your God with all your heart and with all your soul.

The LORD will not forsake his people for his great name's sake: because it hath pleased the LORD to make you his people.—Can a woman forget her sucking child, that she should not have compassion on the son of her womb? yea, they may forget, yet will I not forget thee.—Happy *is he* that *hath* the God of Jacob for his help, whose hope *is* in the LORD his God.

Shall not God avenge his own elect, which cry day and night unto him, though he bear long with them? I tell you that he will avenge them speedily.

Ezr. 9.9; 1 Pe. 4.12; He. 12.7–8 § Deu. 13.3
§ 1 Sa. 12.22; Isa. 49.15; Ps. 146.5 § Lu. 18.7–8

He that overcometh
shall inherit all things.

If in this life only we have hope in Christ, we are of all men most miserable.—Now they desire a better *country*, that is, an heavenly: wherefore God is not ashamed to be called their God: for he hath prepared for them a city.— An inheritance incorruptible, and undefiled, and that fadeth not away, reserved in heaven for you.

All things are yours…the world, or life, or death, or things present, or things to come; all are yours.—Eye hath not seen, nor ear heard, neither have entered into the heart of man, the things which God hath prepared for them that love him. But God hath revealed *them* unto us by his Spirit.

Look to yourselves, that we lose not those things which we have wrought, but that we receive a full reward.—Let us lay aside every weight, and the sin which doth so easily beset *us*, and let us run with patience the race that is set before us.

Rev. 21.7; 1 Co. 15.19; He. 11.16; 1 Pe. 1.4
§ 1 Co. 3.21,22; 1 Co. 2.9–10 § 2 Jn. 8; He. 12.1

It is good for me
to draw near to God.

LORD, I have loved the habitation of thy house, and the place where thine honour dwelleth.—A day in thy courts *is* better than a thousand. I had rather be a door-keeper in the house of my God, than to dwell in the tents of wickedness.—Blessed *is the man whom* thou choosest, and causest to approach *unto thee, that* he may dwell in thy courts: we shall be satisfied with the goodness of thy house, *even* of thy holy temple.

The LORD *is* good unto them that wait for him, to the soul *that* seeketh him.—Therefore will the LORD wait, that he may be gracious unto you, and therefore will he be exalted, that he may have mercy upon you: for the LORD *is* a God of judgment: blessed *are* all they that wait for him.

Having therefore, brethren, boldness to enter into the holiest by the blood of Jesus, by a new and living way, which he hath consecrated for us…let us draw near with a true heart in full assurance of faith, having our hearts sprinkled from an evil conscience.

Ps. 73.28; Ps. 26.8; Ps. 84.10; Ps. 65.4 § Lam. 3.25; Isa. 30.18 § He. 10.19–20,22

Ye know the grace of our Lord Jesus Christ.

The Word was made flesh, and dwelt among us, (and we beheld his glory, the glory as of the only begotten of the Father,) full of grace and truth.—Thou art fairer than the children of men: grace is poured into thy lips.—All bare him witness, and wondered at the gracious words which proceeded out of his mouth.

Ye have tasted that the Lord *is* gracious.—He that believeth on the Son of God hath the witness in himself.—We speak that we do know, and testify that we have seen.

O taste and see that the LORD *is* good: blessed *is* the man *that* trusteth in him.—I sat down under his shadow with great delight, and his fruit *was* sweet to my taste.

He said unto me, My grace is sufficient for thee: for my strength is made perfect in weakness.—Unto every one of us is given grace according to the measure of the gift of Christ.—As every man hath received the gift, *even so* minister the same one to another, as good stewards of the manifold grace of God.

2 Co. 8.9; Jn. 1.14; Ps. 45.2; Lu. 4.22 § 1 Pe. 2.3;
1 Jn. 5.10; Jn. 3.11 § Ps. 34.8; Song 2.3 § 2 Co. 12.9;
Eph. 4.7; 1 Pe. 4.10

**Let patience have *her* perfect work,
that ye may be perfect and entire,
wanting nothing.**

Now for a season, if need be, ye are in heaviness through manifold temptations: that the trial of your faith, being much more precious than of gold that perisheth, though it be tried with fire, might be found unto praise and honour and glory at the appearing of Jesus Christ.—We glory in tribulations…knowing that tribulation worketh patience; and patience, experience; and experience, hope.

It is good that *a man* should both hope and quietly wait for the salvation of the LORD.—Ye have in heaven a better and an enduring substance. Cast not away therefore your confidence, which hath great recompence of reward. For ye have need of patience, that, after ye have done the will of God, ye might receive the promise.— Our Lord Jesus Christ himself, and God, even our Father, which hath loved us, and hath given *us* everlasting consolation and good hope through grace, comfort your hearts.

Jas. 1.4; 1 Pe. 1.6–7; Ro. 5.3–4 § Lam. 3.26;
He. 10.34–36; 2 Th. 2.16–17

God shall judge the secrets of men
by Jesus Christ.

Judge nothing before the time, until the Lord come, who both will bring to light the hidden things of darkness, and will make manifest the counsels of the hearts: and then shall every man have praise of God.—The Father judgeth no man, but hath committed all judgment unto the Son...because he is the Son of man.—The Son of God...hath his eyes like unto a flame of fire.

They say, How doth God know? and is there knowledge in the most High?—These *things* hast thou done, and I kept silence; thou thoughtest that I was altogether *such an one* as thyself: *but* I will reprove thee, and set *them* in order before thine eyes.—There is nothing covered, that shall not be revealed; neither hid, that shall not be known.

Lord, all my desire *is* before thee; and my groaning is not hid from thee.—Examine me, O LORD, and prove me; try my reins and my heart.

Ro. 2.16; 1 Co. 4.5; Jn. 5.22,27; Rev. 2.18 § Ps. 73.11; Ps. 50.21; Lu. 12.2 § Ps. 38.9; Ps. 26.2

A God of truth and without iniquity, just and right *is* he.

Him that judgeth righteously.—We must all appear before the judgment seat of Christ; that every one may receive the things *done* in *his* body, according to that he hath done, whether *it be* good or bad.—Every one of us shall give account of himself to God.—The soul that sinneth, it shall die.

Awake, O sword, against my shepherd, and against the man *that is* my fellow, saith the LORD of hosts: smite the shepherd.—The LORD hath laid on him the iniquity of us all.—Mercy and truth are met together; righteousness and peace have kissed *each other*.—Mercy rejoiceth against judgment.—The wages of sin *is* death; but the gift of God *is* eternal life through Jesus Christ our Lord.

A just God and a Saviour; *there is* none beside me.—Just, and the justifier of him which believeth in Jesus.—Justified freely by his grace through the redemption that is in Christ Jesus.

Deu. 32.4; 1 Pe. 2.23; 2 Co. 5.10; Ro. 14.12; Ezek. 18.4
§ Zech. 13.7; Isa. 53.6; Ps. 85.10; Jas. 2.13; Ro. 6.23
§ Isa. 45.21; Ro. 3.26; Ro. 3.24

Death is swallowed up in victory.

Thanks *be* to God, which giveth us the victory through our Lord Jesus Christ.

Forasmuch...as the children are partakers of flesh and blood, he also himself likewise took part of the same; that through death he might destroy him that had the power of death, that is, the devil; and deliver them who through fear of death were all their lifetime subject to bondage.

If we be dead with Christ, we believe that we shall also live with him: knowing that Christ being raised from the dead dieth no more; death hath no more dominion over him. For in that he died, he died unto sin once: but in that he liveth, he liveth unto God.

Likewise reckon ye also yourselves to be dead indeed unto sin, but alive unto God through Jesus Christ our Lord.

In all these things we are more than conquerors through him that loved us.

1 Co. 15.54; 1 Co. 15.57 § He. 2.14–15 § Ro. 6.8–10 § Ro. 6.11 § Ro. 8.37

Humble yourselves...
under the mighty hand of God,
that he may exalt you in due time.

Every one *that is* proud in heart *is* an abomination to the LORD: *though* hand *join* in hand, he shall not be unpunished.

O LORD, thou *art* our father; we *are* the clay, and thou our potter; and we all *are* the work of thy hand. Be not wroth very sore, O LORD, neither remember iniquity for ever: behold, see, we beseech thee, we *are* all thy people.—Thou hast chastised me, and I was chastised, as a bullock unaccustomed *to the yoke:* turn thou me, and I shall be turned; for thou *art* the LORD my God. Surely after that I was turned, I repented; and after that I was instructed, I smote upon *my* thigh: I was ashamed, yea, even confounded, because I did bear the reproach of my youth.—*It is* good for a man that he bear the yoke in his youth.

Affliction cometh not forth of the dust, neither doth trouble spring out of the ground; yet man is born unto trouble, as the sparks fly upward.

---

1 Pe. 5.6;   Pro. 16.5 § Isa. 64.8–9;   Jer. 31.18–19; Lam. 3.27 § Job 5.6–7

Yea, hath God said?

When the tempter came to [Jesus], he said, If thou be the Son of God... But [Jesus] answered and said, It is written...it is written...it is written... Then the devil leaveth him.

I may not return with thee... For it was said to me by the word of the LORD, Thou shalt eat no bread nor drink water there... He said unto him, I *am* a prophet also as thou *art;* and an angel spake unto me by the word of the LORD, saying, Bring him back with thee into thine house, that he may eat bread and drink water. *But* he lied unto him. So he went back with him... The man of God...was disobedient unto the word of the LORD: therefore the LORD hath delivered him unto the lion, which hath torn him, and slain him, according to the word of the LORD.—Though we, or an angel from heaven, preach any other gospel unto you than that which we have preached unto you, let him be accursed.—Thy word have I hid in mine heart, that I might not sin against thee.

Ge. 3.1; Mt. 4.3,4,7,10,11 § 1 Ki. 13.16,17,18–19,26; Ga. 1.8; Ps. 119.11

They shall put my name upon the children of Israel; and I will bless them.

O LORD our God, *other* lords beside thee have had dominion over us: *but* by thee only will we make mention of thy name.—We are *thine:* thou never barest rule over them; they were not called by thy name.

All people of the earth shall see that thou art called by the name of the LORD; and they shall be afraid of thee.—The LORD will not forsake his people for his great name's sake: because it hath pleased the LORD to make you his people.

O Lord, hear; O Lord, forgive; O Lord, hearken and do; defer not, for thine own sake, O my God: for thy city and thy people are called by thy name.—Help us, O God of our salvation, for the glory of thy name: and deliver us, and purge away our sins, for thy name's sake. Wherefore should the heathen say, Where *is* their God?—The name of the LORD *is* a strong tower: the righteous runneth into it, and is safe.

Nu. 6.27; Isa. 26.13; Isa. 63.19 § Deu. 28.10; 1 Sa. 12.22 § Dan. 9.19; Ps. 79.9–10; Pro. 18.10

**The heavens declare the glory of God;
and the firmament sheweth his handywork.**

The invisible things of him from the creation of the world are clearly seen, being understood by the things that are made, *even* his eternal power and Godhead.—He left not himself without witness.—Day unto day uttereth speech, and night unto night sheweth knowledge. *There is* no speech nor language, *where* their voice is not heard.

When I consider thy heavens, the work of thy fingers, the moon and the stars, which thou hast ordained; what is man, that thou art mindful of him? and the son of man, that thou visitest him?

There is one glory of the sun, and another glory of the moon, and another glory of the stars: for *one* star differeth from *another* star in glory. So also *is* the resurrection of the dead.—They that be wise shall shine as the brightness of the firmament; and they that turn many to righteousness as the stars for ever and ever.

Ps. 19.1; Ro. 1.20; Ac. 14.17; Ps. 19.2–3 § Ps. 8.3–4
§ 1 Co. 15.41–42; Dan. 12.3

**Hereby perceive we the love *of God*,
because he laid down his life for us.**

The love of Christ, which passeth knowledge.—
Greater love hath no man than this, that a man lay down
his life for his friends.—Ye know the grace of our Lord
Jesus Christ, that, though he was rich, yet for your sakes
he became poor, that ye through his poverty might be
rich.—Beloved, if God so loved us, we ought also to love
one another.—Be ye kind one to another, tenderhearted, forgiving one another, even as God for Christ's sake
hath forgiven you.—Forbearing one another, and forgiving one another, if any man have a quarrel against
any: even as Christ forgave you, so also *do* ye.—For even
the Son of man came not to be ministered unto, but to
minister, and to give his life a ransom for many.—
Christ…suffered for us, leaving us an example, that ye
should follow his steps.

Ye also ought to wash one another's feet. For I have
given you an example, that ye should do as I have done
to you.—We ought to lay down *our* lives for the
brethren.

1 Jn. 3.16;   Eph. 3.19;   Jn. 15.13;   2 Co. 8.9;   1 Jn. 4.11;
Eph. 4.32;   Col. 3.13;   Mk. 10.45;   1 Pe. 2.21
§ Jn. 13.14–15;   1 Jn. 3.16

The Son can do nothing of himself, but what he seeth the Father do: for what things soever he doeth, these also doeth the Son likewise.

The LORD giveth wisdom: out of his mouth *cometh* knowledge and understanding.—I will give you a mouth and wisdom, which all your adversaries shall not be able to gainsay nor resist.

Wait on the LORD: be of good courage, and he shall strengthen thine heart.—My grace is sufficient for thee: for my strength is made perfect in weakness.

Them that are sanctified by God the Father.—He that sanctifieth and they who are sanctified *are* all of one: for which cause he is not ashamed to call them brethren.

Do not I fill heaven and earth? saith the LORD.—The fulness of him that filleth all in all.

I, *even* I, *am* the LORD; and beside me *there is* no saviour.—This is indeed the Christ, the Saviour of the world.

Grace, mercy, *and* peace, from God the Father and the Lord Jesus Christ our Saviour.

Jn. **5.**19; Pro. 2.6; Lu. 21.15 § Ps. 27.14; 2 Co. 12.9
§ Jude 1; He. 2.11 § Jer. 23.24; Eph. 1.23 § Isa. 43.11;
Jn. 4.42 § Titus 1.4

He knoweth the way that I take:
when **he hath tried me,**
I shall come forth as gold.

He knoweth our frame.—He doth not afflict willingly nor grieve the children of men.

The foundation of God standeth sure, having this seal, The Lord knoweth them that are his. And, Let every one that nameth the name of Christ depart from iniquity. But in a great house there are not only vessels of gold and of silver, but also of wood and of earth; and some to honour, and some to dishonour. If a man therefore purge himself from these, he shall be a vessel unto honour, sanctified, and meet for the master's use, *and* prepared unto every good work.

He shall sit *as* a refiner and purifier of silver: and he shall purify the sons of Levi, and purge them as gold and silver, that they may offer unto the LORD an offering in righteousness.—I...will refine them as silver is refined...they shall call on my name, and I will hear them: I will say, It *is* my people: and they shall say, the LORD *is* my God.

Job 23.10;   Ps. 103.14;   Lam. 3.33   § 2 Tim. 2.19–21 § Mal. 3.3;   Zech. 13.9

**Shew me thy ways, O LORD;
teach me thy paths.**

And Moses said unto the LORD... I pray thee, if I have found grace in thy sight, shew me now thy way, that I may know thee... And he said, My presence shall go *with thee*, and I will give thee rest.—He made known his ways unto Moses, his acts unto the children of Israel.

The meek will he guide in judgment: and the meek will he teach his way. What man *is* he that feareth the LORD? him shall he teach in the way *that* he shall choose.—Trust in the LORD with all thine heart; and lean not unto thine own understanding. In all thy ways acknowledge him, and he shall direct thy paths.

Thou wilt shew me the path of life: in thy presence *is* fulness of joy; at thy right hand *there are* pleasures for evermore.—I will instruct thee and teach thee in the way which thou shalt go: I will guide thee with mine eye.—The path of the just *is* as the shining light, that shineth more and more unto the perfect day.

Ps. 25.4; Ex. 33.12,13,14; Ps. 103.7 § Ps. 25.9,12;
Pro. 3.5–6 § Ps. 16.11; Ps. 32.8; Pro. 4.18

The fruit of the Spirit is...temperance.

Every man that striveth for the mastery is temperate in all things. Now they *do it* to obtain a corruptible crown; but we an incorruptible. I therefore so run, not as uncertainly; so fight I, not as one that beateth the air: but I keep under my body, and bring *it* into subjection: lest that by any means, when I have preached to others, I myself should be a castaway.—Be not drunk with wine, wherein is excess; but be filled with the Spirit.

If any *man* will come after me, let him deny himself, and take up his cross, and follow me.

Let us not sleep, as *do* others; but let us watch and be sober. For they that sleep sleep in the night; and they that be drunken are drunken in the night. But let us, who are of the day, be sober.—Denying ungodliness and worldly lusts, we should live soberly, righteously, and godly, in this present world; looking for that blessed hope, and the glorious appearing of the great God and our Saviour Jesus Christ.

Ga. 5.22,23; 1 Co. 9.25–27; Eph. 5.18 § Mt. 16.24 § 1 Th. 5.6–8; Titus 2.12–13

Grow up into him in all things, which is the head, *even* Christ.

First the blade, then the ear, after that the full corn in the ear.—Till we all come in the unity of the faith, and of the knowledge of the Son of God, unto a perfect man, unto the measure of the stature of the fulness of Christ.

They measuring themselves by themselves, and comparing themselves among themselves, are not wise... But he that glorieth, let him glory in the Lord. For not he that commendeth himself is approved, but whom the Lord commendeth.

The body *is* of Christ. Let no man beguile you of your reward in a voluntary humility and worshipping of angels, intruding into those things which he hath not seen, vainly puffed up by his fleshly mind, and not holding the Head from which all the body by joints and bands having nourishment ministered, and knit together, increaseth with the increase of God.

Grow in grace, and *in* the knowledge of our Lord and Saviour Jesus Christ.

Eph. 4.15; Mk. 4.28; Eph. 4.13 § 2 Co. 10.12,17–18
§ Col. 2.17–19 § 2 Pe. 3.18

**The goat shall bear upon him all their iniquities
unto a land not inhabited:
and he shall let go the goat in the wilderness.**

As far as the east is from the west, *so* far hath he removed our transgressions from us.—In those days, and in that time, saith the LORD, the iniquity of Israel shall be sought for, and *there shall be* none; and the sins of Judah, and they shall not be found: for I will pardon them whom I reserve.—Thou wilt cast all their sins into the depths of the sea.—Who *is* a God like unto thee, that pardoneth iniquity?

All we like sheep have gone astray; we have turned every one to his own way; and the LORD hath laid on him the iniquity of us all.—He shall bear their iniquities. Therefore will I divide him *a portion* with the great, and he shall divide the spoil with the strong: because he hath poured out his soul unto death: and he was numbered with the transgressors; and he bare the sin of many, and made intercession for the transgressors.— The Lamb of God, which taketh away the sin of the world.

Lev. 16.22; Ps. 103.12; Jer. 50.20; Mi. 7.19; Mi. 7.18
§ Isa. 53.6; Isa. 53.11–12; Jn. 1.29

**Who maketh thee to differ *from another*?
and what hast thou that thou didst not receive?**

By the grace of God I am what I am.—Of his own will begat he us with the word of truth.—*It is* not of him that willeth, nor of him that runneth, but of God that sheweth mercy.—Where *is* boasting then? It is excluded.—Christ Jesus…is made unto us wisdom, and righteousness, and sanctification, and redemption… He that glorieth, let him glory in the Lord.

You *hath he quickened*, who were dead in trespasses and sins; wherein in time past ye walked according to the course of this world, according to the prince of the power of the air, the spirit that now worketh in the children of disobedience: among whom also we all had our conversation in times past in the lusts of our flesh, fulfilling the desires of the flesh and of the mind; and were by nature the children of wrath, even as others.—Ye are washed…ye are sanctified…ye are justified in the name of the Lord Jesus, and by the Spirit of our God.

1 Co. 4.7; 1 Co. 15.10; Jas. 1.18; Ro. 9.16; Ro. 3.27;
1 Co. 1.30,31 § Eph. 2.1–3; 1 Co. 6.11

Unto him that loved us, and washed us from our sins in his own blood.

Love *is* strong as death... Many waters cannot quench love, neither can the floods drown it.—Greater love hath no man than this, that a man lay down his life for his friends.

Who his own self bare our sins in his own body on the tree, that we, being dead to sins, should live unto righteousness: by whose stripes ye were healed.—In whom we have redemption through his blood, the forgiveness of sins, according to the riches of his grace.

Ye are washed...ye are sanctified...ye are justified in the name of the Lord Jesus, and by the Spirit of our God.—Ye *are* a chosen generation, a royal priesthood, an holy nation, a peculiar people; that ye should shew forth the praises of him who hath called you out of darkness into his marvellous light.—I beseech you...brethren, by the mercies of God, that ye present your bodies a living sacrifice, holy, acceptable unto God, *which is* your reasonable service.

Rev. 1.5; Song 8.6,7; Jn. 15.13 § 1 Pe. 2.24; Eph. 1.7 § 1 Co. 6.11; 1 Pe. 2.9; Ro. 12.1

**There are differences of administrations,
but the same Lord.**

Over the king's treasures *was* Azmaveth the son of Adiel: and over the storehouses...Jehonathan... And over them that did the work of the field for tillage of the ground *was* Ezri... And over the vineyards *was* Shimei... These *were* the rulers of the substance which *was* king David's.

God hath set some in the church, first apostles, secondarily prophets, thirdly teachers, after that miracles, then gifts of healings, helps, governments, diversities of tongues.—All these worketh that one and the selfsame Spirit, dividing to every man severally as he will.

As every man hath received the gift, *even so* minister the same one to another, as good stewards of the manifold grace of God. If any man speak, *let him speak* as the oracles of God; if any man minister, *let him do it* as of the ability which God giveth: that God in all things may be glorified through Jesus Christ, to whom be praise and dominion for ever and ever.

1 Co. 12.5; 1 Chr. 27.25,26,27,31 § 1 Co. 12.28;
1 Co. 12.11 § 1 Pe. 4.10–11

Moses wist not that the skin of his face shone while he talked with him.

Not unto us, O LORD, not unto us, but unto thy name give glory.—Lord, when saw we thee an hungred, and fed *thee?* or thirsty, and gave *thee* drink?—In lowliness of mind let each esteem other better than themselves.—Be clothed with humility.

[Jesus] was transfigured before them: and his face did shine as the sun, and his raiment was white as the light.—All that sat in the council, looking stedfastly on [Stephen], saw his face as it had been the face of an angel.—The glory which thou gavest me I have given them.—We all, with open face beholding as in a glass the glory of the Lord, are changed into the same image from glory to glory, *even* as by the Spirit of the Lord.

Ye are the light of the world. A city that is set on a hill cannot be hid. Neither do men light a candle, and put it under a bushel, but on a candlestick; and it giveth light unto all that are in the house.

Ex. 34.29; Ps. 115.1; Mt. 25.37; Phil. 2.3; 1 Pe. 5.5
§ Mt. 17.2; Ac. 6.15; Jn. 17.22; 2 Co. 3.18
§ Mt. 5.14–15

**There are diversities of operations,
but it is the same God which worketh all in all.**

There fell *some* of Manasseh to David... And they helped David against the band *of the rovers:* for they *were* all mighty men of valour.—The manifestation of the Spirit is given to every man to profit withal.

Of the children of Issachar, *which were men* that had understanding of the times, to know what Israel ought to do.—To one is given by the Spirit the word of wisdom; to another the word of knowledge by the same Spirit.

Of Zebulun, such as went forth to battle, expert in war, with all instruments of war, fifty thousand, which could keep rank: *they were* not of double heart.—A double minded man *is* unstable in all his ways.

There should be no schism in the body; but...the members should have the same care one for another. And whether one member suffer, all the members suffer with it; or one member be honoured, all the members rejoice with it.

One Lord, one faith, one baptism.

---

1 Co. 12.6; 1 Chr. 12.19,21; 1 Co. 12.7 § 1 Chr. 12.32; 1 Co. 12.8 § 1 Chr. 12.33; Jas. 1.8 § 1 Co. 12.25–26 § Eph. 4.5

**Call upon me in the day of trouble:
I will deliver thee, and thou shalt glorify me.**

Why art thou cast down, O my soul? and why art thou disquieted within me? hope thou in God: for I shall yet praise him, *who is* the health of my countenance, and my God.—LORD, thou hast heard the desire of the humble: thou wilt prepare their heart, thou wilt cause thine ear to hear.—For thou, Lord, *art* good, and ready to forgive; and plenteous in mercy unto all them that call upon thee.

Jacob said unto his household... Let us arise, and go up to Beth-el; and I will make there an altar unto God, who answered me in the day of my distress, and was with me in the way which I went.—Bless the LORD, O my soul, and forget not all his benefits.

I love the LORD, because he hath heard my voice *and* my supplications. Because he hath inclined his ear unto me, therefore will I call upon *him* as long as I live. The sorrows of death compassed me, and the pains of hell gat hold upon me: I found trouble and sorrow. Then called I upon the name of the LORD.

Ps. 50.15; Ps. 42.11; Ps. 10.17; Ps. 86.5 § Ge. 35.2,3;
Ps. 103.2 § Ps. 116.1–4

**Yet a little while,
and he that shall come will come,
and will not tarry.**

Write the vision, and make *it* plain upon tables, that he may run that readeth it. For the vision *is* yet for an appointed time, but at the end it shall speak, and not lie: though it tarry, wait for it; because it will surely come, it will not tarry.

Beloved, be not ignorant of this one thing, that one day *is* with the Lord as a thousand years, and a thousand years as one day. The Lord is not slack concerning his promise, as some men count slackness; but is longsuffering to us-ward, not willing that any should perish, but that all should come to repentance.—Thou, O Lord, *art* a God full of compassion, and gracious, longsuffering, and plenteous in mercy and truth.—Oh that thou wouldest rend the heavens, that thou wouldest come down... For since the beginning of the world *men* have not heard, nor perceived by the ear, neither hath the eye seen, O God, beside thee, *what* he hath prepared for him that waiteth for him.

He. 10.37; Hab. 2.2–3 § 2 Pe. 3.8–9; Ps. 86.15;
Isa. 64.1,4

The Lord God omnipotent reigneth.

I know that thou canst do every *thing*.—The things which are impossible with men are possible with God.—He doeth according to his will in the army of heaven, and *among* the inhabitants of the earth: and none can stay his hand, or say unto him, What doest thou?—*There is* none that can deliver out of my hand: I will work, and who shall let it?—Abba, Father, all things *are* possible unto thee.

Believe ye that I am able to do this? They said unto him, Yea, Lord. Then touched he their eyes, saying, According to your faith be it unto you.—Lord, if thou wilt, thou canst make me clean. And Jesus put forth *his* hand, and touched him, saying, I will; be thou clean.— The mighty God.—All power is given unto me in heaven and in earth.

Some *trust* in chariots, and some in horses: but we will remember the name of the LORD our God.—Be strong and courageous, be not afraid nor dismayed… *there be* more with us than with him.

Rev. 19.6; Job 42.2; Lu. 18.27; Dan. 4.35; Isa. 43.13; Mk. 14.36 § Mt. 9.28–29; Mt. 8.2–3; Isa. 9.6; Mt. 28.18 § Ps. 20.7; 2 Chr. 32.7

What *is* the thing that *the* LORD hath said unto thee?

He hath shewed thee, O man, what *is* good; and what doth the LORD require of thee, but to do justly, and to love mercy, and to walk humbly with thy God?—To keep the commandments of the LORD, and his statutes, which I command thee this day for thy good.

As many as are of the works of the law are under the curse: for it is written, Cursed *is* every one that continueth not in all things which are written in the book of the law to do them. But that no man is justified by the law in the sight of God, *it is* evident: for, The just shall live by faith… Wherefore then *serveth* the law? It was added because of transgressions, till the seed should come to whom the promise was made.

God, who at sundry times and in divers manners spake in time past unto the fathers by the prophets, hath in these last days spoken unto us by *his* Son.

Speak, LORD; for thy servant heareth.

---

1 Sa. 3.17; Mi. 6.8; Deu. 10.13 § Ga. 3.10–11,19
§ He. 1.1–2 § 1 Sa. 3.9

The meek will he teach his way.

Blessed *are* the meek.

I returned, and saw under the sun, that the race *is* not to the swift, nor the battle to the strong, neither yet bread to the wise, nor yet riches to men of understanding, nor yet favour to men of skill.—A man's heart deviseth his way: but the LORD directeth his steps.

Unto thee lift I up mine eyes, O thou that dwellest in the heavens. Behold, as the eyes of servants *look* unto the hand of their masters, *and* as the eyes of a maiden unto the hand of her mistress; so our eyes *wait* upon the LORD our God.—Cause me to know the way wherein I should walk; for I lift up my soul unto thee.

O our God, wilt thou not judge them? for we have no might against this great company that cometh against us; neither know we what to do: but our eyes *are* upon thee.

If any of you lack wisdom, let him ask of God, that giveth to all *men* liberally, and upbraideth not; and it shall be given him.

When he, the Spirit of truth, is come, he will guide you into all truth.

Ps. 25.9;   Mt. 5.5   § Ec. 9.11;   Pro. 16.9   § Ps. 123.1–2; Ps. 143.8   § 2 Chr. 20.12   § Jas. 1.5   § Jn. 16.13

O Lord God…
with thy blessing let the house of thy servant
be blessed for ever.

Thou blessest, O LORD, and *it shall be* blessed for ever.—The blessing of the LORD, it maketh rich, and he addeth no sorrow with it.

Remember the words of the Lord Jesus, how he said, It is more blessed to give than to receive.—When thou makest a feast, call the poor, the maimed, the lame, the blind: and thou shalt be blessed; for they cannot recompense thee: for thou shalt be recompensed at the resurrection of the just.—Come, ye blessed of my Father, inherit the kingdom prepared for you from the foundation of the world: for I was an hungred, and ye gave me meat: I was thirsty, and ye gave me drink: I was a stranger, and ye took me in: naked, and ye clothed me: I was sick, and ye visited me: I was in prison, and ye came unto me.

Blessed *is* he that considereth the poor: the LORD will deliver him in time of trouble.

The LORD God *is* a sun and shield.

---

2 Sa. 7.29; 1 Chr. 17.27; Pro. 10.22 § Ac. 20.35;
Lu. 14.13–14; Mt. 25.34–36 § Ps. 41.1 § Ps. 84.11

I will not fear what man shall do unto me.

Who shall separate us from the love of Christ? *shall* tribulation, or distress, or persecution, or famine, or nakedness, or peril, or sword?... Nay, in all these things we are more than conquerors through him that loved us.

Be not afraid of them that kill the body, and after that have no more that they can do. But I will forewarn you whom ye shall fear: Fear him, which after he hath killed hath power to cast into hell; yea, I say unto you, Fear him.

Blessed *are* they which are persecuted for righteousness' sake: for their's is the kingdom of heaven. Blessed are ye, when *men* shall revile you, and persecute *you*, and shall say all manner of evil against you falsely, for my sake. Rejoice, and be exceeding glad: for great *is* your reward in heaven.—None of these things move me, neither count I my life dear unto myself, so that I might finish my course with joy.—I will speak of thy testimonies...before kings, and will not be ashamed.

He. 13.6;   Ro. 8.35,37   § Lu. 12.4–5   § Mt. 5.10–12; Ac. 20.24;   Ps. 119.46

He...set my feet upon a rock.

That Rock was Christ.—Simon Peter...said, Thou art the Christ, the Son of the living God. And Jesus answered and said... Upon this rock I will build my church; and the gates of hell shall not prevail against it.—Neither is there salvation in any other: for there is none other name under heaven given among men, whereby we must be saved.

Let us draw near...in full assurance of faith...faith without wavering.—Let him ask in faith, nothing wavering... He that wavereth is like a wave of the sea driven with the wind and tossed.

Who shall separate us from the love of Christ? *shall* tribulation, or distress, or persecution, or famine, or nakedness, or peril, or sword?... Nay, in all these things we are more than conquerors through him that loved us. For I am persuaded, that neither death, nor life, nor angels, nor principalities, nor powers, nor things present, nor things to come, nor height, nor depth, nor any other creature, shall be able to separate us from the love of God, which is in Christ Jesus our Lord.

Ps. 40.2; 1 Co. 10.4; Mt. 16.16,17–18; Ac. 4.12
§ He. 10.22,23; Jas. 1.6 § Ro. 8.35,37–39

**Thou *art* a God ready to pardon,
gracious and merciful.**

The Lord is not slack concerning his promise, as some men count slackness; but is longsuffering to us-ward, not willing that any should perish, but that all should come to repentance.—The longsuffering of our Lord *is* salvation.

For this cause I obtained mercy, that in me first Jesus Christ might shew forth all longsuffering, for a pattern to them which should hereafter believe on him to life everlasting.—Whatsoever things were written aforetime were written for our learning, that we through patience and comfort of the scriptures might have hope.

Despisest thou the riches of his goodness and forbearance and longsuffering; not knowing that the goodness of God leadeth thee to repentance?—Rend your heart, and not your garments, and turn unto the LORD your God: for he *is* gracious and merciful, slow to anger, and of great kindness, and repenteth him of the evil.

Ne. 9.17; 2 Pe. 3.9; 2 Pe. 3.15 § 1 Tim. 1.16; Ro. 15.4 § Ro. 2.4; Joel 2.13

The words of the Lord *are* pure words.

Thy word is very pure: therefore thy servant loveth it.—The statutes of the LORD *are* right, rejoicing the heart: the commandment of the LORD *is* pure, enlightening the eyes.—Every word of God *is* pure: he *is* a shield unto them that put their trust in him. Add thou not unto his words, lest he reprove thee, and thou be found a liar.

Thy word have I hid in mine heart, that I might not sin against thee... I will meditate in thy precepts, and have respect unto thy ways.—Brethren, whatsoever things are true, whatsoever things *are* honest, whatsoever things *are* just, whatsoever things *are* pure, whatsoever things *are* lovely, whatsoever things *are* of good report, if *there be* any virtue, and if *there be* any praise, think on these things.—As newborn babes, desire the sincere milk of the word, that ye may grow thereby.

We are not as many, which corrupt the word of God: but as of sincerity, but as of God, in the sight of God speak we in Christ.—Nor handling the word of God deceitfully.

Ps. 12.6; Ps. 119.140; Ps. 19.8; Pro. 30.5–6
§ Ps. 119.11,15; Phil. 4.8; 1 Pe. 2.2 § 2 Co. 2.17;
2 Co. 4.2

The whole family in heaven and earth.

One God and Father of all, who *is* above all, and through all, and in you all.—Ye are all the children of God by faith in Christ Jesus.—That in the dispensation of the fulness of times he might gather together in one all things in Christ, both which are in heaven, and which are on earth; *even* in him.

He is not ashamed to call them brethren.—Behold my mother and my brethren! For whosoever shall do the will of my Father which is in heaven, the same is my brother, and sister, and mother.—Go to my brethren, and say unto them, I ascend unto my Father, and your Father.

I saw under the altar the souls of them that were slain for the word of God, and for the testimony which they held…and white robes were given unto every one of them; and it was said unto them, that they should rest yet for a little season, until their fellowservants also and their brethren, that should be killed as they *were*, should be fulfilled.—That they without us should not be made perfect.

Eph. 3.15; Eph. 4.6; Ga. 3.26; Eph. 1.10 § He. 2.11; Mt. 12.49–50; Jn. 20.17 § Rev. 6.9,10–11; He. 11.40

After this manner...pray ye:
Our Father which art in heaven.

Jesus...lifted up his eyes to heaven, and said, Father.—
My Father, and your Father.

Ye are all the children of God by faith in Christ
Jesus.—Ye have not received the spirit of bondage again
to fear; but ye have received the Spirit of adoption,
whereby we cry, Abba, Father. The Spirit itself beareth
witness with our spirit, that we are the children of God.

Because ye are sons, God hath sent forth the Spirit of
his Son into your hearts, crying, Abba, Father.
Wherefore thou art no more a servant, but a son.

Verily, verily, I say unto you, Whatsoever ye shall ask
the Father in my name, he will give *it* you. Hitherto have
ye asked nothing in my name: ask, and ye shall receive,
that your joy may be full.

I will receive you, and will be a Father unto you, and
ye shall be my sons and daughters, saith the Lord
Almighty.

Mt. 6.9; Jn. 17.1; Jn. 20.17 § Ga. 3.26; Ro. 8.15–16
§ Ga. 4.6,7 § Jn. 16.23–24 § 2 Co. 6.17–18

Be not far from me; for trouble *is* near.

How long wilt thou forget me, O LORD? for ever? how long wilt thou hide thy face from me? How long shall I take counsel in my soul, *having* sorrow in my heart daily?—Hide not thy face *far* from me; put not thy servant away in anger: thou hast been my help; leave me not, neither forsake me, O God of my salvation.

He shall call upon me, and I will answer him: I *will be* with him in trouble; I will deliver him, and honour him.—The LORD *is* nigh unto all them that call upon him, to all that call upon him in truth. He will fulfil the desire of them that fear him: he also will hear their cry, and will save them.

I will not leave you comfortless: I will come to you.—Lo, I am with you alway, *even* unto the end of the world.

God *is* our refuge and strength, a very present help in trouble.—Truly my soul waiteth upon God: from him *cometh* my salvation.—My soul, wait thou only upon God; for my expectation *is* from him.

Ps. 22.11; Ps. 13.1–2; Ps. 27.9 § Ps. 91.15; Ps. 145.18–19 § Jn. 14.18; Mt. 28.20 § Ps. 46.1; Ps. 62.1; Ps. 62.5

Hallowed be thy name.

Thou shalt worship no other god: for the LORD, whose name *is* Jealous, *is* a jealous God.

Who *is* like unto thee, O LORD, among the gods? who *is* like thee, glorious in holiness, fearful *in* praises, doing wonders?—Holy, holy, holy, Lord God Almighty.

Worship the LORD in the beauty of holiness.—I saw…the Lord sitting upon a throne, high and lifted up, and his train filled the temple. Above it stood the seraphims… And one cried unto another, and said, Holy, holy, holy, *is* the LORD of hosts: the whole earth *is* full of his glory… Then said I, Woe *is* me! for I am undone.—I have heard of thee by the hearing of the ear: but now mine eye seeth thee. Wherefore I abhor *myself*.

The blood of Jesus Christ his Son cleanseth us from all sin.—That *we* might be partakers of his holiness.—Having therefore, brethren, boldness to enter into the holiest by the blood of Jesus…let us draw near with a true heart.

Mt. 6.9; Ex. 34.14 § Ex. 15.11; Rev. 4.8 § 1 Chr. 16.29; Isa. 6.1–3,5; Job 42.5–6 § 1 Jn. 1.7; He. 12.10; He. 10.19,22

God was in Christ, reconciling the world unto himself, not imputing their trespasses unto them.

It pleased *the Father* that in him should all fulness dwell; and, having made peace through the blood of his cross, by him to reconcile all things unto himself.— Mercy and truth are met together; righteousness and peace have kissed *each other*.

I know the thoughts that I think toward you, saith the LORD, thoughts of peace, and not of evil.—Come now, and let us reason together, saith the LORD: though your sins be as scarlet, they shall be as white as snow; though they be red like crimson, they shall be as wool.

Who *is* a God like unto thee, that pardoneth iniquity?

Acquaint now thyself with him, and be at peace.— Work out your own salvation with fear and trembling. For it is God which worketh in you both to will and to do of *his* good pleasure.—LORD, thou wilt ordain peace for us: for thou also hast wrought all our works in us.

---

2 Co. 5.19; Col. 1.19–20; Ps. 85.10 § Jer. 29.11; Isa. 1.18 § Mi. 7.18 § Job 22.21; Phil. 2.12–13; Isa. 26.12

Thy kingdom come.

In the days of these kings shall the God of heaven set up a kingdom, which shall never be destroyed: and the kingdom shall not be left to other people, *but* it shall break in pieces and consume all these kingdoms, and it shall stand for ever.—A stone...cut out without hands.—Not by might, nor by power, but by my spirit, saith the LORD of hosts.—The kingdom of God cometh not with observation: neither shall they say, Lo here! or, lo there! for, behold, the kingdom of God is within you.

Unto you it is given to know the mystery of the kingdom of God... So is the kingdom of God, as if a man should cast seed into the ground; and should sleep, and rise night and day, and the seed should spring and grow up, he knoweth not how... But when the fruit is brought forth, immediately he putteth in the sickle, because the harvest is come.

Be ye...ready: for in such an hour as ye think not the Son of man cometh.

The Spirit and the bride say, Come. And let him that heareth say, Come.

Mt. 6.10; Dan. 2.44; Dan. 2.34; Zech. 4.6; Lu. 17.20–21 § Mk. 4.11,26–27,29 § Mt. 24.44 § Rev. 22.17

**From the first day that thou didst
set thine heart to understand,
and to chasten thyself before thy God,
thy words were heard.**

Thus saith the high and lofty One that inhabiteth eternity, whose name *is* Holy; I dwell in the high and holy *place*, with him also *that is* of a contrite and humble spirit, to revive the spirit of the humble, and to revive the heart of the contrite ones.—The sacrifices of God *are* a broken spirit: a broken and a contrite heart, O God, thou wilt not despise.—Though the LORD *be* high, yet hath he respect unto the lowly: but the proud he knoweth afar off.—Humble yourselves therefore under the mighty hand of God, that he may exalt you in due time.—God resisteth the proud, but giveth grace unto the humble. Submit yourselves therefore to God.

Thou, Lord, *art* good, and ready to forgive; and plenteous in mercy unto all them that call upon thee. Give ear, O LORD, unto my prayer; and attend to the voice of my supplications. In the day of my trouble I will call upon thee: for thou wilt answer me.

Dan. 10.12; Isa. 57.15; Ps. 51.17; Ps. 138.6; 1 Pe. 5.6; Jas. 4.6–7 § Ps. 86.5–7

Thy will be done in earth,
as *it is* in heaven.

Understanding what the will of the Lord *is*.

It is not the will of your Father which is in heaven, that one of these little ones should perish.

This is the will of God, *even* your sanctification.—That he no longer should live the rest of *his* time in the flesh to the lusts of men, but to the will of God.—Of his own will begat he us with the word of truth... Wherefore lay apart all filthiness.

Be ye holy; for I am holy.—[Jesus said] Whosoever shall do the will of God, the same is my brother, and my sister, and mother.—Whosoever heareth these sayings of mine, and doeth them, I will liken him unto a wise man, which built his house upon a rock: and the rain descended, and the floods came, and the winds blew, and beat upon that house; and it fell not: for it was founded upon a rock.—The world passeth away, and the lust thereof: but he that doeth the will of God abideth for ever.

Mt. 6.10; Eph. 5.17 § Mt. 18.14 § 1 Th. 4.3; 1 Pe. 4.2; Jas. 1.18,21 § 1 Pe. 1.16; Mk. 3.35; Mt. 7.24–25; 1 Jn. 2.17

Christ both died,
and rose, and revived, that he might be
Lord both of the dead and living.

It pleased the LORD to bruise him; he hath put *him* to grief: when thou shalt make his soul an offering for sin, he shall see *his* seed, he shall prolong *his* days, and the pleasure of the LORD shall prosper in his hand. He shall see of the travail of his soul, *and* shall be satisfied: by his knowledge shall my righteous servant justify many; for he shall bear their iniquities.—Ought not Christ to have suffered these things, and to enter into his glory?—We thus judge, that if one died for all, then were all dead: and *that* he died for all, that they which live should not henceforth live unto themselves, but unto him which died for them, and rose again.

Let all the house of Israel know assuredly, that God hath made that same Jesus, whom ye have crucified, both Lord and Christ.—Who verily was foreordained before the foundation of the world, but was manifest in these last times for you, who by him do believe in God.

Ro. 14.9; Isa. 53.10–11; Lu. 24.26; 2 Co. 5.14–15
§ Ac. 2.36; 1 Pe. 1.20–21

Give us this day our daily bread.

I have been young, and *now* am old; yet have I not seen the righteous forsaken, nor his seed begging bread.—Bread shall be given him; his waters *shall be* sure.—The ravens brought him bread and flesh in the morning, and bread and flesh in the evening; and he drank of the brook.

My God shall supply all your need according to his riches in glory by Christ Jesus.—*Be* content with such things as ye have: for he hath said, I will never leave thee, nor forsake thee.

He humbled thee, and suffered thee to hunger, and fed thee with manna…that he might make thee know that man doth not live by bread only, but by every *word* that proceedeth out of the mouth of the LORD doth man live.—Jesus said unto them, Verily, verily, I say unto you, Moses gave you not that bread from heaven; but my Father giveth you the true bread from heaven. For the bread of God is he which cometh down from heaven, and giveth life unto the world. Then said they unto him, Lord, evermore give us this bread.

Mt. **6.11**; Ps. 37.25; Isa. 33.16; 1 Ki. 17.6 § Phil. 4.19; He. 13.5 § Deu. 8.3; Jn. 6.32–34

God *is* my defence.

The LORD *is* my rock, and my fortress, and my deliverer; the God of my rock; in him will I trust: *he is* my shield, and the horn of my salvation, my high tower, and my refuge, my saviour.—The LORD *is* my strength and my shield; my heart trusted in him, and I am helped: therefore my heart greatly rejoiceth; and with my song will I praise him.

When the enemy shall come in like a flood, the Spirit of the LORD shall lift up a standard against him.—We may boldly say, The Lord *is* my helper, and I will not fear what man shall do unto me.

The LORD *is* my light and my salvation; whom shall I fear? the LORD *is* the strength of my life; of whom shall I be afraid?—*As* the mountains *are* round about Jerusalem, so the LORD *is* round about his people from henceforth even for ever.—Because thou hast been my help, therefore in the shadow of thy wings will I rejoice.

For thy name's sake lead me, and guide me.

Ps. 59.9; 2 Sa. 22.2–3; Ps. 28.7 § Isa. 59.19; He. 13.6 § Ps. 27.1; Ps. 125.2; Ps. 63.7 § Ps. 31.3

Forgive us our debts,
as we forgive our debtors.

Lord, how oft shall my brother sin against me, and I forgive him? till seven times? Jesus saith unto him, I say not unto thee, Until seven times: but, Until seventy times seven.—O thou wicked servant, I forgave thee all that debt, because thou desiredst me: shouldest not thou also have had compassion on thy fellowservant, even as I had pity on thee? And his lord was wroth, and delivered him to the tormentors, till he should pay all that was due unto him. So likewise shall my heavenly Father do also unto you, if ye from your hearts forgive not every one his brother their trespasses.—Be ye kind one to another, tenderhearted, forgiving one another, even as God for Christ's sake hath forgiven you.—You...hath he quickened...having forgiven you all trespasses; blotting out the handwriting of ordinances that was against us, which was contrary to us, and took it out of the way, nailing it to his cross.—Even as Christ forgave you, so also *do* ye.

Mt. 6.12; Mt. 18.21–22; Mt. 18.32–35; Eph. 4.32;
Col. 2.13–14; Col. 3.13

Not slothful in business;
fervent in spirit; serving the Lord.

Whatsoever thy hand findeth to do, do *it* with thy might; for *there is* no work, nor device, nor knowledge, nor wisdom, in the grave, whither thou goest.—Whatsoever ye do, do *it* heartily, as to the Lord, and not unto men; knowing that of the Lord ye shall receive the reward of the inheritance: for ye serve the Lord Christ.—Whatsoever good thing any man doeth, the same shall he receive of the Lord.

I must work the works of him that sent me, while it is day: the night cometh, when no man can work.—Wist ye not that I must be about my Father's business?—The zeal of thine house hath eaten me up.

Brethren, give diligence to make your calling and election sure: for if ye do these things, ye shall never fall.—We desire that every one of you do shew the same diligence to the full assurance of hope unto the end: that ye be not slothful, but followers of them who through faith and patience inherit the promises.—So run, that ye may obtain.

Ro. 12.11; Ec. 9.10; Col. 3.23–24; Eph. 6.8 § Jn. 9.4; Lu. 2.49; Jn. 2.17 § 2 Pe. 1.10; He. 6.11–12; 1 Co. 9.24

Lead us not into temptation,
but deliver us from evil.

He that trusteth in his own heart is a fool: but whoso walketh wisely, he shall be delivered.

Let no man say when he is tempted, I am tempted of God: for God cannot be tempted with evil, neither tempteth he any man: but every man is tempted, when he is drawn away of his own lust, and enticed.— Wherefore come out from among them, and be ye separate, saith the Lord, and touch not the unclean *thing;* and I will receive you.

Lot lifted up his eyes, and beheld all the plain of Jordan, that it *was* well watered every where...*even* as the garden of the LORD... Then Lot chose him all the plain of Jordan... But the men of Sodom *were* wicked and sinners before the LORD exceedingly.—[God] delivered just Lot, vexed with the filthy conversation of the wicked... The Lord knoweth how to deliver the godly out of temptations.—Yea, he shall be holden up: for God is able to make him stand.

Mt. 6.13; Pro. 28.26 § Jas. 1.13–14; 2 Co. 6.17
§ Ge. 13.10,11,13; 2 Pe. 2.7,9; Ro. 14.4

**In thy name shall they rejoice all the day:
and in thy righteousness shall they be exalted.**

In the LORD have I righteousness and strength: *even* to him shall *men* come; and all that are incensed against him shall be ashamed. In the LORD shall all the seed of Israel be justified, and shall glory.—Be glad in the LORD, and rejoice, ye righteous: and shout for joy, all *ye that are* upright in heart.

The righteousness of God without the law is manifested, being witnessed by the law and the prophets; even the righteousness of God *which is* by faith of Jesus Christ unto all and upon all them that believe... To declare...at this time his righteousness: that he might be just, and the justifier of him which believeth in Jesus.

Rejoice in the Lord alway: *and* again I say, Rejoice.— Whom having not seen, ye love; in whom, though now ye see *him* not, yet believing, ye rejoice with joy unspeakable and full of glory.

Ps. 89.16; Isa. 45.24–25; Ps. 32.11 § Ro. 3.21–22,26
§ Phil. 4.4; 1 Pe. 1.8

Thine is the kingdom,
and the power, and the glory, for ever.

The LORD reigneth, he is clothed with majesty… Thy throne *is* established of old: thou *art* from everlasting.

The LORD *is*…great in power.—If God *be* for us, who *can be* against us?—Our God whom we serve is able to deliver us…and he will deliver *us.*—My Father, which gave *them* me, is greater than all; and no *man* is able to pluck *them* out of my Father's hand.—Greater is he that is in you, than he that is in the world.

Not unto us, O LORD, not unto us, but unto thy name give glory.—Thine, O LORD, *is* the greatness, and the power, and the glory, and the victory, and the majesty: for all *that is* in the heaven and in the earth *is thine;* thine *is* the kingdom, O LORD, and thou art exalted as head above all… Now therefore, our God, we thank thee, and praise thy glorious name. But who *am* I, and what *is* my people, that we should be able to offer so willingly after this sort? for all things *come* of thee, and of thine own have we given thee.

Mt. 6.13; Ps. 93.1,2 § Na. 1.3; Ro. 8.31; Dan. 3.17; Jn. 10.29; 1 Jn. 4.4 § Ps. 115.1; 1 Chr. 29.11,13–14

**One of the soldiers with a spear pierced his side,
and forthwith came there out blood and water.**

Behold the blood of the covenant, which the LORD hath made with you.—The life of the flesh *is* in the blood: and I have given it to you upon the altar to make an atonement for your souls.—*It is* not possible that the blood of bulls and of goats should take away sins.

And [Jesus] said unto them, This is my blood of the new testament, which is shed for many.—By his own blood he entered in once into the holy place, having obtained eternal redemption *for us.*—Peace through the blood of his cross.

Ye know that ye were not redeemed with corruptible things, *as* silver and gold…but with the precious blood of Christ, as of a lamb without blemish and without spot…manifest in these last times for you.

Then will I sprinkle clean water upon you, and ye shall be clean…from all your idols, will I cleanse you.— Let us draw near with a true heart in full assurance of faith, having our hearts sprinkled from an evil conscience.

Jn. **19.**34; Ex. 24.8; Lev. 17.11; He. 10.4 § Mk. 14.24;
He. 9.12; Col. 1.20 § 1 Pe. 1.18,19,20 § Ezek. 36.25;
He. 10.22

Amen.

Amen: the LORD God...say so *too*.—He who blesseth himself in the earth shall bless himself in the God of truth [*Heb.* God of Amen] and he that sweareth in the earth shall swear by the God of truth [*Heb.* God of Amen].

When God made promise to Abraham, because he could swear by no greater, he sware by himself... For men verily swear by the greater: and an oath for confirmation *is* to them an end of all strife. Wherein God, willing more abundantly to shew unto the heirs of promise the immutability of his counsel, confirmed *it* by an oath: that by two immutable things, in which *it was* impossible for God to lie, we might have a strong consolation, who have fled for refuge to lay hold upon the hope set before us.

These things saith the Amen, the faithful and true witness.—For all the promises of God in him *are* yea, and in him Amen, unto the glory of God by us.

Blessed *be* the LORD God, the God of Israel, who only doeth wondrous things. And blessed *be* his glorious name for ever...Amen, and Amen.

Mt. 6.13; 1 Ki. 1.36; Isa. 65.16 § He. 6.13,16–18
§ Rev. 3.14; 2 Co. 1.20 § Ps. 72.18–19

The LORD shall be thy confidence, and shall keep thy foot from being taken.

Surely the wrath of man shall praise thee: the remainder of wrath shalt thou restrain.—The king's heart *is* in the hand of the LORD, *as* the rivers of water: he turneth it whithersoever he will.—When a man's ways please the LORD, he maketh even his enemies to be at peace with him.

I wait for the LORD, my soul doth wait, and in his word do I hope. My soul *waiteth* for the Lord more than they that watch for the morning: *I say, more than* they that watch for the morning.—I sought the LORD, and he heard me, and delivered me from all my fears.

The eternal God *is thy* refuge, and underneath *are* the everlasting arms: and he shall thrust out the enemy from before thee; and shall say, Destroy *them*.—Blessed *is* the man that trusteth in the LORD, and whose hope the LORD is.

What shall we then say to these things? If God *be* for us, who *can be* against us?

Pro. 3.26; Ps. 76.10; Pro. 21.1; Pro. 16.7 § Ps. 130.5–6; Ps. 34.4 § Deu. 33.27; Jer. 17.7 § Ro. 8.31

Consolation in Christ…
comfort of love…fellowship of the Spirit.

Man *that is* born of a woman *is* of few days, and full of trouble. He cometh forth like a flower, and is cut down: he fleeth also as a shadow, and continueth not.— My flesh and my heart faileth: *but* God *is* the strength of my heart, and my portion for ever.

The Father…shall give you another Comforter, that he may abide with you for ever…the Comforter *which is* the Holy Ghost, whom the Father will send in my name.—Blessed *be* God, even the Father of our Lord Jesus Christ, the Father of mercies, and the God of all comfort; who comforteth us in all our tribulation, that we may be able to comfort them which are in any trouble, by the comfort wherewith we ourselves are comforted of God.

If we believe that Jesus died and rose again, even so them also which sleep in Jesus will God bring with him… And so shall we ever be with the Lord. Wherefore comfort one another with these words.

Phil. 2.1; Job 14.1–2; Ps. 73.26 § Jn. 14.16,26; 2 Co. 1.3,4 § 1 Th. 4.14,17–18

I delight in the law of God
after the inward man.

O how love I thy law! it *is* my meditation all the day.—
Thy words were found, and I did eat them; and thy word
was unto me the joy and rejoicing of mine heart.—I sat
down under his shadow with great delight, and his fruit
was sweet to my taste.—I have esteemed the words of his
mouth more than my necessary *food*.

I delight to do thy will, O my God: yea, thy law *is*
within my heart.—My meat is to do the will of him that
sent me, and to finish his work.

The statutes of the LORD *are* right, rejoicing the
heart: the commandment of the LORD *is* pure, enlightening the eyes… More to be desired *are they* than gold,
yea, than much fine gold: sweeter also than honey and
the honeycomb.—Be ye doers of the word, and not
hearers only, deceiving your own selves. For if any be a
hearer of the word, and not a doer, he is like unto a man
beholding his natural face in a glass.

Ro. 7.22; Ps. 119.97; Jer. 15.16; Song 2.3; Job 23.12
§ Ps. 40.8; Jn. 4.34 § Ps. 19.8,10; Jas. 1.22–23

The LORD thy God accept thee.

Wherewith shall I come before the LORD, *and* bow myself before the high God? shall I come before him with burnt offerings, with calves of a year old? Will the LORD be pleased with thousands of rams, *or* with ten thousands of rivers of oil? shall I give my firstborn *for* my transgression, the fruit of my body *for* the sin of my soul? He hath shewed thee, O man, what *is* good; and what doth the LORD require of thee, but to do justly, and to love mercy, and to walk humbly with thy God?

We are all as an unclean *thing*, and all our righteousnesses *are* as filthy rags.—There is none righteous, no, not one... For all have sinned, and come short of the glory of God; being justified freely by his grace through the redemption that is in Christ Jesus: whom God hath set forth *to be* a propitiation through faith in his blood...To declare...at this time his righteousness: that he might be just, and the justifier of him which believeth in Jesus.

Accepted in the beloved.—Ye are complete in him.

2 Sa. 24.23; Mi. 6.6–8 § Isa. 64.6; Ro. 3.10,23–25,26 § Eph. 1.6; Col. 2.10

**Of his fulness have all we received,
and grace for grace.**

This is my beloved Son, in whom I am well pleased.—
Behold, what manner of love the Father hath bestowed
upon us, that we should be called the sons of God.

His Son, whom he hath appointed heir of all
things.—If children, then heirs; heirs of God, and joint-
heirs with Christ; if so be that we suffer with *him*, that
we may be also glorified together.

I and *my* Father are one. The Father *is* in me, and I
in him.—My Father, and your Father; and...my God,
and your God.—I in them, and thou in me, that they
may be made perfect in one.

The church, which is his body, the fulness of him
that filleth all in all.

Having...these promises, dearly beloved, let us
cleanse ourselves from all filthiness of the flesh and spirit, perfecting holiness in the fear of God.

Jn. 1.16; Mt. 17.5; 1 Jn. 3.1 § He. 1.2; Ro. 8.17
§ Jn. 10.30,38; Jn. 20.17; Jn. 17.23 § Eph. 1.22–23
§ 2 Co. 7.1

**The servant is not greater than his lord;
neither he that is sent greater than he that sent him.
If ye know these things, happy are ye if ye do them.**

There was...a strife among them, which of them should be accounted the greatest. And he said unto them, The kings of the Gentiles exercise lordship over them; and they that exercise authority upon them are called benefactors. But ye *shall* not *be* so: but he that is greatest among you, let him be as the younger; and he that is chief, as he that doth serve. For whether *is* greater, he that sitteth at meat, or he that serveth? *is* not he that sitteth at meat? but I am among you as he that serveth.—Even as the Son of man came not to be ministered unto, but to minister, and to give his life a ransom for many.

Jesus...riseth from supper, and laid aside his garments; and took a towel, and girded himself. After that he poureth water into a bason, and began to wash the disciples' feet, and to wipe *them* with the towel wherewith he was girded.

Jn. 13.16,17; Lu. 22.24–27; Mt. 20.28 § Jn. 13.3,4–5

O God, my heart is fixed.

The LORD *is* my light and my salvation; whom shall I fear? the LORD *is* the strength of my life; of whom shall I be afraid?

Thou wilt keep *him* in perfect peace, *whose* mind *is* stayed *on thee:* because he trusteth in thee.—He shall not be afraid of evil tidings: his heart is fixed, trusting in the LORD. His heart *is* established, he shall not be afraid, until he see *his desire* upon his enemies.

What time I am afraid, I will trust in thee.—In the time of trouble he shall hide me in his pavilion: in the secret of his tabernacle shall he hide me; he shall set me up upon a rock. And now shall mine head be lifted up above mine enemies round about me: therefore will I offer in his tabernacle sacrifices of joy; I will sing, yea, I will sing praises unto the LORD.

The God of all grace, who hath called us unto his eternal glory by Christ Jesus, after that ye have suffered a while, make you perfect, stablish, strengthen, settle *you.* To him *be* glory and dominion for ever and ever.

Ps. 108.1; Ps. 27.1 § Isa. 26.3; Ps. 112.7–8 § Ps. 56.3; Ps. 27.5–6 § 1 Pe. 5.10–11

The LORD hath prepared his throne in the heavens; and his kingdom ruleth over all.

The lot is cast into the lap; but the whole disposing thereof *is* of the LORD.—Shall there be evil in a city, and the LORD hath not done it?

I *am* the LORD, and *there is* none else, *there is* no God beside me: I girded thee, though thou hast not known me: that they may know from the rising of the sun, and from the west, that *there is* none beside me. I *am* the LORD, and *there is* none else. I form the light, and create darkness: I make peace, and create evil: I the LORD do all these *things*.

He doeth according to his will in the army of heaven, and *among* the inhabitants of the earth: and none can stay his hand, or say unto him, What doest thou?—If God *be* for us, who *can be* against us?

He must reign, till he hath put all enemies under his feet.—Fear not, little flock; for it is your Father's good pleasure to give you the kingdom.

Ps. 103.19; Pro. 16.33; Am. 3.6 § Isa. 45.5–7
§ Dan. 4.35; Ro. 8.31 § 1 Co. 15.25; Lu. 12.32

**A man's life consisteth not in the abundance of
the things which he possesseth.**

A little that a righteous man hath *is* better than the
riches of many wicked.—Better *is* little with the fear of
the LORD than great treasure and trouble therewith.—
Godliness with contentment is great gain…having food
and raiment let us be therewith content.

Give me neither poverty nor riches; feed me with
food convenient for me: lest I be full, and deny *thee*, and
say, Who *is* the LORD? or lest I be poor, and steal, and
take the name of my God *in vain*.—Give us this day our
daily bread.

Take no thought for your life, what ye shall eat, or
what ye shall drink; nor yet for your body, what ye shall
put on. Is not the life more than meat, and the body
than raiment?—When I sent you without purse, and
scrip, and shoes, lacked ye any thing? And they said,
Nothing.—*Let your* conversation *be* without covetousness; *and be* content with such things as ye have: for he
hath said, I will never leave thee, nor forsake thee.

Lu. 12.15; Ps. 37.16; Pro. 15.16; 1 Tim. 6.6,8
§ Pro. 30.8–9; Mt. 6.11 § Mt. 6.25; Lu. 22.35; He. 13.5

It is the spirit that quickeneth.

The first man Adam was made a living soul; the last Adam *was made* a quickening spirit.—That which is born of the flesh is flesh; and that which is born of the Spirit is spirit.—Not by works of righteousness which we have done, but according to his mercy he saved us, by the washing of regeneration, and renewing of the Holy Ghost.

If any man have not the Spirit of Christ, he is none of his. And if Christ *be* in you, the body *is* dead because of sin; but the Spirit *is* life because of righteousness. But if the Spirit of him that raised up Jesus from the dead dwell in you, he that raised up Christ from the dead shall also quicken your mortal bodies by his Spirit that dwelleth in you.

I live; yet not I, but Christ liveth in me: and the life which I now live in the flesh I live by the faith of the Son of God.—Reckon ye...yourselves to be dead indeed unto sin, but alive unto God through Jesus Christ our Lord.

Jn. 6.63; 1 Co. 15.45; Jn. 3.6; Titus 3.5 § Ro. 8.9–11 § Ga. 2.20; Ro. 6.11

**I am cast out of thy sight;
yet I will look again toward thy holy temple.**

Zion said, The LORD hath forsaken me, and my Lord hath forgotten me. Can a woman forget her sucking child, that she should not have compassion on the son of her womb? yea, they may forget, yet will I not forget thee.

I forgat prosperity. And I said, My strength and my hope is perished from the LORD.—Awake, why sleepest thou, O Lord? arise, cast *us* not off for ever.—Why sayest thou, O Jacob, and speakest, O Israel, My way is hid from the LORD, and my judgment is passed over from my God?—In a little wrath I hid my face from thee for a moment; but with everlasting kindness will I have mercy on thee, saith the LORD thy Redeemer.

Why art thou cast down, O my soul? and why art thou disquieted within me? hope in God: for I shall yet praise him, *who is* the health of my countenance.—*We are* troubled on every side, yet not distressed; *we are* perplexed, but not in despair; persecuted, but not forsaken; cast down, but not destroyed.

Jon. 2.4; Isa. 49.14–15 § Lam. 3.17–18; Ps. 44.23; Isa. 40.27; Isa. 54.8 § Ps. 43.5; 2 Co. 4.8–9

When the poor and needy seek water,
and *there is* none,
and their tongue faileth for thirst,
I the LORD will hear them.

There be many that say, Who will shew us *any* good?—
All *is* vanity and vexation of spirit…What hath man of
all his labour, and of the vexation of his heart, wherein
he hath laboured under the sun? For all his days *are* sorrows, and his travail grief; yea, his heart taketh not rest
in the night.—They have forsaken me the fountain of
living waters, *and* hewed them out cisterns, broken cisterns, that can hold no water.

Him that cometh to me I will in no wise cast out.—
I will pour water upon him that is thirsty.—Blessed *are*
they which do hunger and thirst after righteousness: for
they shall be filled.

O God, thou *art* my God; early will I seek thee: my
soul thirsteth for thee, my flesh longeth for thee in a dry
and thirsty land, where no water is.

Isa. 41.17; Ps. 4.6; Ec. 2.17,22–23; Jer. 2.13 § Jn. 6.37;
Isa. 44.3; Mt. 5.6 § Ps. 63.1

Lo, I am with you alway,
even unto the end of the world.

If two of you shall agree on earth as touching any thing that they shall ask, it shall be done for them of my Father which is in heaven. For where two or three are gathered together in my name, there am I in the midst of them.—He that hath my commandments, and keepeth them, he it is that loveth me: and he that loveth me shall be loved of my Father, and I will love him, and will manifest myself to him.

Lord, how is it that thou wilt manifest thyself unto us, and not unto the world?…If a man love me, he will keep my words: and my Father will love him, and we will come unto him, and make our abode with him.

Unto him that is able to keep you from falling, and to present *you* faultless before the presence of his glory with exceeding joy, to the only wise God our Saviour, *be* glory and majesty, dominion and power, both now and ever. Amen.

Mt. 28.20; Mt. 18.19–20; Jn. 14.21 § Jn. 14.22,23 § Jude 24–25

The end of all things is at hand.

I saw a great white throne, and him that sat on it, from whose face the earth and the heaven fled away.—The heavens and the earth, which are now...are kept in store, reserved unto fire against the day of judgment.

God *is* our refuge and strength, a very present help in trouble. Therefore will not we fear, though the earth be removed, and though the mountains be carried into the midst of the sea; *though* the waters thereof roar *and* be troubled, *though* the mountains shake with the swelling thereof.—Ye shall hear of wars and rumours of wars: see that ye be not troubled.

We have a building of God, an house not made with hands, eternal in the heavens.—We, according to his promise, look for new heavens and a new earth, wherein dwelleth righteousness. Wherefore, beloved, seeing that ye look for such things, be diligent that ye may be found of him in peace, without spot, and blameless.

---

1 Pe. 4.7; Rev. 20.11; 2 Pe. 3.7 § Ps. 46.1–3; Mt. 24.6
§ 2 Co. 5.1; 2 Pe. 3.13–14

The LORD reigneth.

Fear ye not me? saith the LORD: will ye not tremble at my presence, which have placed the sand *for* the bound of the sea by a perpetual decree, that it cannot pass it: and though the waves thereof toss themselves, yet can they not prevail; though they roar, yet can they not pass over it?—Promotion *cometh* neither from the east, nor from the west, nor from the south. But God *is* the judge: he putteth down one, and setteth up another.

He changeth the times and the seasons: he removeth kings, and setteth up kings: he giveth wisdom unto the wise, and knowledge to them that know understanding.—Ye shall hear of wars and rumours of wars: see that ye be not troubled.

If God *be* for us, who *can be* against us?—Are not two sparrows sold for a farthing? and one of them shall not fall on the ground without your Father. But the very hairs of your head are all numbered. Fear ye not therefore, ye are of more value than many sparrows.

Ps. 99.1; Jer. 5.22; Ps. 75.6–7 § Dan. 2.21; Mt. 24.6 § Ro. 8.31; Mt. 10.29–31

Take heed to your spirit.

Master, we saw one casting out devils in thy name; and we forbad him, because he followeth not with us. And Jesus said unto him, Forbid *him* not: for he that is not against us is for us... Lord, wilt thou that we command fire to come down from heaven, and consume them, even as Elias did? But he...rebuked them, and said, Ye know not what manner of spirit ye are of.

Eldad and Medad do prophesy in the camp. And Joshua the son of Nun...answered and said, My lord Moses, forbid them. And Moses said unto him, Enviest thou for my sake? would God that all the LORD's people were prophets, *and* that the LORD would put his spirit upon them!

The fruit of the Spirit is love, joy, peace, longsuffering, gentleness, goodness, faith, meekness, temperance.—And they that are Christ's have crucified the flesh with the affections and lusts. If we live in the Spirit, let us also walk in the Spirit. Let us not be desirous of vain glory, provoking one another, envying one another.

Mal. 2.15; Lu. 9.49–50,54–55 § Nu. 11.27–29
§ Ga. 5.22–23; Ga. 5.24–26

Himself took our infirmities,
and bare *our* sicknesses.

Then shall the priest command to take for him that is to be cleansed two birds alive *and* clean, and cedar wood, and scarlet, and hyssop: and the priest shall command that one of the birds be killed in an earthen vessel over running water: as for the living bird, he shall take it, and the cedar wood, and the scarlet, and the hyssop, and shall dip them and the living bird in the blood of the bird *that was* killed over the running water: and he shall sprinkle upon him that is to be cleansed from the leprosy seven times, and shall pronounce him clean, and shall let the living bird loose into the open field.

Behold a man full of leprosy: who seeing Jesus fell on *his* face, and besought him, saying, Lord, if thou wilt, thou canst make me clean.—And Jesus, moved with compassion, put forth *his* hand, and touched him, and saith unto him, I will; be thou clean. And as soon as he had spoken, immediately the leprosy departed from him, and he was cleansed.

Mt. 8.17; Lev. 14.4–7 § Lu. 5.12; Mk. 1.41–42

He whom thou blessest
is blessed.

Blessed *are* the poor in spirit: for theirs is the kingdom of heaven. Blessed *are* they that mourn: for they shall be comforted. Blessed *are* the meek: for they shall inherit the earth. Blessed *are* they which do hunger and thirst after righteousness: for they shall be filled. Blessed *are* the merciful: for they shall obtain mercy. Blessed *are* the pure in heart: for they shall see God. Blessed *are* the peacemakers: for they shall be called the children of God. Blessed *are* they which are persecuted for righteousness' sake: for theirs is the kingdom of heaven. Blessed are ye, when *men* shall revile you, and persecute *you*, and shall say all manner of evil against you falsely, for my sake. Rejoice, and be exceeding glad: for great *is* your reward in heaven.—Blessed *are* they that hear the word of God, and keep it.

Blessed *are* they that do his commandments, that they may have right to the tree of life, and may enter in through the gates into the city.

Nu. 22.6; Mt. 5.3–12; Lu. 11.28 § Rev. 22.14

He saw that *there was* no man,
and wondered that *there was* no intercessor:
therefore his arm brought salvation unto him.

Sacrifice and offering thou didst not desire; mine ears hast thou opened: burnt offering and sin offering hast thou not required. Then said I, Lo, I come: in the volume of the book *it is* written of me, I delight to do thy will, O my God: yea, thy law *is* within my heart.—I lay down my life, that I might take it again. No man taketh it from me, but I lay it down of myself. I have power to lay it down, and I have power to take it again.

There is no God else beside me; a just God and a Saviour; *there is* none beside me. Look unto me, and be ye saved, all the ends of the earth: for I *am* God, and *there is* none else.—There is none other name under heaven given among men, whereby we must be saved.

Ye know the grace of our Lord Jesus Christ, that, though he was rich, yet for your sakes he became poor, that ye through his poverty might be rich.

Isa. 59.16; Ps. 40.6–8; Jn. 10.17–18 § Isa. 45.21–22; Ac. 4.12 § 2 Co. 8.9

The enemy.

Be sober, be vigilant; because your adversary the devil, as a roaring lion, walketh about, seeking whom he may devour.—Resist the devil, and he will flee from you.

Put on the whole armour of God, that ye may be able to stand against the wiles of the devil. For we wrestle not against flesh and blood, but against principalities, against powers, against the rulers of the darkness of this world, against spiritual wickedness in high *places*. Wherefore take unto you the whole armour of God, that ye may be able to withstand in the evil day, and having done all, to stand. Stand therefore, having your loins girt about with truth, and having on the breastplate of right-eousness; and your feet shod with the preparation of the gospel of peace; above all, taking the shield of faith, wherewith ye shall be able to quench all the fiery darts of the wicked.

Rejoice not against me, O mine enemy: when I fall, I shall arise; when I sit in darkness, the LORD *shall be* a light unto me.

Lu. 10.19; 1 Pe. 5.8; Jas. 4.7 § Eph. 6.11–16 § Mi. 7.8

He *is* altogether lovely.

 My meditation of him shall be sweet.—My beloved *is*…the chiefest among ten thousand.—A chief corner stone, elect, precious: and he that believeth on him shall not be confounded.—Thou art fairer than the children of men: grace is poured into thy lips.—God…hath highly exalted him, and given him a name which is above every name.—It pleased *the Father* that in him should all fulness dwell.

Whom having not seen, ye love; in whom, though now ye see *him* not, yet believing, ye rejoice with joy unspeakable and full of glory.

I count all things *but* loss for the excellency of the knowledge of Christ Jesus my Lord: for whom I have suffered the loss of all things, and do count them *but* dung, that I may win Christ, and be found in him, not having mine own righteousness, which is of the law, but that which is through the faith of Christ, the righteousness which is of God by faith.

Song 5.16; Ps.104.34; Song 5.10; 1 Pe. 2.6; Ps. 45.2; Phil. 2.9; Col. 1.19 § 1 Pe. 1.8 § Phil. 3.8–9

David encouraged himself
in the LORD his God.

Lord, to whom shall we go? thou hast the words of eternal life.—I know whom I have believed, and am persuaded that he is able to keep that which I have committed unto him against that day.

In my distress I called upon the LORD, and cried unto my God: he heard my voice out of his temple, and my cry came before him, *even* into his ears... They prevented me in the day of my calamity: but the LORD was my stay. He brought me forth also into a large place; he delivered me, because he delighted in me.

I will bless the LORD at all times: his praise *shall* continually *be* in my mouth. My soul shall make her boast in the LORD: the humble shall hear *thereof*, and be glad. O magnify the LORD with me, and let us exalt his name together. I sought the LORD, and he heard me, and delivered me from all my fears... O taste and see that the LORD *is* good: blessed *is* the man *that* trusteth in him.

---

1 Sa. 30.6; Jn. 6.68; 2 Tim. 1.12 § Ps. 18.6,18–19
§ Ps. 34.1–4,8

It is good that *a man* should both hope
and quietly wait for the salvation of the LORD.

Hath God forgotten to be gracious? hath he in anger shut up his tender mercies?—I said in my haste, I am cut off from before thine eyes: nevertheless thou heardest the voice of my supplications when I cried unto thee.

Shall not God avenge his own elect, which cry day and night unto him, though he bear long with them? I tell you that he will avenge them speedily.—Wait on the LORD, and he shall save thee.—Rest in the LORD, and wait patiently for him: fret not thyself because of him who prospereth in his way, because of the man who bringeth wicked devices to pass.

Ye shall not *need* to fight in this *battle:* set yourselves, stand ye *still*, and see the salvation of the LORD.

Let us not be weary in well doing…in due season we shall reap, if we faint not.—Behold, the husbandman waiteth for the precious fruit of the earth, and hath long patience for it, until he receive the early and latter rain.

Lam. 3.26; Ps. 77.9; Ps. 31.22 § Lu. 18.7–8; Pro. 20.22; Ps. 37.7 § 2 Chr. 20.17 § Ga. 6.9; Jas. 5.7

Take us the foxes, the little foxes,
that spoil the vines:
for our vines *have* tender grapes.

Who can understand *his* errors? cleanse thou me from secret *faults.*—Looking diligently lest any man fail of the grace of God; lest any root of bitterness springing up trouble *you*, and thereby many be defiled.—Ye did run well; who did hinder you that ye should not obey the truth?

He which hath begun a good work in you will perform *it* until the day of Jesus Christ... Only let your conversation be as it becometh the gospel of Christ.— The tongue is a little member, and boasteth great things. Behold, how great a matter a little fire kindleth! And the tongue *is* a fire, a world of iniquity: so is the tongue among our members, that it defileth the whole body, and setteth on fire the course of nature; and it is set on fire of hell... The tongue can no man tame; *it is* an unruly evil, full of deadly poison.—Let your speech *be* alway with grace, seasoned with salt.

Song 2.15; Ps. 19.12; He. 12.15; Ga. 5.7 § Phil. 1.6,27; Jas. 3.5–6,8; Col. 4.6

Not by might, nor by power,
but by my spirit, saith the LORD of hosts.

Who hath directed the Spirit of the LORD, or *being* his counsellor hath taught him?

God hath chosen the foolish things of the world to confound the wise; and God hath chosen the weak things of the world to confound the things which are mighty; and base things of the world, and things which are despised, hath God chosen, *yea*, and things which are not, to bring to nought things that are: that no flesh should glory in his presence.

The wind bloweth where it listeth, and thou hearest the sound thereof, but canst not tell whence it cometh, and whither it goeth: so is every one that is born of the Spirit.—Born, not of blood, nor of the will of the flesh, nor of the will of man, but of God.

My spirit remaineth among you: fear ye not.—The battle *is* not yours, but God's.

The LORD saveth not with sword and spear: for the battle *is* the LORD's.

Zech. 4.6; Isa. 40.13 § 1 Co. 1.27–29 § Jn. 3.8; Jn. 1.13 § Hag. 2.5; 2 Chr. 20.15 § 1 Sa. 17.47

Do as thou hast said.

Stablish thy word unto thy servant, who *is devoted* to thy fear... So shall I have wherewith to answer him that reproacheth me: for I trust in thy word... Remember the word unto thy servant, upon which thou hast caused me to hope... Thy statutes have been my songs in the house of my pilgrimage... The law of thy mouth *is* better unto me than thousands of gold and silver... For ever, O LORD, thy word is settled in heaven. Thy faithfulness *is* unto all generations.

God, willing more abundantly to shew unto the heirs of promise the immutability of his counsel, confirmed *it* by an oath; that by two immutable things, in which *it was* impossible for God to lie, we might have a strong consolation, who have fled for refuge to lay hold upon the hope set before us: which *hope* we have as an anchor of the soul, both sure and stedfast, and which entereth into that within the veil; whither the forerunner is for us entered, *even* Jesus.

Exceeding great and precious promises.

2 Sa. 7.25; Ps. 119.38,42,49,54,72,89,90 § He. 6.17–20 § 2 Pe. 1.4

**Blessed *is* the man that heareth me, watching daily
at my gates, waiting at the posts of my doors.**

Behold, as the eyes of servants *look* unto the hand of
their masters, *and* as the eyes of a maiden unto the hand
of her mistress; so our eyes *wait* upon the LORD our
God, until that he have mercy upon us.

A continual burnt offering throughout your generations *at* the door of the tabernacle of the congregation
before the LORD: where I will meet you, to speak there
unto thee.—In all places where I record my name I will
come unto thee, and I will bless thee.

Where two or three are gathered together in my
name, there am I in the midst of them.

The hour cometh, and now is, when the true worshippers shall worship the Father in spirit and in truth:
for the Father seeketh such to worship him. God *is* a
Spirit: and they that worship him must worship *him* in
spirit and in truth.

Praying always with all prayer and supplication in
the Spirit.—Pray without ceasing.

Pro. 8.34; Ps. 123.2 § Ex. 29.42; Ex. 20.24 § Mt. 18.20
§ Jn. 4.23–24 § Eph. 6.18; 1 Th. 5.17

His name shall be called…Counsellor.

The spirit of the LORD shall rest upon him, the spirit of wisdom and understanding, the spirit of counsel and might, the spirit of knowledge and of the fear of the LORD; and shall make him of quick understanding in the fear of the LORD.

Doth not wisdom cry? and understanding put forth her voice?… Unto you, O men, I call; and my voice *is* to the sons of man. O ye simple, understand wisdom: and, ye fools, be ye of an understanding heart. Hear; for I will speak of excellent things; and the opening of my lips *shall be* right things… Counsel *is* mine, and sound wisdom: I *am* understanding; I have strength.

The LORD of hosts…is wonderful in counsel, *and* excellent in working.—If any of you lack wisdom, let him ask of God, that giveth to all *men* liberally, and upbraideth not; and it shall be given him.—Trust in the LORD with all thine heart; and lean not unto thine own understanding. In all thy ways acknowledge him, and he shall direct thy paths.

Isa. 9.6; Isa. 11.2–3 § Pro. 8.1,4–6,14 § Isa. 28.29; Jas. 1.5; Pro. 3.5–6

Ever follow that which is good.

For even hereunto were ye called: because Christ also suffered for us, leaving us an example, that ye should follow his steps: who did no sin, neither was guile found in his mouth: who, when he was reviled, reviled not again...but committed *himself* to him that judgeth righteously.—Consider him that endured such contradiction of sinners against himself, lest ye be wearied and faint in your minds.

Let us lay aside every weight, and the sin which doth so easily beset *us*, and let us run with patience the race that is set before us, looking unto Jesus the author and finisher of *our* faith; who for the joy that was set before him endured the cross, despising the shame, and is set down at the right hand of the throne of God.

Finally, brethren, whatsoever things are true, whatsoever things *are* honest, whatsoever things *are* just, whatsoever things *are* pure, whatsoever things *are* lovely, whatsoever things *are* of good report; if *there be* any virtue, and if *there be* any praise, think on these things.

---

1 Th. 5.15;   1 Pe. 2.21–23;   He. 12.3   § He. 12.1–2
§ Phil. 4.8

The mighty God.

Thou art fairer than the children of men: grace is poured into thy lips: therefore God hath blessed thee for ever. Gird thy sword upon *thy* thigh, O *most* mighty, with thy glory and thy majesty. And in thy majesty ride prosperously because of truth and meekness *and* righteousness... Thy throne, O God, *is* for ever and ever: the sceptre of thy kingdom *is* a right sceptre.—Thou spakest in vision to thy holy one, and saidst, I have laid help upon *one that is* mighty.—The man *that is* my fellow, saith the LORD of hosts.

Behold, God *is* my salvation; I will trust, and not be afraid: for the LORD JEHOVAH *is* my strength and *my* song; he also is become my salvation.—Thanks *be* unto God, which always *causeth* us to triumph in Christ.

Now unto him that is able to keep you from falling, and to present *you* faultless before the presence of his glory with exceeding joy, to the only wise God our Saviour, *be* glory and majesty, dominion and power, both now and ever.

Isa. 9.6; Ps. 45.2–4,6; Ps. 89.19; Zech. 13.7 § Isa. 12.2; 2 Co. 2.14 § Jude 24–25

**The ways of the LORD *are* right,
and the just shall walk in them:
but the transgressors shall fall therein.**

Unto you...which believe *he is* precious: but unto them which be disobedient...a stone of stumbling, and a rock of offence.—The way of the LORD *is* strength to the upright: but destruction *shall be* to the workers of iniquity.

He that hath ears to hear, let him hear.—Whoso *is* wise, and will observe these *things*, even they shall understand the lovingkindness of the LORD.—The light of the body is the eye: if therefore thine eye be single, thy whole body shall be full of light.—If any man will do his will, he shall know of the doctrine, whether it be of God.—Whosoever hath, to him shall be given, and he shall have more abundance.

He that is of God heareth God's words: ye therefore hear *them* not, because ye are not of God.—Ye will not come to me, that ye might have life.—My sheep hear my voice, and I know them, and they follow me.

Hos. 14.9; 1 Pe. 2.7,8; Pro. 10.29 § Mt. 11.15;
Ps. 107.43; Mt. 6.22; Jn. 7.17; Mt. 13.12 § Jn. 8.47;
Jn. 5.40; Jn. 10.27

The everlasting Father.

Hear, O Israel: The LORD our God *is* one LORD.

I and *my* Father are one…the Father *is* in me, and I in him.—If ye had known me, ye should have known my Father also.—Philip saith unto him, Lord, shew us the Father, and it sufficeth us. Jesus saith unto him, Have I been so long time with you, and yet hast thou not known me, Philip? he that hath seen me hath seen the Father.—Behold I and the children which God hath given me.—He shall see of the travail of his soul, *and* shall be satisfied.—I am Alpha and Omega, the beginning and the ending, saith the Lord, which is, and which was, and which is to come, the Almighty.—Before Abraham was, I am.—God said unto Moses, I AM THAT I AM: and he said, Thus shalt thou say unto the children of Israel, I AM hath sent me unto you.

Unto the Son *he saith*, Thy throne, O God, *is* for ever and ever.—He is before all things, and by him all things consist.—In him dwelleth all the fulness of the Godhead bodily.

Isa. 9.6; Deu. 6.4 § Jn. 10.30,38; Jn. 8.19; Jn. 14.8–9; He. 2.13; Isa. 53.11; Rev. 1.8; Jn. 8.58; Ex. 3.14 § He. 1.8; Col. 1.17; Col. 2.9

Now for a season, if need be,
ye are in heaviness through manifold temptations.

Beloved, think it not strange concerning the fiery trial which is to try you, as though some strange thing happened unto you: but rejoice, inasmuch as ye are partakers of Christ's sufferings; that, when his glory shall be revealed, ye may be glad also with exceeding joy.—The exhortation…speaketh unto you as unto children, My son, despise not thou the chastening of the Lord, nor faint when thou art rebuked of him.—Now no chastening for the present seemeth to be joyous, but grievous: nevertheless afterward it yieldeth the peaceable fruit of righteousness unto them which are exercised thereby.

We have not an high priest which cannot be touched with the feeling of our infirmities; but was in all points tempted like as *we are, yet* without sin.—For in that he himself hath suffered being tempted, he is able to succour them that are tempted.—God *is* faithful, who will not suffer you to be tempted above that ye are able.

---

1 Pe. 1.6; 1 Pe. 4.12–13; He. 12.5; He. 12.11
§ He. 4.15; He. 2.18; 1 Co. 10.13

The Prince of Peace.

He shall judge thy people with righteousness, and thy poor with judgment. The mountains shall bring peace to the people, and the little hills, by righteousness... He shall come down like rain upon the mown grass: as showers *that* water the earth. In his days shall the righteous flourish; and abundance of peace so long as the moon endureth.—Glory to God...on earth peace, good will toward men.

Through the tender mercy of our God...the dayspring from on high hath visited us, to give light to them that sit in darkness and *in* the shadow of death, to guide our feet into the way of peace.—Peace by Jesus Christ: (he is Lord of all).

These things I have spoken unto you, that in me ye might have peace. In the world ye shall have tribulation: but be of good cheer; I have overcome the world.—Peace I leave with you, my peace I give unto you: not as the world giveth, give I unto you.—The peace of God, which passeth all understanding, shall keep your hearts and minds through Christ Jesus.

Isa. 9.6; Ps. 72.2–3,6–7; Lu. 2.14 § Lu. 1.78–79; Ac. 10.36 § Jn. 16.33; Jn. 14.27; Phil. 4.7

**Take thou also unto thee principal spices…
And thou shalt make it an oil of holy ointment.**

Upon man's flesh shall it not be poured, neither shall ye make *any other* like it, after the composition of it: it *is* holy, *and* it shall be holy unto you.—One Spirit.— Diversities of gifts, but the same Spirit.

God, thy God, hath anointed thee with the oil of gladness above thy fellows.—God anointed Jesus of Nazareth with the Holy Ghost and with power.—God giveth not the Spirit by measure *unto him.*

Of his fulness have all we received.—As the same anointing teacheth you of all things, and is truth, and is no lie, and even as it hath taught you, ye shall abide in him.—He which…hath anointed us, *is* God; who hath also sealed us, and given the earnest of the Spirit in our hearts.

The fruit of the Spirit is love, joy, peace, longsuffering, gentleness, goodness, faith, meekness, temperance: against such there is no law.

Ex. 30.23,25;   Ex. 30.32;   Eph. 4.4;   1 Co. 12.4 § Ps. 45.7; Ac. 10.38;   Jn. 3.34 § Jn. 1.16;   1 Jn. 2.27;   2 Co. 1.21–22 § Ga. 5.22–23

The fashion of this world passeth away.

All the days of Methuselah were nine hundred sixty and nine years: and he died.

Let the brother of low degree rejoice in that he is exalted: but the rich, in that he is made low: because as the flower of the grass he shall pass away. For the sun is no sooner risen with a burning heat, but it withereth the grass, and the flower thereof falleth, and the grace of the fashion of it perisheth: so also shall the rich man fade away in his ways.—For what *is* your life? It is even a vapour, that appeareth for a little time, and then vanisheth away.—The world passeth away, and the lust thereof: but he that doeth the will of God abideth for ever.

LORD, make me to know mine end, and the measure of my days, what it is; that I may know how frail I am.— When they shall say, Peace and safety; then sudden destruction cometh upon them, as travail upon a woman with child; and they shall not escape. But ye, brethren, are not in darkness, that that day should overtake you as a thief.

---

1 Co. 7.31; Ge. 5.27 § Jas. 1.9–11; Jas. 4.14; 1 Jn. 2.17
§ Ps. 39.4; 1 Th. 5.3–4

**When Christ, *who is* our life, shall appear,
then shall ye also appear with him in glory.**

I am the resurrection, and the life: he that believeth in me, though he were dead, yet shall he live.—God hath given to us eternal life, and this life is in his Son. He that hath the Son hath life; *and* he that hath not the Son of God hath not life.

The Lord himself shall descend from heaven with a shout, with the voice of the archangel, and with the trump of God: and the dead in Christ shall rise first: then we which are alive *and* remain shall be caught up together with them in the clouds, to meet the Lord in the air: and so shall we ever be with the Lord. Wherefore comfort one another with these words.—When he shall appear, we shall be like him; for we shall see him as he is.—It is sown in dishonour; it is raised in glory: it is sown in weakness; it is raised in power. It is sown a natural body; it is raised a spiritual body.

If I go and prepare a place for you, I will come again, and receive you unto myself; that where I am, *there* ye may be also.

Col. 3.4; Jn. 11.25; 1 Jn. 5.11,12 § 1 Th. 4.16–18;
1 Jn. 3.2; 1 Co. 15.43–44 § Jn. 14.3

Lead me in thy truth, and teach me.

When he, the Spirit of truth is come, he will guide you into all truth.—Ye have an unction from the Holy One, and ye know all things.

To the law and to the testimony: if they speak not according to this word, *it is* because *there is* no light in them.—The holy scriptures…are able to make thee wise unto salvation through faith which is in Christ Jesus. All scripture *is* given by inspiration of God, and *is* profitable for doctrine, for reproof, for correction, for instruction in righteousness: that the man of God may be perfect, throughly furnished unto all good works.

I will instruct thee and teach thee in the way which thou shalt go: I will guide thee with mine eye.—The light of the body is the eye: if therefore thine eye be single, thy whole body shall be full of light.—If any man will do his will, he shall know of the doctrine, whether it be of God.—The wayfaring men, though fools, shall not err *therein.*

Ps. 25.5; Jn. 16.13; 1 Jn. 2.20 § Isa. 8.20;
2 Tim. 3.15–17 § Ps. 32.8; Mt. 6.22; Jn. 7.17; Isa. 35.8

Oh that *men* would praise the LORD *for* his goodness, and *for* his wonderful works to the children of men!

O taste and see that the LORD *is* good: blessed *is* the man *that* trusteth in him.—How great *is* thy goodness, which thou hast laid up for them that fear thee!

This people have I formed for myself; they shall shew forth my praise.—Having predestinated us unto the adoption of children by Jesus Christ to himself, according to the good pleasure of his will, to the praise of the glory of his grace, wherein he hath made us accepted in the beloved... That we should be to the praise of his glory, who first trusted in Christ.

How great *is* his goodness, and how great *is* his beauty!—The LORD *is* good to all: and his tender mercies *are* over all his works. All thy works shall praise thee, O LORD; and thy saints shall bless thee. They shall speak of the glory of thy kingdom, and talk of thy power; to make known to the sons of men his mighty acts, and the glorious majesty of his kingdom.

Ps. 107.8; Ps. 34.8; Ps. 31.19 § Isa. 43.21; Eph. 1.5–6,12 § Zech. 9.17; Ps. 145.9–12

Behold, we count them happy
which endure.

We glory in tribulations…knowing that tribulation worketh patience; and patience, experience; and experience, hope: and hope maketh not ashamed; because the love of God is shed abroad in our hearts by the Holy Ghost which is given unto us.—No chastening for the present seemeth to be joyous, but grievous: nevertheless afterward it yieldeth the peaceable fruit of righteousness unto them which are exercised thereby.—My brethren, count it all joy when ye fall into divers temptations; knowing *this*, that the trying of your faith worketh patience. But let patience have *her* perfect work, that ye may be perfect and entire, wanting nothing… Blessed *is* the man that endureth temptation: for when he is tried, he shall receive the crown of life, which the Lord hath promised to them that love him.—Most gladly therefore will I rather glory in my infirmities, that the power of Christ may rest upon me…for when I am weak, then am I strong.

Jas. 5.11; Ro. 5.3–5; He. 12.11; Jas. 1.2–4,12; 2 Co. 12.9,10

**Let us, who are of the day, be sober,
putting on the breastplate of faith and love;
and for an helmet, the hope of salvation.**

Gird up the loins of your mind, be sober, and hope to the end for the grace that is to be brought unto you at the revelation of Jesus Christ.—Stand therefore, having your loins girt about with truth, and having on the breastplate of righteousness… Above all, taking the shield of faith, wherewith ye shall be able to quench all the fiery darts of the wicked. And take the helmet of salvation, and the sword of the Spirit, which is the word of God.

He will swallow up death in victory; and the Lord GOD will wipe away tears from off all faces; and the rebuke of his people shall he take away from off all the earth: for the LORD hath spoken *it*. And it shall be said in that day, Lo, this *is* our God; we have waited for him, and he will save us: this *is* the LORD; we have waited for him, we will be glad and rejoice in his salvation.

Faith is the substance of things hoped for, the evidence of things not seen.

---

1 Th. 5.8;   1 Pe. 1.13;   Eph. 6.14,16–17   § Isa. 25.8–9   § He. 11.1

The children of Israel pitched before them like two little flocks of kids; but the Syrians filled the country.

Thus saith the LORD, because the Syrians have said, the LORD *is* God of the hills, but he *is* not God of the valleys, therefore will I deliver all this great multitude into thine hand, and ye shall know that I *am* the LORD. And they pitched one over against the other seven days. And *so* it was, that in the seventh day the battle was joined: and the children of Israel slew of the Syrians an hundred thousand footmen in one day.—Ye are of God, little children, and have overcome them: because greater is he that is in you, than he that is in the world.

Fear thou not; for I *am* with thee: be not dismayed; for I *am* thy God: I will strengthen thee; yea, I will help thee; yea, I will uphold thee with the right hand of my righteousness.

They shall fight against thee; but they shall not prevail against thee; for I *am* with thee, saith the LORD, to deliver thee.

---

1 Ki. 20.27; 1 Ki. 20.28–29; 1 Jn. 4.4 § Isa. 41.10 § Jer. 1.19

I have laid help upon *one that is* mighty;
I have exalted *one* chosen out of the people.

I, *even* I, *am* the LORD; and beside me *there is* no saviour.—*There is* one God, and one mediator between God and men, the man Christ Jesus.—There is none other name under heaven given among men, whereby we must be saved.

The mighty God.—Who...made himself of no reputation, and took upon him the form of a servant, and was made in the likeness of men: and being found in fashion as a man, he humbled himself, and became obedient unto death, even the death of the cross. Wherefore God also hath highly exalted him, and given him a name which is above every name.—We see Jesus, who was made a little lower than the angels for the suffering of death, crowned with glory and honour; that he by the grace of God should taste death for every man.—Forasmuch...as the children are partakers of flesh and blood, he also himself likewise took part of the same.

Ps. 89.19; Isa. 43.11; 1 Tim. 2.5; Ac. 4.12 § Isa. 9.6; Phil. 2.6,7–9; He. 2.9; He. 2.14

**Gather my saints together unto me;
those that have made a covenant with me by sacrifice.**

Christ was once offered to bear the sins of many; and unto them that look for him shall he appear the second time without sin unto salvation.—He is the mediator of the new testament, that by means of death...they which are called might receive the promise of eternal inheritance.

Father, I will that they also, whom thou hast given me, be with me where I am.—Then shall he send his angels, and shall gather together his elect from the four winds, from the uttermost part of the earth to the uttermost part of heaven.—If *any* of thine be driven out unto the outmost *parts* of heaven, from thence will the LORD thy God gather thee, and from thence will he fetch thee.

The dead in Christ shall rise first: then we which are alive *and* remain shall be caught up together with them in the clouds, to meet the Lord in the air: and so shall we ever be with the Lord.

Ps. 50.5; He. 9.28; He. 9.15 § Jn. 17.24; Mk. 13.27; Deu. 30.4 § 1 Th. 4.16–17

Fruitful in every good work,
and increasing in the knowledge of God.

I beseech you…brethren, by the mercies of God, that ye present your bodies a living sacrifice, holy, acceptable unto God, *which is* your reasonable service. And be not conformed to this world: but be ye transformed by the renewing of your mind, that ye may prove what *is* that good, and acceptable, and perfect, will of God.—As ye have yielded your members servants to uncleanness and to iniquity unto iniquity; even so now yield your members servants to righteousness unto holiness.—In Christ Jesus neither circumcision availeth any thing, nor uncircumcision, but a new creature. And as many as walk according to this rule, peace *be* on them, and mercy.

Herein is my Father glorified, that ye bear much fruit; so shall ye be my disciples.—I have chosen you, and ordained you, that ye should go and bring forth fruit, and *that* your fruit should remain: that whatsoever ye shall ask of the Father in my name, he may give it you.

Col. 1.10; Ro. 12.1–2; Ro. 6.19; Ga. 6.15–16 § Jn. 15.8; Jn. 15.16

I sought him, but I found him not.

Return unto the LORD thy God; for thou hast fallen by thine iniquity. Take with you words, and turn to the LORD: say unto him, Take away all iniquity, and receive *us* graciously.

Let no man say when he is tempted, I am tempted of God... But every man is tempted, when he is drawn away of his own lust, and enticed... Do not err, my beloved brethren. Every good gift and every perfect gift is from above, and cometh down from the Father of lights, with whom is no variableness, neither shadow of turning.

Wait on the LORD: be of good courage, and he shall strengthen thine heart: wait, I say, on the LORD.—*It is* good that *a man* should both hope and quietly wait for the salvation of the LORD.—Shall not God avenge his own elect, which cry day and night unto him, though he bear long with them?

Truly my soul waiteth upon God: from him *cometh* my salvation... My soul, wait thou only upon God; for my expectation *is* from him.

Song 3.1; Hos. 14.1–2 § Jas. 1.13,14,16–17 § Ps. 27.14; Lam. 3.26; Lu. 18.7 § Ps. 62.1,5

He led them on safely.

I lead in the way of righteousness, in the midst of the paths of judgment.

Behold, I send an Angel before thee, to keep thee in the way, and to bring thee into the place which I have prepared.—In all their affliction he was afflicted, and the angel of his presence saved them: in his love and in his pity he redeemed them; and he bare them, and carried them all the days of old.

They got not the land in possession by their own sword, neither did their own arm save them: but thy right hand, and thine arm, and the light of thy countenance, because thou hadst a favour unto them.—So didst thou lead thy people, to make thyself a glorious name.

Lead me, O LORD, in thy righteousness because of mine enemies; make thy way straight before my face.— O send out thy light and thy truth: let them lead me; let them bring me unto thy holy hill, and to thy tabernacles. Then will I go unto the altar of God, unto God my exceeding joy: yea, upon the harp will I praise thee, O God my God.

Ps. 78.53; Pro. 8.20 § Ex. 23.20; Isa. 63.9 § Ps. 44.3; Isa. 63.14 § Ps. 5.8; Ps. 43.3–4

Ye are washed…ye are sanctified…ye are justified.

The blood of Jesus Christ his Son cleanseth us from all sin.—The chastisement of our peace *was* upon him; and with his stripes we are healed.

Christ…loved the church, and gave himself for it; that he might sanctify and cleanse it with the washing of water by the word, that he might present it to himself a glorious church, not having spot, or wrinkle, or any such thing; but that it should be holy and without blemish.—To her was granted that she should be arrayed in fine linen, clean and white: for the fine linen is the righteousness of saints.—Let us draw near with a true heart in full assurance of faith, having our hearts sprinkled from an evil conscience, and our bodies washed with pure water.

Who shall lay any thing to the charge of God's elect? *It is* God that justifieth.—Blessed *is he whose* transgression *is* forgiven, *whose* sin is covered. Blessed *is* the man unto whom the LORD imputeth not iniquity, and in whose spirit *there is* no guile.

---

1 Co. 6.11; 1 Jn. 1.7; Isa. 53.5 § Eph. 5.25–27;
Rev. 19.8; He. 10.22 § Ro. 8.33; Ps. 32.1–2

Godly sorrow worketh repentance to salvation not to be repented of.

Peter remembered the word of Jesus, which said unto him, Before the cock crow, thou shalt deny me thrice. And he went out, and wept bitterly.—If we confess our sins, he is faithful and just to forgive us *our* sins, and to cleanse us from all unrighteousness.—The blood of Jesus Christ his Son cleanseth us from all sin.

Mine iniquities have taken hold upon me, so that I am not able to look up; they are more than the hairs of my head: therefore my heart faileth me. Be pleased, O LORD, to deliver me: O LORD, make haste to help me.

Turn thou to thy God: keep mercy and judgment, and wait on thy God continually.

The sacrifices of God *are* a broken spirit: a broken and a contrite heart, O God, thou wilt not despise.—He healeth the broken in heart, and bindeth up their wounds.—He hath shewed thee, O man, what *is* good; and what doth the LORD require of thee, but to do justly, and to love mercy, and to walk humbly with thy God?

---

2 Co. 7.10; Mt. 26.75; 1 Jn. 1.9; 1 Jn. 1.7
§ Ps. 40.12–13 § Hos. 12.6 § Ps. 51.17; Ps. 147.3;
Mi. 6.8

Is it well with thee?…
And she answered, *It is* well.

We having the same spirit of faith.

As chastened, and not killed; as sorrowful, yet alway rejoicing; as poor, yet making many rich; as having nothing, and *yet* possessing all things.

We are troubled on every side, yet not distressed; *we are* perplexed, but not in despair; persecuted, but not forsaken; cast down, but not destroyed; always bearing about in the body the dying of the Lord Jesus, that the life also of Jesus might be made manifest in our body… For which cause we faint not; but though our outward man perish, yet the inward *man* is renewed day by day. For our light affliction, which is but for a moment, worketh for us a far more exceeding *and* eternal weight of glory; while we look not at the things which are seen, but at the things which are not seen.

Beloved, I wish above all things that thou mayest prosper and be in health, even as thy soul prospereth.

---

2 Ki. 4.26; 2 Co. 4.13 § 2 Co. 6.9–10
§ 2 Co. 4.8–10,16–18 § 2 Jn. 2

Christ...
loved the church, and gave himself for it;
that he might sanctify and cleanse it
with the washing of water by the word.

Walk in love, as Christ also hath loved us, and hath given himself for us an offering and a sacrifice to God for a sweetsmelling savour.

Being born again, not of corruptible seed, but of incorruptible, by the word of God, which liveth and abideth for ever.—Sanctify them through thy truth: thy word is truth.—Except a man be born of water and *of* the Spirit, he cannot enter into the kingdom of God.— Not by works of righteousness which we have done, but according to his mercy he saved us, by the washing of regeneration, and renewing of the Holy Ghost.—Thy word hath quickened me.

The law of the LORD *is* perfect, converting the soul: the testimony of the LORD *is* sure, making wise the simple. The statutes of the LORD *are* right, rejoicing the heart: the commandment of the LORD *is* pure, enlightening the eyes.

Eph. 5.25–26; Eph. 5.2 § 1 Pe. 1.23; Jn. 17.17; Jn. 3.5; Titus. 3.5; Ps. 119.50 § Ps. 19.7–8

**Through him we both have access
by one Spirit unto the Father.**

I in them, and thou in me, that they may be made perfect in one.

Whatsoever ye shall ask in my name, that will I do, that the Father may be glorified in the Son. If ye shall ask any thing in my name, I will do *it*... And I will pray the Father, and he shall give you another Comforter, that he may abide with you for ever; *even* the Spirit of truth; whom the world cannot receive, because it seeth him not, neither knoweth him: but ye know him; for he dwelleth with you, and shall be in you.—*There is* one body, and one Spirit, even as ye are called in one hope of your calling; one Lord, one faith, one baptism, one God and Father of all, who *is* above all, and through all, and in you all.—When ye pray, say, Our Father which art in heaven.

Having therefore, brethren, boldness to enter into the holiest by the blood of Jesus, by a new and living way...let us draw near.

Eph. 2.18; Jn. 17.23 § Jn. 14.13–14,16–17; Eph. 4.4–6; Lu. 11.2 § He. 10.19–20,22

**Thou *art* my help and my deliverer;
make no tarrying, O my God.**

The steps of a *good* man are ordered by the LORD: and he delighteth in his way. Though he fall, he shall not be utterly cast down: for the LORD upholdeth *him with* his hand.—In the fear of the LORD *is* strong confidence: and his children shall have a place of refuge.—Who *art* thou, that thou shouldest be afraid of a man *that* shall die, and of the son of man *which* shall be made *as* grass; and forgettest the LORD thy maker?

I *am* with thee to deliver thee.—Be strong and of a good courage, fear not, nor be afraid of them: for the LORD thy God, he *it is* that doth go with thee; he will not fail thee, nor forsake thee.

I will sing of thy power; yea, I will sing aloud of thy mercy in the morning: for thou hast been my defence and refuge in the day of my trouble.—Thou *art* my hiding place; thou shalt preserve me from trouble; thou shalt compass me about with songs of deliverance.

Ps. 40.17; Ps. 37.23–24; Pro. 14.26; Isa. 51.12–13
§ Jer. 1.8; Deu. 31.6 § Ps. 59.16; Ps. 32.7

How wilt thou do in the swelling of Jordan?

For Jordan overfloweth all his banks all the time of harvest.

The priests that bare the ark of the covenant of the LORD stood firm on dry ground in the midst of Jordan, and all the Israelites passed over on dry ground, until all the people were passed clean over Jordan.

We see Jesus, who was made a little lower than the angels for the suffering of death, crowned with glory and honour; that he by the grace of God should taste death for every man.

Though I walk through the valley of the shadow of death, I will fear no evil: for thou *art* with me; thy rod and thy staff they comfort me.—When thou passest through the waters, I *will be* with thee; and through the rivers, they shall not overflow thee.

Fear not; I am the first and the last: *I am* he that liveth, and was dead; and, behold, I am alive for evermore, Amen; and have the keys of hell and of death.

Jer. 12.5; Jos. 3.15 § Jos. 3.17 § He. 2.9 § Ps. 23.4; Isa. 43.2 § Rev. 1.17–18

**God *is* faithful,
by whom ye were called unto
the fellowship of his Son Jesus Christ our Lord.**

Let us hold fast the profession of *our* faith without wavering; (for he *is* faithful that promised).—God hath said, I will dwell in them, and walk in *them;* and I will be their God, and they shall be my people.—Truly our fellowship *is* with the Father, and with his Son Jesus Christ.—Rejoice, inasmuch as ye are partakers of Christ's sufferings; that, when his glory shall be revealed, ye may be glad also with exceeding joy.

That ye, being rooted and grounded in love, may be able to comprehend with all saints what *is* the breadth, and length, and depth, and height; and to know the love of Christ, which passeth knowledge, that ye might be filled with all the fulness of God.

Whosoever shall confess that Jesus is the Son of God, God dwelleth in him, and he in God.—And he that keepeth his commandments dwelleth in him, and he in him.

1 Co. 1.9; He. 10.23; 2 Co. 6.16; 1 Jn. 1.3; 1 Pe. 4.13
§ Eph. 3.17–19 § 1 Jn. 4.15; 1 Jn. 3.24

We are his workmanship.

They brought great stones, costly stones, *and* hewed stones, to lay the foundation of the house.—The house, when it was in building, was built of stone made ready before it was brought thither: so that there was neither hammer nor axe *nor* any tool of iron heard in the house, while it was in building.

Ye also, as lively stones, are built up a spiritual house.—Built upon the foundation of the apostles and prophets, Jesus Christ himself being the chief corner *stone;* in whom all the building fitly framed together groweth unto an holy temple in the Lord: in whom ye also are builded together for an habitation of God through the Spirit.—Which in time past *were* not a people, but *are* now the people of God.

Ye are God's building.—Therefore if any man *be* in Christ, *he is* a new creature: old things are passed away; behold, all things are become new.—Now he that hath wrought us for the selfsame thing *is* God, who also hath given unto us the earnest of the Spirit.

Eph. 2.10; 1 Ki. 5.17; 1 Ki. 6.7 § 1 Pe. 2.5;
Eph. 2.20–22; 1 Pe. 2.10 § 1 Co. 3.9; 2 Co. 5.17;
2 Co. 5.5

Sanctify them through thy truth:
thy word is truth.

Now ye are clean through the word which I have spoken unto you.—Let the word of Christ dwell in you richly in all wisdom.

Wherewithal shall a young man cleanse his way? by taking heed *thereto* according to thy word. With my whole heart have I sought thee: O let me not wander from thy commandments.

When wisdom entereth into thine heart, and knowledge is pleasant unto thy soul; discretion shall preserve thee, understanding shall keep thee.

My foot hath held his steps, his way have I kept, and not declined. Neither have I gone back from the commandment of his lips; I have esteemed the words of his mouth more than my necessary *food.*—I have more understanding than all my teachers: for thy testimonies *are* my meditation.—If ye continue in my word, *then* are ye my disciples indeed; and ye shall know the truth, and the truth shall make you free.

Jn. 17.17; Jn. 15.3; Col. 3.16 § Ps. 119.9–10
§ Pro. 2.10–11 § Job 23.11–12; Ps. 119.99; Jn. 8.31–32

Fellowcitizens with the saints.

Ye are come unto mount Sion, and unto the city of the living God, the heavenly Jerusalem, and to an innumerable company of angels, to the general assembly and church of the firstborn, which are written in heaven, and to God the Judge of all, and to the spirits of just men made perfect.

These all died in faith, not having received the promises, but having seen them afar off, and were persuaded of *them*, and embraced *them*, and confessed that they were strangers and pilgrims on the earth.—Our conversation [*Greek* citizenship] is in heaven; from whence also we look for the Saviour, the Lord Jesus Christ: who shall change our vile body, that it may be fashioned like unto his glorious body, according to the working whereby he is able even to subdue all things unto himself.—The Father…hath delivered us from the power of darkness, and hath translated *us* into the kingdom of his dear Son.

As strangers and pilgrims, abstain from fleshly lusts, which war against the soul.

Eph. 2.19; He. 12.22–23 § He. 11.13; Phil. 3.20–21; Col. 1.12,13 § 1 Pe. 211

Thy thoughts are very deep.

W_e...do not cease to pray for you, and to desire that
ye might be filled with the knowledge of his will in all
wisdom and spiritual understanding.—That ye, being
rooted and grounded in love, may be able to comprehend with all saints what *is* the breadth, and length, and
depth, and height; and to know the love of Christ, which
passeth knowledge, that ye might be filled with all the
fulness of God.

O the depth of the riches both of the wisdom and
knowledge of God! how unsearchable *are* his judgments, and his ways past finding out!—My thoughts *are*
not your thoughts, neither *are* your ways my ways, saith
the LORD. For *as* the heavens are higher than the earth,
so are my ways higher than your ways, and my thoughts
than your thoughts.—Many, O LORD my God, *are* thy
wonderful works *which* thou hast done, and thy
thoughts *which are* to us-ward: they cannot be reckoned
up in order unto thee: *if* I would declare and speak *of
them*, they are more than can be numbered.

Ps. 92.5; Col. 1.9; Eph. 3.17–19 § Ro. 11.33;
Isa. 55.8–9; Ps. 40.5

Whatsoever a man soweth,
that shall he also reap.

They that plow iniquity, and sow wickedness, reap the same.—They have sown the wind, and they shall reap the whirlwind.—He that soweth to his flesh shall of the flesh reap corruption.

To him that soweth righteousness *shall be* a sure reward.—He that soweth to the Spirit shall of the Spirit reap life everlasting. And let us not be weary in well doing: for in due season we shall reap, if we faint not. As we have therefore opportunity, let us do good unto all *men*, especially unto them who are of the household of faith.

There is that scattereth, and yet increaseth; and *there is* that withholdeth more than is meet, but *it tendeth* to poverty. The liberal soul shall be made fat: and he that watereth shall be watered also himself.—He which soweth sparingly shall reap also sparingly; and he which soweth bountifully shall reap also bountifully.

Ga. 6.7; Job 4.8; Hos. 8.7; Ga. 6.8 § Pro. 11.18; Ga. 6.8–10 § Pro. 11.24–25; 2 Co. 9.6

He stayeth his rough wind
in the day of the east wind.

Let us fall now into the hand of the LORD; for his mercies *are* great.—I *am* with thee, saith the LORD, to save thee…I will correct thee in measure, and will not leave thee altogether unpunished.—He will not always chide: neither will he keep *his anger* for ever. He hath not dealt with us after our sins; nor rewarded us according to our iniquities… For he knoweth our frame; he remembereth that we *are* dust.—I will spare them, as a man spareth his own son that serveth him.

God *is* faithful, who will not suffer you to be tempted above that ye are able; but will with the temptation also make a way to escape, that ye may be able to bear *it*.—Satan hath desired *to have* you, that he may sift *you* as wheat: but I have prayed for thee, that thy faith fail not.

Thou hast been a strength to the poor, a strength to the needy in his distress, a refuge from the storm, a shadow from the heat, when the blast of the terrible ones *is* as a storm *against* the wall.

Isa. 27.8; 2 Sa. 24.14; Jer. 30.11; Ps. 103.9,10,14; Mal. 3.17 § 1 Co. 10.13; Lu. 22.31–32 § Isa. 25.4

I believed not the words,
until I came, and mine eyes had seen it:
and, behold, the half was not told me.

The queen of the south shall rise up in the judgment with this generation, and shall condemn it: for she came from the uttermost parts of the earth to hear the wisdom of Solomon; and, behold, a greater than Solomon *is* here.—And the Word was made flesh, and dwelt among us, (and we beheld his glory, the glory as of the only begotten of the Father,) full of grace and truth.

My speech and my preaching *was*…in demonstration of the Spirit and of power: that your faith should not stand in the wisdom of men, but in the power of God… But as it is written, Eye hath not seen, nor ear heard, neither have entered into the heart of man, the things which God hath prepared for them that love him. But God hath revealed *them* unto us by his Spirit: for the Spirit searcheth all things, yea, the deep things of God.

Thine eyes shall see the king in his beauty.—We shall see him as he is.—In my flesh shall I see God.—I shall be satisfied.

---

1 Ki. 10.7; Mt. 12.42; Jn. 1.14 § 1 Co. 2.4–5,9–10
§ Isa. 33.17; 1 Jn. 3.2; Job 19.26; Ps. 17.15

By their fruits ye shall know them.

Little children, let no man deceive you: he that doeth righteousness is righteous, even as he is righteous.— Doth a fountain send forth at the same place sweet *water* and bitter? Can the fig tree, my brethren, bear olive berries? either a vine, figs? so *can* no fountain both yield salt water and fresh. Who *is* a wise man and endued with knowledge among you? let him shew out of a good conversation his works with meekness of wisdom.—Having your conversation honest among the Gentiles: that, whereas they speak against you as evildoers, they may by *your* good works, which they shall behold, glorify God in the day of visitation.

Either make the tree good, and his fruit good; or else make the tree corrupt, and his fruit corrupt: for the tree is known by *his* fruit… A good man out of the good treasure of the heart bringeth forth good things: and an evil man out of the evil treasure bringeth forth evil things.

What could have been done more to my vineyard, that I have not done in it?

Mt. 7.20; 1 Jn. 3.7; Jas. 3.11–13; 1 Pe. 2.12
§ Mt. 12.33,35 § Isa. 5.4

I will make the place of my feet glorious.

Thus saith the LORD, The heaven *is* my throne, and the earth *is* my footstool.

Will God in very deed dwell with men on the earth? behold, heaven and the heaven of heavens cannot contain thee; how much less this house which I have built!

Thus saith the LORD of hosts; Yet once, it *is* a little while, and I will shake the heavens, and the earth, and the sea, and the dry *land;* and I will shake all nations, and the desire of all nations shall come: and I will fill this house with glory, saith the LORD of hosts... The glory of this latter house shall be greater than of the former, saith the LORD of hosts.

I saw a new heaven and a new earth: for the first heaven and the first earth were passed away; and there was no more sea... And I heard a great voice out of heaven, saying, Behold, the tabernacle of God *is* with men, and he will dwell with them, and they shall be his people, and God himself shall be with them, *and be* their God.

Isa. 60.13; Isa. 66.1 § 2 Chr. 6.18 § Hag. 2.6–7,9 § Rev. 21.1,3

When I sit in darkness,
the LORD *shall be* a light unto me.

When thou passest through the waters, I *will be* with thee; and through the rivers, they shall not overflow thee: when thou walkest through the fire, thou shalt not be burned; neither shall the flame kindle upon thee. For I *am* the LORD thy God, the Holy One of Israel, thy Saviour.—I will bring the blind by a way *that* they knew not; I will lead them in paths *that* they have not known: I will make darkness light before them, and crooked things straight. These things will I do unto them, and not forsake them.

Yea, though I walk through the valley of the shadow of death, I will fear no evil: for thou *art* with me; thy rod and thy staff they comfort me.—What time I am afraid, I will trust in thee. In God I will praise his word, in God I have put my trust; I will not fear what flesh can do unto me.—The LORD *is* my light and my salvation; whom shall I fear? the LORD *is* the strength of my life; of whom shall I be afraid?

Mi. 7.8; Isa. 43.2–3; Isa. 42.16 § Ps. 23.4; Ps. 56.3–4; Ps. 27.1

One God,
and one mediator between God and men,
the man Christ Jesus.

Hear, O Israel: The LORD our God *is* one LORD.—A mediator is not *a mediator* of one, but God is one.

We have sinned with our fathers, we have committed iniquity, we have done wickedly. Our fathers understood not thy wonders in Egypt; they remembered not the multitude of thy mercies... Therefore he said that he would destroy them, had not Moses his chosen stood before him in the breach, to turn away his wrath, lest he should destroy *them.*

Wherefore, holy brethren, partakers of the heavenly calling, consider the Apostle and High Priest of our profession, Christ Jesus; who was faithful to him that appointed him, as also Moses *was faithful* in all his house.

He is the mediator of a better covenant, which was established upon better promises... I will be merciful to their unrighteousness, and their sins and their iniquities will I remember no more.

1 Tim. 2.5; Deu. 6.4; Ga. 3.20 § Ps. 106.6–7,23
§ He. 3.1–3 § He. 8.6,12

Him that cometh to me
I will in no wise cast out.

It shall come to pass, when he crieth unto me, that I will hear; for I *am* gracious.—I will not cast them away, neither will I abhor them, to destroy them utterly, and to break my covenant with them: for I *am* the LORD their God.—I will remember my covenant with thee in the days of thy youth, and I will establish unto thee an everlasting covenant.

Come now, and let us reason together, saith the LORD: though your sins be as scarlet, they shall be as white as snow; though they be red like crimson, they shall be as wool.—Let the wicked forsake his way, and the unrighteous man his thoughts: and let him return unto the LORD, and he will have mercy upon him; and to our God, for he will abundantly pardon.—Lord, remember me when thou comest into thy kingdom. And Jesus said unto him, Verily I say unto thee, To day shalt thou be with me in paradise.

A bruised reed shall he not break, and the smoking flax shall he not quench.

Jn. 6.37; Ex. 22.27; Lev. 26.44; Ezek. 16.60 § Isa. 1.18; Isa. 55.7; Lu. 23.42–43 § Isa. 42.3

His dear Son.

Lo a voice from heaven, saying, This is my beloved Son, in whom I am well pleased.—Behold my servant, whom I uphold; mine elect, *in whom* my soul delighteth.—The only begotten Son, which is in the bosom of the Father.

In this was manifested the love of God toward us, because that God sent his only begotten Son into the world, that we might live through him. Herein is love, not that we loved God, but that he loved us, and sent his son *to be* the propitiation for our sins... And we have known and believed the love that God hath to us. God is love.

The glory which thou gavest me I have given them; that they may be one, even as we are one: I in them, and thou in me, that they may be made perfect in one; and that the world may know that thou hast sent me, and hast loved them, as thou hast loved me.—Behold, what manner of love the Father hath bestowed upon us, that we should be called the sons of God.

Col. 1.13; Mt. 3.17; Isa. 42.1; Jn. 1.18 § 1 Jn. 4.9–10,16 § Jn. 17.22–24; 1 Jn. 3.1

Praying in the Holy Ghost.

God *is* a Spirit: and they that worship him must worship *him* in spirit and in truth.—We…have access by one Spirit unto the Father.

O my Father, if it be possible, let this cup pass from me: nevertheless not as I will, but as thou *wilt*.

The Spirit…helpeth our infirmities: for we know not what we should pray for as we ought: but the Spirit itself maketh intercession for us with groanings which cannot be uttered. And he that searcheth the hearts knoweth what *is* the mind of the Spirit, because he maketh intercession for the saints according to *the will of* God.—This is the confidence that we have in him, that, if we ask any thing according to his will, he heareth us.—When he, the Spirit of truth, is come, he will guide you into all truth.

Praying always with all prayer and supplication in the Spirit, and watching thereunto with all perseverance and supplication.

Jude 20; Jn. 4.24; Eph. 2.18 § Mt. 26.39 § Ro. 8.26–27; 1 Jn. 5.14; Jn. 16.13 § Eph. 6.18

**There is hope of a tree, if it be cut down,
that it will sprout again, and that
the tender branch thereof will not cease.**

A bruised reed shall he not break.—He restoreth my soul.

Godly sorrow worketh repentance to salvation not to be repented of: but the sorrow of the world worketh death.—No chastening for the present seemeth to be joyous, but grievous: nevertheless afterward it yieldeth the peaceable fruit of righteousness unto them which are exercised thereby.

Before I was afflicted I went astray: but now have I kept thy word… *It is* good for me that I have been afflicted; that I might learn thy statutes.—After all that is come upon us for our evil deeds, and for our great trespass, seeing that thou our God hast punished us less than our iniquities *deserve*, and hast given us *such* deliverance as this; should we again break thy commandments…?

Rejoice not against me, O mine enemy: when I fall, I shall arise; when I sit in darkness, the LORD *shall be* a light unto me…he will bring me forth to the light, *and* I shall behold his righteousness.

Job 14.7; Isa. 42.3; Ps. 23.3 § 2 Co. 7.10; He. 12.11 § Ps. 119.67,71; Ezr. 9.13–14 § Mi. 7.8–9

Whoso hearkeneth unto me shall dwell safely, and shall be quiet from fear of evil.

LORD, thou hast been our dwelling place in all generations.—He that dwelleth in the secret place of the most High shall abide under the shadow of the Almighty.—His truth *shall be thy* shield and buckler.

Your life is hid with Christ in God.—He that toucheth you toucheth the apple of his eye.—Fear ye not, stand still, and see the salvation of the LORD... The LORD shall fight for you, and ye shall hold your peace.—God *is* our refuge and strength, a very present help in trouble. Therefore will not we fear.—These things I have spoken unto you, that in me ye might have peace. In the world ye shall have tribulation: but be of good cheer; I have overcome the world.

Jesus spake unto them, saying, Be of good cheer; it is I; be not afraid.—Why are ye troubled? and why do thoughts arise in your hearts? Behold my hands and my feet, that it is I myself: handle me, and see; for a spirit hath not flesh and bones, as ye see me have.—I know whom I have believed, and am persuaded that he is able to keep that which I have committed unto him against that day.

Pro. 1.33; Ps. 90.1; Ps. 91.1; Ps. 91.4 § Col. 3.3; Zech. 2.8; Ex. 14.13–14; Ps. 46.1,2; Jn. 16.33 § Mt. 14.27; Lu. 24.38–39; 2 Tim. 1.12

My kingdom is not of this world.

This man, after he had offered one sacrifice for sins for ever, sat down on the right hand of God; from henceforth expecting till his enemies be made his footstool.—Hereafter shall ye see the Son of man sitting on the right hand of power, and coming in the clouds of heaven.

He must reign, till he hath put all enemies under his feet.

Thanks *be* to God, which giveth us the victory through our Lord Jesus Christ.—He raised him from the dead, and set *him* at his own right hand in the heavenly *places*, far above all principality, and power, and might, and dominion, and every name that is named, not only in this world, but also in that which is to come: and hath put all *things* under his feet, and gave him *to be* the head over all *things* to the church, which is his body, the fulness of him that filleth all in all.—He shall shew, *who is* the blessed and only Potentate, the King of kings, and Lord of lords.

Jn. 18.36; He. 10.12–13; Mt. 26.64 § 1 Co. 15.25
§ 1 Co. 15.57; Eph. 1.20–23; 1 Tim. 6.15

**My mother and my brethren are these
which hear the word of God, and do it.**

Both he that sanctifieth and they who are sanctified *are* all of one: for which cause he is not ashamed to call them brethren, saying, I will declare thy name unto my brethren, in the midst of the church will I sing praise unto thee.—In Jesus Christ neither circumcision availeth any thing, nor uncircumcision; but faith which worketh by love.—Ye are my friends, if ye do whatsoever I command you.—Blessed *are* they that hear the word of God, and keep it.

Not every one that saith unto me, Lord, Lord, shall enter into the kingdom of heaven; but he that doeth the will of my Father which is in heaven.—My meat is to do the will of him that sent me.—If we say that we have fellowship with him, and walk in darkness, we lie, and do not the truth.—Whoso keepeth his word, in him verily is the love of God perfected: hereby know we that we are in him.

Lu. 8.21;   He. 2.11–12;   Ga. 5.6;   Jn. 15.14;   Lu. 11.28
§ Mt. 7.21;   Jn. 4.34;   1 Jn. 1.6;   1 Jn. 2.5

What doest thou here, Elijah?

He knoweth the way that I take.—O LORD, thou hast searched me, and known *me*. Thou knowest my down-sitting and mine uprising, thou understandest my thought afar off. Thou compassest my path and my lying down, and art acquainted *with* all my ways... Whither shall I go from thy spirit? or whither shall I flee from thy presence?... *If* I take the wings of the morning, *and* dwell in the uttermost parts of the sea; even there shall thy hand lead me, and thy right hand shall hold me.

Elias was a man subject to like passions as we are.—The fear of man bringeth a snare: but whoso putteth his trust in the LORD shall be safe.—Though he fall, he shall not be utterly cast down: for the LORD upholdeth *him with* his hand.—A just *man* falleth seven times, and riseth up again.

Let us not be weary in well doing: for in due season we shall reap, if we faint not.—The spirit indeed *is* willing, but the flesh *is* weak.—Like as a father pitieth *his* children, *so* the LORD pitieth them that fear him.

1 Ki. 19.9; Job 23.10; Ps. 139.1–3,7,9–10 § Jas. 5.17; Pro. 29.25; Ps. 37.24; Pro. 24.16 § Ga. 6.9; Mt. 26.41; Ps. 103.13

Being…made free from sin,
ye became the servants of righteousness.

Ye cannot serve God and mammon.—When ye were the servants of sin, ye were free from righteousness. What fruit had ye then in those things whereof ye are now ashamed? for the end of those things *is* death. But now being made free from sin, and become servants to God, ye have your fruit unto holiness, and the end everlasting life.

Christ *is* the end of the law for righteousness to every one that believeth.

If any man serve me, let him follow me; and where I am, there shall also my servant be: if any man serve me, him will *my* Father honour.—Take my yoke upon you, and learn of me; for I am meek and lowly in heart: and ye shall find rest unto your souls. For my yoke *is* easy, and my burden is light.

O LORD our God, *other* lords beside thee have had dominion over us: *but* by thee only will we make mention of thy name.—I will run the way of thy commandments, when thou shalt enlarge my heart.

Ro. 6.18; Mt. 6.24; Ro. 6.20–22 § Ro. 10.4 § Jn. 12.26; Mt. 11.29–30 § Isa. 26.13; Ps. 119.32

Whosoever shall call
on the name of the Lord
shall be saved.

Manasseh…did *that which was* evil in the sight of the LORD, after the abominations of the heathen…and he reared up altars for Baal…and he built altars for all the host of heaven in the two courts of the house of the LORD. And he made his son pass through the fire, and observed times, and used enchantments, and dealt with familiar spirits and wizards: he wrought much wickedness in the sight of the LORD, to provoke *him* to anger.—And when he was in affliction, he besought the LORD his God, and humbled himself greatly before the God of his fathers, and prayed unto him: and he was intreated of him, and heard his supplication.

Come now, and let us reason together, saith the LORD: though your sins be as scarlet, they shall be as white as snow; though they be red like crimson, they shall be as wool.—The Lord…is longsuffering to usward, not willing that any should perish.

Ac. 2.21; 2 Ki. 21.1,2,3,5–6; 2 Chr. 33.12–13
§ Isa. 1.18; 2 Pe. 3.9

The LORD delighteth in thee.

Thus saith the LORD that created thee... Fear not: for I have redeemed thee, I have called *thee* by thy name; thou *art* mine.—Can a woman forget her sucking child, that she should not have compassion on the son of her womb? yea, they may forget, yet will I not forget thee. Behold, I have graven thee upon the palms of *my* hands: thy walls *are* continually before me.

The steps of a *good* man are ordered by the LORD: and he delighteth in his way.—My delights *were* with the sons of men.—The LORD taketh pleasure in them that fear him, in those that hope in his mercy.—They shall be mine, saith the LORD of hosts, in that day when I make up my jewels; and I will spare them, as a man spareth his own son that serveth him.

You, that were sometime alienated and enemies in *your* mind by wicked works, yet now hath he reconciled in the body of his flesh through death, to present you holy and unblameable and unreproveable in his sight.

Isa. 62.4;   Isa. 43.1;   Isa. 49.15–16   § Ps. 37.23;   Pro. 8.31; Ps. 147.11;   Mal. 3.17   § Col. 1.21–22

The sorrow of the world worketh death.

When Ahithophel saw that his counsel was not followed, he saddled *his* ass, and arose, and gat him home to his house, to his city, and put his household in order, and hanged himself, and died.—A wounded spirit who can bear?

Is there no balm in Gilead; *is there* no physician there? why then is not the health of the daughter of my people recovered?—The LORD hath anointed me to preach good tidings unto the meek; he hath sent me to bind up the brokenhearted…to comfort all that mourn; to appoint unto them that mourn in Zion, to give unto them beauty for ashes, the oil of joy for mourning, the garment of praise for the spirit of heaviness.—Come unto me, all *ye* that labour and are heavy laden, and I will give you rest. Take my yoke upon you, and learn of me; for I am meek and lowly in heart: and ye shall find rest unto your souls. For my yoke *is* easy, and my burden is light.

Philip…preached unto him Jesus.—He healeth the broken in heart, and bindeth up their wounds.

2 Co. 7.10; 2 Sa. 17.23; Pro. 18.14 § Jer. 8.22;
Isa. 61.1,2–3; Mt. 11.28–30 § Ac. 8.35; Ps. 147.3

The glory which thou gavest me
I have given them.

I saw...the Lord sitting upon a throne, high and lifted up, and his train filled the temple. Above it stood the seraphims... And one cried unto another, and said, Holy, holy, holy, *is* the LORD of hosts: the whole earth *is* full of his glory.—These things said Esaias, when he saw his glory, and spake of him.—Upon the likeness of the throne *was* the likeness...of a man above upon it... As the appearance of the bow that is in the cloud in the day of rain, so *was* the appearance of the brightness round about. This *was* the appearance of the likeness of the glory of the LORD.

I beseech thee, shew me thy glory... And he said, Thou canst not see my face: for there shall no man see me, and live.—No man hath seen God at any time; the only begotten Son, which is in the bosom of the Father, he hath declared *him*.—God, who commanded the light to shine out of darkness, hath shined in our hearts, to *give* the light of the knowledge of the glory of God in the face of Jesus Christ.

Jn. 17.22;   Isa. 6.1–2,3;   Jn. 12.41;   Ezek. 1.26,28
§ Ex. 33.18,20;   Jn. 1.18;   2 Co. 4.6

My son, if sinners entice thee, consent thou not.

She took of the fruit thereof, and did eat, and gave also unto her husband with her; and he did eat.—Did not Achan the son of Zerah commit a trespass in the accursed thing, and wrath fell on all the congregation of Israel? and that man perished not alone in his iniquity.

Thou shalt not follow a multitude to *do* evil.

Wide *is* the gate, and broad *is* the way, that leadeth to destruction, and many there be which go in thereat.

None of us liveth to himself.—Brethren, ye have been called unto liberty; only *use* not liberty for an occasion to the flesh, but by love serve one another.—Take heed lest by any means this liberty of yours become a stumblingblock to them that are weak...when ye sin so against the brethren, and wound their weak conscience, ye sin against Christ.

All we like sheep have gone astray; we have turned every one to his own way; and the LORD hath laid on him the iniquity of us all.

Pro. 1.10; Ge. 3.6; Jos. 22.20 § Ex. 23.2 § Mt. 7.13 § Ro. 14.7; Ga. 5.13; 1 Co. 8.9,12 § Isa. 53.6

**As the body without the spirit is dead,
so faith without works is dead also.**

Not every one that saith...Lord, Lord, shall enter into the kingdom of heaven; but he that doeth the will of my Father which is in heaven.—Holiness, without which no man shall see the Lord.—Add to your faith virtue; and to virtue knowledge; and to knowledge temperance; and to temperance patience; and to patience godliness; and to godliness brotherly kindness; and to brotherly kindness charity. For if these things be in you, and abound, they make *you that ye shall* neither *be* barren nor unfruitful in the knowledge of our Lord Jesus Christ. But he that lacketh these things is blind, and cannot see afar off, and hath forgotten that he was purged from his old sins. Wherefore the rather, brethren, give diligence to make your calling and election sure: for if ye do these things, ye shall never fall.

By grace are ye saved through faith; and that not of yourselves: *it is* the gift of God: not of works, lest any man should boast.

Jas. 2.26; Mt. 7.21; He. 12.14; 2 Pe. 1.5–10
§ Eph. 2.8–9

As the children are partakers of flesh and blood, he also himself likewise took part of the same; that through death he might…deliver them who through fear of death were all their lifetime subject to bondage.

O death, where *is* thy sting? O grave, where *is* thy victory?… Thanks *be* to God, which giveth us the victory through our Lord Jesus Christ.—For which cause we faint not; but though our outward man perish, yet the inward *man* is renewed day by day.

We know that if our earthly house of *this* tabernacle were dissolved, we have a building of God, an house not made with hands, eternal in the heavens… Therefore *we are* always confident, knowing that, whilst we are at home in the body, we are absent from the Lord…and willing rather to be absent from the body, and to be present with the Lord.

Let not your heart be troubled: ye believe in God, believe also in me. In my Father's house are many mansions: if *it were* not *so*, I would have told you. I go to prepare a place for you.

He. 2.14,15; 1 Co. 15.55,57; 2 Co. 4.16 § 2 Co. 5.1,6,8
§ Jn. 14.1–3

We shall be satisfied with the goodness of thy house.

One *thing* have I desired of the LORD, that will I seek after; that I may dwell in the house of the LORD all the days of my life, to behold the beauty of the LORD, and to enquire in his temple.

Blessed *are* they which do hunger and thirst after righteousness: for they shall be filled.—He hath filled the hungry with good things; and the rich he hath sent empty away.

He satisfieth the longing soul, and filleth the hungry soul with goodness.—I am the bread of life: he that cometh to me shall never hunger; and he that believeth on me shall never thirst.

How excellent *is* thy lovingkindness, O God! therefore the children of men put their trust under the shadow of thy wings. They shall be abundantly satisfied with the fatness of thy house; and thou shalt make them drink of the river of thy pleasures. For with thee *is* the fountain of life: in thy light shall we see light.—Thy lovingkindness is better than life

Ps. 65.4; Ps. 27.4 § Mt. 5.6; Lu. 1.53 § Ps. 107.9; Jn. 6.35 § Ps. 36.7–9; Ps. 63.3

Do ye now believe?

What *doth it* profit, my brethren, though a man say he hath faith, and have not works? can faith save him?…faith, if it hath not works, is dead, being alone.

By faith Abraham, when he was tried, offered up Isaac: and he that had received the promises offered up his only begotten *son*…accounting that God *was* able to raise *him* up, even from the dead.—Was not Abraham our father justified by works, when he had offered Isaac his son upon the altar?… Ye see then how that by works a man is justified, and not by faith only.

Whoso looketh into the perfect law of liberty, and continueth *therein*, he being not a forgetful hearer, but a doer of the work, this man shall be blessed in his deed.

By their fruits ye shall know them. Not every one that saith unto me, Lord, Lord, shall enter into the kingdom of heaven; but he that doeth the will of my Father which is in heaven.—If ye know these things, happy are ye if ye do them.

Jn. 16.31;   Jas. 2.14,17   § He. 11.17,19;   Jas. 2.21,24   § Jas. 1.25   § Mt. 7.20–21;   Jn. 13.17

The Lord of peace himself
give you peace always by all means.
The Lord *be* with you all.

Peace, from him which is, and which was, and which is to come.—The peace of God, which passeth all understanding, shall keep your hearts and minds through Christ Jesus.

Jesus himself stood in the midst of them, and saith unto them, Peace *be* unto you.—Peace I leave with you, my peace I give unto you: not as the world giveth, give I unto you. Let not your heart be troubled, neither let it be afraid.

The Comforter...*even* the Spirit of truth.—The fruit of the Spirit is love, joy, peace.—The Spirit itself beareth witness with our spirit, that we are the children of God.

My presence shall go *with thee,* and I will give thee rest. And he said unto him, If thy presence go not *with me*, carry us not up hence. For wherein shall it be known here that I and thy people have found grace in thy sight? *is it* not in that thou goest with us?

2 Th. 3.16; Rev. 1.4; Phil. 4.7 § Lu. 24.36; Jn. 14.27
§ Jn. 15.26; Ga. 5.22; Ro. 8.16 § Ex. 33.14–16

We glory in tribulations.

If in this life only we have hope in Christ, we are of all men most miserable.—These things have I spoken unto you, that ye should not be offended. They shall put you out of the synagogues: yea, the time cometh, that whosoever killeth you will think that he doeth God service. And these things will they do unto you, because they have not known the Father, nor me.

Beloved, think it not strange concerning the fiery trial which is to try you, as though some strange thing happened unto you: but rejoice, inasmuch as ye are partakers of Christ's sufferings; that, when his glory shall be revealed, ye may be glad also with exceeding joy.—Sorrowful, yet alway rejoicing.

Rejoice in the Lord alway: *and* again I say, Rejoice.—They departed from the presence of the council, rejoicing that they were counted worthy to suffer shame for his name.

The God of hope fill you with all joy and peace in believing.

Although the fig tree shall not blossom, neither *shall* fruit *be* in the vines; the labour of the olive shall fail, and the fields shall yield no meat; the flock shall be cut off from the fold, and *there shall be* no herd in the stalls: yet I will rejoice in the LORD, I will joy in the God of my salvation.

Ro. 5.3; 1 Co. 15.19; Jn. 16.1–3 § 1 Pe. 4.12–13;
2 Co. 6.10 § Phil. 4.4; Ac. 5.41 § Ro. 15.13 § Hab. 3.17–18

**A man shall be as an hiding place from the wind,
and a covert from the tempest.**

Forasmuch...as the children are partakers of flesh and blood, he also himself likewise took part of the same.—The man *that is* my fellow, saith the LORD of hosts.—I and *my* Father are one.

He that dwelleth in the secret place of the most High shall abide under the shadow of the Almighty.—There shall be a tabernacle for a shadow in the daytime from the heat, and for a place of refuge, and for a covert from storm and from rain.—The LORD *is* thy shade upon thy right hand. The sun shall not smite thee by day, nor the moon by night.

When my heart is overwhelmed: lead me to the rock *that* is higher than I.—Thou *art* my hiding place; thou shalt preserve me from trouble.—Thou hast been a strength to the poor, a strength to the needy in his distress, a refuge from the storm, a shadow from the heat, when the blast of the terrible ones *is* as a storm *against* the wall.

Isa. 32.2; He. 2.14; Zech. 13.7; Jn. 10.30 § Ps. 91.1;
Isa. 4.6; Ps. 121.5–6 § Ps. 61.2; Ps. 32.7; Isa. 25.4

Behold, I create new heavens and a new earth.

The new heavens and the new earth, which I will make, shall remain before me...so shall your seed and your name remain.

We, according to his promise, look for new heavens and a new earth, wherein dwelleth righteousness.

I saw a new heaven and a new earth: for the first heaven and the first earth were passed away; and there was no more sea. And I John saw the holy city, new Jerusalem, coming down from God out of heaven, prepared as a bride adorned for her husband. And I heard a great voice out of heaven saying, Behold, the tabernacle of God *is* with men, and he will dwell with them, and they shall be his people, and God himself shall be with them, *and be* their God. And God shall wipe away all tears from their eyes; and there shall be no more death, neither sorrow, nor crying, neither shall there be any more pain: for the former things are passed away. And he that sat upon the throne said, Behold, I make all things new.

Isa. 65.17; Isa. 66.22 § 2 Pe. 3.13 § Rev. 21.1–5

**Ye have an unction from the Holy One,
and ye know all things.**

God anointed Jesus of Nazareth with the Holy Ghost and with power.—It pleased *the Father* that in him should all fulness dwell.—Of his fulness have all we received, and grace for grace.

Thou anointest my head with oil.—The anointing which ye have received of him abideth in you, and ye need not that any man teach you: but as the same anointing teacheth you of all things, and is truth, and is no lie, and even as it hath taught you, ye shall abide in him.

The Comforter, *which is* the Holy Ghost, whom the Father will send in my name, he shall teach you all things, and bring all things to your remembrance, whatsoever I have said unto you.

The Spirit also helpeth our infirmities: for we know not what we should pray for as we ought: but the Spirit itself maketh intercession for us with groanings which cannot be uttered.

1 Jn. 2.20; Ac. 10.38; Col. 1.19; Jn. 1.16 § Ps. 23.5;
1 Jn. 2.27 § Jn. 14.26 § Ro. 8.26

Having our hearts
sprinkled from an evil conscience.

If the blood of bulls and of goats, and the ashes of an heifer sprinkling the unclean, sanctifieth to the purifying of the flesh: How much more shall the blood of Christ, who through the eternal Spirit offered himself without spot to God, purge your conscience from dead works to serve the living God?—The blood of sprinkling, that speaketh better things than *that of* Abel.

We have redemption through his blood, the forgiveness of sins, according to the riches of his grace.

When Moses had spoken every precept to all the people according to the law, he took the blood of calves and of goats, with water, and scarlet wool, and hyssop, and sprinkled both the book, and all the people... Moreover he sprinkled with blood both the tabernacle, and all the vessels of the ministry. And almost all things are by the law purged with blood; and without shedding of blood is no remission.

He. 10.22; He. 9.13,14; He. 12.24 § Eph. 1.7
§ He. 9.19,21–22

I would seek unto God,
and unto God would I commit my cause.

Is any thing too hard for the LORD?—Commit thy way unto the LORD; trust also in him; and he shall bring *it* to pass.—Be careful for nothing; but in every thing by prayer and supplication with thanksgiving let your requests be made known unto God.—Casting all your care upon him; for he careth for you.

Hezekiah received the letter from the hand of the messengers, and read it: and Hezekiah went up unto the house of the LORD, and spread it before the LORD. And Hezekiah prayed unto the LORD.

It shall come to pass, that before they call, I will answer; and while they are yet speaking, I will hear.—The effectual fervent prayer of a righteous man availeth much.

I love the LORD, because he hath heard my voice *and* my supplications. Because he hath inclined his ear unto me, therefore will I call upon *him* as long as I live.

Job 5.8; Ge. 18.14; Ps. 37.5; Phil. 4.6; 1 Pe. 5.7
§ Isa. 37.14–15 § Isa. 65.24; Jas. 5.16 § Ps. 116.1–2

Our bodies washed with pure water.

Thou shalt...make a laver *of* brass...and thou shalt put it between the tabernacle of the congregation and the altar, and thou shalt put water therein. For Aaron and his sons shall wash their hands and their feet thereat: when they go into the tabernacle of the congregation, they shall wash with water, that they die not...they shall wash their hands and their feet, that they die not.—Your body is the temple of the Holy Ghost *which is* in you.—If any man defile the temple of God, him shall God destroy; for the temple of God is holy, which *temple* ye are.

In my flesh shall I see God: whom I shall see for myself, and mine eyes shall behold, and not another.—There shall in no wise enter into it any thing that defileth.—*Thou art* of purer eyes than to behold evil, and canst not look on iniquity.—I beseech you therefore, brethren, by the mercies of God, that ye present your bodies a living sacrifice, holy, acceptable unto God, *which is* your reasonable service.

He. 10.22; Ex. 30.18–20,21; 1 Co. 6.19; 1 Co. 3.17
§ Job 19.26–27; Rev. 21.27; Hab. 1.13; Ro. 12.1

Where shall wisdom be found?…
Behold the fear of the Lord, that is wisdom.

If any of you lack wisdom, let him ask of God, that giveth to all *men* liberally, and upbraideth not; and it shall be given him. But let him ask in faith, nothing wavering.—Trust in the LORD with all thine heart; and lean not unto thine own understanding. In all thy ways acknowledge him, and he shall direct thy paths.—The only wise God.—Be not wise in thine own eyes.

Ah, Lord GOD! behold, I cannot speak: for I *am* a child. But the Lord said unto me, Say not, I *am* a child: for thou shalt go to all that I shall send thee, and whatsoever I command thee thou shalt speak. Be not afraid of their faces: for I *am* with thee to deliver thee, saith the LORD.

Whatsoever ye shall ask the Father in my name, he will give *it* you. Hitherto have ye asked nothing in my name: ask, and ye shall receive, that your joy may be full.—All things, whatsoever ye shall ask in prayer, believing, ye shall receive.—To the law and to the testimony: if they speak not according to this word, *it is* because *there is* no light in them.

Job 28.12,28; Jas. 1.5–6; Pro. 3.5–6; 1 Tim. 1.17; Pro. 3.7 § Jer. 1.6–8 § Jn. 16.23–24; Mt. 21.22; Isa. 8.20

I would not live alway.

And I said, O that I had wings like a dove! *for then* would I fly away, and be at rest... I would hasten my escape from the windy storm *and* tempest.

In this we groan, earnestly desiring to be clothed upon with our house which is from heaven... For we that are in *this* tabernacle do groan, being burdened: not for that we would be unclothed, but clothed upon, that mortality might be swallowed up of life.—Having a desire to depart, and to be with Christ; which is far better.

Let us run with patience the race that is set before us, looking unto Jesus the author and finisher of *our* faith; who for the joy that was set before him endured the cross, despising the shame, and is set down at the right hand of the throne of God. For consider him that endured such contradiction of sinners against himself, lest ye be wearied and faint in your minds.

Let not your heart be troubled, neither let it be afraid.

Job 7.16; Ps. 55.6,8 § 2 Co. 5.2,4; Phil. 1.23 § He. 12.1–3 § Jn. 14.27

It is **good for me that I have been afflicted;
that I might learn thy statutes.**

Though he were a Son, yet learned he obedience by the things which he suffered.—We suffer with *him*, that we may be also glorified together. For I reckon that the sufferings of this present time *are* not worthy *to be compared* with the glory which shall be revealed in us.

He knoweth the way that I take: *when* he hath tried me, I shall come forth as gold. My foot hath held his steps, his way have I kept, and not declined.

Thou shalt remember all the way which the LORD thy God led thee these forty years in the wilderness, to humble thee, *and* to prove thee, to know what *was* in thine heart, whether thou wouldest keep his commandments, or no... Thou shalt also consider in thine heart, that, as a man chasteneth his son, *so* the LORD thy God chasteneth thee. Therefore thou shalt keep the commandments of the LORD thy God, to walk in his ways, and to fear him.—For whom the Lord loveth he chasteneth.

Ps. 119.71; He. 5.8; Ro. 8.17–18 § Job 23.10–11
§ Deu. 8.2,5–6; He. 12.6

By strength shall no man prevail.

Then said David to the Philistine, Thou comest to me with a sword, and with a spear, and with a shield: but I come to thee in the name of the LORD of hosts, the God of the armies of Israel, whom thou hast defied... And David put his hand in his bag, and took thence a stone, and slang *it*... So David prevailed over the Philistine with a sling and with a stone.

There is no king saved by the multitude of an host: a mighty man is not delivered by much strength... Behold, the eye of the LORD *is* upon them that fear him, upon them that hope in his mercy.—Both riches and honour *come* of thee, and thou reignest over all; and in thine hand *is* power and might; and in thine hand *it is* to make great, and to give strength unto all.

I...glory in my infirmities, that the power of Christ may rest upon me. Therefore I take pleasure in infirmities, in reproaches, in necessities, in persecutions, in distresses for Christ's sake: for when I am weak, then am I strong.—Not by might, nor by power, but by my spirit, saith the LORD of hosts.

1 Sa. 2.9; 1 Sa. 17.45,49,50 § Ps. 33.16,18; 1 Chr. 29.12 § 2 Co. 12.9–10; Zech. 4.6

It is God
which worketh in you.

Not that we are sufficient of ourselves to think any thing as of ourselves; but our sufficiency *is* of God.—A man can receive nothing, except it be given him from heaven.—No man can come to me, except the Father which hath sent me draw him: and I will raise him up at the last day.—And I will give them one heart, and one way, that they may fear me for ever.

Do not err, my beloved brethren. Every good gift and every perfect gift is from above, and cometh down from the Father of lights, with whom is no variableness, neither shadow of turning. Of his own will begat he us with the word of truth, that we should be a kind of firstfruits of his creatures.

For we are his workmanship, created in Christ Jesus unto good works, which God hath before ordained that we should walk in them.

LORD, thou wilt ordain peace for us: for thou also hast wrought all our works in us.

Phil. 2.13; 2 Co. 3.5; Jn. 3.27; Jn. 6.44; Jer. 32.39 § Jas. 1.16–18 § Eph. 2.10 § Isa. 26.12

The spirit indeed *is* willing,
but the flesh *is* weak.

In the way of thy judgments, O LORD, have we waited for thee; the desire of *our* soul *is* to thy name, and to the remembrance of thee. With my soul have I desired thee in the night; yea, with my spirit within me will I seek thee early.

I know that in me (that is, in my flesh,) dwelleth no good thing: for to will is present with me; but *how* to perform that which is good I find not... For I delight in the law of God after the inward man: but I see another law in my members, warring against the law of my mind, and bringing me into captivity to the law of sin which is in my members.—The flesh lusteth against the Spirit, and the Spirit against the flesh: and these are contrary the one to the other: so that ye cannot do the things that ye would.

I can do all things through Christ which strengtheneth me.—Our sufficiency *is* of God.—My grace is sufficient for thee.

Mt. 26.41; Isa. 26.8–9 § Ro. 7.18,22–23; Ga. 5.17
§ Phil. 4.13; 2 Co. 3.5; 2 Co. 12.9

**He hath made him *to be* sin for us,
who knew no sin; that we might be made
the righteousness of God in him.**

The LORD hath laid on him the iniquity of us all.—
Who his own self bare our sins in his own body on the
tree, that we, being dead to sins, should live unto righteousness: by whose stripes ye were healed.—As by one
man's disobedience many were made sinners, so by the
obedience of one shall many be made righteous.

After that the kindness and love of God our Saviour
toward man appeared, not by works of righteousness
which we have done, but according to his mercy he
saved us, by the washing of regeneration, and renewing
of the Holy Ghost; which he shed on us abundantly
through Jesus Christ our Saviour; that being justified by
his grace, we should be made heirs according to the
hope of eternal life.—*There is* therefore now no condemnation to them which are in Christ Jesus, who walk
not after the flesh, but after the Spirit.

THE LORD OUR RIGHTEOUSNESS.

2 Co. 5.21; Isa. 53.6; 1 Pe. 2.24; Ro. 5.19 § Titus 3.4–7;
Ro. 8.1 § Jer. 23.6

I will be as the dew unto Israel.

The meekness and gentleness of Christ.—His favour *is* as dew upon the grass.

A bruised reed shall he not break, and the smoking flax shall he not quench.

The Spirit of the Lord *is* upon me, because he hath anointed me to preach the gospel to the poor; he hath sent me to heal the brokenhearted, to preach deliverance to the captives, and recovering of sight to the blind, to set at liberty them that are bruised, to preach the acceptable year of the Lord… And he began to say unto them, This day is this scripture fulfilled in your ears. And all bare him witness, and wondered at the gracious words which proceeded out of his mouth.

And the Lord turned, and looked upon Peter. And Peter remembered the word of the Lord, how he had said unto him, Before the cock crow, thou shalt deny me thrice. And Peter went out, and wept bitterly.

He shall feed his flock like a shepherd: he shall gather the lambs with his arm, and carry *them* in his bosom, *and* shall gently lead those that are with young.

Hos. 14.5; 2 Co. 10.1; Pro. 19.12 § Isa. 42.3
§ Lu. 4.18–19,21–22 § Lu. 22.61–62 § Isa. 40.11

By love serve one another.

Brethren, if a man be overtaken in a fault, ye which are spiritual, restore such an one in the spirit of meekness; considering thyself, lest thou also be tempted. Bear ye one another's burdens, and so fulfil the law of Christ.

Brethren, if any of you do err from the truth, and one convert him; let him know, that he which converteth the sinner from the error of his way shall save a soul from death, and shall hide a multitude of sins.—Seeing ye have purified your souls in obeying the truth through the Spirit unto unfeigned love of the brethren, *see that ye* love one another with a pure heart fervently.—Owe no man any thing, but to love one another; for he that loveth another hath fulfilled the law.—*Be* kindly affectioned one to another with brotherly love; in honour preferring one another.—Yea, all *of you* be subject one to another, and be clothed with humility: for God resisteth the proud, and giveth grace to the humble.

We...that are strong ought to bear the infirmities of the weak, and not to please ourselves.

Ga. 5.13; Ga. 6.1–2 § Jas. 5.19–20; 1 Pe. 1.22;
Ro. 13.8; Ro. 12.10; 1 Pe. 5.5 § Ro. 15.1

Then shall the dust return to the earth as it was.

It is sown in corruption…it is sown in dishonour…it is sown in weakness…it is sown a natural body.—The first man *is* of the earth, earthy.

Dust thou *art*, and unto dust shalt thou return.—One dieth in his full strength, being wholly at ease and quiet… And another dieth in the bitterness of his soul, and never eateth with pleasure. They shall lie down alike in the dust, and the worms shall cover them.

My flesh…shall rest in hope.—*Though* after my skin *worms* destroy this *body*, yet in my flesh shall I see God.—The Lord Jesus Christ…shall change our vile body, that it may be fashioned like unto his glorious body, according to the working whereby he is able even to subdue all things unto himself.

LORD, make me to know mine end, and the measure of my days, what it *is; that* I may know how frail I *am.*—So teach *us* to number our days, that we may apply *our* hearts unto wisdom.

Ec. 12.7; 1 Co. 15.42,43,44; 1 Co. 15.47 § Ge. 3.19;
Job 21.23,25–26 § Ps. 16.9; Job 19.26; Phil. 3.20,21
§ Ps. 39.4; Ps. 90.12

**To do justice and judgment
is more acceptable to the LORD than sacrifice.**

He hath shewed thee, O man, what *is* good; and what doth the LORD require of thee, but to do justly, and to love mercy, and to walk humbly with thy God?—Hath the LORD *as great* delight in burnt offerings and sacrifices, as in obeying the voice of the LORD? Behold, to obey *is* better than sacrifice, *and* to hearken than the fat of rams.—To love him with all the heart, and with all the understanding, and with all the soul, and with all the strength, and to love *his* neighbour as himself, is more than all whole burnt offerings and sacrifices.

Therefore turn thou to thy God: keep mercy and judgment, and wait on thy God continually.—Mary...sat at Jesus' feet, and heard his word... One thing is needful: and Mary hath chosen that good part, which shall not be taken away from her.

It is God which worketh in you both to will and to do of *his* good pleasure.

Pro. 21.3; Mi. 6.8; 1 Sa. 15.22; Mk. 12.33 § Hos. 12.6; Lu. 10.39,42 § Phil. 2.13

The spirit shall return unto God who gave it.

The LORD God formed man *of* the dust of the ground, and breathed into his nostrils the breath of life; and man became a living soul.—*There is* a spirit in man: and the inspiration of the Almighty giveth them understanding.—The first man Adam was made a living soul.—The spirit of man that goeth upward.

Whilst we are at home in the body, we are absent from the Lord… We are confident…and willing rather to be absent from the body, and to be present with the Lord.—With Christ; which is far better.—I would not have you to be ignorant, brethren, concerning them which are asleep, that ye sorrow not, even as others which have no hope. For if we believe that Jesus died and rose again, even so them also which sleep in Jesus will God bring with him.

I go to prepare a place for you. And if I go and prepare a place for you, I will come again, and receive you unto myself; that where I am, *there* ye may be also.

Ec. 12.7; Ge. 2.7; Job 32.8; 1 Co. 15.45; Ec. 3.21
§ 2 Co. 5.6,8; Phil. 1.23; 1 Th. 4.13–14 § Jn. 14.2–3

No *man* is able to pluck *them* out of my Father's hand.

I know whom I have believed, and am persuaded that he is able to keep that which I have committed unto him against that day.—The Lord shall deliver me from every evil work, and will preserve *me* unto his heavenly kingdom.—We are more than conquerors through him that loved us. For I am persuaded, that neither death, nor life, nor angels, nor principalities, nor powers, nor things present, nor things to come, nor height, nor depth, nor any other creature, shall be able to separate us from the love of God, which is in Christ Jesus our Lord.—Your life is hid with Christ in God.

Hath not God chosen the poor of this world rich in faith, and heirs of the kingdom which he hath promised to them that love him?

Our Lord Jesus Christ himself, and God, even our Father, which hath loved us, and hath given *us* everlasting consolation and good hope through grace, comfort your hearts, and stablish you in every good word and work.

Jn. 10.29; 2 Tim. 1.12; 2 Tim. 4.18; Ro. 8.37–39;
Col. 3.3 § Jas. 2.5 § 2 Th. 2.16–17

The perfect law of liberty.

Ye shall know the truth, and the truth shall make you free... Verily, verily, I say unto you, Whosoever committeth sin is the servant of sin... If the Son therefore shall make you free, ye shall be free indeed.

Stand fast therefore in the liberty wherewith Christ hath made us free, and be not entangled again with the yoke of bondage... For, brethren, ye have been called unto liberty; only *use* not liberty for an occasion to the flesh, but by love serve one another. For all the law is fulfilled in one word, *even* in this; Thou shalt love thy neighbour as thyself.—Being then made free from sin, ye became the servants of righteousness.—For the woman which hath an husband is bound by the law to *her* husband so long as he liveth; but if the husband be dead, she is loosed from the law of *her* husband.

The law of the Spirit of life in Christ Jesus hath made me free from the law of sin and death.—I will walk at liberty: for I seek thy precepts.

Jas. 1.25; Jn. 8.32,34,36 § Ga. 5.1,13–14; Ro. 6.18; Ro. 7.2 § Ro. 8.2; Ps. 119.45

Let not...your good be evil spoken of.

Abstain from all appearance of evil.—Providing for honest things, not only in the sight of the Lord, but also in the sight of men.—For so is the will of God, that with well doing ye may put to silence the ignorance of foolish men.

But let none of you suffer as a murderer, or *as* a thief, or *as* an evildoer, or as a busybody in other men's matters. Yet if *any man suffer* as a Christian, let him not be ashamed; but let him glorify God on this behalf.

Brethren, ye have been called unto liberty; only *use* not liberty for an occasion to the flesh, but by love serve one another.—Take heed lest by any means this liberty of yours become a stumblingblock to them that are weak.—Whoso shall offend one of these little ones which believe in me, it were better for him that a millstone were hanged about his neck, and *that* he were drowned in the depth of the sea.—Inasmuch as ye have done *it* unto one of the least of these my brethren, ye have done *it* unto me.

Ro. 14.16; 1 Th. 5.22; 2 Co. 8.21; 1 Pe. 2.15
§ 1 Pe. 4.15–16 § Ga. 5.13; 1 Co. 8.9; Mt. 18.6;
Mt. 25.40

Awake thou that sleepest, and arise from the dead, and Christ shall give thee light.

*I*t *is* high time to awake out of sleep: for now *is* our salvation nearer than when we believed.—Therefore let us not sleep, as *do* others; but let us watch and be sober. For they that sleep sleep in the night; and they that be drunken are drunken in the night. But let us, who are of the day, be sober, putting on the breastplate of faith and love; and for an helmet, the hope of salvation.

Arise, shine; for thy light is come, and the glory of the LORD is risen upon thee. For, behold, the darkness shall cover the earth, and gross darkness the people: but the LORD shall arise upon thee, and his glory shall be seen upon thee.

Wherefore gird up the loins of your mind, be sober, and hope to the end for the grace that is to be brought unto you at the revelation of Jesus Christ.—Let your loins be girded about, and *your* lights burning; and ye yourselves like unto men that wait for their lord.

Eph. 5.14; Ro. 13.11; 1 Th. 5.6–8 § Isa. 60.1–2 § 1 Pe. 1.13; Lu. 12.35–36

**The king of Israel, *even* the LORD,
is in the midst of thee. —Emmanuel…God with us.**

Fear thou not; for I *am* with thee: be not dismayed; for I *am* thy God: I will strengthen thee; yea, I will help thee; yea, I will uphold thee with the right hand of my righteousness.—Strengthen ye the weak hands, and confirm the feeble knees. Say to them *that are* of a fearful heart, Be strong, fear not: behold, your God will come *with* vengeance, *even* God *with* a recompence; he will come and save you.—The LORD thy God in the midst of thee *is* mighty; he will save, he will rejoice over thee with joy; he will rest in his love, he will joy over thee with singing.—Wait on the LORD: be of good courage, and he shall strengthen thine heart.

I heard a great voice out of heaven saying, Behold, the tabernacle of God *is* with men, and he will dwell with them, and they shall be his people, and God himself shall be with them, *and be* their God. And God shall wipe away all tears from their eyes; and there shall be no more death, neither sorrow, nor crying, neither shall there be any more pain.

Zeph. 3.15; Mt. 1.23; Isa. 41.10; Isa. 35.3–4; Zeph. 3.17; Ps. 27.14 § Rev. 21.3–4

Wherefore criest thou unto me? speak unto the children of Israel, that they go forward.

Be of good courage, and let us behave ourselves valiantly for our people, and for the cities of our God: and let the LORD do *that which is* good in his sight.—We made our prayer unto our God, and set a watch against them day and night.

Not every one that saith unto me, Lord, Lord, shall enter into the kingdom of heaven; but he that doeth the will of my Father which is in heaven.—If any man will do his will, he shall know of the doctrine, whether it be of God.—Then shall we know, *if* we follow on to know the LORD.

Watch and pray, that ye enter not into temptation.— Watch ye, stand fast in the faith, quit you like men, be strong.—Not slothful in business; fervent in spirit; serving the Lord.

Strengthen ye the weak hands, and confirm the feeble knees. Say to them *that are* of a fearful heart, Be strong, fear not.

Ex. 14.15; 1 Chr. 19.13; Ne. 4.9 § Mt. 7.21; Jn. 7.17; Hos. 6.3 § Mt. 26.41; 1 Co. 16.13; Ro. 12.11 § Isa. 35.3–4

Be strong in the grace that is in Christ Jesus.

Strengthened with all might, according to his glorious power.—As ye have therefore received Christ Jesus the Lord, *so* walk ye in him: rooted and built up in him, and stablished in the faith, as ye have been taught, abounding therein with thanksgiving.—Trees of righteousness, the planting of the LORD, that he might be glorified.—Built upon the foundation of the apostles and prophets, Jesus Christ himself being the chief corner *stone;* in whom all the building fitly framed together groweth unto an holy temple in the Lord: in whom ye also are builded together for an habitation of God through the Spirit.

I commend you to God, and to the word of his grace, which is able to build you up, and to give you an inheritance among all them which are sanctified.—Being filled with the fruits of righteousness, which are by Jesus Christ, unto the glory and praise of God.

Fight the good fight of faith.—In nothing terrified by your adversaries.

---

2 Tim. 2.1;   Col. 1.11;   Col. 2.6–7;   Isa. 61.3;
Eph. 2.20–22 § Ac. 20.32;   Phil. 1.11 § 1 Tim. 6.12;
Phil. 1.28

Thou renderest to every man
according to his work.

Other foundation can no man lay than that is laid, which is Jesus Christ... If any man's work abide which he hath built thereupon, he shall receive a reward. If any man's work shall be burned, he shall suffer loss: but he himself shall be saved; yet so as by fire.—We must all appear before the judgment seat of Christ; that every one may receive the things *done* in *his* body, according to that he hath done, whether *it be* good or bad.

When thou doest alms, let not thy left hand know what thy right hand doeth: that thine alms may be in secret: and thy Father which seeth in secret himself shall reward thee openly.—After a long time the lord of those servants cometh, and reckoneth with them.

Not that we are sufficient of ourselves to think any thing as of ourselves; but our sufficiency *is* of God.— LORD, thou wilt ordain peace for us: for thou also hast wrought all our works in us.

Ps. 62.12; 1 Co. 3.11,14–15; 2 Co. 5.10 § Mt. 6.3–4; Mt. 25.19 § 2 Co. 3.5; Isa. 26.12

Make his praise glorious.

This people have I formed for myself; they shall shew forth my praise.—I will cleanse them from all their iniquity, whereby they have sinned against me; and I will pardon all their iniquities, whereby they have sinned, and whereby they have transgressed against me. And it shall be to me a name of joy, a praise and an honour before all the nations of the earth.—By him therefore let us offer the sacrifice of praise to God continually, that is, the fruit of *our* lips giving thanks to his name.

I will praise thee, O Lord my God, with all my heart: and I will glorify thy name for evermore. For great *is* thy mercy toward me: and thou hast delivered my soul from the lowest hell.—Who *is* like unto thee, O LORD...glorious in holiness, fearful *in* praises, doing wonders?—I will praise the name of God with a song, and will magnify him with thanksgiving.—They sing the song of Moses the servant of God, and the song of the Lamb, saying, Great and marvellous *are* thy works, Lord God Almighty.

Ps. 66.2; Isa. 43.21; Jer. 33.8,9; He. 13.15
§ Ps. 86.12–13; Ex. 15.11; Ps. 69.30; Rev. 15.3

By nature the children of wrath, even as others.

 We ourselves also were sometimes foolish, disobedient, deceived, serving divers lusts and pleasures, living in malice and envy, hateful, *and* hating one another.— Marvel not that I said unto thee, Ye must be born again.

The LORD said unto Satan, Hast thou considered my servant Job, that *there is* none like him in the earth, a perfect and an upright man, one that feareth God, and escheweth evil?—Job answered the LORD, and said, Behold, I am vile; what shall I answer thee? I will lay mine hand upon my mouth.

Behold, I was shapen in iniquity; and in sin did my mother conceive me.—David...to whom also he gave testimony, and said, I have found David the *son* of Jesse, a man after mine own heart, which shall fulfil all my will.

I thank Christ Jesus our Lord, who hath enabled me, for that he counted me faithful, putting me into the ministry; who was before a blasphemer, and a persecutor, and injurious: but I obtained mercy.

That which is born of the flesh is flesh; and that which is born of the Spirit is spirit.

Eph. 2.3; Titus 3.3; Jn. 3.7 § Job 1.8; Job 40.3,4 § Ps. 51.5; Ac. 13.22 § 1 Tim. 1.12–13 § Jn. 3.6

**Bear ye one another's burdens,
and so fulfil the law of Christ.—
The reproaches of them that reproached thee
are fallen upon me.**

Look not every man on his own things, but every man also on the things of others. Let this mind be in you, which was also in Christ Jesus: who...took upon him the form of a servant.—Even the Son of man came not to be ministered unto, but to minister, and to give his life a ransom for many.—He died for all, that they which live should not henceforth live unto themselves, but unto him which died for them, and rose again.

When Jesus...saw her weeping, and the Jews also weeping which came with her, he groaned in the spirit, and was troubled.—Jesus wept.—Rejoice with them that do rejoice, and weep with them that weep.

Be ye all of one mind, having compassion one of another, love as brethren, *be* pitiful, *be* courteous: not rendering evil for evil, or railing for railing; but contrariwise blessing; knowing that ye are thereunto called, that ye should inherit a blessing.

Ga. 6.2; Ps. 69.9; Phil. 2.4–6,7; Mk. 10.45; 2 Co. 5.15
§ Jn. 11.33; Jn. 11.35; Ro. 12.15 § 1 Pe. 3.8–9

Son, go work to day in my vineyard.

Thou art no more a servant, but a son; and if a son, then an heir of God through Christ.

Reckon ye...yourselves to be dead indeed unto sin, but alive unto God through Jesus Christ our Lord. Let not sin therefore reign in your mortal body, that ye should obey it in the lusts thereof. Neither yield ye your members *as* instruments of unrighteousness unto sin: but yield yourselves unto God, as those that are alive from the dead, and your members *as* instruments of righteousness unto God.—As obedient children, not fashioning yourselves according to the former lusts in your ignorance: but as he which hath called you is holy, so be ye holy in all manner of conversation; because it is written, Be ye holy; for I am holy.—Sanctified, and meet for the master's use, *and* prepared unto every good work.

Therefore, my beloved brethren, be ye stedfast, unmoveable, always abounding in the work of the Lord, forasmuch as ye know that your labour is not in vain in the Lord.

Mt. 21.28; Ga. 4.7 § Ro. 6.11–13; 1 Pe. 1.14–15; 2 Tim. 2.21 § 1 Co. 15.58

**Having loved his own which were in the world,
he loved them unto the end.**

I pray for them: I pray not for the world, but for them which thou hast given me; for they are thine. And all mine are thine, and thine are mine; and I am glorified in them... I pray not that thou shouldest take them out of the world, but that thou shouldest keep them from the evil. They are not of the world, even as I am not of the world.

As the Father hath loved me, so have I loved you: continue ye in my love.—Greater love hath no man than this, that a man lay down his life for his friends. Ye are my friends, if ye do whatsoever I command you.—A new commandment I give unto you, That ye love one another; as I have loved you, that ye also love one another.

He which hath begun a good work in you will perform *it* until the day of Jesus Christ.—Christ...loved the church, and gave himself for it; that he might sanctify and cleanse it with the washing of water by the word.

Jn. 13.1; Jn. 17.9–10,15–16 § Jn. 15.9; Jn. 15.13–14; Jn. 13.34 § Phil. 1.6; Eph. 5.25–26

The deep things of God.

Henceforth I call you not servants; for the servant knoweth not what his lord doeth: but I have called you friends; for all things that I have heard of my Father I have made known unto you.—It is given unto you to know the mysteries of the kingdom of heaven.—The secret *things belong* unto the LORD our God: but those *things which are* revealed *belong* unto us and to our children for ever, that *we* may do all the words of this law.

We have received, not the spirit of the world, but the Spirit which is of God; that we might know the things that are freely given to us of God.

For this cause I bow my knees unto the Father of our Lord Jesus Christ, of whom the whole family in heaven and earth is named, that he would grant you, according to the riches of his glory, to be strengthened with might by his Spirit in the inner man…that ye, being rooted and grounded in love, may be able to comprehend with all saints what *is* the breadth, and length, and depth, and height; and to know the love of Christ, which passeth knowledge, that ye might be filled with all the fulness of God.

---

1 Co. 2.10; Jn. 15.15; Mt. 13.11; Deu. 29.29
§ 1 Co. 2.12 § Eph. 3.14–16,17–19

Quicken us,
and we will call upon thy name.

It is the spirit that quickeneth.—The Spirit also helpeth our infirmities: for we know not what we should pray for as we ought: but the Spirit itself maketh intercession for us with groanings which cannot be uttered. And he that searcheth the hearts knoweth what *is* the mind of the Spirit, because he maketh intercession for the saints according to *the will of* God.—Praying always with all prayer and supplication in the Spirit, and watching thereunto with all perseverance.

I will never forget thy precepts: for with them thou hast quickened me.—The words that I speak unto you, *they* are spirit, and *they* are life.—The letter killeth, but the spirit giveth life.—If ye abide in me, and my words abide in you, ye shall ask what ye will, and it shall be done unto you.—This is the confidence that we have in him, that, if we ask any thing according to his will, he heareth us.

No man can say that Jesus is the Lord, but by the Holy Ghost.

Ps. 80.18; Jn. 6.63; Ro. 8.26–27; Eph. 6.18 § Ps. 119.93; Jn. 6.63; 2 Co. 3.6; Jn. 15.7; 1 Jn. 5.14 § 1 Co. 12.3

**Have no fellowship with
the unfruitful works of darkness,
but rather reprove *them*.**

Be not deceived: evil communications corrupt good manners.

Know ye not that a little leaven leaveneth the whole lump? Purge out therefore the old leaven… I wrote unto you in an epistle not to company with fornicators: yet not altogether with the fornicators of this world, or with the covetous, or extortioners, or with idolaters; for then must ye needs go out of the world… I have written unto you not to keep company, if any man that is called a brother be a fornicator, or covetous, or an idolater, or a railer, or a drunkard, or an extortioner; with such an one no not to eat.—That ye may be blameless and harmless, the sons of God, without rebuke, in the midst of a crooked and perverse nation, among whom ye shine as lights in the world.

In a great house there are not only vessels of gold and of silver, but also of wood and of earth; and some to honour, and some to dishonour.

Eph. 5.11;   1 Co. 15.33   § 1 Co. 5.6–7,9–10,11;
Phil. 2.15   § 2 Tim. 2.20

Let us...come boldly unto the throne of grace,
that we may obtain mercy,
and find grace to help in time of need.

Be careful for nothing; but in every thing by prayer and supplication with thanksgiving let your requests be made known unto God. And the peace of God, which passeth all understanding, shall keep your hearts and minds through Christ Jesus.—Ye have not received the spirit of bondage again to fear; but ye have received the Spirit of adoption, whereby we cry, Abba, Father.

I said not unto the seed of Jacob, Seek ye me in vain.—Having therefore...boldness to enter into the holiest by the blood of Jesus, by a new and living way, which he hath consecrated for us, through the veil, that is to say, his flesh; and *having* an high priest over the house of God; let us draw near with a true heart in full assurance of faith, having our hearts sprinkled from an evil conscience, and our bodies washed with pure water.—We may boldly say, The Lord *is* my helper, and I will not fear what man shall do unto me.

He. 4.16; Phil. 4.6–7; Ro. 8.15 § Isa. 45.19;
He. 10.19,22; He. 13.6

**Ye shall know the truth,
and the truth shall make you free.**

Where the Spirit of the Lord *is*, there *is* liberty.—The law of the Spirit of life in Christ Jesus hath made me free from the law of sin and death.—If the Son…shall make you free, ye shall be free indeed.

Brethren, we are not children of the bondwoman, but of the free.—Knowing that a man is not justified by the works of the law, but by the faith of Jesus Christ, even we have believed in Jesus Christ, that we might be justified by the faith of Christ, and not by the works of the law: for by the works of the law shall no flesh be justified.

Whoso looketh into the perfect law of liberty, and continueth *therein*, he being not a forgetful hearer, but a doer of the work, this man shall be blessed in his deed.—Stand fast therefore in the liberty wherewith Christ hath made us free, and be not entangled again with the yoke of bondage.

Jn. **8.32**; 2 Co. 3.17; Ro. 8.2; Jn. 8.36 § Ga. 4.31; Ga. 2.16 § Jas. 1.25; Ga. 5.1

Unto the upright there ariseth
light in the darkness.

Who *is* among you that feareth the LORD, that obeyeth the voice of his servant, that walketh *in* darkness, and hath no light? let him trust in the name of the LORD, and stay upon his God.—Though he fall, he shall not be utterly cast down: for the LORD upholdeth *him with* his hand.—The commandment *is* a lamp; and the law *is* light.

Rejoice not against me, O mine enemy: when I fall, I shall arise; when I sit in darkness, the LORD *shall be* a light unto me. I will bear the indignation of the LORD, because I have sinned against him, until he plead my cause, and execute judgment for me: he will bring me forth to the light, *and* I shall behold his righteousness.

The light of the body is the eye: if therefore thine eye be single, thy whole body shall be full of light. But if thine eye be evil, thy whole body shall be full of darkness. If therefore the light that is in thee be darkness, how great *is* that darkness!

Ps. 112.4; Isa. 50.10; Ps. 37.24; Pro. 6.23 § Mi. 7.8–9 § Mt. 6.22–23

He shall feed his flock like a shepherd:
he shall gather the lambs with his arm,
and carry them in his bosom, and shall
gently lead those that are with young.

I have compassion on the multitude, because they continue with me now three days, and have nothing to eat...I will not send them away fasting, lest they faint in the way.—We have not an high priest which cannot be touched with the feeling of our infirmities.

They brought young children to him...and he took them up in his arms, put *his* hands upon them, and blessed them.—Yea; have ye never read, Out of the mouth of babes and sucklings thou hast perfected praise?

I have gone astray like a lost sheep; seek thy servant.—The Son of man is come to seek and to save that which was lost.—Ye were as sheep going astray; but are now returned unto the Shepherd and Bishop of your souls.

Fear not, little flock; for it is your Father's good pleasure to give you the kingdom.—I will feed my flock, and I will cause them to lie down, saith the Lord GOD.

Isa. 40.11; Mt. 15.32; He. 4.15 § Mk. 10.13,16;
Mt. 21.16 § Ps. 119.176; Lu. 19.10; 1 Pe. 2.25
§ Lu. 12.32; Ezek. 34.15

He hath chosen us in him
before the foundation of the world.

That we should be holy and without blame before him in love.

God hath from the beginning chosen you to salvation through sanctification of the Spirit and belief of the truth: whereunto he called you…to the obtaining of the glory of our Lord Jesus Christ.—Whom he did foreknow, he also did predestinate *to be* conformed to the image of his Son, that he might be the firstborn among many brethren. Moreover whom he did predestinate, them he also called: and whom he called, them he also justified: and whom he justified, them he also glorified.—Elect according to the foreknowledge of God the Father, through sanctification of the Spirit, unto obedience and sprinkling of the blood of Jesus Christ.

A new heart also will I give you, and a new spirit will I put within you: and I will take away the stony heart out of your flesh, and I will give you an heart of flesh.—God hath not called us unto uncleanness, but unto holiness.

Eph. 1.4; Eph. 1.4 § 2 Th. 2.13–14; Ro. 8.29–30; 1 Pe. 1.2 § Ezek. 36.26; 1 Th. 4.7

_If_ the LORD would make windows in heaven, might this thing be?

Have faith in God.—Without faith _it is_ impossible to please _him._—With God all things are possible.

Is my hand shortened at all, that it cannot redeem? or have I no power to deliver?

My thoughts _are_ not your thoughts, neither _are_ your ways my ways, saith the LORD. For _as_ the heavens are higher than the earth, so are my ways higher than your ways, and my thoughts than your thoughts.—Prove me now herewith, saith the LORD of hosts, if I will not open you the windows of heaven, and pour you out a blessing, that _there shall_ not _be room_ enough _to receive it._

Behold, the LORD's hand is not shortened, that it cannot save; neither his ear heavy, that it cannot hear.— LORD, _it is_ nothing with thee to help, whether with many, or with them that have no power.

But we had the sentence of death in ourselves, that we should not trust in ourselves, but in God which raiseth the dead: who delivered us from so great a death, and doth deliver us: in whom we trust that he will yet deliver _us._

---

2 Ki. 7.2; Mk. 11.22; He. 11.6; Mt. 19.26 § Isa. 50.2
§ Isa. 55.8–9; Mal. 3.10 § Isa. 59.1; 2 Chr. 14.11
§ 2 Co. 1.9–10

The days of thy mourning
shall be ended.

In the world ye shall have tribulation.—The whole creation groaneth and travaileth in pain together until now. And not only *they*, but ourselves also, which have the firstfruits of the Spirit, even we ourselves groan within ourselves, waiting for the adoption, *to wit*, the redemption of our body.—We that are in *this* tabernacle do groan, being burdened: not for that we would be unclothed, but clothed upon, that mortality might be swallowed up of life.

These are they which came out of great tribulation, and have washed their robes, and made them white in the blood of the Lamb. Therefore are they before the throne of God, and serve him day and night in his temple: and he that sitteth on the throne shall dwell among them. They shall hunger no more, neither thirst any more; neither shall the sun light on them, nor any heat. For the Lamb which is in the midst of the throne shall feed them, and shall lead them unto living fountains of waters: and God shall wipe away all tears from their eyes.

Isa. 60.20; Jn. 16.33; Ro. 8.22–23; 2 Co. 5.4
§ Rev. 7.14–17

Master, carest thou not that we perish?

The LORD *is* good to all: and his tender mercies *are* over all his works.

Every moving thing that liveth shall be meat for you; even as the green herb have I given you all things.—While the earth remaineth, seedtime and harvest, and cold and heat, and summer and winter, and day and night shall not cease.

The LORD *is* good, a strong hold in the day of trouble; and he knoweth them that trust in him.—God heard the voice of the lad; and the angel of God called to Hagar out of heaven, and said unto her, What aileth thee, Hagar? fear not; for God hath heard the voice of the lad where he *is*... And God opened her eyes, and she saw a well of water; and she went, and filled the bottle with water, and gave the lad drink.

Take no thought, saying, What shall we eat? or, What shall we drink?...for your heavenly Father knoweth that ye have need of all these things.—Trust...in the living God, who giveth us richly all things to enjoy.

Casting all your care upon him; for he careth for you.

Mk. 4.38; Ps. 145.9 § Ge. 9.3; Ge. 8.22 § Na.1.7; Ge. 21.17,19 § Mt. 6.31,32; 1 Tim. 6.17 § 1 Pe. 5.7

Your work of faith.

This is the work of God, that ye believe on him whom he hath sent.

Faith, if it hath not works, is dead, being alone.— Faith...worketh by love.—He that soweth to his flesh shall of the flesh reap corruption; but he that soweth to the Spirit shall of the Spirit reap life everlasting.—We are his workmanship, created in Christ Jesus unto good works, which God hath before ordained that we should walk in them.—Who gave himself for us, that he might redeem us from all iniquity, and purify unto himself a peculiar people, zealous of good works.

We are bound to thank God always for you, brethren, as it is meet, because that your faith groweth exceedingly, and the charity of every one of you all toward each other aboundeth... Wherefore also we pray always for you, that our God would count you worthy of *this* calling, and fulfil all the good pleasure of *his* goodness, and the work of faith with power.—It is God which worketh in you both to will and to do of *his* good pleasure.

1 Th. 1.3; Jn. 6.29 § Jas. 2.17; Ga. 5.6; Ga. 6.8; Eph. 2.10; Titus 2.14 § 2 Th. 1.3,11; Phil. 2.13

Where is the promise
of his coming?

Enoch...the seventh from Adam, prophesied of these, saying, Behold, the Lord cometh with ten thousands of his saints, to execute judgment upon all.—Behold, he cometh with clouds; and every eye shall see him, and they *also* which pierced him: and all kindreds of the earth shall wail because of him.

The Lord himself shall descend from heaven with a shout, with the voice of the archangel, and with the trump of God: and the dead in Christ shall rise first: then we which are alive *and* remain shall be caught up together with them in the clouds, to meet the Lord in the air: and so shall we ever be with the Lord.

The grace of God that bringeth salvation hath appeared to all men, teaching us that, denying ungodliness and worldly lusts, we should live soberly, righteously, and godly, in this present world; looking for that blessed hope, and the glorious appearing of the great God and our Saviour Jesus Christ.

---

2 Pe. 3.4; Jude 14,15; Rev. 1.7 § 1 Th. 4.16–17
§ Titus 2.11–13

> Let him take hold of my strength,
> *that* he may make peace with me.

I know the thoughts that I think toward you, saith the LORD, thoughts of peace, and not of evil.—*There is* no peace, saith the LORD, unto the wicked.

In Christ Jesus ye who sometimes were far off are made nigh by the blood of Christ. For he is our peace.

It pleased *the Father* that in him should all fulness dwell; and, having made peace through the blood of his cross, by him to reconcile all things unto himself.—Christ Jesus: whom God hath set forth *to be* a propitiation through faith in his blood, to declare his righteousness for the remission of sins that are past…that he might be just, and the justifier of him which believeth in Jesus.—If we confess our sins, he is faithful and just to forgive us *our* sins, and to cleanse us from all unrighteousness.

Trust ye in the LORD for ever: for in the LORD JEHO-VAH *is* everlasting strength.

Isa. 27.5; Jer. 29.11; Isa. 48.22 § Eph. 2.13–14
§ Col. 1.19–20; Ro. 3.24–25,26; 1 Jn. 1.9 § Isa. 26.4

God hath given to us eternal life,
and this life is in his Son.

As the Father raiseth up the dead, and quickeneth *them;* even so the Son quickeneth whom he will... As the Father hath life in himself; so hath he given to the Son to have life in himself.

I am the resurrection, and the life: he that believeth in me, though he were dead, yet shall he live: and whosoever liveth and believeth in me shall never die.— I am the good shepherd: the good shepherd giveth his life for the sheep... I lay down my life, that I might take it again. No man taketh it from me, but I lay it down of myself. I have power to lay it down, and I have power to take it again. This commandment have I received of my Father.—No man cometh unto the Father, but by me.—He that hath the Son hath life; *and* he that hath not the Son of God hath not life.—For ye are dead, and your life is hid with Christ in God. When Christ, *who is* our life, shall appear, then shall ye also appear with him in glory.

1 Jn. 5.11; Jn. 5.21,26 § Jn. 11.25–26; Jn. 10.11,17–18; Jn. 14.6; 1 Jn. 5.12; Col. 3.3–4

If ye live after the flesh, ye shall die:
but if ye through the Spirit
do mortify the deeds of the body,
ye shall live.

Now the works of the flesh are manifest, which are *these;* Adultery, fornication...and such like: of the which I tell you before, as I have also told *you* in time past, that they which do such things shall not inherit the kingdom of God. But the fruit of the Spirit is love, joy, peace, longsuffering, gentleness, goodness, faith, meekness, temperance: against such there is no law. And they that are Christ's have crucified the flesh with the affections and lusts. If we live in the Spirit, let us also walk in the Spirit.

The grace of God that bringeth salvation hath appeared to all men, teaching us that, denying ungodliness and worldly lusts, we should live soberly, righteously, and godly, in this present world; looking for that blessed hope, and the glorious appearing of the great God and our Saviour Jesus Christ; who gave himself for us, that he might redeem us from all iniquity.

Ro. 8.13;   Ga. 5.19,21–25 § Titus 2.11–14

**Then said the princes of the Philistines,
What *do* these Hebrews *here*?**

If ye be reproached for the name of Christ, happy *are ye*; for the spirit of glory and of God resteth upon you: on their part he is evil spoken of, but on your part he is glorified. But let none of you suffer as a murderer, or *as* a thief...or as a busybody in other men's matters.

Let not...your good be evil spoken of.—Having your conversation honest among the Gentiles.

Be ye not unequally yoked together with unbelievers: for what fellowship hath righteousness with unrighteousness? and what communion hath light with darkness?...ye are the temple of the living God... Wherefore come out from among them, and be ye separate, saith the Lord, and touch not the unclean *thing*.

Ye *are* a chosen generation, a royal priesthood, an holy nation, a peculiar people; that ye should shew forth the praises of him who hath called you out of darkness into his marvellous light.

1 Sa. 29.3; 1 Pe. 4.14–15 § Ro. 14.16; 1 Pe. 2.12
§ 2 Co. 6.14,16,17 § 1 Pe. 2.9

The kindness and love of God our Saviour toward man appeared.

I have loved thee with an everlasting love.

In this was manifested the love of God toward us, because that God sent his only begotten Son into the world, that we might live through him. Herein is love, not that we loved God, but that he loved us, and sent his Son *to be* the propitiation for our sins.

When the fulness of the time was come, God sent forth his Son, made of a woman, made under the law, to redeem them that were under the law, that we might receive the adoption of sons.—The Word was made flesh, and dwelt among us, (and we beheld his glory, the glory as of the only begotten of the Father,) full of grace and truth.—Great is the mystery of godliness: God was manifest in the flesh.

As the children are partakers of flesh and blood, he also himself likewise took part of the same; that through death he might destroy him that had the power of death, that is, the devil.

Titus 3.4; Jer. 31.3 § 1 Jn. 4.9–10 § Ga. 4.4–5; Jn. 1.14; 1 Tim. 3.16 § He. 2.14

Thanks *be* unto God
for his unspeakable gift.

Make a joyful noise unto the LORD, all ye lands. Serve the LORD with gladness: come before his presence with singing... Enter into his gates with thanksgiving, *and* into his courts with praise: be thankful unto him, *and* bless his name.—For unto us a child is born, unto us a son is given: and the government shall be upon his shoulder: and his name shall be called Wonderful, Counsellor, The mighty God, The everlasting Father, The Prince of Peace.

He...spared not his own Son, but delivered him up for us all.—Having yet...one son, his wellbeloved, he sent him.

Oh that *men* would praise the LORD *for* his goodness, and *for* his wonderful works to the children of men!— Bless the LORD, O my soul: and all that is within me, *bless* his holy name.

My soul doth magnify the Lord, and my spirit hath rejoiced in God my Saviour.

2 Co. **9.15**; Ps. 100.1–2,4; Isa. 9.6–7 § Ro. 8.32; Mk. 12.6 § Ps. 107.21; Ps. 103.1 § Lu. 1.46–47

Be ye stedfast, unmoveable,
always abounding in the work of the Lord.

Ye know that your labour is not in vain in the Lord.—
As ye have…received Christ Jesus the Lord, *so* walk ye in
him: rooted and built up in him, and stablished in the
faith, as ye have been taught, abounding therein with
thanksgiving.—He that shall endure unto the end, the
same shall be saved.—That on the good ground are
they, which in an honest and good heart, having heard
the word, keep *it*, and bring forth fruit with patience.

By faith ye stand.

I must work the works of him that sent me, while it
is day: the night cometh, when no man can work.

He that soweth to his flesh shall of the flesh reap corruption; but he that soweth to the Spirit shall of the
Spirit reap life everlasting. And let us not be weary in
well doing: for in due season we shall reap, if we faint
not. As we have therefore opportunity, let us do good
unto all *men*, especially unto them who are of the
household of faith.

1 Co. 15.58; 1 Co. 15.58; Col. 2.6–7; Mt. 24.13;
Lu. 8.15 § 2 Co. 1.24 § Jn. 9.4 § Ga. 6.8–10

**He is able…
to save them to the uttermost
that come unto God by him.**

I am the way, the truth, and the life: no man cometh unto the Father, but by me.—Neither is there salvation in any other: for there is none other name under heaven given among men, whereby we must be saved.

My sheep hear my voice, and I know them, and they follow me: and I give unto them eternal life; and they shall never perish, neither shall any *man* pluck them out of my hand.—He which hath begun a good work in you will perform *it* until the day of Jesus Christ.—Is any thing too hard for the LORD?

Now unto him that is able to keep you from falling, and to present *you* faultless before the presence of his glory with exceeding joy, to the only wise God our Saviour, *be* glory and majesty, dominion and power, both now and ever. Amen.

He. 7.25; Jn. 14.6; Ac. 4.12 § Jn. 10.27–28; Phil. 1.6; Ge. 18.14 § Jude 24–25

> We look not at the things which are seen,
> but at the things which are not seen:
> for the things which are seen *are* temporal;
> but the things which are not seen *are* eternal.

Here have we no continuing city.—Ye have in heaven a better and an enduring substance.

Fear not, little flock; for it is your Father's good pleasure to give you the kingdom.

Now for a season, if need be, ye are in heaviness through manifold temptations.—There the wicked cease *from* troubling; and there the weary be at rest.

We that are in *this* tabernacle do groan, being burdened.—God shall wipe away all tears from their eyes; and there shall be no more death, neither sorrow, nor crying, neither shall there be any more pain: for the former things are passed away.

The sufferings of this present time *are* not worthy *to be compared* with the glory which shall be revealed in us.—Our light affliction, which is but for a moment, worketh for us a far more exceeding *and* eternal weight of glory.

---

2 Co. 4.18;   He. 13.14;   He. 10.34   § Lu. 12.32
§ 1 Pe. 1.6;   Job 3.17   § 2 Co. 5.4;   Rev. 21.4
§ Ro. 8.18;   2 Co. 4.17

He is our peace.

God was in Christ, reconciling the world unto himself, not imputing their trespasses unto them... For he hath made him *to be* sin for us, who knew no sin; that we might be made the righteousness of God in him.—Having made peace through the blood of his cross, by him to reconcile all things unto himself... And you, that were sometime alienated and enemies in *your* mind by wicked works, yet now hath he reconciled in the body of his flesh through death, to present you holy and unblameable and unreproveable in his sight.—Blotting out the handwriting of ordinances that was against us, which was contrary to us, and took it out of the way, nailing it to his cross.—Having abolished in his flesh the enmity, *even* the law of commandments *contained* in ordinances; for to make in himself of twain one new man, *so* making peace.

Peace I leave with you, my peace I give unto you: not as the world giveth, give I unto you. Let not your heart be troubled, neither let it be afraid.

Eph. 2.14; 2 Co. 5.19,21; Col. 1.20,21–22; Col. 2.14; Eph. 2.15 § Jn. 14.27

Thy sins be forgiven thee.

I will forgive their iniquity, and I will remember their sin no more.—Who can forgive sins but God only?

I, *even* I, *am* he that blotteth out thy transgressions for mine own sake, and will not remember thy sins.—Blessed *is he whose* transgression *is* forgiven, *whose* sin *is* covered. Blessed *is* the man unto whom the LORD imputeth not iniquity.—Who *is* a God like unto thee, that pardoneth iniquity?

God for Christ's sake hath forgiven you.—The blood of Jesus Christ his Son cleanseth us from all sin. If we say that we have no sin, we deceive ourselves, and the truth is not in us. If we confess our sins, he is faithful and just to forgive us *our* sins, and to cleanse us from all unrighteousness.

As far as the east is from the west, *so* far hath he removed our transgressions from us.—Sin shall not have dominion over you: for ye are not under the law, but under grace... Being then made free from sin, ye became the servants of righteousness.

Mk. 2.5; Jer. 31.34; Mk. 2.7 § Isa. 43.25; Ps. 32.1–2; Mi. 7.18 § Eph. 4.32; 1 Jn. 1.7–9 § Ps. 103.12; Ro. 6.14,18

We would see Jesus.

Yea, in the way of thy judgments, O LORD, have we waited for thee; the desire of *our* soul *is* to thy name, and to the remembrance of thee.

The LORD *is* nigh unto all them that call upon him, to all that call upon him in truth.

Where two or three are gathered together in my name, there am I in the midst of them.—I will not leave you comfortless: I will come to you.—Lo, I am with you alway, *even* unto the end of the world.

Let us run with patience the race that is set before us, looking unto Jesus the author and finisher of *our* faith.

Now we see through a glass, darkly; but then face to face.—Having a desire to depart, and to be with Christ; which is far better.

Beloved, now are we the sons of God, and it doth not yet appear what we shall be: but we know that, when he shall appear, we shall be like him; for we shall see him as he is. And every man that hath this hope in him purifieth himself, even as he is pure.

Jn. 12.21; Isa. 26.8 § Ps. 145.18 § Mt. 18.20; Jn. 14.18; Mt. 28.20 § He. 12.1–2 § 1 Co. 13.12; Phil. 1.23 § 1 Jn. 3.2–3

Understanding what the will of the Lord *is*.

This is the will of God, *even* your sanctification.—Acquaint now thyself with him, and be at peace: thereby good shall come unto thee.—This is life eternal, that they might know thee the only true God, and Jesus Christ, whom thou hast sent.—We know that the Son of God is come, and hath given us an understanding, that we may know him that is true, and we are in him that is true, *even* in his Son Jesus Christ. This is the true God, and eternal life.

We…do not cease to pray for you, and to desire that ye might be filled with the knowledge of his will in all wisdom and spiritual understanding.—The God of our Lord Jesus Christ, the Father of glory…give unto you the spirit of wisdom and revelation in the knowledge of him: the eyes of your understanding being enlightened; that ye may know what is the hope of his calling, and what the riches of the glory of his inheritance in the saints, and what *is* the exceeding greatness of his power to us-ward who believe.

Eph. 5.17; 1 Th. 4.3; Job 22.21; Jn. 17.3; 1 Jn. 5.20
§ Col. 1.9; Eph. 1.17–19

Draw nigh to God, and he will draw nigh to you.

Enoch walked with God.—Can two walk together, except they be agreed?—*It is* good for me to draw near to God.

The LORD *is* with you, while ye be with him; and if ye seek him, he will be found of you; but if ye forsake him, he will forsake you... When they in their trouble did turn unto the LORD God of Israel, and sought him, he was found of them.—Abide with us: for it is toward evening, and the day is far spent. And he went in to tarry with them.

For I know the thoughts that I think toward you, saith the LORD, thoughts of peace, and not of evil, to give you an expected end. Then shall ye call upon me, and ye shall go and pray unto me, and I will hearken unto you. And ye shall seek me, and find *me*, when ye shall search for me with all your heart.

Having therefore, brethren, boldness to enter into the holiest by the blood of Jesus, by a new and living way...and *having* an high priest over the house of God; let us draw near with a true heart in full assurance of faith.

Jas 4.8; Ge. 5.24; Am. 3.3; Ps. 73.28 § 2 Chr. 15.2,4; Lu. 24.29 § Jer. 29.11–13 § He. 10.19–20,21–22

Blameless in the day of our Lord Jesus Christ.

You, that were sometime alienated and enemies in *your* mind by wicked works, yet now hath he reconciled in the body of his flesh through death, to present you holy and unblameable and unreproveable in his sight: if ye continue in the faith grounded and settled, and *be* not moved away from the hope of the gospel.—That ye may be blameless and harmless, the sons of God, without rebuke, in the midst of a crooked and perverse nation, among whom ye shine as lights in the world.

Wherefore, beloved, seeing that ye look for such things, be diligent that ye may be found of him in peace, without spot, and blameless.—Sincere and without offence till the day of Christ.

Now unto him that is able to keep you from falling, and to present *you* faultless before the presence of his glory with exceeding joy, to the only wise God our Saviour, *be* glory and majesty, dominion and power, both now and ever. Amen.

1 Co. 1.8;   Col. 1.21–23;   Phil. 2.15   § 2 Pe. 3.14;
Phil. 1.10   § Jude 24–25

He will keep the feet of his saints.

IIf we say that we have fellowship with him, and walk in darkness, we lie, and do not the truth: but if we walk in the light, as he is in the light, we have fellowship one with another, and the blood of Jesus Christ his Son cleanseth us from all sin.—He that is washed needeth not save to wash *his* feet, but is clean every whit.

I have taught thee in the way of wisdom; I have led thee in right paths. When thou goest, thy steps shall not be straitened; and when thou runnest, thou shalt not stumble... Enter not into the path of the wicked, and go not in the way of evil *men*. Avoid it, pass not by it, turn from it, and pass away... Let thine eyes look right on, and let thine eyelids look straight before thee. Ponder the path of thy feet, and let all thy ways be established. Turn not to the right hand nor to the left: remove thy foot from evil.

The Lord shall deliver me from every evil work, and will preserve *me* unto his heavenly kingdom: to whom *be* glory for ever and ever. Amen.

1 Sa. 2.9; 1 Jn. 1.6–7; Jn. 13.10
§ Pro. 4.11–12,14–15,25–27 § 2 Tim. 4.18

**The LORD thy God bare thee, as a man doth bear
his son, in all the way that ye went,
until ye came into this place.**

I bare you on eagles' wings, and brought you unto myself.—In his love and in his pity he redeemed them; and he bare them, and carried them all the days of old.—As an eagle stirreth up her nest, fluttereth over her young, spreadeth abroad her wings, taketh them, beareth them on her wings: *so* the LORD alone did lead him.

Even to *your* old age I *am* he; and *even* to hoar hairs will I carry *you:* I have made, and I will bear; even I will carry, and will deliver *you.*—This God *is* our God for ever and ever: he will be our guide *even* unto death.

Cast thy burden upon the LORD, and he shall sustain thee.—Take no thought for your life, what ye shall eat, or what ye shall drink; nor yet for your body, what ye shall put on… For your heavenly Father knoweth that ye have need of all these things.

Hitherto hath the LORD helped us.

Deu. 1.31;　Ex. 19.4;　Isa. 63.9;　Deu. 32.11–12
§ Isa. 46.4;　Ps. 48.14　§ Ps. 55.22;　Mt. 6.25,32
§ 1 Sa. 7.12

There remaineth yet
very much land to be possessed.

Not as though I had already attained, either were already perfect: but I follow after, if that I may apprehend that for which also I am apprehended of Christ Jesus.

Be ye therefore perfect.—Giving all diligence, add to your faith virtue; and to virtue knowledge; and to knowledge temperance; and to temperance patience; and to patience godliness; and to godliness brotherly kindness; and to brotherly kindness charity.

I pray, that your love may abound yet more and more in knowledge and *in* all judgment.

Eye hath not seen, nor ear heard, neither have entered into the heart of man, the things which God hath prepared for them that love him. But God hath revealed *them* unto us by his Spirit.

There remaineth…a rest to the people of God.— Thine eyes shall see the king in his beauty: they shall behold the land that is very far off.

Jos. 13.1; Phil. 3.12 § Mt. 5.48; 2 Pe. 1.5–7 § Phil. 1.9 § 1 Co. 2.9–10 § He. 4.9; Isa. 33.17

For Special Occasions

They cry unto the LORD in their trouble,
and he saveth them out of their distresses…
Oh that *men* would praise the LORD
for his goodness, and *for* his wonderful
works to the children of men!

Were there not ten cleansed? but where *are* the nine?—Forget not all his benefits.—God, who answered me in the day of my distress.

I sought the LORD, and he heard me, and delivered me from all my fears.—I love the LORD, because he hath heard my voice *and* my supplications. Because he hath inclined his ear unto me, therefore will I call upon *him* as long as I live.—My heart trusted in him, and I am helped: therefore my heart greatly rejoiceth; and with my song will I praise him.

Call upon me in the day of trouble: I will deliver thee, and thou shalt glorify me… Whoso offereth praise glorifieth me.

Giving thanks always for all things unto God and the Father in the name of our Lord Jesus Christ.

Ps. 107.19,21; Lu. 17.17; Ps. 103.2; Ge. 35.3 § Ps. 34.4; Ps. 116.1–2; Ps. 28.7 § Ps. 50.15,23 § Eph. 5.20

They shall not be ashamed that wait for me.

Said I not unto thee, that, if thou wouldest believe, thou shouldest see the glory of God?

O Daniel, servant of the living God, is thy God, whom thou servest continually, able to deliver thee?... No manner of hurt was found upon him, because he believed in his God.

I prayed; and the LORD hath given me my petition which I asked of him.—My heart rejoiceth in the LORD.—Come *and* hear, all ye that fear God, and I will declare what he hath done for my soul... Blessed *be* God, which hath not turned away my prayer, nor his mercy from me.—I thank thee, and praise thee, O thou God of my fathers, who hast given me wisdom and might.

When the waves thereof arise, thou stillest them.— He maketh the storm a calm, so that the waves thereof are still... So he bringeth them unto their desired haven. Oh that *men* would praise the LORD *for* his goodness.— Blessed *is* the man *that* trusteth in him.

Isa. 49.23; Jn. 11.40 § Dan. 6.20,23 § 1 Sa. 1.27;
1 Sa. 2.1; Ps. 66.16,20; Dan. 2.23 § Ps. 89.9;
Ps. 107.29,30–31; Ps. 34.8

The Lord bless thee, and keep thee.

The LORD that made heaven and earth bless thee.—God, even our Father.—The living God, who giveth us richly all things to enjoy.

Humble yourselves in the sight of the Lord, and he shall lift you up...ye know not what *shall be* on the morrow. For what *is* your life? It is even a vapour, that appeareth for a little time, and then vanisheth away.

No good *thing* will he withhold from them that walk uprightly.—He layeth up sound wisdom for the righteous: *he is* a buckler to them that walk uprightly. —Blessed *are* they that keep his testimonies, *and that* seek him with the whole heart.

He that keepeth thee will not slumber. Behold, he that keepeth Israel shall neither slumber nor sleep... The LORD shall preserve thee from all evil: he shall preserve thy soul. The LORD shall preserve thy going out and thy coming in from this time forth, and even for evermore.—The LORD shall be thy confidence, and shall keep thy foot from being taken.—Thou wilt keep *him* in perfect peace, *whose* mind *is* stayed *on thee:* because he trusteth in thee.

The Lord of peace himself give you peace always by all means.

Nu. 6.24; Ps. 134.3; 2 Th. 2.16; 1 Tim. 6.17
§ Jas. 4.10,14 § Ps. 84.11; Pro. 2.7; Ps. 119.2
§ Ps. 121.3–4,7–8; Pro. 3.26; Isa. 26.3 § 2 Th. 3.16

**The steps of a *good* man are ordered by the LORD:
and he delighteth in his way. Though he fall,
he shall not be utterly cast down:
for the LORD upholdeth *him with* his hand.**

Lord, thou hast been our dwelling place in all generations... For a thousand years in thy sight *are but* as yesterday
when it is past, and *as* a watch in the night... So teach *us* to
number our days, that we may apply *our* hearts unto wisdom... Make us glad according to the days *wherein* thou hast
afflicted us, *and* the years *wherein* we have seen evil. Let thy
work appear unto thy servants, and thy glory unto their children. And let the beauty of the LORD our God be upon us:
and establish thou the work of our hands upon us; yea, the
work of our hands establish thou it.

Oh how great *is* thy goodness, which thou hast laid up for
them that fear thee... Thou shalt hide them in the secret of
thy presence from the pride of man: thou shalt keep them
secretly in a pavilion from the strife of tongues.—He that
dwelleth in the secret place of the most High shall abide
under the shadow of the Almighty.

It is better to go to the house of mourning, than to go to
the house of feasting: for that *is* the end of all men; and the
living will lay *it* to his heart.—The redeemed of the LORD
shall return, and come with singing unto Zion; and everlasting joy *shall be* upon their head: they shall obtain gladness
and joy; *and* sorrow and mourning shall flee away.

Ps. 37.23–24; Ps. 90.1,4,12,15–17 § Ps. 31.19,20;
Ps. 91.1 § Ec. 7.2; Isa. 51.11

Jesus was called, and his disciples, to the marriage.

Marriage *is* honourable in all.—The LORD God said, *It is* not good that the man should be alone; I will make him an help meet for him.... Therefore shall a man leave his father and his mother, and shall cleave unto his wife: and they shall be one flesh.—Every creature of God *is* good, and nothing to be refused, if it be received with thanksgiving: for it is sanctified by the word of God and prayer.

The blessing of the LORD, it maketh rich, and he addeth no sorrow with it.—The living God...giveth us richly all things to enjoy.—Who crowneth thee with lovingkindness and tender mercies; who satisfieth thy mouth with good *things*.

Christ...loved the Church, and gave himself for it.— Ye are not your own.

Brethren, the time *is* short: it remaineth, that both they that have wives be as though they had none...and they that rejoice, as though they rejoiced not...and they that use this world, as not abusing *it*: for the fashion of this world passeth away.—Set your affection on things above.

Jn. 2.2; He. 13.4; Ge. 2.18,24; 1 Tim. 4.4–5
§ Pro. 10.22; 1 Tim. 6.17; Ps. 103.4–5 § Eph. 5.25;
1 Co. 6.19 § 1 Co. 7.29,30,31; Col. 3.2

THE NEW HOME

I will walk within my house with a perfect heart.

As for me and my house, we will serve the LORD.

Seek ye first the kingdom of God, and his righteousness; and all these things shall be added unto you.—No servant can serve two masters... Ye cannot serve God and mammon.

Being heirs together of the grace of life; that your prayers be not hindered.—Two *are* better than one... for if they fall, the one will lift up his fellow.—Let us consider one another to provoke unto love and to good works.

Husbands, love *your* wives.—That...the young women...love their husbands.—Not easily provoked.— Be ye kind one to another, tenderhearted, forgiving one another, even as God for Christ's sake hath forgiven you.

Our sufficiency *is* of God.—I the LORD thy God will hold thy right hand, saying unto thee, Fear not; I will help thee.

Ps. 101.2; Jos. 24.15 § Mt. 6.33; Lu. 16.13 § 1 Pe. 3.7;
Ec. 4.9,10; He. 10.24 § Col. 3.19; Titus 2.4; 1 Co. 13.5;
Eph. 4.32 § 2 Co. 3.5; Isa. 41.13

Neither know we what to do:
but our eyes *are* upon thee.

O God, thou knowest my foolishness; and my sins are not hid from thee.—Teach me to do thy will; for thou *art* my God.—Lead me, O LORD, in thy righteousness...make thy way straight before my face.—My times *are* in thy hand.

If any of you lack wisdom, let him ask of God, that giveth to all *men* liberally, and upbraideth not; and it shall be given him. But let him ask in faith, nothing wavering.—Who *is* among you that feareth the LORD...that walketh *in* darkness, and hath no light? let him trust in the name of the LORD, and stay upon his God.

In the multitude of my thoughts within me thy comforts delight my soul.—Why art thou cast down, O my soul? and *why* art thou disquieted in me? hope thou in God.

And he said unto them, Why are ye so fearful? how is it that ye have no faith?—Now faith is...the evidence of things not seen.

---

2 Chr. 20.12; Ps. 69.5; Ps. 143.10; Ps. 5.8; Ps. 31.15 § Jas. 1.5–6; Isa. 50.10 § Ps. 94.19; Ps. 42.5 § Mk. 4.40; He. 11.1

Fear not; I will help thee.

Come unto me, all *ye* that labour and are heavy laden, and I will give you rest.—All the promises of God in him *are* yea, and in him Amen.

He shall call upon me, and I will answer him: I *will be* with him in trouble.—I have made, and I will bear; even I will carry, and will deliver *you*.—I *will be* with thee.

Be careful for nothing; but in every thing by prayer and supplication with thanksgiving let your requests be made known unto God. And the peace of God, which passeth all understanding, shall keep your hearts and minds through Christ Jesus.

I will instruct thee and teach thee in the way which thou shalt go: I will guide thee with mine eye.—I will never leave thee, nor forsake thee.—Lo, I am with you alway, *even* unto the end of the world.

Fear not; I am the first and the last.

Isa. 41.13; Mt. 11.28; 2 Co. 1.20 § Ps. 91.15; Isa. 46.4; Isa. 43.2 § Phil. 4.6–7 § Ps. 32.8; He.13.5; Mt. 28.20 § Rev. 1.17

O my God, my soul is cast down within me.

Mine eyes fail *with looking* upward: O LORD, I am oppressed; undertake for me. What shall I say? he hath both spoken unto me, and himself hath done *it.*

Why art thou cast down, O my soul? and why art thou disquieted within me? hope thou in God: for I shall yet praise him, *who is* the health of my countenance, and my God.

If I say, Surely the darkness shall cover me; even the night shall be light about me. Yea, the darkness hideth not from thee; but the night shineth as the day: the darkness and the light *are* both alike *to thee...* I will praise thee; for I am fearfully *and* wonderfully made: marvellous *are* thy works; and *that* my soul knoweth right well.

Will the Lord cast off for ever? and will he be favourable no more? Is his mercy clean gone for ever? doth *his* promise fail for evermore?... And I said, This *is* my infirmity: *but I will remember* the years of the right hand of the most High. I will remember the works of the LORD: surely I will remember thy wonders of old. I will meditate also of all thy work, and talk of thy doings.

Joseph *is* not, and Simeon *is* not, and ye will take Benjamin *away*: all these things are against me.—When he saw the wagons which Joseph had sent to carry him, the spirit of Jacob their father revived.

From the end of the earth will I cry unto thee, when my heart is overwhelmed: lead me to the rock *that* is higher than I.

Ps. 42.6; Isa. 38.14–15 § Ps. 42.11 § Ps. 139.11–12,14 § Ps. 77.7–8,10–12 § Ge. 42.36; Ge. 45.27 § Ps. 61.2

He giveth power to the faint;
and to *them that have* no might
he increaseth strength.

Even the youths shall faint and be weary, and the young men shall utterly fall: but they that wait upon the LORD shall renew *their* strength; they shall mount up with wings as eagles; they shall run, and not be weary; *and* they shall walk, and not faint.

He shall not fail nor be discouraged.

Who *is* among you that feareth the LORD, that obeyeth the voice of his servant, that walketh *in* darkness, and hath no light? let him trust in the name of the LORD, and stay upon his God.

My grace is sufficient for thee: for my strength is made perfect in weakness. Most gladly therefore will I rather glory in my infirmities, that the power of Christ may rest upon me...for when I am weak, then am I strong.

And you...now hath he reconciled in the body of his flesh through death, to present you holy and unblameable and unreproveable in his sight: if ye continue in the faith grounded and settled, and *be* not moved away from the hope of the gospel, which ye have heard.

Isa. 40.29; Isa. 40.30–31 § Isa. 42.4 § Isa. 50.10 § 2 Co. 12.9,10 § Col. 1.21–23

**Save me, O God; for the waters
are come in unto *my* soul.**

Is any among you afflicted? let him pray.

O my Father, if it be possible, let this cup pass from me: nevertheless not as I will, but as thou *wilt*.—Being in an agony he prayed more earnestly.—Jesus wept.

Surely he hath borne our griefs, and carried our sorrows.—We have not an high priest which cannot be touched with the feeling of our infirmities; but was in all points tempted like as *we are*, *yet* without sin. Let us therefore come boldly unto the throne of grace, that we may…find grace to help in time of need.

He careth for you.—I have called *thee* by thy name; thou *art* mine. When thou passest through the waters, I *will be* with thee; and through the rivers, they shall not overflow thee.—I will never leave thee, nor forsake thee.

Though he slay me, yet will I trust in him.—My flesh and my heart faileth: *but* God *is* the strength of my heart, and my portion for ever.

Ps. 69.1; Jas. 5.13 § Mt. 26.39; Lu. 22.44; Jn. 11.35
§ Isa. 53.4; He. 4.15–16 § 1 Pe. 5.7; Isa. 43.1–2;
He. 13.5 § Job 13.15; Ps. 73.26

I, *even* I, *am* he that comforteth you.

His compassions fail not... For he doth not afflict willingly nor grieve the children of men.—What I do thou knowest not now; but thou shalt know hereafter.—Lo, these *are* parts of his ways: but how little a portion is heard of him?

The Lord is very pitiful, and of tender mercy.—The Father of mercies, and the God of all comfort; who comforteth us in all our tribulation, that we may be able to comfort them which are in any trouble, by the comfort wherewith we ourselves are comforted of God.

He hath sent me to bind up the brokenhearted.—A man of sorrows, and acquainted with grief.—I will not leave you comfortless.

Another Comforter...*even* the Spirit of truth.

The eternal God *is thy* refuge, and underneath *are* the everlasting arms.—As one whom his mother comforteth, so will I comfort you.

Isa. 51.12; Lam. 3.22,33; Jn. 13.7; Job 26.14 § Jas. 5.11;
2 Co. 1.3–4 § Isa. 61.1; Isa. 53.3; Jn. 14.18
§ Jn. 14.16,17 § Deu. 33.27; Isa. 66.13

Lord, behold,
he whom thou lovest is sick.

Surely he hath borne our griefs, and carried our sorrows.—Himself took our infirmities, and bare *our* sicknesses.—He, *being* full of compassion.—Like as a father pitieth *his* children, *so* the LORD pitieth them that fear him. For he knoweth our frame.

Who shall separate us from the love of Christ? *shall* tribulation, or distress?—Whom the Lord loveth he chasteneth... Now no chastening for the present seemeth to be joyous, but grievous: nevertheless afterward it yieldeth the peaceable fruit of righteousness unto them which are exercised thereby.—We know that all things work together for good to them that love God.

And he said unto me, My grace is sufficient for thee: for my strength is made perfect in weakness. Most gladly therefore will I rather glory in my infirmities, that the power of Christ may rest upon me.

Jn. 11.3; Isa. 53.4; Mt. 8.17; Ps. 78.38; Ps. 103.13–14
§ Ro. 8.35; He. 12.6,11; Ro. 8.28 § 2 Co. 12.9

Have mercy upon me, O LORD; for I *am* weak:
O LORD, heal me.

When my heart is overwhelmed: lead me to the rock *that* is higher than I.—He giveth power to the faint; and to *them that have* no might he increaseth strength.— The LORD *is* the strength of my life.

Be not far from me; for trouble *is* near.—Thou *art* near, O LORD.—Thou hast heard my voice... Thou drewest near in the day *that* I called upon thee: thou saidst, Fear not.—A very present help in trouble.

Look upon mine affliction and my pain; and forgive all my sins.—O LORD, I am oppressed; undertake for me.—A bruised reed shall he not break.—Yea, though I walk through the valley of the shadow of death, I will fear no evil: for thou *art* with me.—Underneath *are* the everlasting arms.

Now our Lord Jesus Christ himself, and God, even our Father, which hath loved us, and hath given *us* ever- lasting consolation and good hope through grace, comfort your hearts.

Ps. 6.2; Ps. 61.2; Isa. 40.29; Ps. 27.1 § Ps. 22.11; Ps. 119.151; Lam. 3.56,57; Ps. 46.1 § Ps. 25.18; Isa. 38.14; Mt. 12.20; Ps. 23.4; Deu. 33.27 § 2 Th. 2.16–17

Father, I will that they also, whom thou hast given me, be with me where I am.

He shall return no more to his house, neither shall his place know him any more.

Whilst we are at home in the body, we are absent from the Lord: we are…willing rather to be absent from the body, and to be present with the Lord.—I am in a strait betwixt two, having a desire to depart, and to be with Christ; which is far better.—Whether we live…or die, we are the Lord's.

Ye have in heaven a better and an enduring substance.—It doth not yet appear what we shall be: but we know that, when he shall appear, we shall be like him; for we shall see him as he is.—Now we see through a glass, darkly; but then face to face.—I will behold thy face in righteousness: I shall be satisfied, when I awake, with thy likeness.

So shall we ever be with the Lord. Wherefore comfort one another with these words.

Jn. 17.24; Job 7.10 § 2 Co. 5.6,8; Phil. 1.23; Ro. 14.8
§ He. 10.34; 1 Jn. 3.2; 1 Co. 13.12; Ps. 17.15
§ 1 Th. 4.17–18

Asleep.

Fallen asleep.—Them...which sleep in Jesus.—Asleep in Christ.

Our friend...sleepeth... Howbeit Jesus spake of his death.—They stoned Stephen...and...he fell asleep.

Our Saviour Jesus Christ...hath abolished death.—That through death he might...deliver them who through fear of death were all their lifetime subject to bondage.—That he by the grace of God should taste death for every man.

Precious in the sight of the LORD *is* the death of his saints.—Death is swallowed up in victory. O death, where *is* thy sting? O grave, where *is* thy victory? The sting of death *is* sin; and the strength of sin *is* the law. But thanks *be* to God, which giveth us the victory through our Lord Jesus Christ. Therefore, my beloved brethren, be ye stedfast, unmoveable, always abounding in the work of the Lord, forasmuch as ye know that your labour is not in vain in the Lord.

---

1 Th. 4.13; 1 Co. 15.6; 1 Th. 4.14; 1 Co. 15.18 § Jn. 11.11,13; Ac. 7.59,60 § 2 Tim. 1.10; He. 2.14,15; He. 2.9 § Ps. 116.15; 1 Co. 15.54–58

**Shall we receive good at the hand of God,
and shall we not receive evil?**

He shall not be afraid of evil tidings: his heart is fixed, trusting in the LORD.—What I do thou knowest not now; but thou shalt know hereafter.—And we know that all things work together for good to them that love God, to them who are the called according to *his* purpose.

And there came a messenger unto Job, and said, The oxen were plowing, and the asses feeding beside them: and the Sabeans fell *upon them*, and took them away...there came also another, and said, The fire of God is fallen from heaven, and hath burned up the sheep, and the servants, and consumed them...there came also another, and said, Thy sons and thy daughters *were* eating and drinking wine in their eldest brother's house: and, behold, there came a great wind from the wilderness, and smote the four corners of the house, and it fell upon the young men, and they are dead; and I only am escaped alone to tell thee.

It *is* the LORD: let him do what seemeth him good.

Job 2.10; Ps. 112.7; Jn. 13.7; Ro. 8.28
§ Job 1.14–15,16,18–19 § 1 Sa. 3.18

That which I see not teach thou me.

I have yet many things to say unto you, but ye cannot bear them now.

There came a messenger to David, saying, The hearts of the men of Israel are after Absalom. And David said… Arise, and let us flee; for we shall not *else* escape from Absalom.—And the king said unto Zadok, Carry back the ark of God into the city: if I shall find favour in the eyes of the LORD, he will bring me again, and shew me *both* it, and his habitation: but if he thus say, I have no delight in thee; behold, *here am* I, let him do to me as seemeth good unto him… And David went up by the ascent of *mount* Olivet, and wept as he went up.— Weeping may endure for a night, but joy *cometh* in the morning.—I will make an everlasting covenant with you, *even* the sure mercies of David.

The LORD blessed the latter end of Job more than his beginning.—Beloved, think it not strange concerning the fiery trial which is to try you, as though some strange thing happened unto you: but rejoice, inasmuch as ye are partakers of Christ's sufferings.

Job 34.32; Jn. 16.12 § 2 Sa. 15.13–14;
2 Sa. 15.25–26,30; Ps. 30.5; Isa. 55.3 § Job 42.12;
1 Pe. 4.12–13

Mizpah.

The LORD watch between me and thee, when we are absent one from another…God *is* witness betwixt me and thee.

Pray… But I beseech *you* the rather to do this, that I may be restored to you the sooner.—But we, brethren, being taken from you for a short time in presence, not in heart, endeavoured the more abundantly to see your face with great desire. Wherefore we would have come unto you, even I Paul, once and again; but Satan hindered us.

Sorrow hath filled your heart. Nevertheless I tell you the truth; It is expedient for you that I go away.

Who shall separate us from the love of Christ?… For I am persuaded, that neither death, nor life, nor angels, nor principalities, nor powers, nor things present, nor things to come, nor height, nor depth, nor any other creature, shall be able to separate us from the love of God, which is in Christ Jesus our Lord.

He hath said, I will never leave thee, nor forsake thee. So that we may boldly say, The Lord *is* my helper, and I will not fear what man shall do unto me.—Lo, I am with you alway, *even* unto the end of the world.

Ge. 31.49; Ge. 31.49,50 § He.13.18,19; 1 Th. 2.17–18 § Jn. 16.6–7 § Ro. 8.35,38–39 § He.13.5–6; Mt. 28.20

I will not leave you comfortless:
I will come to you.

As cold waters to a thirsty soul, so *is* good news from a far country.

And they went up out of Egypt, and came into the land of Canaan unto Jacob their father, and told him, saying, Joseph *is* yet alive, and he *is* governor over all the land of Egypt. And Jacob's heart fainted, for he believed them not. And they told him all the words of Joseph, which he had said unto them: and when he saw the wagons which Joseph had sent to carry him, the spirit of Jacob their father revived: and Israel said, *It is* enough; Joseph my son *is* yet alive: I will go and see him before I die.

And now, behold, I know that ye all, among whom I have gone preaching the kingdom of God, shall see my face no more... And when he had thus spoken, he kneeled down, and prayed with them all. And they all wept sore, and fell on Paul's neck, and kissed him, sorrowing most of all for the words which he spake, that they should see his face no more. And they accompanied him unto the ship.

Jn. 14.18; Pro. 25.25 § Ge. 45.25–28 § Ac. 20.25,36–38

I will see you again.

And Israel said unto Joseph, I had not thought to see thy face: and, lo, God hath shewed me also thy seed.

When the LORD turned again the captivity of Zion, we were like them that dream. Then was our mouth filled with laughter, and our tongue with singing: then said they among the heathen, The LORD hath done great things for them. The LORD hath done great things for us; *whereof* we are glad... He that goeth forth and weepeth, bearing precious seed, shall doubtless come again with rejoicing, bringing his sheaves *with him.*

And when they were come, and had gathered the church together, they rehearsed all that God had done with them, and how he had opened the door of faith unto the Gentiles.

I go to prepare a place for you. And if I go and prepare a place for you, I will come again, and receive you unto myself; that where I am, *there* ye may be also.—For yet a little while, and he that shall come will come, and will not tarry.

Jn. 16.22; Ge. 48.11 § Ps. 126.1–3,6 § Ac. 14.27
§ Jn. 14.2–3; He.10.37

Sorrow and sighing shall flee away.

And Jacob lifted up his eyes, and looked, and, behold, Esau came, and with him four hundred men... And Esau ran to meet him, and embraced him, and fell on his neck, and kissed him: and they wept... And Jacob said...if now I have found grace in thy sight, then receive my present at my hand: for therefore I have seen thy face, as though I had seen the face of God, and thou wast pleased with me.

Joseph made himself known unto his brethren... And he said, I *am* Joseph your brother, whom ye sold into Egypt. Now therefore be not grieved, nor angry with yourselves, that ye sold me hither: for God did send me before you to preserve life... And ye shall tell my father of all my glory in Egypt...and ye shall haste and bring down my father hither.

Peter...was kept in prison: but prayer was made without ceasing of the church unto God for him... He...declared unto them how the Lord had brought him out of the prison.

Isa. 35.10; Ge. 33.1,4,10 § Ge. 45.1,4–5,13 § Ac. 12.5,17

I *am* the LORD that healeth thee.

I shall not die, but live, and declare the works of the LORD. The LORD hath chastened me sore: but he hath not given me over unto death.

Bless the LORD, O my soul, and forget not all his benefits: who forgiveth all thine iniquities; who healeth all thy diseases.—In those days was Hezekiah sick unto death... Then Hezekiah...prayed unto the LORD, and said, Remember now, O LORD, I beseech thee, how I have walked before thee in truth and with a perfect heart, and have done *that which is* good in thy sight. And Hezekiah wept sore. Then came the word of the LORD to Isaiah, saying, Go, and say to Hezekiah, Thus saith the LORD, the God of David thy father, I have heard thy prayer, I have seen thy tears: behold, I will add unto thy days fifteen years.

And, behold, there came a leper and worshipped him, saying, Lord, if thou wilt, thou canst make me clean. And Jesus put forth *his* hand, and touched him, saying, I will; be thou clean. And immediately his leprosy was cleansed.

Ex. 15.26; Ps. 118.17–18 § Ps. 103.2–3; Isa. 38.1,2–5 § Mt. 8.2–3

The prayer of faith shall save the sick.

This sickness is not unto death, but for the glory of God.—He knoweth the way that I take: *when* he hath tried me, I shall come forth as gold.

I supposed it necessary to send to you Epaphroditus, my brother, and companion in labour, and fellowsoldier, but your messenger, and he that ministered to my wants. For he longed after you all, and was full of heaviness, because that ye had heard that he had been sick. For indeed he was sick nigh unto death: but God had mercy on him; and not on him only, but on me also, lest I should have sorrow upon sorrow…hold such in reputation: because for the work of Christ he was nigh unto death, not regarding his life, to supply your lack of service toward me.

And he said unto me, My grace is sufficient for thee: for my strength is made perfect in weakness. Most gladly therefore will I rather glory in my infirmities, that the power of Christ may rest upon me.

Jas. 5.15; Jn. 11.4; Job 23.10 **§** Phil. 2.25–27,29–30 **§** 2 Co. 12.9

**Rest in the LORD,
and wait patiently for him.**

And he said unto them, Come ye yourselves apart into a desert place, and rest a while.—And they came to Elim, where *were* twelve wells of water, and threescore and ten palm trees: and they encamped there by the waters.

And as he lay and slept under a juniper tree, behold, then an angel touched him, and said unto him, Arise *and* eat. And he looked, and, behold, *there was* a cake baken on the coals, and a cruse of water at his head. And he did eat and drink, and laid him down again. And the angel of the LORD came again the second time, and touched him, and said, Arise *and* eat; because the journey *is* too great for thee. And he arose, and did eat and drink, and went in the strength of that meat forty days and forty nights unto Horeb the mount of God.

The Lord *is* my shepherd; I shall not want. He maketh me to lie down in green pastures: he leadeth me beside the still waters. He restoreth my soul.

Ps. 37.7; Mk. 6.31; Ex. 15.27 § 1 Ki. 19.5–8
§ Ps. 23.1–3

The LORD *is* thy shade upon thy right hand.

Hast thou not known? hast thou not heard, *that* the everlasting God, the LORD, the Creator of the ends of the earth, fainteth not, neither is weary? *there is* no searching of his understanding. He giveth power to the faint; and to *them that have* no might he increaseth strength. Even the youths shall faint and be weary, and the young men shall utterly fall: but they that wait upon the LORD shall renew *their* strength; they shall mount up with wings as eagles; they shall run, and not be weary; *and* they shall walk, and not faint.

Thy youth is renewed like the eagle's... Like as a father pitieth *his* children, *so* the LORD pitieth them that fear him. For he knoweth our frame; he remembereth that we *are* dust.

We have this treasure in earthen vessels, that the excellency of the power may be of God, and not of us... For our light affliction, which is but for a moment, worketh for us a far more exceeding *and* eternal weight of glory.

Ps. 121.5; Isa. 40.28–31 § Ps. 103.5,13–14
§ 2 Co. 4.7,17

In the day of adversity consider.

*I*f thou faint in the day of adversity, thy strength *is* small.—Behold, I have refined thee, but not with silver; I have chosen thee in the furnace of affliction.—We must through much tribulation enter into the kingdom of God.

Although the fig tree shall not blossom, neither *shall* fruit *be* in the vines; the labour of the olive shall fail, and the fields shall yield no meat; the flock shall be cut off from the fold, and *there shall be* no herd in the stalls: yet I will rejoice in the LORD, I will joy in the God of my salvation.

Blessed *be* God, even the Father of our Lord Jesus Christ, the Father of mercies, and the God of all comfort; who comforteth us in all our tribulation, that we may be able to comfort them which are in any trouble, by the comfort wherewith we ourselves are comforted of God.

We glory in tribulations also.—I have learned, in whatsoever state I am…to be content.—Your sorrow shall be turned into joy.

Ec. 7.14; Pro. 24.10; Isa. 48.10; Ac. 14.22
§ Hab. 3.17–18 § 2 Co. 1.3–4 § Ro. 5.3; Phil. 4.11;
Jn. 16.20

Tribulation worketh patience.

Why art thou cast down, O my soul? and *why* art thou disquieted in me? hope thou in God: for I shall yet praise him *for* the help of his countenance.

For I was envious at the foolish, *when* I saw the prosperity of the wicked... When I thought to know this, it *was* too painful for me; until I went into the sanctuary of God; *then* understood I their end.—Cast thy burden upon the LORD, and he shall sustain thee.

At my first answer no man stood with me, but all *men* forsook me: *I pray God* that it may not be laid to their charge. Notwithstanding the Lord stood with me, and strengthened me...and I was delivered out of the mouth of the lion.

For *it was* not an enemy *that* reproached me; then I could have borne *it*... But *it was* thou, a man mine equal, my guide, and mine acquaintance. We took sweet counsel together, *and* walked unto the house of God in company.—He faileth not.

Ro. 5.3; Ps. 42.5 § Ps. 73.3,16–17; Ps. 55.22
§ 2 Tim. 4.16–17 § Ps. 55.12,13–14; Zeph. 3.5

In the day of prosperity be joyful.

And the LORD was with Joseph, and he was a prosperous man.—Let the LORD be magnified, which hath pleasure in the prosperity of his servant.

Blessed *is* the man that walketh not in the counsel of the ungodly, nor standeth in the way of sinners, nor sitteth in the seat of the scornful. But his delight *is* in the law of the LORD; and in his law doth he meditate day and night. And he shall be like a tree planted by the rivers of water, that bringeth forth his fruit in his season; his leaf also shall not wither; and whatsoever he doeth shall prosper.

This book of the law shall not depart out of thy mouth; but thou shalt meditate therein day and night, that thou mayest observe to do according to all that is written therein: for then thou shalt make thy way prosperous, and then thou shalt have good success.

And the LORD was with him; *and* he prospered whithersoever he went forth.—And in every work that he began…to seek his God, he did *it* with all his heart, and prospered.

Ec. 7.14; Ge. 39.2; Ps. 35.27 § Ps. 1.1–3 § Jos. 1.8 § 2 Ki. 18.7; 2 Chr. 31.21

If God *be* for us, who *can be* against us?

Beloved, I wish above all things that thou mayest prosper and be in health, even as thy soul prospereth.

Upon the first *day* of the week let every one of you lay by him in store, as *God* hath prospered him.—Bring ye all the tithes into the storehouse, that there may be meat in mine house, and prove me now herewith, saith the LORD of hosts, if I will not open you the windows of heaven, and pour you out a blessing, that *there shall* not *be room* enough *to receive it.*

Both riches and honour *come* of thee, and thou reignest over all.—Then Solomon sat on the throne of the LORD as king instead of David his father, and prospered.— Seek ye first the kingdom of God, and his righteousness; and all these things shall be added unto you.

Lay not up for yourselves treasures upon earth, where moth and rust doth corrupt, and where thieves break through and steal: but lay up for yourselves treasures in heaven… For where your treasure is, there will your heart be also.

Ro. 8.31; 3 Jn. 2 § 1 Co. 16.2; Mal. 3.10 § 1 Chr. 29.12; 1 Chr. 29.23; Mt. 6.33 § Mt. 6.19–20,21

If riches increase, set not your heart *upon them*.

Thou shalt remember the LORD thy God: for *it is* he that giveth thee power to get wealth.—The blessing of the LORD, it maketh rich, and he addeth no sorrow with it.—Let not the rich *man* glory in his riches: but let him that glorieth glory in this, that he understandeth and knoweth me, that I *am* the LORD.

Riches certainly make themselves wings; they fly away.—Charge them that are rich in this world, that they be not highminded, nor trust in uncertain riches, but in the living God, who giveth us richly all things to enjoy.—And I have also given thee that which thou hast not asked, both riches, and honour: so that there shall not be any…like unto thee all thy days.—Riches *are* not for ever.

Give me neither poverty nor riches; feed me with food convenient for me.—Honour the Lord with thy substance, and with the first fruits of all thine increase: so shall thy barns be filled with plenty, and thy presses shall burst out with new wine.

Ps. 62.10; Deu. 8.18; Pro. 10.22; Jer. 9.23–24
§ Pro. 23.5; 1 Tim. 6.17; 1 Ki. 3.13; Pro. 27.24
§ Pro. 30.8; Pro. 3.9–10

Whatsoever he saith unto you, do *it*.

Without me ye can do nothing.

When he had left speaking, he said unto Simon, Launch out into the deep, and let down your nets for a draught. And Simon answering said unto him, Master, we have toiled all the night, and have taken nothing: nevertheless at thy word I will let down the net. And when they had this done, they inclosed a great multitude of fishes: and their net brake. And they beckoned unto *their* partners, which were in the other ship, that they should come and help them. And they came, and filled both the ships, so that they began to sink. When Simon Peter saw *it*, he fell down at Jesus' knees, saying, Depart from me; for I am a sinful man, O Lord. For he was astonished, and all that were with him, at the draught of the fishes which they had taken.

In my prosperity I said, I shall never be moved. LORD, by thy favour thou hast made my mountain to stand strong.

Therefore, my beloved brethren, be ye stedfast, unmoveable, always abounding in the work of the Lord, forasmuch as ye know that your labour is not in vain in the Lord.

Jn. 2.5; Jn. 15.5 § Lu. 5.4–9 § Ps. 30.6–7 § 1 Co. 15.58

**For this child I prayed; and the LORD hath given me
my petition which I asked of him.**

Lo, children *are* an heritage of the LORD: *and* the fruit
of the womb *is his* reward.

A little child shall lead them.—Train up a child in
the way he should go: and when he is old, he will not
depart from it.—For I know him, that he will command
his children and his household after him, and they shall
keep the way of the LORD, to do justice and judgment.—
Thy children like olive plants round about thy
table.—He took a child, and set him in the midst of
them: and when he had taken him in his arms, he said
unto them, Whosoever shall receive one of such children in my name, receiveth me: and whosoever shall
receive me, receiveth not me, but him that sent me.

Jesus...said... Suffer the little children to come
unto me, and forbid them not: for of such is the kingdom of God.

Take heed that ye despise not one of these little ones;
for I say unto you, That in heaven their angels do always
behold the face of my Father which is in heaven.

---

1 Sa. 1.27; Ps. 127.3 § Isa.11.6; Pro. 22.6; Ge. 18.19;
Ps. 128.3; Mk. 9.36–37 § Mk. 10.14 § Mt. 18.10

Thanks *be* unto God for his unspeakable gift.

In this was manifested the love of God toward us, because that God sent his only begotten Son into the world, that we might live through him.

And she brought forth her firstborn son, and wrapped him in swaddling clothes, and laid him in a manger; because there was no room for them in the inn.

And there were in the same country shepherds... keeping watch over their flock by night. And, lo, the angel of the Lord came upon them, and the glory of the Lord shone round about them: and they were sore afraid. And the angel said unto them, Fear not: for, behold, I bring you good tidings of great joy, which shall be to all people. For unto you is born this day in the city of David a Saviour, which is Christ the Lord. And this *shall be* a sign unto you; Ye shall find the babe wrapped in swaddling clothes, lying in a manger.

And suddenly there was with the angel a multitude of the heavenly host praising God, and saying, Glory to God in the highest, and on earth peace, good will toward men.

2 Co. 9.15; 1 Jn. 4.9 § Lu. 2.7 § Lu. 2.8–12
§ Lu. 2.13–14

Ye shall hallow the fiftieth year

And proclaim liberty throughout *all* the land unto all the inhabitants thereof: it shall be a jubile unto you; and ye shall return every man unto his possession, and ye shall return every man unto his family.

And ye shall know the truth, and the truth shall make you free… If the Son therefore shall make you free, ye shall be free indeed.—And thou shalt remember all the way which the LORD thy God led thee.—He found him in a desert land, and in the waste howling wilderness; he led him about, he instructed him, he kept him as the apple of his eye.

Happy *is he* that *hath* the God of Jacob for his help, whose hope *is* in the LORD his God.—Who redeemeth thy life from destruction; who crowneth thee with lovingkindness and tender mercies.—I will sing unto the LORD as long as I live: I will sing praise to my God while I have my being. My meditation of him shall be sweet: I will be glad in the LORD.

Lev. 25.10; Lev. 25.10 § Jn. 8.32,36; Deu. 8.2;
Deu. 32.10 § Ps. 146.5; Ps. 103.4; Ps. 104.33–34

A jubile shall that fiftieth year be unto you.

It *is* the jubile; it shall be holy unto you... In the year of this jubile ye shall return every man unto his possession... The land shall not be sold for ever: for the land *is* mine.—Then shalt thou cause the trumpet of the jubile to sound.

Rejoice in the Lord alway: *and* again I say, Rejoice.— Stand fast therefore in the liberty wherewith Christ hath made us free, and be not entangled again with the yoke of bondage.

Jesus Christ the same yesterday, and to day, and for ever.—I will extol thee, my God, O king; and I will bless thy name for ever and ever. Every day will I bless thee... Great *is* the LORD, and greatly to be praised; and his greatness *is* unsearchable. One generation shall praise thy works to another, and shall declare thy mighty acts... They shall abundantly utter the memory of thy great goodness, and shall sing of thy righteousness.

Praise ye the LORD... Praise him for his mighty acts: praise him according to his excellent greatness.

Lev. 25.11; Lev. 25.12,13,23; Lev. 25.9 § Phil. 4.4; Ga. 5.1 § He. 13.8; Ps. 145.1–2,3–4,7 § Ps. 150.1,2

With the ancient *is* wisdom;
and in length of days understanding.

The days of our years *are* threescore years and ten; and if by reason of strength *they be* fourscore years, yet *is* their strength labour and sorrow; for it is soon cut off, and we fly away... So teach *us* to number our days, that we may apply *our* hearts unto wisdom.—And *even* to *your* old age I *am* he; and *even* to hoar hairs will I carry *you*: I have made, and I will bear; even I will carry, and will deliver *you*.

The beauty of old men *is* the gray head.—Happy *is* the man *that* findeth wisdom, and the man *that* getteth understanding. For the merchandise of it *is* better than the merchandise of silver, and the gain thereof than fine gold. She *is* more precious than rubies: and all the things thou canst desire are not to be compared unto her. Length of days *is* in her right hand; *and* in her left hand riches and honour.

From a child thou hast known the holy scriptures, which are able to make thee wise unto salvation through faith which is in Christ Jesus.

Job 12.12; Ps. 90.10,12; Isa. 46.4 § Pro. 20.29;
Pro. 3.13–16 § 2 Tim. 3.15

They shall still bring forth fruit in old age.

He shall be like a tree planted by the rivers of water, that bringeth forth his fruit in his season.

He that dwelleth in the secret place of the most High shall abide under the shadow of the Almighty... With long life will I satisfy him, and shew him my salvation.

Honour thy father and thy mother: that thy days may be long upon the land which the LORD thy God giveth thee.

Thou shalt rise up before the hoary head, and honour the face of the old man, and fear thy God: I *am* the LORD.—That thou mayest love the LORD thy God, *and* that thou mayest obey his voice, and that thou mayest cleave unto him: for he *is* thy life, and the length of thy days.—Thou shalt have a perfect and just weight, a perfect and just measure shalt thou have: that thy days may be lengthened in the land.

Trust in the LORD with all thine heart; and lean not unto thine own understanding. In all thy ways acknowledge him, and he shall direct thy paths.—The path of the just *is* as the shining light, that shineth more and more unto the perfect day.

Ps. 92.14; Ps. 1.3 § Ps. 91.1,16 § Ex. 20.12 § Lev. 19.32; Deu. 30.20; Deu. 25.15 § Pro. 3.5–6; Pro. 4.18

**Thou shalt guide me with thy counsel,
and afterward receive me *to* glory.**

Thou in thy mercy hast led forth the people *which* thou hast redeemed: thou hast guided *them* in thy strength unto thy holy habitation... Thou shalt bring them in, and plant them in the mountain of thine inheritance, *in* the place, O LORD, *which* thou hast made for thee to dwell in, *in* the Sanctuary, O LORD, *which* thy hands have established.

Not one thing hath failed of all the good things which the LORD your God spake concerning you; all are come to pass unto you, *and* not one thing hath failed thereof.

The God which fed me all my life long unto this day.—In thy presence *is* fulness of joy; at thy right hand *there are* pleasures for evermore.—Surely goodness and mercy shall follow me all the days of my life: and I will dwell in the house of the LORD for ever.

Lord, now lettest thou thy servant depart in peace, according to thy word: for mine eyes have seen thy salvation.

Ps. 73.24; Ex. 15.13,17 § Jos. 23.14 § Ge. 48.15;
Ps. 16.11; Ps. 23.6 § Lu. 2.29–30

In my Father's house are many mansions.

So teach *us* to number our days, that we may apply *our* hearts unto wisdom.—For so an entrance shall be ministered unto you abundantly into the everlasting kingdom of our Lord and Saviour Jesus Christ.—In whom we have redemption through his blood, the forgiveness of sins, according to the riches of his grace.

For we know in part, and we prophesy in part. But when that which is perfect is come, then that which is in part shall be done away... For now we see through a glass, darkly; but then face to face: now I know in part; but then shall I know even as also I am known.—And God shall wipe away all tears from their eyes; and there shall be no more death, neither sorrow, nor crying, neither shall there be any more pain: for the former things are passed away.

Thine eyes shall see the king in his beauty.—Behold, I shew you a mystery; We shall not all sleep, but we shall all be changed.—We shall be like him; for we shall see him as he is.

Jn. 14.2; Ps. 90.12; 2 Pe. 1.11; Eph. 1.7
§ 1 Co. 13.9–10,12; Rev. 21.4 § Isa. 33.17; 1 Co. 15.51;
1 Jn. 3.2